Jon Chase

Amartya Sen was born in 1933 and grew up in Santiniketan and in Dhaka (now the capital of Bangladesh). As a student in India and then at Trinity College, Cambridge, he "seriously flirted, in turn, with Sanskrit, mathematics, and physics before settling for the eccentric charms of economics," as he has written. Now Lamont University Professor at Harvard, he was Master of Trinity College from 1998 to 2004, and has taught at many other universities in Britain, the United States, and India. When Professor Sen was awarded the Nobel Prize in Economics in 1998, he was the first Asian to be so honored.

Also by Amartya Sen

Choice of Techniques
Collective Choice and Social Welfare
On Economic Inequality
Poverty and Famines
Choice, Welfare and Measurement
Resources, Values and Development
Commodities and Capabilities
On Ethics and Economics
Inequality Reexamined
Development as Freedom
Rationality and Freedom
Identity and Violence

The Argumentative Indian

THE ARGUMENTATIVE INDIAN

WRITINGS ON INDIAN HISTORY, CULTURE AND IDENTITY

AMARTYA SEN

PICADOR

FARRAR, STRAUS AND GIROUX

NEW YORK

 Printed in the United States of America. For information, address Picador, 175 Fifth Avenue, New York, N.Y. 10010.

www.picadorusa.com

For information on Picador Reading Group Guides, as well as ordering, please contact Picador.
Phone: 646-307-5629
Fax: 212-253-9627
E-mail: readinggroupguides@picadorusa.com

Earlier versions of some of the essays in this book have appeared in the following publications: The New York Review of Books, *Essays 5, 8, 13; as* Our Culture, Their Culture *(Calcutta: Nandan, 1996), Essay 6 (abridged earlier version);* The New Republic, *Essays 6 (abridged earlier version), 12;* Daedalus, *Essay 7;* Financial Times, *Essay 9; Kaushik Basu and Sanjay Subrahmanyam, eds.,* Unravelling the Nation: Sectarian Conflict and India's Secular Identity *(Delhi: Penguin, 1996), Essay 14;* Little Magazine, *Essay 15.*

The publishers are grateful for permission to reproduce the following illustrations: Tagore and Gandhi at Santiniketan, © Akg-Images; 'Xuanzang [Hiuan-tsang] returning to China with Sanskrit manuscripts from India in 645 AD', © Fujita Museum of Art, Osaka; 'Arjuna hits the target', © British Library, London.

Library of Congress Cataloging-in-Publication Data

Sen, Amartya.
The argumentative Indian : writings on Indian history, culture and identity / by Amartya Sen.
p. cm.
Includes index.
ISBN-13: 978-0-312-42602-6
ISBN-10: 0-312-42602-X
1. India—Civilization. I. Title.

DS423 .S338 2005
954—dc22

2005049460

Originally published in Great Britain by Penguin Books Ltd.
First published in the United States by Farrar, Straus and Giroux

10 9 8 7 6

To my sister, Supurna Datta

Contents

PART FOUR

Reason and Identity

Preface

These essays on India were written over the last decade – about half of them over the last couple of years. The first four, which make up the first part of the collection, introduce and explain the principal themes pursued in this book, related to India's long argumentative tradition.

India is an immensely diverse country with many distinct pursuits, vastly disparate convictions, widely divergent customs and a veritable feast of viewpoints. Any attempt to talk about the culture of the country, or about its past history or contemporary politics, must inescapably involve considerable selection. I need not, therefore, labour the point that the focus on the argumentative tradition in this work is also a result of choice. It does not reflect a belief that this is the only reasonable way of thinking about the history or culture or politics of India. I am very aware that there are other ways of proceeding.

The selection of focus here is mainly for three distinct reasons: the long history of the argumentative tradition in India, its contemporary relevance, and its relative neglect in ongoing cultural discussions. It can in addition be claimed that the simultaneous flourishing of many different convictions and viewpoints in India has drawn substantially on the acceptance – explicitly or by implication – of heterodoxy and dialogue. The reach of Indian heterodoxy is remarkably extensive and ubiquitous.

Consider the politically charged issue of the role of so-called 'ancient India' in understanding the India of today. In contemporary politics, the enthusiasm for ancient India has often come from the Hindutva movement – the promoters of a narrowly Hindu view of

Indian civilization – who have tried to separate out the period preceding the Muslim conquest of India (from the third millennium BCE to the beginning of the second millennium CE). In contrast, those who take an integrationist approach to contemporary India have tended to view the harking back to ancient India with the greatest of suspicion. For example, the Hindutva activists like invoking the holy Vedas, composed in the second millennium BCE, to define India's 'real heritage'. They are also keen on summoning the *Rāmāyaṇa*, the great epic, for many different purposes, from delineating Hindu beliefs and convictions to finding alleged justification for the forcible demolition of a mosque – the Babri masjid – that is situated at the very spot where the 'divine' Rama, it is claimed, was born. The integrationists, by contrast, have tended to see the Vedas and the *Rāmāyaṇa* as unwelcome intrusions of some specific Hindu beliefs into the contemporary life of secular India.

The integrationists are not wrong to question the factional nature of the choice of 'Hindu classics' over other products of India's long and diverse history. They are also right to point to the counterproductive role that such partisan selection can play in the secular, multireligious life of today's India. Even though more than 80 per cent of Indians may be Hindu, the country has a very large Muslim population (the third largest among all the countries in the world – larger than the entire British and French populations put together), and a great many followers of other faiths: Christians, Sikhs, Jains, Parsees and others.

However, even after noting the need for integration and for a multicultural perspective, it has to be accepted that these old books and narratives have had an enormous influence on Indian literature and thought. They have deeply influenced literary and philosophical writings on the one hand, and folk traditions of storytelling and critical dialectics on the other. The difficulty does not lie in the importance of the Vedas or the *Rāmāyaṇa*, but in the understanding of their role in Indian culture. When the Muslim Pathan rulers of Bengal arranged for making good Bengali translations of the Sanskrit *Mahābhārata* and *Rāmāyaṇa* in the fourteenth century (on which see Essay 3), their enthusiasm for the ancient Indian epics reflected their love of culture, rather than any conversion to Hinduism.* It would be as difficult to ignore their general importance in Indian culture (on some allegedly 'secular' ground) as it would be to insist on viewing them through the narrow prism of a particularly raw version of Hindu religiosity.

The Vedas may be full of hymns and religious invocations, but they also tell stories, speculate about the world and – true to the argumentative propensity already in view – ask difficult questions. A basic doubt concerns the very creation of the world: did someone make it, was it a spontaneous emergence, and is there a God who knows what really happened? As is discussed in Essay 1, the *Rigveda* goes on to express radical doubts on these issues: 'Who really knows? Who will here proclaim it? Whence was it produced? Whence is this creation? . . . perhaps it formed itself, or perhaps it did not – the one who looks down on it, in the highest heaven, only he knows – or perhaps he does not know.' These doubts from the second millennium BCE would recur again and again in India's long argumentative history, along with a great many other questions about epistemology and ethics (as is discussed in Essay 1). They survive side by side with intense religious beliefs and deeply respectful faith and devotion.

Similarly, the adherents of Hindu politics – especially those who are given to vandalizing places of worship of other religions – may take Rama to be divine, but in much of the *Rāmāyaṇa*, Rama is treated primarily as a hero – a great 'epic hero' – with many good qualities and some weaknesses, including a tendency to harbour suspicions about his wife Sītā's faithfulness. A pundit who gets considerable space in the *Rāmāyaṇa*, called Jāvāli, not only does not treat Rama as God, he calls his actions 'foolish' ('especially for', as Jāvāli puts it, 'an intelligent and wise man'). Before he is persuaded to withdraw his allegations, Jāvāli gets time enough in the *Rāmāyaṇa* to explain in detail

*As is also discussed in Essay 3, the first translation of the Upaniṣads – the most philosophical part of the Vedic Hindu literature – that caught the attention of European intellectuals was the Persian translation produced in the seventeenth century by the Moghal prince Dara Shikoh, the eldest son (and legitimate heir) of Emperor Shah Jahan and of Mumtaz Mahal (the beautiful queen on whose tomb the Taj Mahal would be built). Dara was killed by his more sectarian brother, Aurangzeb, to seize the Moghal throne.

that 'there is no after-world, nor any religious practice for attaining that', and that 'the injunctions about the worship of gods, sacrifice, gifts and penance have been laid down in the śāstras [scriptures] by clever people, just to rule over [other] people.'* The problem with invoking the *Rāmāyaṇa* to propagate a reductionist account of Hindu religiosity lies in the way the epic is deployed for this purpose – as a document of supernatural veracity, rather than as 'a marvellous parable' (as Rabindranath Tagore describes it) and a widely enjoyed part of India's cultural heritage.

The roots of scepticism in India go back a long way, and it would be hard to understand the history of Indian culture if scepticism were to be jettisoned. Indeed, the resilient reach of the tradition of dialectics can be felt throughout Indian history, even as conflicts and wars have led to much violence. Given the simultaneous presence of dialogic encounters and bloody battles in India's past, the tendency to concentrate only on the latter would miss something of real significance.

It is indeed important to understand the long tradition of accepted heterodoxy in India. In resisting the attempts by the Hindutva activists to capture ancient India as their home ground (and to see it as the unique cradle of Indian civilization), it is not enough to point out that India has many other sources of culture as well. It is necessary also to see how much heterodoxy there has been in Indian thoughts and beliefs from very early days. Not only did Buddhists, Jains, agnostics and atheists compete with each other and with adherents of what we now call Hinduism (a much later term) in the India of the first millennium BCE, but also the dominant religion in India was Buddhism for nearly a thousand years. The Chinese in the first millennium CE standardly referred to India as 'the Buddhist kingdom' (the far-reaching effects of the Buddhist connections between the two largest countries in the world are discussed in Essay 8). Ancient India cannot be fitted into the narrow box where the Hindutva activists want to incarcerate it.

It was indeed a Buddhist emperor of India, Ashoka, who, in the third century BCE, not only outlined the need for toleration and the richness of heterodoxy, but also laid down what are perhaps the oldest rules for conducting debates and disputations, with the opponents

*See Essays 1 and 3 for fuller discussions of these and other examples of ancient scepticism and dialogic combats.

being 'duly honoured in every way on all occasions'. That political principle figures a great deal in later discussions in India, but the most powerful defence of toleration and of the need for the state to be equidistant from different religions came from a Muslim Indian emperor, Akbar. This was of course much later, but those principles of religious toleration, enunciated in the 1590s, were still early enough at a time when the Inquisition was in full swing in Europe.

The contemporary relevance of the dialogic tradition and of the acceptance of heterodoxy is hard to exaggerate. Discussions and arguments are critically important for democracy and public reasoning. They are central to the practice of secularism and for even-handed treatment of adherents of different religious faiths (including those who have no religious beliefs). Going beyond these basic structural priorities, the argumentative tradition, if used with deliberation and commitment, can also be extremely important in resisting social inequalities and in removing poverty and deprivation. Voice is a crucial component of the pursuit of social justice.

It is sometimes asserted that the use of dialectics is largely confined to the more affluent and more literate, and is thus of no value to the common people. The elitism that is rampant in such a belief is not only extraordinary, it is made more exasperating through the political cynicism and impassivity it tends to encourage. The critical voice is the traditional ally of the aggrieved, and participation in arguments is a general opportunity, not a particularly specialized skill (like composing sonnets or performing trapeze acts).

Just before the Indian general elections in the spring of 2004, when I visited a Bengali village not far from my own home, I was told by a villager, who was barely literate and certainly very poor: 'It is not very hard to silence us, but that is not because we cannot speak.' Indeed, even though the recording and preservation of arguments tend to be biased in the direction of the articulations of the powerful and the well schooled, many of the most interesting accounts of arguments from the past involve members of disadvantaged groups (as is discussed in Essays 1 and 2).

The nature and strength of the dialogic tradition in India is sometimes ignored because of the much championed belief that India is the land of religions, the country of uncritical faiths and unquestioned practices. Some cultural theorists, allegedly 'highly sympathetic', are particularly keen on showing the strength of the faith-based and unreasoning culture of India and the East, in contrast with the 'shallow rationalism' and scientific priorities of the West. This line of argument may well be inspired by sympathy, but it can end up suppressing large parts of India's intellectual heritage. In this pre-selected 'East–West' contrast, meetings are organized, as it were, between Aristotle and Euclid on the one hand, and wise and contented Indian peasants on the other. This is not, of course, an uninteresting exercise, but it is not pre-eminently a better way of understanding the 'East–West' cultural contrast than by arranging meetings between, say, Āryabhaṭa (the mathematician) and Kauṭilya (the political economist) on the one hand, and happily determined Visigoths on the other. If the immediate motivation for this book is social and political understanding in India, it has, I believe, some relevance also for the way the classification of the cultures of the world has become cemented into a shape that pays little or no attention to a great deal of our past and present.*

The four essays in Part I outline the nature, reach and relevance of the argumentative tradition in India. This includes, as is particularly discussed in Essays 1 and 2, the part that pluralism and the dialogic tradition play in supporting democracy, secularism and the pursuit of mathematics and science, and the use that can be made of dialectics in seeking social justice, against the barriers of class, caste, community and gender. Essay 3 discusses the relevance of a capacious understanding of a large and heterodox India, contrasted with the drastically downsized view of the country that appeals to some religious activists, who combine it with a severely miniaturized understanding of Hinduism.† These discussions have relevance, as is discussed in Essay 4, for the way Indian identity can be understood, and the diagnostic issues are relevant not only for Indians in India but also for the large (at least 20 million strong) Indian diaspora across the world.

*I was impressed to find, on arriving at Harvard in the late 1980s, that all books on India in the bookshop of the famous 'Harvard Coop' were kept in the section called 'Religions'.

†In my Foreword to the reissue of my grandfather K. M. Sen's book on Hinduism (London: Penguin Books, 2005), I discuss the different ways in which that capacious religion can be seen.

The essays in Part II deal with the role of communication in the development and understanding of cultures. The discussions in Essays 5 and 6 try to follow and to develop the insights on this subject that emerge from the works of the visionary poet and writer Rabindranath Tagore and the great film director Satyajit Ray. The emergence of different versions of 'imagined India' in Western perceptions is investigated in Essay 7, along with the impact that these misconceptions, in turn, have had on the way Indians have tended to see themselves in the colonial or post-colonial period. Essay 8 is devoted to examining the close and extensive intellectual relations (covering science, mathematics, engineering, literature, music, and public health care and administration) that China and India had – along with religion and trade – for a thousand years, beginning in the early part of the first millennium, and the lessons that emerge from all this for contemporary China and India.

Part III is concerned with the politics of deprivation (poverty, class and caste divisions, gender inequality) and with the precariousness of human security in the subcontinent as a result of the development of nuclear weapons in India and Pakistan. Essays 9–12 investigate what has happened and is happening right now, and what issues can appropriately be taken up for critical examination.

The role of reasoning in the identity of Indians is the subject matter of the last part of the book, which begins with an essay on the reach of reasoning, including a rejection of the often-aired claim that analytical reasoning and critique are quintessentially 'Western' or 'European' traditions. The contribution that reasoned assessment can make to the troubled world in which we live is also examined. Essay 14 subjects the debates on secularism to critical scrutiny, which has implications for the way Indians can see themselves in a multi-religious and multicultural India. India's multicultural history is wonderfully reflected in the profusion of the well-designed and well-developed calendars that exist, each with a long history. This is the subject matter of Essay 15. That essay also discusses how these calendrical variations have allowed agreement on a 'principal meridian' for India – fixed at Ujjain – from the fifth century CE onwards, which still serves as the basis of 'Indian standard time' – an odd five and a half hours ahead of Greenwich Mean Time (though it was fixed rather earlier than the GMT was born). The final essay is based on the Dorab Tata Lectures I gave in 2001, on the Indian identity, and it returns briefly to the very general issues taken up at the beginning of the book.

I have benefited from the comments and suggestions of many friends and colleagues, and their contributions are acknowledged individually in some of the essays. For the book as a whole, I have also greatly benefited from many helpful suggestions from Sugata Bose, Antara Dev Sen, Jean Drèze, Ayesha Jalal, Martha Nussbaum, V. K. Ramachandran, Kumar Rana and Emma Rothschild. In addition I would like to thank, for advice and comments, Montek Singh Ahluwalia, Sudhir Anand, Pranab Bardhan, Kaushik Basu, Homi Bhabha, Akeel Bilgrami, Gayatri Chakravarti Spivak, Nimai Chatterji, Deependranath Datta, Supurna Datta, Meghnad Desai, Nabaneeta Dev Sen, Krishna Dutta, Nathan Glazer, Sulochana Glazer, Craig Jamieson, Armando Massarenti, Patricia Mirrlees, Pranati Mukhopadhyaya, Siddiq Osmani, Mozaffar Qizilbash, Anisur Rahman, Andrew Robinson, Indrani Sen, Arjun Sengupta, Jagdish Sharma, Robert Silvers, Rehman Sobhan, Leon Wieseltier and Nur Yalman. I must also record my appreciation of the inspiration provided by the analyses of parts of the corpus of Sanskrit literature by Sukumari Bhattacharji and the late Bimal Matilal.

I would also like to express my appreciation of the general guidance I have received from discussions on the structure and content of the book with my editor, Stuart Proffitt, at Penguin. He has also made a number of important suggestions on individual articles. I would also like to acknowledge gratefully the extremely helpful copy-editing done by Elizabeth Stratford. For excellent research assistance I am much indebted to Rosie Vaughan at the Centre for History and Economics in Cambridge. Finally, I am grateful for the joint support from the Ford Foundation, the Rockefeller Foundation and the Mellon Foundation in meeting some of the material costs of my research on this and related subjects.

I end with three final remarks. First, since this is a collection of essays (eight new ones and eight previously published), there are some overlaps between them, particularly involving empirical illustrations (though they often illustrate different points). I have eliminated some overlaps, but others could not be dropped without making the individual essays incoherent or obscure. I have tried to give cross-references when they could help. Immediately relevant references are given in the footnotes; other citations are in the Notes at the end of the book.

Second, even though I have had to use diacritical marks for the English spelling of Sanskrit words, I have invoked them in extreme moderation (see the explanations on pp. xix–xx). I have used none for some Sanskrit words and names that are by now commonly used in English, such as Raja, Rani, Rama, Krishna, Ashoka, Brahmin, Vedas, Vedantic or Tantric, not to mention the word Sanskrit itself.

The final remark concerns the style of writing. The book aims to be, at one level, an academic study done by a detached observer, but at another level I am caught within the domain of my subject matter. As an involved Indian citizen, who is very concerned with Indian culture, history and politics – and also with general life in India – it is hard for me to refer to Indians as 'they' rather than 'we'. So, 'we' it has been, not the distant 'they'. Further, given my sense of subcontinental identity, particularly with Bangladesh (from where my family comes), the domain of personal affiliation has sometimes been wider than that of India alone. I need not apologize for this, but the reader is entitled to an explanation of my departure from academic impersonality.

AMARTYA SEN
15 August 2004

Diacritical Notation for Sanskrit Words

Longer vowels have been denoted by a bar on top: ā as in *father*, ī as in *police*, and ū as in *rule*. Regarding sibilants, s stands for the unaspirate, as in *sun*, whereas the corresponding aspirate sound is shown as ṣ, as in *shun*, and the strongly palatal s as ś, as in *shanti* (achieved through placing one's tongue on the upper palate).

Retroflex consonants in the so-called 't group' have been shown with a dot below, such as ṭ, ṭh, ḍ, ḍh and ṇ, in contrast with dental t, th, d, dh and n, which are unencumbered. That distinction, which is not captured well in English but is quite critical in Sanskrit, can be illustrated with the difference between the retroflex ṭ in *tiny* and the Italian-inspired dental t in *pasta*. The unaspirated ch as in *China* in English is shown, in line with the standard diacritical convention, by the unadorned c, as in Italian pronunciation when c is followed by an e or an i (e.g. *cento*), with its aspirate variation being shown with ch.

I have eschewed some of the other distinctions, showing for example the Sanskrit semivowel *rhi* simply as *ri*, as in *Rigveda* (rather than the more austere rendering in the form of *Ṛgveda*). The nasalization symbols used here are: the guttural ṅ (as in *aṅga*), the palatal ñ (as in *jñana*), the retroflex ṇ (as in *varṇa*), the dental n (as in *nava*) and the labial m (as in *mantra*). The somewhat varying use of the nasalizing *anusvāra* is denoted by ṃ, as in *ahiṃsa*.

As is explained in the Preface, I have withheld diacritical marks altogether for those Sanskrit words or names which have become familiar expressions in English, such as Raja, Rani, Rama, Krishna, Ashoka, Aryan, Brahmin, Tantric, Vedantic or (for that matter) Sanskrit.

All this involves some shortcuts, but the long route would have been unduly protracted for a book that is aimed at contributing to public discussion. Also, diacritical marks are reserved for Sanskrit words only, and I have not used them at all for words in the modern Indian languages, such as Hindi or Bengali.

PART ONE

Voice and Heterodoxy

I

The Argumentative Indian

Prolixity is not alien to us in India. We are able to talk at some length. Krishna Menon's record of the longest speech ever delivered at the United Nations (nine hours non-stop), established half a century ago (when Menon was leading the Indian delegation), has not been equalled by anyone from anywhere. Other peaks of loquaciousness have been scaled by other Indians. We do like to speak.

This is not a new habit. The ancient Sanskrit epics the *Rāmāyaṇa* and the *Mahābhārata*, which are frequently compared with the *Iliad* and the *Odyssey*, are colossally longer than the works that the modest Homer could manage. Indeed, the *Mahābhārata* alone is about seven times as long as the *Iliad* and the *Odyssey* put together. The *Rāmāyaṇa* and the *Mahābhārata* are certainly great epics: I recall with much joy how my own life was vastly enriched when I encountered them first as a restless youngster looking for intellectual stimulation as well as sheer entertainment. But they proceed from stories to stories woven around their principal tales, and are engagingly full of dialogues, dilemmas and alternative perspectives. And we encounter masses of arguments and counterarguments spread over incessant debates and disputations.

Dialogue and Significance

The arguments are also, often enough, quite substantive. For example, the famous *Bhagavad Gītā*, which is one small section of the *Mahābhārata*, presents a tussle between two contrary moral positions – Krishna's emphasis on doing one's duty, on one side, and Arjuna's focus on avoiding bad consequences (and generating good ones), on the other. The debate occurs on the eve of the great war that is a central event in the *Mahābhārata*. Watching the two armies readying for war, profound doubts about the correctness of what they are doing are raised by Arjuna, the peerless and invincible warrior in the army of the just and honourable royal family (the Pāṇḍavas) who are about to fight the unjust usurpers (the Kauravas). Arjuna questions whether it is right to be concerned only with one's duty to promote a just cause and be indifferent to the misery and the slaughter – even of one's kin – that the war itself would undoubtedly cause. Krishna, a divine incarnation in the form of a human being (in fact, he is also Arjuna's charioteer), argues against Arjuna. His response takes the form of articulating principles of action – based on the priority of doing one's duty – which have been repeated again and again in Indian philosophy. Krishna insists on Arjuna's duty to fight, irrespective of his evaluation of the consequences. It is a just cause, and, as a warrior and a general on whom his side must rely, Arjuna cannot waver from his obligations, no matter what the consequences are.

Krishna's hallowing of the demands of duty wins the argument, at least as seen in the religious perspective.[1] Indeed, Krishna's conversations with Arjuna, the *Bhagavad Gītā*, became a treatise of great theological importance in Hindu philosophy, focusing particularly on the 'removal' of Arjuna's doubts. Krishna's moral position has also been eloquently endorsed by many philosophical and literary commentators across the world, such as Christopher Isherwood and T. S. Eliot. Isherwood in fact translated the *Bhagavad Gītā* into English.[2] This admiration for the *Gītā*, and for Krishna's arguments in particular, has been a lasting phenomenon in parts of European culture. It was spectacularly praised in the early nineteenth century by Wilhelm von Humboldt as 'the most beautiful, perhaps the only true philosophical song existing in any known tongue'.[3] In a poem in *Four Quartets*, Eliot summarizes Krishna's view in the form of an admonishment: 'And do not think of the fruit of action. / Fare forward.' Eliot explains: 'Not fare well, / But fare forward, voyagers.'[4]

And yet, as a debate in which there are two reasonable sides, the epic *Mahābhārata* itself presents, sequentially, each of the two contrary arguments with much care and sympathy.[5] Indeed, the tragic desolation that the post-combat and post-carnage land – largely the Indo-Gangetic plain – seems to face towards the end of the *Mahābhārata* can even be seen as something of a vindication of Arjuna's profound doubts. Arjuna's contrary arguments are not really vanquished, no matter what the 'message' of the *Bhagavad Gītā* is meant to be. There remains a powerful case for 'faring well', and not just 'forward'.*

J. Robert Oppenheimer, the leader of the American team that developed the ultimate 'weapon of mass destruction' during the Second World War, was moved to quote Krishna's words ('I am become death, the destroyer of worlds') as he watched, on 16 July 1945, the awesome force of the first nuclear explosion devised by man.[6] Like the advice that Arjuna had received about his duty as a warrior fighting for a just cause, Oppenheimer the physicist could well find justification in his technical commitment to develop a bomb for what was clearly the right side. Scrutinizing – indeed criticizing – his own actions, Oppenheimer said later on: 'When you see something that is technically sweet, you go ahead and do it and you argue about what to do about it only after you have had your technical success.'[7] Despite that compulsion to 'fare forward', there was reason also for reflecting on Arjuna's concerns: How can good come from killing so many people? And why should I seek victory, kingdom or happiness for my own side?

These arguments remain thoroughly relevant in the contemporary world. The case for doing what one sees as one's duty must be strong, but how can we be indifferent to the consequences that may follow from our doing what we take to be our just duty? As we reflect on the manifest problems of our global world (from terrorism, wars and violence to epidemics, insecurity and gruelling poverty), or on India's special concerns (such as economic development, nuclear confrontation or regional peace), it is important to take on board Arjuna's conse-

*As a high-school student, when I asked my Sanskrit teacher whether it would be permissible to say that the divine Krishna got away with an incomplete and unconvincing argument, he replied: 'Maybe you could say that, but you must say it with adequate respect.' I have presented elsewhere a critique – I hope with adequate respect – of Krishna's deontology, along with a defence of Arjuna's consequential perspective, in 'Consequential Evaluation and Practical Reason', *Journal of Philosophy* 97 (Sept. 2000).

quential analysis, in addition to considering Krishna's arguments for doing one's duty. The univocal 'message of the *Gītā*' requires supplementation by the broader argumentative wisdom of the *Mahābhārata*, of which the *Gītā* is only one small part.

There will be an opportunity in this essay, and in the others to follow, to examine the reach and significance of many of the debates and altercations that have figured prominently in the Indian argumentative tradition. We have to take note not only of the opinions that won – or allegedly won – in the debates, but also of the other points of view that were presented and are recorded or remembered. A defeated argument that refuses to be obliterated can remain very alive.

Gender, Caste and Voice

There is, however, a serious question to be asked as to whether the tradition of arguments and disputations has been confined to an exclusive part of the Indian population – perhaps just to the members of the male elite. It would, of course, be hard to expect that argumentational participation would be uniformly distributed over all segments of the population, but India has had deep inequalities along the lines of gender, class, caste and community (on which more presently). The social relevance of the argumentative tradition would be severely limited if disadvantaged sections were effectively barred from participation. The story here is, however, much more complex than a simple generalization can capture.

I begin with gender. There can be little doubt that men have tended, by and large, to rule the roost in argumentative moves in India. But despite that, the participation of women in both political leadership and intellectual pursuits has not been at all negligible. This is obvious enough today, particularly in politics. Indeed, many of the dominant political parties in India – national as well as regional – are currently led by women and have been so led in the past. But even in the national movement for Indian independence, led by the Congress Party, there were many more women in positions of importance than in the Russian and Chinese revolutionary movements put together. It is also perhaps worth noting that Sarojini Naidu, the first woman

President of the Indian National Congress, was elected in 1925, fifty years earlier than the election of the first woman leader of a major British political party (Margaret Thatcher in 1975).* The second woman head of the Indian National Congress, Nellie Sengupta, was elected in 1933.

Earlier or later, these developments are products of relatively recent times. But what about the distant past? Women's traditional role in debates and discussions has certainly been much less pronounced than that of men in India (as would also be true of most countries in the world). But it would be a mistake to think that vocal leadership by women is completely out of line with anything that has happened in India's past. Indeed, even if we go back all the way to ancient India, some of the most celebrated dialogues have involved women, with the sharpest questionings often coming from women interlocutors. This can be traced back even to the Upaniṣads – the dialectical treatises that were composed from about the eighth century BCE and which are often taken to be foundations of Hindu philosophy.

For example, in the *Brihadāraṇyaka Upaniṣad* we are told about the famous 'arguing combat' in which Yājñavalkya, the outstanding scholar and teacher, has to face questions from the assembled gathering of pundits, and here it is a woman scholar, Gārgī, who provides the sharpest edge to the intellectual interrogation. She enters the fray without any special modesty: 'Venerable Brahmins, with your permission I shall ask him two questions only. If he is able to answer those questions of mine, then none of you can ever defeat him in expounding the nature of God.'[8]

Even though Gārgī, as an intellectual and pedagogue, is no military leader (in the mode, for example, of the Rani of Jhansi – another fem-

*The Presidentship of the Congress Party was not by any means a formal position only. Indeed, the election of Subhas Chandra Bose (the fiery spokesman of the increasing – and increasingly forceful – resistance to the British Raj) as the President of Congress in 1938 and in 1939 led to a great inner-party tussle, with Mohandas Gandhi working tirelessly to oust Bose. This was secured – not entirely with propriety or elegance – shortly after Bose's Presidential Address proposing a strict 'time limit' for the British to quit India or to face a less nonviolent opposition. The role of the Congress President in directing the Party has remained important. In the general elections in 2004, when Sonia Gandhi emerged victorious as the President of Congress, she chose to remain in that position, rather than take up the role of Prime Minister.

inine hero – who fought valiantly along with the 'mutineers' in the middle of the nineteenth century against British rule – one of the great 'warrior-queens' of the world, as Antonia Fraser describes her[9]), her use of imagery is strikingly militant: 'Yājñavalkya, I have two questions for you. Like the ruler of Videha or Kāśī [Benares], coming from a heroic line, who strings his unstrung bow, takes in hand two penetrating arrows and approaches the enemy, so do I approach you with two questions, which you have to answer.' Yājñavalkya does, however, manage to satisfy Gārgī with his answers (I am not competent to examine the theological merits of this interchange and will refrain from commenting on the substantive content of their discussion). Gārgī acknowledges this handsomely, but again without undue modesty: 'Venerable Brahmins, you should consider it an achievement if you can get away after bowing to him. Certainly, none of you can ever defeat him in expounding the nature of God.'

Interestingly, Yājñavalkya's wife Maitreyī raises a profoundly important motivational question when the two discuss the reach of wealth in the context of the problems and predicaments of human life, in particular what wealth can or cannot do for us. Maitreyī wonders whether it could be the case that if 'the whole earth, full of wealth' were to belong just to her, she could achieve immortality through it. 'No,' responds Yājñavalkya, 'like the life of rich people will be your life. But there is no hope of immortality by wealth.' Maitreyī remarks: 'What should I do with that by which I do not become immortal?'[10]

Maitreyī's rhetorical question has been repeatedly cited in Indian religious philosophy to illustrate both the nature of the human predicament and the limitations of the material world. But there is another aspect of this exchange that has, in some ways, more immediate interest. This concerns the relation – and the distance – between income and achievement, between the commodities we can buy and the actual capabilities we can enjoy, between our economic wealth and our ability to live as we would like.* While there is a connection

*Maitreyī's central question ('What should I do with that by which I do not become immortal?') was useful for me to motivate and explain an understanding of development that is not parasitic on judging development by the growth of GNP or GDP; see my *Development as Freedom* (New York: Knopf, and Oxford: Oxford University Press, 1999), p. 1.

between opulence and our ability to achieve what we value, the linkage may or may not be very close. Maitreyī's worldly worries might well have some transcendental relevance (as Indian religious commentators have discussed over many centuries), but they certainly have worldly interest as well. If we are concerned with the freedom to live long and live well, our focus has to be directly on life and death, and not just on wealth and economic opulence.

The arguments presented by women speakers in epics and classical tales, or in recorded history, do not always conform to the tender and peace-loving image that is often assigned to women. In the epic story of the *Mahābhārata*, the good King Yudhiṣṭhira, reluctant to engage in a bloody battle, is encouraged to fight the usurpers of his throne with 'appropriate anger', and the most eloquent instigator is his wife, Draupadī.[11]

In the sixth-century version of this dialogue, presented in the *Kirātārjunīya* by Bhāravi, Draupadī speaks thus:

> For a woman to advise men like you
> is almost an insult.
> And yet, my deep troubles compel me
> to overstep the limits of womanly conduct,
> make me speak up.
>
> The kings of your race, brave as Indra,
> have for a long time ruled the earth without a break.
> But now with your own hand
> you have thrown it away,
> like a rutting elephant tearing off
> his garland with his trunk. . . .
>
> If you choose to reject heroic action
> and see forbearance as the road to future happiness,
> then throw away your bow, the symbol of royalty,
> wear your hair matted in knots,
> stay here and make offerings in the sacred fire![12]

It is not hard to see which side Draupadī was on in the Arjuna–Krishna debate, which deals with a later stage of the same sequence of events, by which time Yudhiṣṭhira had made his choice to fight (rather than embrace the life of a local hermit, mockingly assigned to him by his wife, with unconcealed derision).

If it is important not to see the Indian argumentative tradition as the exclusive preserve of men, it is also necessary to understand that the use of argumentative encounters has frequently crossed the barriers of class and caste. Indeed, the challenge to religious orthodoxy has often come from spokesmen of socially disadvantaged groups. Disadvantage is, of course, a comparative concept. When Brahminical orthodoxy was disputed in ancient India by members of other groups (including merchants and craftsmen), the fact that the protesters were often quite affluent should not distract attention from the fact that, in the context of Brahmin-dominated orthodoxy, they were indeed distinctly underprivileged. This may be particularly significant in understanding the class basis of the rapid spread of Buddhism, in particular, in India. The undermining of the superiority of the priestly caste played quite a big part in these initially rebellious religious movements, which include Jainism as well as Buddhism. It included a 'levelling' feature that is not only reflected in the message of human equality for which these movements stood, but is also captured in the nature of the arguments used to undermine the claim to superiority of those occupying exalted positions. Substantial parts of early Buddhist and Jain literatures contain expositions of protest and resistance.

Movements against caste divisions that have figured repeatedly in Indian history, with varying degrees of success, have made good use of engaging arguments to question orthodox beliefs. Many of these counterarguments are recorded in the epics, indicating that opposition to hierarchy was not absent even in the early days of caste arrangements. We do not know whether the authors to whom the sceptical arguments are attributed were the real originators of the doubts expressed, or mere vehicles of exposition of already established questioning, but the prominent presence of these anti-inequality arguments in the epics as well as in other classical documents gives us a fuller insight into the reach of the argumentative tradition than a monolithic exposition of the so-called 'Hindu point of view' can possibly provide.

For example, when, in the *Mahābhārata*, Bhrigu tells Bharadvāja that caste divisions relate to differences in physical attributes of different human beings, reflected in skin colour, Bharadvāja responds not only by pointing to the considerable variations in skin colour *within* every caste ('if different colours indicate different castes, then all castes are mixed castes'), but also by the more profound question: 'We all seem to be affected by desire, anger, fear, sorrow, worry, hunger, and labour; how do we have caste differences then?'[13] There is also a genealogical scepticism expressed in another ancient document, the *Bhaviṣya Purāṇa*: 'Since members of all the four castes are children of God, they all belong to the same caste. All human beings have the same father, and children of the same father cannot have different castes.' These doubts do not win the day, but nor are their expressions obliterated in the classical account of the debates between different points of view.

To look at a much later period, the tradition of 'medieval mystical poets', well established by the fifteenth century, included exponents who were influenced both by the egalitarianism of the Hindu Bhakti movement and by that of the Muslim Sufis, and their far-reaching rejection of social barriers brings out sharply the reach of arguments across the divisions of caste and class. Many of these poets came from economically and socially humble backgrounds, and their questioning of social divisions as well as of the barriers of disparate religions reflected a profound attempt to deny the relevance of these artificial restrictions. It is remarkable how many of the exponents of these heretical points of views came from the working class: Kabir, perhaps the greatest poet of them all, was a weaver, Dadu a cotton-carder, Ravi-das a shoe-maker, Sena a barber, and so on.* Also, many leading figures in these movements were women, including of course the famous Mira Bai (whose songs are still very popular, after four hundred years), but also Andal, Daya-bai, Sahajo-bai and Ksema, among others.

In dealing with issues of contemporary inequality, which will be discussed in the next essay, the relevance and reach of the argumentative tradition must be examined in terms of the contribution it can

*On this, see Kshiti Mohan Sen, *Medieval Mysticism of India*, with a Foreword by Rabindranath Tagore, trans. from Bengali by Manomohan Ghosh (London: Luzac, 1930).

make today in resisting and undermining these inequities which characterize so much of contemporary Indian society. It would be a great mistake in that context to assume that because of the possible effectiveness of well-tutored and disciplined arguments, the argumentative tradition must, in general, favour the privileged and the well-educated, rather than the dispossessed and the deprived. Some of the most powerful arguments in Indian intellectual history have, in fact, been about the lives of the least privileged groups, which have drawn on the substantive force of these claims, rather than on the cultivated brilliance of well-trained dialectics.

Democracy as Public Reasoning

Does the richness of the tradition of argument make much difference to subcontinental lives today? I would argue it does, and in a great many different ways. It shapes our social world and the nature of our culture. It has helped to make heterodoxy the natural state of affairs in India (more on this presently): persistent arguments are an important part of our public life. It deeply influences Indian politics, and is particularly relevant, I would argue, to the development of democracy in India and the emergence of its secular priorities.

The historical roots of democracy in India are well worth considering, if only because the connection with public argument is often missed, through the temptation to attribute the Indian commitment to democracy simply to the impact of British influence (despite the fact that such an influence should have worked similarly for a hundred other countries that emerged from an empire on which the sun used not to set). The point at issue, however, is not specific to India only: in general, the tradition of public reasoning is closely related to the roots of democracy across the globe. But since India has been especially fortunate in having a long tradition of public arguments, with toleration of intellectual heterodoxy, this general connection has been particularly effective in India. When, more than half a century ago, independent India became the first country in the non-Western world to choose a resolutely democratic constitution, it not only used what it had learned from the institutional experiences in Europe and America (particularly Great Britain), it also drew on its own tradition of public reasoning and argumentative heterodoxy.

India's unusual record as a robust, non-Western democracy includes not just its popular endorsement, following independence from the British Raj, of the democratic form of government, but also the tenacious persistence of that system, in contrast to many other countries where democracy has intermittently made cameo appearances. It includes, importantly in this context, the comprehensive acceptance by the armed forces (differently from the military in many other countries in Asia and Africa) as well as by the political parties (from the Communist left to the Hindu right, across the political spectrum) of the priority of civilian rule – no matter how inefficient and awkward (and how temptingly replaceable) democratic governance might have seemed.

The decisive experiences in India also include the unequivocal rejection by the Indian electorate of a very prominent attempt, in the 1970s, to dilute democratic guarantees in India (on the alleged ground of the seriousness of the 'emergency' that India then faced). The officially sponsored proposal was massively rebuffed in the polls in 1977.[14] Even though Indian democracy remains imperfect and flawed in several different ways (more on that later, in Essays 9–12), the ways and means of overcoming those faults can draw powerfully on the argumentational tradition.

It is very important to avoid the twin pitfalls of (1) taking democracy to be just a gift of the Western world that India simply accepted when it became independent, and (2) assuming that there is something unique in Indian history that makes the country singularly suited to democracy. The point, rather, is that democracy is intimately connected with public discussion and interactive reasoning. Traditions of public discussion exist across the world, not just in the West.[15] And to the extent that such a tradition can be drawn on, democracy becomes easier to institute and also to preserve.

Even though it is very often repeated that democracy is a quintessentially Western idea and practice, that view is extremely limited because of its neglect of the intimate connections between public reasoning and the development of democracy – a connection that has been profoundly explored by contemporary philosophers, most notably John Rawls.[16] Public reasoning includes the opportunity for citizens to participate in political discussions and to influence public choice. Balloting can be seen as only one of the ways – albeit a very important way – to make public discussions effective, when the opportunity to vote is combined with the opportunity to speak and listen, without fear. The reach – and effectiveness – of voting depend critically on the opportunity for open public discussion.

A broader understanding of democracy – going well beyond the freedom of elections and ballots – has emerged powerfully, not only in contemporary political philosophy, but also in the new disciplines of 'social choice theory' and 'public choice theory', influenced by economic reasoning as well as by political ideas.* In addition to the fact that open discussions on important public decisions can vastly enhance information about society and about our respective priorities, they can also provide the opportunity for revising the chosen priorities in response to public discussion. Indeed, as James Buchanan, the founder of the contemporary discipline of public choice theory, has argued: 'the definition of democracy as "government by discussion" implies that individual values can and do change in the process of decision-making.'[17] The role of the argumentative tradition of India applies not merely to the public expression of values, but also to the interactive formation of values, illustrated for example by the emergence of the Indian form of secularism (to be discussed in the next section).

Long traditions of public discussion can be found across the world, in many different cultures, as I have discussed elsewhere.[18] But here India does have some claim to distinction – not unrelated to the major theme of this essay. The Greek and Roman heritage on public discussion is, of course, rightly celebrated, but the importance attached to public deliberation also has a remarkable history in India. As it happens, even the world-conquering Alexander received

*I have tried to present critical assessments of the contributions of social choice theory and of public choice theory in my Presidential Address to the American Economic Association ('Rationality and Social Choice', *American Economic Review*, 85, 1995) and in my Nobel Lecture ('The Possibility of Social Choice', *American Economic Review*, 89, 1999). Both are included in a collection of my essays: *Rationality and Freedom* (Cambridge, Mass.: Harvard University Press, 2002).

some political lecturing as he roamed around north-west India in the fourth century BCE. For example, when Alexander asked a group of Jain philosophers why they were paying so little attention to the great conqueror, he got the following – broadly anti-imperial – reply (as reported by Arrian):

> King Alexander, every man can possess only so much of the earth's surface as this we are standing on. You are but human like the rest of us, save that you are always busy and up to no good, travelling so many miles from your home, a nuisance to yourself and to others! . . . You will soon be dead, and then you will own just as much of the earth as will suffice to bury you.*

In the history of public reasoning in India, considerable credit must be given to the early Indian Buddhists, who had a great commitment to discussion as a means of social progress. That commitment produced, among other results, some of the earliest open general meetings in the world. The so-called 'Buddhist councils', which aimed at settling disputes between different points of view, drew delegates from different places and from different schools of thought. The first of the four principal councils was held in Rājagriha shortly after Gautama Buddha's death; the second about a century later in Vaiśālī; and the last occurred in Kashmir in the second century CE. But the third – the largest and the best known of these councils – occurred under the patronage of Emperor Ashoka in the third century BCE, in the then capital of India, Pāṭaliputra (now called Patna).[19] These councils were primarily concerned with resolving differences in religious principles and practices, but they evidently also addressed the demands of social and civic duties, and furthermore helped, in a general way, to consolidate and promote the tradition of open discussion on contentious issues.

The association of Ashoka, who ruled over the bulk of the Indian subcontinent (stretching into what is now Afghanistan), with the largest of these councils is of particular interest, since he was strongly

*Alexander, we learn from Arrian, responded to this egalitarian reproach with the same kind of admiration that he had shown in his encounter with Diogenes, even though his own conduct remained altogether unchanged ('the exact opposite of what he then professed to admire'). See Peter Green, *Alexander of Macedon, 356–323 B.C.: A Historical Biography* (Berkeley: University of California Press, 1992), p. 428.

committed to making sure that public discussion could take place without animosity or violence. Ashoka tried to codify and propagate what must have been among the earliest formulations of rules for public discussion – a kind of ancient version of the nineteenth-century 'Robert's Rules of Order'.[20] He demanded, for example, 'restraint in regard to speech, so that there should be no extolment of one's own sect or disparagement of other sects on inappropriate occasions, and it should be moderate even on appropriate occasions'. Even when engaged in arguing, 'other sects should be duly honoured in every way on all occasions'.

Ashoka's championing of public discussion has had echoes in the later history of India, but none perhaps as strong as the Moghal Emperor Akbar's sponsorship and support for dialogues between adherents of different faiths, nearly two thousand years later. Akbar's overarching thesis that 'the pursuit of reason' rather than 'reliance on tradition' is the way to address difficult problems of social harmony included a robust celebration of reasoned dialogues.[21] A royal sponsorship is not essential for the practice of public reasoning, but it adds another dimension to the reach of the argumentative history of India. In the deliberative conception of democracy, the role of open discussion, with or without sponsorship by the state, has a clear relevance. While democracy must also demand much else,[22] public reasoning, which is central to participatory governance, is an important part of a bigger picture. I shall have occasion to return to this connection later.

Understanding Secularism

The long history of heterodoxy has a bearing not only on the development and survival of democracy in India, it has also richly contributed, I would argue, to the emergence of secularism in India, and even to the form that Indian secularism takes, which is not exactly the same as the way secularism is defined in parts of the West.[23] The tolerance of religious diversity is implicitly reflected in India's having served as a shared home – in the chronology of history – for Hindus, Buddhists, Jains, Jews, Christians, Muslims, Parsees, Sikhs, Baha'is and others. The Vedas, which date back at least to the middle of the second millennium BCE, paved the way to what is now called Hinduism (that term was devised much later by Persians and Arabs, after the river Sindhu or Indus). Buddhism and Jainism had both emerged by the sixth century BCE. Buddhism, the practice of which is now rather sparse in India, was the dominant religion of the country for nearly a thousand years. Jainism, on the other hand, born at the same time as Buddhism, has survived as a powerful Indian religion over two and a half millennia.

Jews came to India, it appears, shortly after the fall of Jerusalem, though there are other theories as well (including the claim that members of the Bene Israeli community first arrived in the eighth century BCE, and, more plausibly, that they came in 175 BCE).[24] Jewish arrivals continued in later waves, in the fifth and sixth centuries from southern Arabia and Persia until the last wave of Baghdadi Jews from Iraq and Syria, mostly to Bombay and Calcutta, in the eighteenth and nineteenth centuries. Christians, too, came very early, and by the fourth century there were large Christian communities in what is now Kerala.[25] Parsees started arriving in the late seventh century, as soon as persecution of Zoroastrianism began in Persia. The Baha'is were among the last groups to seek refuge in India, in the last century. Over this long period there were other migrations, including the settlement of Muslim Arab traders, which began on India's western coast in the eighth century, well before the invasions that came from other Muslim countries via the more warlike north-western routes. There were in addition many conversions, especially to Islam. Each religious community managed to retain its identity within India's multi-religious spectrum.*

The toleration of diversity has also been explicitly defended by strong arguments in favour of the richness of variation, including fulsome praise of the need to interact with each other, in mutual respect, through dialogue. In the last section, I discussed the contributions made to public reasoning by two of the grandest of Indian

*One of the reflections of this diversity can be seen in the survival of the different calendars that are respectively associated with Buddhism, Jainism, Judaism, Christianity, Zoroastrianism and Islam, which have all been flourishing for a very long time in India, along with the different Hindu calendars (as is discussed in Essay 15 below).

emperors, Ashoka and Akbar. How relevant are their ideas and policies for the content and reach of Indian secularism?

Ashoka, as was mentioned earlier, wanted a general agreement on the need to conduct arguments with 'restraint in regard to speech': 'a person must not do reverence to his own sect or disparage the beliefs of another without reason.' He went on to argue: 'Depreciation should be for specific reasons only, because the sects of other people all deserve reverence for one reason or another.' Ashoka supplemented this general moral and political principle by a dialectical argument based on enlightened self-interest: 'For he who does reverence to his own sect while disparaging the sects of others wholly from attachment to his own sect, in reality inflicts, by such conduct, the severest injury on his own sect.'[26]

Akbar not only made unequivocal pronouncements on the priority of tolerance, but also laid the formal foundations of a secular legal structure and of religious neutrality of the state, which included the duty to ensure that 'no man should be interfered with on account of religion, and anyone is to be allowed to go over to a religion that pleases him.'[27] Despite his deep interest in other religions and his brief attempt to launch a new religion, Din-ilahi (God's religion), based on a combination of good points chosen from different faiths, Akbar did remain a good Muslim himself. Indeed, when Akbar died in 1605, the Islamic theologian Abdul Haq, who had been quite critical of Akbar's lapses from orthodoxy, concluded with some satisfaction that, despite his 'innovations', Akbar had remained a proper Muslim.[28]

The meetings that Akbar arranged in the late sixteenth century for public dialogue (referred to in the last section) involved members of different religious faiths (including Hindus, Muslims, Christians, Parsees, Jains, Jews and even atheists). While the historical background of Indian secularism can be traced to the trend of thinking that had begun to take root well before Akbar, the politics of secularism received a tremendous boost from Akbar's championing of pluralist ideals, along with his insistence that the state should be completely impartial between different religions. Akbar's own political decisions also reflected his pluralist commitments, well exemplified even by his insistence on filling his court with non-Muslim intellectuals and artists (including the great Hindu musician Tansen) in addition to Muslim ones, and, rather remarkably, by his trusting a Hindu former king (Raja Man Singh), who had been defeated earlier by Akbar, to serve as the general commander of his armed forces.[29]

The tolerance of variation in different walks of life has also had other – if less regal – support throughout Indian history, including in Sanskrit drama, with criticism and ridicule of narrow-minded persecution, for example in Śūdraka's *Mricchakaṭikam* (The Little Clay Cart) and *Mudrārākṣasam* (The Signet of the Minister). It finds expression also in Sanskrit poetry, with celebration of diversity, perhaps most elegantly expressed in Kālidāsa's *Meghadūtam* (The Cloud Messenger), which applauds the beauty of varieties of human customs and behaviour through the imagined eyes of a cloud that carries a message of longing from a banished husband to his beloved wife, as the cloud slowly journeys across fifth-century India. A similar commitment to accepting – and exalting – diversity can be seen in many other writings, from the prose and poetry of Amir Khusrau, a Muslim scholar and poet in the fourteenth century, to the rich culture of non-sectarian religious poetry which flourished from around that time, drawing on both Hindu (particularly Bhakti) and Muslim (particularly Sufi) traditions. Indeed, interreligious tolerance is a persistent theme in the poetry of Kabir, Dadu, Ravi-das, Sena and others, a circle which, as was discussed earlier, also included a number of distinguished women poets, such as the remarkable Mira Bai in the sixteenth century.[30]

Secularism in contemporary India, which received legislative formulation in the post-independence constitution of the Indian Republic, contains strong influences of Indian intellectual history, including the championing of intellectual pluralism. One reflection of this historical connection is that Indian secularism takes a somewhat different form and makes rather different demands from the more austere Western versions, such as the French interpretation of secularism which is supposed to prohibit even personal display of religious symbols or conventions in state institutions at work. Indeed, there are two principal approaches to secularism, focusing respectively on (1) *neutrality* between different religions, and (2) *prohibition* of religious associations in state activities. Indian secularism has tended to emphasize neutrality in particular, rather than prohibition in general.*

It is the 'prohibitory' aspect that has been the central issue in the recent French decision to ban the wearing of headscarves by Muslim women students, on the ground that it violates secularism. It can, however, be argued that such a prohibition could not be justified specifically on grounds of secularism, if we accept the 'neutrality' interpretation of secularism that has powerfully emerged in India. The secular demand that the state be 'equidistant' from different religions (including agnosticism and atheism) need not disallow any person individually – irrespective of his or her religion – from deciding what to wear, so long as members of different faiths are treated symmetrically.

The immediate issue here is not so much whether the French ban is the wrong policy. It could, quite possibly, be justified for some other reason (other than the alleged violation of secularism), for example on the grounds that the headscarves are symbols of gender inequality and can be seen as demeaning to women, or that women (especially young girls) do not really have the freedom to decide what to wear, and that dress decisions are imposed on them by more powerful members of families (with male dominance).† Those can be important concerns (I shall not undertake here a critical scrutiny of

*As will be discussed in the essays that follow, Indian secularism has drawn very severe criticism in recent years from Hindu political activists. While some parts of that attack are based, explicitly or implicitly, on demanding a special place for Hinduism in Indian polity (thereby going against the principle of neutrality), another part of the critique has taken the form of arguing that Indian constitution and practice have not been adequately neutral, and have allowed special treatment of Muslims, for example in exempting some Muslim conventions (such as polygamy) from the legal reach of the civil code that applies to members of all the other communities in India. The issues involved in this critique are discussed – and assessed – in Essay 14. What is important to note here is that the focus of that debate is on the 'neutrality' aspect of secularism, rather than on the 'prohibition' of all religious associations.

†The phenomenon of 'choice inhibition', when the individual is, in principle, free to choose, but cannot in practice exercise that choice (given the totality of social concerns and asymmetries of implicit power), is an important issue in the analysis of liberty in 'social choice theory', which I have tried to investigate elsewhere: 'Liberty and Social Choice', *Journal of Philosophy*, 80 (Jan. 1983); 'Minimal Liberty', *Economica*, 59 (1992); and *Rationality and Freedom*.

their comparative relevance and force), but they are distinct from the demands of secularism itself.

The point is that the banning of an individual's freedom to choose what to wear could not be justified on the ground of secularism as such when that principle is interpreted in terms of the need for the state to be neutral between the different faiths. Being equidistant between different religions does involve a rejection of favouring one religion over another, and this could be taken to imply that state schools should not follow an asymmetrical policy of brandishing symbols from one religion, while excluding others, in the school's own display.* But it need not rule against the freedom of each person individually to make his or her own decisions on what to wear – decisions that others should be willing to respect.

As Ashoka put it in the third century BCE: 'concord, therefore, is meritorious, to wit, hearkening and hearkening *willingly* to the Law of Piety as accepted by other people.'[31] The form as well as the interpretation and understanding of secularism in India can be linked to the history of the acceptance of heterodoxy.

Sceptics, Agnostics and Atheists

The long tradition of arguing also has considerable bearing on the reading of India's past, along with the understanding of contemporary India. Recognizing the history of heterodoxy in India is critically important for coming to grips with the cross-current of ideas, including intellectual processes and scrutinized convictions, that have survived through the turbulence and turmoil of Indian history. Underestimation of that heterodoxy, which alas is far too common, can prevent an adequate understanding of Indian traditions. Let me illustrate this with the status and relevance of religion in India, in

*When I attended a degree-giving convocation, which was described as 'secular', at Dhaka University in Bangladesh in 1999, I was struck by the fact that we had ten minutes each of readings from Muslim, Hindu, Christian and Buddhist texts. While this was a lot of religious thinking at one go, I could see that the ceremony could indeed be described as a 'secular' function under the 'neutrality' interpretation of secularism (I suppose agnostics would have had to free-ride on the scepticism of Buddhism).

particular the need to understand the long heritage of religious scepticism in India.

The powerful presence of religious scepticism in India goes – or at least may appear to go – against a standard characterization of Indian culture, which is exceedingly common, that takes the form of focusing particularly on religion in interpreting Indian traditions. The religious connection is certainly there. For example, it is indeed the case that India has a massive religious literature – perhaps more voluminous than any other country. This is among the reasons for associating the understanding of Indian civilization with religiosity – not merely at the level of popular practice but also that of intellectual engagement. As the Reverend A. C. Bouquet, an accomplished expert on comparative religion, has pointed out: 'India in particular furnishes within its limits examples of every conceivable type of attempt at the solution of the religious problem.'[32]

And so it does. However, these grand explorations of every possible religious belief coexist with deeply sceptical arguments that are also elaborately explored (sometimes within the religious texts themselves), going back all the way to the middle of the second millennium BCE. The so-called 'song of creation' (or the 'creation hymn', as it is sometimes called) in the authoritative Vedas ends with the following radical doubts:

> Who really knows? Who will here proclaim it? Whence was it produced? Whence is this creation? The gods came afterwards, with the creation of this universe. Who then knows whence it has arisen?
>
> Whence this creation has arisen – perhaps it formed itself, or perhaps it did not – the one who looks down on it, in the highest heaven, only he knows – or perhaps he does not know.*

**Rigveda*, 10. 129. English translation by Wendy Doniger O'Flaherty, in *The Rig Veda: An Anthology* (Harmondsworth: Penguin Books, 1981), pp. 25–6. The Vedas also contain many engaging discussions of worldly affairs. For example – in hymn 34 of *Rigveda* – we get a critical, but rather sympathetic, examination of the many problems that the compulsive gambler faces, who grumbles ('my mother-in-law hates me'; 'my wife pushes me away') and resolves to reform ('I will not gamble in the future, I am looked down on by my friends'), but who finds it hard to change his old habits ('I show up there like an adulteress visiting the appointed place') yet easy to advise others ('Do not play with dice. Cultivate your field and remain content with whatsoever you earn').

These 3,500-year-old doubts would recur in Indian critical debates again and again. Indeed, Sanskrit not only has a bigger body of religious literature than exists in any other classical language, it also has a larger volume of agnostic or atheistic writings than in any other classical language. There are a great many discussions and compositions of different kinds, conforming to the loquaciousness of the argumentative tradition.

Indian texts include elaborate religious expositions and protracted defence. They also contain lengthy and sustained debates among different religious schools. But there are, in addition, a great many controversies between defenders of religiosity on one side, and advocates of general scepticism on the other. The doubts sometimes take the form of agnosticism, sometimes that of atheism, but there is also Gautama Buddha's special strategy of combining his theoretical scepticism about God with a practical subversion of the significance of the question by making the choice of good behaviour completely independent of any God – real or imagined.* Indeed, different forms of godlessness have had a strong following throughout Indian history, as they do today.

The 'Lokāyata' philosophy of scepticism and materialism flourished from the first millennium BCE, possibly even in Buddha's own time (judging from some references in the early Buddhist literature), some two and a half millennia ago.[33] There is even some evidence of the influence of that line of thinking in the Upaniṣads.[34] Atheism and materialism continued to attract adherents and advocates over many centuries, and were increasingly associated with the exposition of the

*Gautama's own position on this is, of course, a far cry from the practice of attributing divinity to Buddha himself in some versions of later Buddhism, led by the *nirmāṇa-kāya* doctrine in Mahāyāna teaching. There is also the more general problem, which Ian Mabbett discusses, that 'in analyzing the rise of Buddhism we cannot deny a very important role to the way in which the proponents of *dhamma* interacted with the scattered population of the villages and forest hamlets. From the beginning, Buddhism had to come to terms with these populations' belief in special beings and special powers, of a sort that we normally call supernatural' (Ian Mabbett, 'Early Indian Buddhism and the Supernatural', in Dipak Bhattacharya, Moinul Hassan and Kumkum Ray (eds.), *India and Indology: Professor Sukumari Bhattacharji Felicitation Volume* (Kolkata [Calcutta]: National Book Agency, 2004), p. 503).

intellectually combative Cārvāka.* That 'undercurrent of Indian thought', as D. N. Jha has described it, finds later expression in other texts, for example in the 'materialist philosophical text . . . *Tattopalavasimha* written by a certain Jayarishi in the eighth century'.[35] In the fourteenth century when Mādhava Ācārya (himself a Vedantist Hindu) wrote his authoritative 'Collection of All Philosophies' (*Sarvadarśanasaṃgraha*), the 'Cārvāka system' had the distinction of receiving an elaborately sympathetic defence in the first chapter of the compilation, consisting of a reasoned defence of atheism and materialism.[36] After being expounded and defended in the first chapter, the atheistic claims are subjected to counterarguments in the following chapter, in line with the dialectical strategy of the book, in which each chapter defends a particular school of thought, followed by counterarguments in later chapters.

The exposition of the Cārvāka system begins with a strong assertion: 'how can we attribute to the Divine Being the giving of supreme facility, when such a notion has been utterly abolished by Cārvāka, the crest-gem of the atheistic school?'[37] In addition to the denial of God, there is also a rejection of the soul, and an assertion of the material basis of the mind: '[from these material elements] alone, when transformed into the body, intelligence is produced, just as the inebriating power is developed from the mixing of certain ingredients; and when these are destroyed, intelligence at once perishes also.'[38] Along with these radical beliefs about the nature of life and mind, there is also a philosophy of value, which concentrates on identifiable pleasure, not any 'happiness in a future world'. There is recurrent advice on how to live: 'While life is yours, live joyously!' There is also an acrid and cynical explanation of the cultivated survival of religious illusions among people: 'There is no heaven, no final liberation, nor any soul in another world . . . it is only as a means of livelihood that Brahmins have established here all the ceremonies for the dead – there is no other fruit anywhere.'[39]

*We find references to Cārvāka in the epics also. In the *Mahābhārata*, Cārvāka causes some shock in the establishment by reproaching Yudhiṣṭhira for killing his clansmen in the central battle of that epic (a persistent subject of moral discussion which we have already encountered twice, in the context, respectively, of the Krishna–Arjuna debates and of Draupadī's arguments to Yudhiṣṭhira, encouraging him to fight).

The active presence of atheism and materialism continued through the regimes of Muslim kings. Indeed, even in the late sixteenth century, when the Moghal emperor Akbar held his multi-religious dialogic encounters in Agra, the Cārvāka school of atheism was well represented among the alternative positions that were selected for presentation (as Akbar's adviser and chronicler Abul Fazl noted). In philosophical discourses throughout Indian history, atheists and sceptics make frequent appearances, and even though, in many cases, their points of view are ultimately rejected, they do get their say.

An adequately inclusive understanding of Indian heterodoxy is particularly important for appreciating the reach and range of heterodoxy in the country's intellectual background and diverse history. This is especially critical because of the relative neglect of the rationalist parts of the Indian heritage in the contemporary accounts of India's past, in favour of concentrating on India's impressive religiosity. That selective inattention has, in fact, produced a substantial bias in the interpretation of Indian thought, and through that in the understanding of the intellectual heritage of contemporary India.*

The exaggerated focus on religiosity has also contributed to an underestimation of the reach of public reasoning in India and the diversity of its coverage. For example, Kauṭilya's classic treatise on political economy and governance, *Arthaśāstra* (translatable as 'Economics'), initially composed in the fourth century BCE, is basically a secular treatise, despite the respectful gestures it makes to religious and social customs.[40]

The neglect has also led to the long tradition of rational assessment, central for Indian science and mathematics, being underestimated.† That particular connection is worth discussing, and I turn to that in the next section.

*On this general issue, see my 'The Reach of Reason: East and West', *New York Review of Books*, 47 (20 July 2000), repr. as Essay 13. See also Martha Nussbaum and Amartya Sen, 'Internal Criticism and Indian Rationalist Traditions', in Michael Krausz (ed.), *Relativism: Interpretation and Confrontation* (Notre Dame, Ind.: University of Notre Dame Press, 1988), and Bimal Matilal, *Perception: An Essay on Classical Indian Theories of Knowledge* (Oxford: Clarendon Press, 1986).

†In fairness to Western expertise on India, it must be conceded that there has never been any lack of Occidental interest in what may be called the 'carnal sciences', led by the irrepressible *Kāmasūtra* and *Anaṇgaraṇga*.

Science, Epistemology and Heterodoxy

It is not hard to see that the possibility of scientific advance is closely connected with the role of heterodoxy, since new ideas and discoveries have to emerge initially as heterodox views, which differ from, and may be in conflict with, established understanding. The history of scientific contributions across the world – the experiences of Copernicus, or Galileo, or Newton, or Darwin – shows many examples of the part that resolute heterodoxy has to play, in scrutinizing, and when necessary rejecting, the views that are standardly accepted. We can argue that the flowering of Indian science and mathematics that began in the Gupta period (led particularly by Āryabhaṭa in the fifth century CE, Varāhamihira in the sixth, and Brahmagupta in the seventh) benefited from the tradition of scepticism and questioning which had been flourishing in India at that time.[41] There are also methodological departures in this period in epistemology and in investigating the ways and means of advancing the knowledge of the phenomenal world.[42]

In the *Rāmāyaṇa*, Jāvāli, a sceptical pundit, lectures Rama, the hero of the epic, on how he should behave, but in the process supplements his religious scepticism by an insistence that we must rely only on what we can observe and experience. His denunciation of religious practices ('the injunctions about the worship of gods, sacrifice, gifts and penance have been laid down in the śāstras [scriptures] by clever people, just to rule over [other] people') and his debunking of religious beliefs ('there is no after-world, nor any religious practice for attaining that') are fortified by the firm epistemological advice that Jāvāli gives Rama: 'Follow what is within your experience and do not trouble yourself with what lies beyond the province of human experience.'[43]

This observational focus is, of course, in line with the materialism of Lokāyata and the Cārvāka system. In fact, however, the Cārvāka system went further and suggested the need for methodological scrutiny of knowledge that is derived – directly or indirectly – from perception. We are told that perception is of two kinds: external and internal. Internal perception is obviously dubious because 'you cannot establish that the mind has any power to act independently towards an external object, since all allow that it is dependent on external senses'.[44] But we must be cautious, for a different reason, about relying also on external perception: it depends on how we use this perception. 'Although it is possible that the actual contact of the sense and the object will produce the knowledge of the particular object', often we shall have to rely on propositions that link and connect one object that we may fail to see to another that we can see (such as an unseen fire presumed on the basis of observed smoke). Indeed, there can be no direct observation of objects in the past or in the future, about which we may seek knowledge, and we then have to trace alleged connections over time.

And yet the basis of this type of extension from direct observation remains, it is argued, problematic. While we may be tempted to rely on such connections, 'there might arise a doubt as to the existence of the invariable connection in this particular case (as, for instance, in this particular smoke as implying fire)'.[45] The use of inference is hard to make rigorous, since inference itself requires justification, and this may take us further and further back: 'Nor can *inference* be the means of knowledge of the universal proposition, since in the case of this inference we should also require another inference to establish it, and so on, and hence would arise the fallacy of an *ad infinitum* retrogression.'[46]

If the Lokāyata approach comes through as being intensely argumentative and very dedicated to raising methodological doubts (going well beyond merely disputing the basis of religious knowledge), that is probably a just conclusion. Indeed, Buddhaghoṣa, a Buddhist philosopher in fifth-century India, thought that even though Lokāyata can be literally interpreted as the discipline that bases knowledge only on 'the material world', it could perhaps be better described as the 'discipline of arguments and disputes'.[47] In this respect, the rationale of the Lokāyata approach is quite close to a methodological point that Francis Bacon would make with compelling clarity in 1605 in his treatise *The Advancement of Learning*. 'The registering and proposing of doubts has a *double* use,' Bacon said. One use is straightforward: it guards us 'against errors'. The second use, Bacon argued, involved the role of doubts in initiating and furthering a process of enquiry, which has the effect of enriching our investigations. Issues that 'would have been passed by lightly without intervention', Bacon noted, end up being 'attentively and carefully observed' precisely because of the 'intervention of doubts'.[48]

If epistemological departures from orthodoxy provided methodological help for the cultivation of observational science, so did a catholicity of approach that allowed Indian mathematicians and scientists to learn about the works in these fields in Babylon, Greece and Rome, which were extensively used in Indian astronomy (particularly in the Siddhāntas) which preceded the flowering of Indian science and mathematics from the fifth century CE onwards. There has been a tendency in the new 'nationalism' of the Hindutva movement (discussed further in Essay 3) to deny the importance of global interactions going in different directions (in favour of what can be called 'indigenous sufficiency'). But that reflects a basic misunderstanding of how science proceeds and why the borders of scientific knowledge are not drawn along geographical lines. As it happens, a great many departures in science and mathematics occurred in India from the early centuries of the first millennium which altered the state of knowledge in the world. The interactive openness of Indian work involved both give and take. Indian trigonometry and astronomy, in particular, are of special interest both because of their historical importance and because of the way in which they influenced (as is discussed in Essays 6 and 8) India's relations with other civilizations, particularly the Arab world and China.

In fact, Indian mathematics and astronomy had a particularly profound impact on Arab work (including Iranian work in Arabic) to both of which Arabs and Iranians gave generous acknowledgement. This applied to foundational departures in mathematics (particularly in the development and use of the decimal system and in trigonometry) and also to new ideas and measurements in astronomy. Indeed, the departures presented in Āryabhaṭa's pioneering book, completed in 499 CE, not only generated extensive responses within India (starting with the works of Varāhamihira, Brahmagupta and Bhāskara), but they were also much discussed in their Arabic translations.

In addition to the mathematical advances reflected in Āryabhaṭa's work, the astronomical departures included, among a number of other contributions, the following:

(1) an explanation of lunar and solar eclipses in terms respectively of the earth's shadow on the moon and the moon's obscuring of the sun, combined with methods of predicting the timing and duration of eclipses;
(2) rejection of the standard view of an orbiting sun that went around the earth, in favour of the diurnal motion of the earth;
(3) an identification of the force of gravity to explain why objects are not thrown out as the earth rotates; and
(4) a proposal of the situational variability of the idea of 'up' and 'down' depending on where one is located on the globe, undermining the 'high above' status of heavenly objects (but directly in line with the philosophy of relying on what Jāvāli called 'the province of human experience').

In addition to contributing to scientific understanding, these astronomical advances also involved sharp departures from the established religious orthodoxy. Āryabhaṭa's insistence on working on these issues and on publicizing his findings involved considerable courage and determination.

As Alberuni, the Iranian astronomer, wrote in the early eleventh century, not all of Āryabhaṭa's disciples who followed his scientific lead and algorithmic methods were similarly courageous. Indeed, Brahmagupta, whom Alberuni judged to be the best mathematician of his time (Alberuni even produced a second Arabic translation of Brahmagupta's Sanskrit treatise *Brahmasiddhānta*, having judged the earlier translation, made in the eighth century, to be rather imperfect), clearly lacked Āryabhaṭa's fortitude and uprightness. Brahmagupta played up to religious orthodoxy by criticizing Āryabhaṭa for apostasy in rejecting the established theological astrology, even though Brahmagupta himself continued to use Āryabhaṭa's scientific methods and procedures.

In a remarkable eleventh-century rebuke, Alberuni noted the self-contradiction here, to wit that Brahmagupta, too, followed Āryabhaṭa's scientific methods in predicting eclipses while spinelessly kowtowing to orthodoxy through bad-mouthing Āryabhaṭa:

We shall not argue with him [Brahmagupta], but only whisper into his ear: . . . Why do you, after having spoken such [harsh] words [against Āryabhaṭa and his followers], then begin to calculate the diameter of the moon in order to explain the eclipsing of the sun, and the diameter of the shadow of the earth in order to explain its eclipsing the moon? Why do you compute both eclipses in agreement with the theory of those heretics, and not according to the views of those with whom you think it is proper to agree?[49]

In terms of mathematics and astronomical practice, Brahmagupta was indeed a great follower of the innovative Āryabhaṭa, and as good a mathematician as Āryabhaṭa (possibly even better), but Alberuni doubted that he could have been as fearless a pioneer as Āryabhaṭa clearly was. The constructive role of heterodoxy and of the courage to disagree is not any less pivotal in science than it is in the fostering of public reasoning and in constructing the roots of political democracy.

The Importance of Arguments

Before closing this essay, I should make clear what is and, no less important, what is not being claimed. There is, in particular, no proposal here to seek a single-factor explanation of India's 'past and present' through an exclusive and separate focus on one particular feature out of a multitude that can be found in India's constantly evolving traditions. To recognize the importance of an argumentative heritage and of the history of heterodoxy does not in any way do away with the need to look at the impact of other influences, nor obviate the necessity of investigating the interactions of different influences.

It also definitely does not encourage us to think of any social feature as an unchanging, perennial characteristic of an 'eternal India'. India has undergone radical developments and changes over its long history which cannot be understood without bringing in a variety of factors, circumstances and causal connections that have had – and are continuing to have – their impact. The particular point of the focus on heterodoxy and loquaciousness is not so much to elevate the role of tradition in the development of India, but to seek a fuller reading of Indian traditions, which have interacted with other factors in the dynamism of Indian society and culture.

Consider the relevance of ongoing traditions for the development of democracy – an issue that was briefly discussed earlier. In his autobiography, *Long Walk to Freedom*, Nelson Mandela notes that as a young boy he learned about the importance of democracy from the practice of the local African meetings that were held in the regent's house in Mqhekezweni:

> Everyone who wanted to speak did so. It was democracy in its purest form. There may have been a hierarchy of importance among the speakers, but everyone was heard, chief and subject, warrior and medicine man, shopkeeper and farmer, landowner and laborer. . . . The foundation of self-government was that all men were free to voice their opinions and equal in their value as citizens.[50]

In arguing that his 'long walk to freedom' began at home, Mandela was not claiming that nothing else mattered in taking him towards the fight for democracy, nor that democracy would have no relevance to South Africa had its social heritage been different. The point is, rather, that the traditions Mandela saw at home were momentous, and they interacted with other significant factors that influenced him – and others – in South Africa. And since the democratic precursors in Africa had been fairly widely neglected in discussions on politics and colonial history, it was particularly important for Mandela to bring out the role of Africa's historical traditions.[51]

It is in this broad context that one can see the importance of the contributions made by India's argumentative tradition to its intellectual and social history, and why they remain relevant today. Despite the complexity of the processes of social change, traditions have their own interactive influence, and it is necessary to avoid being imprisoned in formulaic interpretations that are constantly, but often uncritically, repeated in intellectual as well as political discussions on historical traditions. For example, seeing Indian traditions as overwhelmingly religious, or deeply anti-scientific, or exclusively hierarchical, or fundamentally unsceptical (to consider a set of diagnoses that have received some championing in cultural categorizations) involves significant oversimplification of India's past and present. And in so far as traditions are important, these mischaracterizations tend to have a seriously diverting effect on the analysis of contemporary India as well as of its complex history. It is in that broad context that the corrective on which this essay concentrates comes particularly into its own. The claim is that the chosen focus here is useful and instructive, not that it is uniquely enlightening.

It is in this broad context that it becomes particularly important to note that heterodoxy has been championed in many different ways throughout Indian history, and the argumentative tradition remains very much alive today. This tradition has received understanding and support from many of the modern leaders of India – not only political leaders such as Mohandas Gandhi, but also people in other walks of life, such as Rabindranath Tagore. Tagore, who was proud of the fact that his family background reflected 'a confluence of three cultures, Hindu, Mohammedan and British',[52] emphasized the need to be vigilant in defence of this open-minded tradition and to help it to flower more fully.

Like Akbar's championing of *rahi aql* (the path of reason), Tagore emphasized the role of deliberation and reasoning as the foundation of a good society:

Where the mind is without fear and the head is held high;
Where knowledge is free;
Where the world has not been broken up into fragments by narrow
    domestic walls; . . .
Where the clear stream of reason has not lost its way into the dreary desert
    sand of dead habit; . . .
Into that heaven of freedom, my Father, let my country awake.[53]

That task, momentous as it is, is made easier, I have argued, by the long history and consummate strength of our argumentative tradition, which we have reason to celebrate and to defend.

I end on a positive (if somewhat light-hearted) note, by recollecting a nineteenth-century Bengali poem by Ram Mohun Roy which bears on the subject matter of this essay.* Roy explains what is really dreadful about death:

*Ram Mohun Roy was one of the pioneering reformers in nineteenth-century India, whose intellectual contributions matched his public work and leadership. In his far-reaching history of the emergence of the modern world, C. A. Bayly illuminatingly discusses the role of Ram Mohun Roy, 'who made in two decades an astonishing leap from the status of a late-Moghul state intellectual to that of the first Indian liberal', and who 'independently broached themes that were being simultaneously developed in Europe by Garibaldi and Saint-Simon' (*The Birth of the Modern World 1780–1914*, Oxford: Blackwell, 2004, p. 293). Ram Mohun Roy's love of reasoned arguments combined well with the independence and reach of his mind.

Just consider how terrible the day of your death will be.
Others will go on speaking, and you will not be able to argue back.

We are told, in line with our loquacious culture, that the real hardship of death consists of the frustrating – *very* frustrating – inability to argue. There is, actually, an interesting vision behind this extraordinary diagnosis.

2

Inequality, Instability and Voice

The tradition of heterodoxy has clear relevance for democracy and secularism in India, and may have helped Indian philosophy, mathematics and science, but there are also other issues with which we have reason to be concerned. Does it do anything much in resisting inequality and stratification, or in helping the unity of the country, or in making it easier to pursue regional peace?

Recognition and Inequality

I begin with inequality. India has a terrible record in social asymmetry, of which the caste system is only one reflection. This must be adequately recognized first, even when we resist the temptation to accept over-simple generalizations about an allegedly basic dichotomy between an instinctively even-handed West and a perennially hierarchical India (the stomping ground of what Louis Dumont has called 'homo hierarchicus').[1] To acknowledge the long-standing presence of remarkable societal inequality in India, we do not have to endorse radical oversimplifications about cultural – not to mention genetic – predispositions towards asymmetry in India.

But how does the tradition of heterodoxy and arguing touch on this aspect of Indian social life? I begin with heterodoxy and inclusiveness, and will take up later on the relevance of arguing. The inclusiveness of pluralist toleration in India has tended mainly to take the form of accepting different groups of persons as authentic members of the society, with a right to follow their own beliefs and own customs (which may be very different from those of others). It is basically a right of 'recognition', to invoke a somewhat ambiguous idea with Hegelian heritage, which has received much discussion in contemporary social and cultural theory.[2] Since the idea of recognition can be given different interpretations, and may sometimes suggest that all groups are taken to be equal in status and standing, it is important to clarify that something rather less than that is involved in what may be called 'the equity of recognition'.

Indeed, rather than sticking to the overused expression 'recognition', which can stand for many different things, I will use the Sanskrit word *swīkriti*, in the sense of 'acceptance', in particular the acknowledgement that the people involved are entitled to lead their own lives. The idea of *swīkriti* need not, of course, convey any affirmation of equality of the standing of one 'accepted' group compared with another.

Acceptance, in this elementary sense, might not seem like much, but the political value of pluralism has much to do with acceptance – that indeed is the domain in which *swīkriti* delivers a lot.* If the inclusiveness of India made it easy for Christians, Jews, Parsees and other immigrants to settle in India to lead 'their own lives', coming from places where they had been persecuted, the principle that is involved in this 'equity of toleration' is one of acceptance – of *swīkriti* – rather than equality in any broader sense. This remains a substantial issue today, since the extremist parts of the Hindutva movement in contemporary Indian politics threaten – explicitly or by implication – precisely the *swīkriti* of non-Hindus, particularly Muslims.

Swīkriti is thus a momentous issue, in its own right. But, separated from other objectives and priorities, it does little to guarantee – or advance – the cause of social equality or distributive justice. India's record in these areas is indeed quite appalling.† And this remains so

*This is indeed a central issue in 'multiculturalism' which has become a matter of much contention in contemporary Europe and America. The denial of *swīkriti* can be illustrated, for example, by the persecution of Turkish immigrants in Germany and by Lord Tebbit's more amiable 'cricket yardstick', to wit, you cannot be accepted to be truly settled in England unless you support the English cricket team in test matches.

†On class- and gender-based inequalities, see Essays 10 and 11 below. I have discussed a particularly elementary – and brutal – aspect of gender inequality in 'Missing Women', *British Medical Journal*, 304 (7 Mar. 1992), and 'Missing Women Revisited', *British Medical Journal*, 327 (6 Dec. 2003), and in my joint book with Jean Drèze, *India: Development and Participation* (Delhi and Oxford: Oxford University Press, 2002). See also the large literature on these inequalities that is cited in these works.

even after more than half a century of independence and the practice of democratic politics.* Inequalities related to class, caste or gender can continue vigorously without being trimmed in any way by recognition or *swīkriti*. If the norm of acceptance and of participation leads naturally, in the context of a contemporary society, to *political* equality within the broad structure of a democracy (that translation is easy enough), it does not in any automatic way extend that political symmetry into the promotion of *social* and *economic* equality.

In fact, B. R. Ambedkar, who chaired the committee that drafted India's democratic constitution, concluded his presentation with a powerful pointer: 'On the 26th January 1950 [the founding of the Indian Republic with its new constitution], we are going to enter into a life of contradictions. In politics we will have equality and in social and economic life we will have inequality.'[3] There is, however, a connection between the two – between democratic politics and resistance to economic inequality. This is not a mechanical certainty (as indeed India's very slow progress in removing social and economic inequality brings out), but it can be made more effective through committed public action and participatory activities.

The right to comprehensive participation in democratic politics can be the basis of social and political use of 'voice' – through arguments and agitations – to advance the cause of equality in different spheres of life. India's democratic practice has been less than vigorous in some of these issues, and these lacunae are among the major inadequacies in the use of democracy in India today. The future of stratifications related to class, caste, gender and other barriers will depend critically on how they are addressed in political engagement and participatory social actions in the country.[4] Despite the frustration with democracy expressed by many people, disappointed particularly by the slow progress against societal inequality, what is really needed is a more vigorous practice of democracy, rather than the absence of it.[5]

The Indian constitution itself points to the importance of taking up these issues in democratic freedoms. The constitution not only identi-

*Many of the 'challenges' that India faces in the new millennium link closely with continuing inequalities in India; see Romila Thapar (ed.), *India: Another Millennium* (New Delhi and London: Penguin Books, 2000).

fies certain 'fundamental rights', such as freedom of speech and association and equality before the law, but also delineates a set of specific social and economic entitlements under the 'Directive Principles of State Policy', including 'the right to an adequate means of livelihood', 'free and compulsory education for all children', and 'the right to work'.* These rights have been the basis in recent years both of legal decisions by the Supreme Court, and of widespread popular agitation, for example for midday meals in schools, for a general employment guarantee, and other such public arrangements. In a limited way, public voice has already begun to show its effectiveness.

The argumentative tradition can be a strong ally of the underdog, particularly in the context of democratic practice. As was discussed in the first essay, voices of dissent – social as well as philosophical – have often come across barriers of caste, class and gender, and they have not been entirely ineffective. But it is the intermediation of democratic politics that makes the voices of dissent particularly effective in practical affairs. For example, the high proportion of women in leadership positions in Indian nationalist politics and in the post-independence period (discussed earlier) reflects a combination of Indian women's ability to use their voice and the actual opportunities of public politics (as it happens, in this case, originally within the colonial system of the British Raj, in the form of a national movement *against* it).

Something similar can be said about the involvement of political leaders from disadvantaged classes and castes in Indian politics today. Counterarguments to the caste system may have had intellectual force in early disputations, even in parts of the Hindu classics (as was discussed earlier), with clear articulation of sceptical questions in various forms: 'We all seem to be affected by desire, anger, fear, sorrow, worry, hunger, and labour; how do we have caste differences then?' Or, to consider another classical disputation: 'Since members of all the four castes are children of God, they all belong to the same caste. All human beings have the same father, and children of the same father cannot have different castes.'[6] But the practical impact of such criticisms of societal practice can be quite negligible, unless arguments and dissents are reflected in a politically effective voice and in constructive

*See the discussion of these 'rights' and their practical usability in Drèze and Sen, *India: Development and Participation*, especially pp. 184–8, 336–40, 369–79.

public discussions. It would be just as much of a mistake to treat the argumentative tradition as being of no relevance whatever to contemporary Indian society as it would be to regard that tradition as powerfully effective on its own, irrespective of arrangements for politics, particularly of democratic politics.

One of the penalties of the increased focus on religious and communal identities, which has recently gone hand in hand with the deliberate fostering of sectarian politics in India, is a weakening of the pursuit of egalitarian commitments, which requires a more integrated focus on the interests and freedoms of deprived groups taken together (related to economic, social and gender-based stratifications).* While political organizations that unite all the lower castes can – and often do – help the underdogs in general,† that end is not served by the divisive politics of rivalry between different lower-caste groups (fighting each other, rather than confronting together the top dogs of society), or by religious sectarianism (for example, by the congregation of upper- and lower-caste Hindus carefully set up to jointly push and shove the non-Hindus). The newly erected communal boundary lines are not only divisive in themselves, they also add to the social and political difficulties in removing the old barriers of hardened inequality.

The demands *of* justice in India are also demands *for* more use of voice in the pursuit of equity. The argumentative heritage may be an important asset (as I believe it is), but its effectiveness depends on its use. Much would depend on the political deployment of the

*There is also the further issue of the undermining of the role of deprived groups, for example women, through the belittling ideology of sectarian politics. In the context of the Hindutva movement, see the problems identified in Tanika Sarkar, *Hindu Wife, Hindu Nation: Religion, Community, Cultural Nationalism* (Delhi: Permanent Black, and Indian University Press, 2001), and also Tanika Sarkar and Urvashi Butalia (eds.), *Women and the Hindu Right* (Delhi: Kali for Women, 1995), among other contributions in this area.

†General anti-upper-caste movements, in fact, played an important part in the transformation of Kerala in the nineteenth and early twentieth centuries, by working for more egalitarian sharing of social benefits, for example of basic education and healthcare. On this, see V. K. Ramachandran, 'Kerala's Development Achievements', in Jean Drèze and Amartya Sen (eds.), *Indian Development: Selected Regional Perspectives* (Delhi and Oxford: Oxford University Press, 1996).

argumentative voice in opposition to societal inequity and asymmetry, and the actual use that is made of the opportunities of democratic articulation and of political engagement. Silence is a powerful enemy of social justice.

The Unity of India

I turn now to a different issue, that of the unity of India. We can distinguish between two distinct features of the intercommunity discussions arranged by Akbar in Agra in the late sixteenth century. The first was the 'acceptance of plurality', embracing the regular presence of a multitude of beliefs and convictions. The second was the 'dialogic commitment' in the form of Akbar's visionary insistence on the need to have conversations and interchanges among holders of different beliefs and convictions. They are interlinked features of a rich and integrated understanding of a diverse society.

Consider, first, the far-reaching relevance of the former – the more elementary – feature of Akbar's vision, the acknowledgement and recognition of the internal diversity of India. The extent of that diversity has baffled many. Indeed, many centuries later, when Winston Churchill made the momentous announcement that India was no more a country than was the Equator, it was evident that his intellectual imagination was severely strained by the difficulty of seeing how so much diversity could fit into the conception of one country. The British belief, very common in imperial days and not entirely absent now, that it was the Raj that somehow 'created' India reflects not only a pride in alleged authorship, but also some bafflement about the possibility of accommodating so much heterogeneity within the coherent limits of what could be taken to be a pre-existing country.

Yet, as is discussed in Essays 7, 8 and 15, general statements about India and Indians can be found throughout history, from the ancient days of Alexander the Great, of Megasthenes (author of the *Indika*, in the third century BCE), and of Apollonius of Tyana (an India-expert in the first century CE) to the 'medieval' days of Arab and Iranian visitors (who, like Alberuni, wrote so much about the land and the people of India), all the way to the Enlightenment and post-Enlightenment

Europe (with heroic generalizations about India presented by Herder, Schelling, Schlegel and Schopenhauer, among many others). It is also interesting to note that, in the seventh century CE, as the Chinese scholar Yi Jing returned to China after spending ten years in India, he was moved to ask the question: 'Is there anyone, in the five parts of India, who does not admire China?'[7] That rhetorical – and somewhat optimistic – question is an attempt at seeing a unity of attitudes in the country as a whole, despite its divisions, including its 'five parts'.

Akbar was one of the ambitious and energetic emperors of India (along with Candragupta Maurya, Ashoka, the later Candragupta of the Gupta dynasty, Alauddin Khilji, and others) who would not accept that their regime was complete until the bulk of what they took to be one country was under their unified rule.* The wholeness of India, despite all its variations, has consistently invited recognition and response. This was not entirely irrelevant to the British conquerors either, who – even in the eighteenth century – had a more integrated conception of India than Churchill would have been able to construct around the Equator.[8]

The features of India's unity vary greatly with the context. Some of them are more often recollected than others, though they all have their specific relevance. Consider, for example, the emergence, far less often discussed than it should be, of the city of Ujjain, in the early centuries of the first millennium CE, as the location of the 'principal meridian' for Indian calendars, serving for Indian astronomers as something like an Indian Greenwich.† As is discussed in Essay 15, it is still the base of the Indian standard time today, nearly two thousand years later, an awkward five and a half hours ahead of Greenwich Mean Time. That technical development clearly had much to do with the location of imperial power as well as scientific research at that time. Ujjain (or Ujjayinī, as it was then called), as an ancient Indian city, moved from

*There was, of course, some plasticity about the exact borders of what counts as India, but such ambiguity is a common feature of nearly all territorial delineations. Indeed, there is considerable dispute even today about where, say, India ends and China begins, on the northern borders.

†Ujjain had to compete initially with Benares, which is an older city. The early astronomical work *Paulisa Siddhānta*, which preceded Āryabhaṭa's major breakthrough in the fifth century, focused its attention on longitudes at three places in the world: Ujjain, Benares and Alexandria.

its role as the capital of Avanti (later, Malwa) in the seventh century BCE, to become the capital of the Śaka royalty, and most prominently served as the base of the later Gupta dynasty, in the period of the flowering of Indian mathematics and science.

Ujjain was, as it happens, also the home of many leaders of India's literary and cultural world, including the poet Kālidāsa, in the fifth century. It was this connection, rather than the scientific one, that attracted E. M. Forster – that profound observer of India – to Ujjain in 1914. He was struck by the lack of contemporary interest in the history of that ancient city: 'Old buildings are buildings, ruins are ruins.'[9] In Kālidāsa's long poem *Meghadūtam*, described in Essay 1 (as giving a united view of India as a country with very rich variations), a banished husband, who asks a cloud to carry across India his message of love and longing to his far-away wife, insists that the cloud must undertake a detour to see the magnificence of Ujjain. Of course, here too – as elsewhere in Kālidāsa's sensuous writings – he cannot resist dwelling on the feminine charm that could be found. As he visits modern Ujjain, E. M. Forster recollects Kālidāsa's description of the beauty of Ujjayinī women, and how the fifth-century city livened up in the evening as 'women steal to their lovers' through 'darkness that a needle might divide'. The cloud is firmly instructed:

> Though it diverts you on your way northward,
> Do not fail to see the roofs of Ujjayinī's stuccoed palaces –
> If you are not enchanted there by the way the city women's eyes
> Tremble in alarm at your bolts of lightning,
> You are cheated.[10]

Kālidāsa combines his observation of diverse charms and beauties across India with a determination to provide a full view of the entire land that lies on the way from one end of India to another on the route that the poet determines for the messenger cloud.

Similarly, Akbar not only noted the variations across India, but also made serious attempts at some standardization. Indeed, both his abortive move to initiate an integrated calendar for India, the 'Tarikh-ilahi', and his unsuccessful efforts to have a synthetic religion, the 'Din-ilahi', drawing on the different religions known in India, reflected a constructive search for an overarching unity, combined with a firm acknowledgement of plurality. The recognition of heterogeneity has much to do with an understanding of India's qualified solidarity that emerges in these diverse literary, scientific and political efforts. Neither a homogeneous conception of a unitary India, nor a view of isolated segments, could take the place of the idea of a pluralist India that was firmly established well before Lord Clive began erecting the foundations of the Raj.

Solidarity and the Subcontinent

The earlier conceptions of India as a country have had to undergo some cutbacks over the last century, through the partition of 1947.[11] But there are clearly many shared elements in the subcontinental heritage, drawing as they do on the multicultural history of the region. These elements have a widespread bearing on the search, now extremely important, for a safer and more prosperous South Asia.[12] They apply in particular to the fostering of discussions and dialogues to counteract the tensions created by – and the actual dangers resulting from – the development of nuclear bombs and deadly missiles in both India and Pakistan, and of course to resolving long-standing differences on Kashmir.*

Hopeful developments have recently occurred in the dialogic direction. There are constructive intergovernmental initiatives and one hopes that they will be more stable and resilient than past attempts in that direction. For the strength of the dialogic process, it is important that the dialogues involve civil societies as well as government. There have, in fact, been important and constructive moves through citizens' seminars and colloquys for peace and human rights in South Asia, initiated by non-governmental regional organizations. There is much

*Essay 12 goes specifically into the nuclear issue. See also the literature cited there, and also Drèze and Sen, *India: Development and Participation,* ch. 8, Arundhati Roy, *War Talk* (Cambridge, Mass.: South End Press, 2003), and other recent writings on the terrible insecurities involved. Pervez Hoodbhoy's documentary film *Pakistan and India: Under the Nuclear Shadow* and Anand Patwardhan's film *War and Peace* also provide well-informed and well-reasoned critiques of the nuclear policies of the two countries and bring out starkly the seriousness of the problem both countries face.

reason for hope in the fact that these citizens' meetings, whenever organized, tend to attract extensive participation even in the most unfavourable circumstances. For example, there was a meeting of South Asians for Human Rights, a remarkable inter-country citizens' organization (led by Asma Jahangir and I. K. Gujral), in New Delhi in November 2001, attended by more than 700 citizens from different parts of the subcontinent (of whom I was one), just as India and Pakistan seemed to be heading for a violent military confrontation. The media, too, has a critically important role to play in advancing a dialogic approach.*

There are also important issues to be addressed in the other inter-country affairs in the subcontinent. For example, relations between Sri Lanka and India have been vitiated by much misunderstanding about what India should – or can – do to help resolve the issue of Tamil separatism. Similarly, relations between Bangladesh and India demand much subtlety of perception, linked as the two countries are not only by history, but also by language and literature (Bengali culture flourishes on both sides of the border), religion (the Muslim minority in India constitutes about the same proportion of the Indian population as the Hindu minority does of the Bangladeshi population), migration (fairly extensive, taking the illegal with the legal), politics (both secular but with a substantial presence of religious sectarianism in both countries), and economics (great potentiality of close economic ties that continue to remain largely unrealized). There are manifest problems to be addressed on the basis of a fuller understanding, and the use of the deliberative approach – with a long heritage in the joint history of India and Bangladesh – has much to offer here as well.

The dialogic commitment related to the long multicultural history of the subcontinent is indeed deeply relevant for regional solidarity as well as national unity and social justice. Even though this book is

*The Indian press can take some pride in its reach and independence over a long period. However, the rapid expansion of the breadth and coverage of parts of the Pakistani news media is among the most significant developments in South Asia. The tradition of non-sectarianism, particularly advanced by periodicals led by the excellent *Friday Times* and the *Herald*, finds considerable reflection in the daily papers, including the *Dawn*, the *Daily Times*, the *Nation* and others.

mainly concerned with the problems of India in particular, I should emphasize the importance of drawing on the dialogic heritage both of India and of the region as a whole. We are indeed fortunate that this tradition exists and is reasonably well established in the subcontinent. There is basis for some hope for the future in the lines identified by that remarkable observer of the subcontinent Octavio Paz in his book *In Light of India*:

> Of course, it is impossible to foresee the future turn of events. In politics and history, perhaps in everything, that unknown power the ancients called Fate is always at work. Without forgetting this, I must add that, in politics as well as in private life, the surest method for resolving conflicts, however slowly, is dialogue.*

The argumentative route has its uses. We can try to out-talk the 'unknown' – and dumb – power of Fate.

*Octavio Paz, *In Light of India* (New York: Harcourt Brace, 1997), p. 133.

3

India: Large and Small

Some Personal Memories

This is a general book on India, and should perhaps be uncompromisingly impersonal. However, I will take the liberty of talking a little, with due apology, about some personal memories. Many of my childhood years were spent in my grandparents' home at Santiniketan, where I studied at the school that Rabindranath Tagore had established and where my grandfather, Kshiti Mohan Sen, taught. He was, among other things, a well-known Sanskritist (he was even officially titled a 'Pundit', related to his accomplishments at traditional centres of Sanskritic education in Benares), and he was also a major expert on Hinduism, focusing both on its formidable classical heritage and on the medieval religious literature and other devotional poetry (such as that of Kabir, Dadu, the Bauls of Bengal).* We did not have any religious rituals at home, but my grandparents had fairly firm religious convictions, in line with a contemplative and rather non-ceremonial version of Hinduism. Also, Kshiti Mohan was often asked to speak at heterodox religious meetings in Santiniketan, Calcutta and elsewhere.

*See Kshiti Mohan Sen, *Medieval Mysticism of India*, with a Foreword by Rabindranath Tagore, trans. from Bengali by Manomohan Ghosh (London: Luzac, 1930), and *Hinduism* (Harmondsworth: Penguin, 1961, 2005). His Bengali books include not only investigations of the ancient Hindu texts (often focusing on social issues), but also of the 'medieval' religious schools that drew on both Hinduism and Islam. His Bengali books are still very widely read, particularly those on Kabir, Dadu and the Bauls, and on the scriptural diversities on the subject of the caste system and women's social status.

Since my childhood thoughts – for what they were worth – did not attract me at all to religion, I asked my grandfather whether I should be concerned that religion did not appeal to me. He told me, 'No, in fact there is no case for having religious convictions until you are able to think seriously for yourself – it will come with time.' Since, in my case, it did not come at all (my scepticism seemed to mature with age), I told my grandfather, some years later, that he had been absolutely wrong. 'Not at all,' replied my grandfather, 'you have addressed the religious question, and you have placed yourself, I see, in the atheistic – the Lokāyata – part of the Hindu spectrum!'

I remember reflecting on that large view of Hinduism when, some years later, I was helping my grandfather to produce and edit the English version of a book on Hinduism which he had written in Bengali (he knew little English), at the invitation of Penguin Books.* This book, published in 1961, was a great success, both in English (with many reprints on both sides of the Atlantic), and in translations into other languages (French, Dutch, Spanish, but also Farsi and Japanese). Among its substantive accomplishments, Kshiti Mohan's book brought out with much clarity the heterodoxy of beliefs that Hinduism allowed, with a rich variety of well-developed but diverse religious arguments. Kshiti Mohan identified an overarching liberality as being part and parcel of the basic Hindu approach, and saw it as one of its intellectual contributions to the world of thought: 'Hinduism also points out that a difference of metaphysical doctrine need not prevent the development of an accepted basic code of conduct. The important thing about a man is his *dharma* [roughly, the personal basis of behaviour], not necessarily his religion.'[1] That pride in liberality and tolerance contrasts rather sharply with the belligerently sectarian interpretation of Hinduism which is now becoming common through its politicization.

I shall not enter here into the difficult question of the role Hindu tradition may have played in sustaining a dialogic culture and the tolerance of heterodoxy in India, with which this book is much concerned. Some of the most articulate and ardent advocates of tolerance

*This book, called *Hinduism* and first published in 1961, will be reissued soon by Penguin Books, with a new Foreword, written by the present author.

and mutual respect in India were not themselves Hindu, such as Ashoka, who was a Buddhist, and Akbar, who was a Muslim, but they too belonged to a broad culture in which Hindu heterodoxy was vigorously present. As was discussed in the first essay, there is a long tradition of tolerating doubts and disagreements within Hinduism, going back to the ancient Vedas, some three and a half thousand years ago, which made room for profound scepticism: 'Who really knows? Who will here proclaim it? Whence was it produced? . . . Whence this creation has arisen – perhaps it formed itself, or perhaps it did not?'

Indeed, as was discussed in Essay 1, in some of the controversies (for example, between Rama and Jāvāli in the *Rāmāyaṇa* and between Krishna and Arjuna in the *Mahābhārata*), intricate arguments against Rama's and Krishna's orthodox views are elaborately accommodated and carefully preserved in the body of the established texts themselves. Even though orthodoxy is shown to win at the end, the vanquished scepticism lives on, well conserved in the dialogic account. The *Rāmāyaṇa* notes that Jāvāli describes the decisions taken by the epic hero Rama – the same Rama whose divinity has been an act of faith in recently politicized Hinduism – as extremely 'foolish', especially for (to quote Jāvāli) 'an intelligent and wise man'. Jāvāli is given the opportunity in the epic to spell out why he comes to that negative judgement: 'I am really anxious for those who, disregarding all tangible duties and works that lie within the province of perception, busy themselves with ethereal virtue alone. They just suffer various miseries here on earth, preceding their annihilation by death.'[2] The elaborate presentation of alternative points of views draws attention to the plurality of perspectives and arguments, and this tradition of accommodating heterodoxy receives, as was discussed in Essay 1, extensive support within well-established Hindu documents (for example in the fourteenth-century study *Sarvadarśanasaṃgraha* ('Collection of All Philosophies'), where sixteen contrary and competing viewpoints are sequentially presented in as many chapters).

In contrast with this large view, many Hindu political activists today seem bent on doing away with the broad and tolerant parts of the Hindu tradition in favour of a uniquely ascertained – and often fairly crude – view which, they demand, must be accepted by all. The piously belligerent army of Hindu politics would rather take us away from these engagingly thoughtful discussions and would have us embrace instead their much-repeated public proclamations, for example that Rama, the epic hero, is an incarnation of God; that all Hindus worship him; and that he was born on a well-identified spot 'nine lakh [900,000] years ago'.[3] We are thus not allowed to see the *Rāmāyaṇa* as 'a marvellous parable' (as Rabindranath Tagore saw it),* but as a historical document which cannot be questioned. It is also taken to have enough legal status to give actively destructive Hindu politicians a licence to tear down a place of worship of other people (the Babri mosque, in this case, demolished in December 1992) to build a temple to Rama, in celebration of his alleged birth exactly there.

There is also a further claim that, before it was demolished by the Hindu activists, the Babri mosque (or masjid) stood precisely at the site of an earlier Hindu temple, allegedly destroyed to build the mosque. This historical claim (whether or not correct), the authenticity of which is currently under scrutiny (by no less a body than the Supreme Court of India), has to be distinguished from the more gigantic claim that Rama, the divine incarnation, was born there, before recorded history began.

Why any of these theories – historical or religious – even if they were accepted, would give a licence for religious vandalism or sectarian destruction is not at all clear. But in addition, even within the orthodoxy of Hinduism, the insistence that the religious claims of a particular group must be accepted as indisputable truth would be a remarkably constricted view. Many Hindu schools of thought do not mention Rama at all, and, among the texts that do, many hardly portray him in the spectacular light of divinity in which the present-day Hindutva activists insist on seeing him. Indeed, the *Rāmāyaṇa* itself, as just discussed, makes room for those who totally disagree with Rama to articulate, rather elaborately, their doubts.†

*Rabindranath Tagore was keen to preserve the obvious distinction between mythological tales and historical truths: 'the story of the Rāmāyaṇa' is not to be interpreted as 'a matter of historical fact' but 'in the plane of ideas', as a marvellous parable of 'reconciliation' (*A Vision of India's History*, Calcutta: Visva-Bharati, 1951, p. 10).

†There are also several distinct versions of the *Rāmāyaṇa*, varying with region and community within India, offering somewhat different accounts of what was meant to have happened in this epic story. The versions of the *Rāmāyaṇa* known in South-East Asia, for example in Thailand and Indonesia, include further variations.

In addition to favouring narrowly religious certainty, Hindu political activists clearly prefer to dwell on inter-religious confrontations, rather than on the tradition of the peaceful presence of different faiths, side by side. Indians – Hindus as well as others – can actually take some pride in the fact that persecuted minorities (such as Jews, Christians, Parsees) from abroad have come to India over many centuries, seeking a new and unpersecuted life, and have, by and large, found it possible. A continuation of that tolerant and receptive tradition can also be found in the liberal writings of modern-day political or literary leaders, such as Gandhi or Tagore. It is well represented in the speeches and religious writings of many non-aggressive Hindu leaders of our own time, such as Vivekananda.[4]

It is not, however, particularly worthwhile to enter into a debate over whether the liberal, tolerant and receptive traditions within Hinduism may in any sense be taken to be more authentic than the narrower and more combative interpretations that have been forcefully championed by present-day Hindu politics. It is sufficient to note here that there is a well-established capacious view of a broad and generous Hinduism, which contrasts sharply with the narrow and bellicose versions that are currently on political offer, led particularly by parts of the Hindutva movement.

The Emergence of Hindutva

How old is the Hindutva movement? It is a relatively new development in Indian politics, but it has become a powerful force. The Bharatiya Janata Party (BJP), the political party that represents the Hindutva movement in the Indian parliament, was in office in New Delhi between 1998 and 2004, through leading a coalition government, until its electoral defeat in May 2004.

Although Hinduism is an ancient religion, Hindutva is quite a recent political movement. A political party called the 'Hindu Mahasabha' did exist before India's independence, and its successor, the 'Jan Sangh', commanded the loyalty of a small proportion of Hindus. But neither party was a political force to reckon with in the way the BJP and its associates have now become. With its coalition partners, which include largely secular but regional parties from different parts of India (some with only local support) and a relatively tiny militant Hindu party (the Shiv Sena, with a local base in the state of Maharashtra), the BJP took control of the central government in 1998, and, after some defections, formed a new coalition to secure a joint electoral win again, in 1999.

The BJP's rise has been meteoric. In the Lok Sabha (the powerful lower house) of the Indian parliament, the BJP had just two seats in 1984. In 1989 it won 85 seats. By 1991 it had managed to get 119 seats, by 1998 it had 182 seats, and in 1999 it again captured 182 seats. While that was still a minority, in a house of 543 seats in all, it was adequate for the BJP, as the largest single party, to be the leading partner of a coalition (National Democratic Alliance) that ruled India until 2004. In the May 2004 elections, however, the BJP went down from 182 seats to only 138, with the Indian National Congress emerging as the largest party in parliament (with 145 seats), commanding majority support with its own allies (218 seats in all) and the backing of the parties of the left (60 seats).

If the BJP suffered a substantial decline, losing a quarter of its parliamentary seats, most of the 'secular' parties in the BJP-led alliance suffered a catastrophic debacle, with the AIDMK in Tamil Nadu losing all its seats, the Trinamool in West Bengal losing all but one, and the economically dynamic Telegu Desom Party of Andhra Pradesh being reduced to 5 seats from a previous total of 29. The voters seem to have been particularly harsh on most of the secular collaborators of the BJP.

Even though the BJP is no longer dominant, in the way it was over the last few years, it remains a politically powerful force, and is working hard to return to office before long. The BJP has maximally received around a quarter of the votes cast in Indian general elections. This happened in 1998 – its vote share fell from a peak of 26 per cent in 1998 to 24 per cent in 1999, and down to 22 per cent in 2004, with Congress getting 27 per cent. Yet the BJP does have loyal support from a committed group of supporters, and it is an important part of the contemporary Indian political scene. But since the BJP is dependent on its coalitions to get into office, its effective strength depends on its ability to attract support from beyond the immediate BJP fold.

The BJP's powerful role in mainstream Indian politics and the might of the Hindutva movement are parts of the new political reality in India. In the early years after independence, the broad and inclusive concept of an Indian identity which had emerged during the long struggle for freedom commanded sweeping allegiance.[5] The determination to preserve that capacious identity was strengthened by the deep sense of tragedy associated with the partitioning of the subcontinent, and also by considerable national pride in the fact that despite the political pressure for 'an exchange of people', the bulk of the large Muslim population in independent India chose to stay in India rather than move to Pakistan. This inclusive identity, which acknowledged and embraced internal heterogeneity and celebrated the richness of diversity, went with an adamant refusal to prioritize the different religious communities against each other.

It is this spacious and absorptive idea of Indianness that has been severely challenged over recent decades.[6] At the risk of slight oversimplification, it can be said that the movement sees Hindutva (literally, 'the quality of Hinduism') as a quintessential guide to 'Indianness'. Even though the movement had relatively little public support at the time of Indian independence, the idea of 'Hindutva' as a political ideology had already been launched more than two decades earlier. Indeed, the concept of Hindutva was elaborately discussed in a book of that name, published in 1923, authored by Vinayak Damodar Savarkar, often called 'Veer' (valiant) Savarkar, a Hindu chauvinist leader of remarkable energy.[7] While it is often assumed that in pre-partition India the claim that the Hindus and Muslims formed 'two distinct nations' – not two parts of the same Indian nation – was formulated by Muhammad Ali Jinnah (in the context of making a case for the partition of the country on religious lines), it was in fact Savarkar who had floated the idea well before – more than fifteen years earlier than – Jinnah's first invoking of the idea. Nathuram Godse, who murdered Mahatma Gandhi for his failure to support the demands of Hindu politics of the day, was a disciple of Savarkar.[8]

The BJP gets political support from a modest minority of Indians, and, no less to the point, a limited minority of the Hindus. As was noted earlier, the proportion of total votes in Indian parliamentary elections that the BJP has maximally managed to get has been only about 26 per cent (as was mentioned earlier, it has now fallen to

22 per cent), in a country where more than 80 per cent of the total population happen to belong to the Hindu community. It is certainly not the party of choice of most Hindus – far from it. There is also a distinctly regional pattern in the political divisions in India. Indeed, there are several Indian states in which the BJP has never won even a single parliamentary seat.

The politics of Hindutva is promoted by a family of Hindu political organizations of which the BJP is only one part. The 'Sangh Parivar', as it is called, is led by the Rashtriya Swayam Sevak Sangh (RSS) or 'organization of national volunteers', which is in many ways the core organization of the *parivār* (Sanskrit for family). The RSS provides theoretical analyses as well as functional activities in the promotion of Hindutva. The Sangh Parivar also includes the 'Vishwa Hindu Parishad' (VHP), or the World Council of Hindus, devoted not just to religion (as the name indicates) but to intensely religious politics championing what they see as Hinduism. It also includes the 'Sewa Bharti', dedicated to welfare programmes linked with the Hindutva movement. There is in addition the 'Bajrang Dal', the violently energetic youth wing of the Vishwa Hindu Parishad, which has been accused – by the international Human Rights Watch as well as the Indian Human Rights Commission – of direct involvement in the killing of Muslims in the Gujarat riots in 2002. The BJP is the official political arm of the Sangh Parivar, and most of the major leaders of the BJP have been members of the RSS for a long time.

The Hindutva movement has had a strong effect on recent political developments in India, and has added very substantially to the politics of sectarianism.[9] It is therefore important to investigate the nature of the intellectual claims it makes and the arguments it presents. Since the Hindutva movement has been accompanied by violent physical actions, including the killing and terrorizing of minorities (as happened in Bombay in 1992–3 and in Gujarat in 2002), it is difficult to have patience with its intellectual beliefs and public proclamations. But losing patience is not a useful way of addressing any problem – even one with such violent associations. The heterogeneity reflected by the different components of the Hindutva movement also demands that its intellectual wing should receive attention, notwithstanding what their more violent comrades prefer to do.

In fact, while the hard core of 'Hindutva' advocates is relatively small in number, around them cluster a very much larger group, whom I will call 'proto-Hindutva' enthusiasts. They are typically less zealous than the Hindutva champions and are opposed to violence in general (and are typically quite put off by it),[10] but they nevertheless see a basic asymmetry between the pre-eminence of Hinduism in India and the claims of other religions which are 'also present' in India. They agree, thus, with the ideology of Hindutva in giving a primary status to the Hindus in India, compared with the adherents of other faiths.

The argument for this asymmetry seems to draw on two facts:

(1) the *statistical* fact that the Hindus form an overwhelming majority of Indians (no other community comes anywhere close to it numerically), and

(2) the *historical and cultural* fact that the Hindu tradition goes back more than three thousand years in Indian history (at least to the Vedas) and that nearly every part of the Indian culture bears the historical imprint of Hindu thoughts and practices.

Both are undoubtedly weighty considerations and deserve serious attention and scrutiny.

Numbers and Classification

The statistical argument starts clearly with a correct premise: more than four-fifths of the Indian citizens are Hindus in terms of standard classification, even though the beliefs of Hindus, as already discussed, are often thoroughly diverse (the 'official' number of Hindus includes even agnostics and atheists of Hindu social background). This statistical fact has appeared to many – not just the Hindutva enthusiasts – to be grounds enough for an immediate identification of India as a pre-eminently Hindu country. That summary reductionism appeals also to many international journalists – even of the leading newspapers in Europe and America – who persistently describe India as a 'mainly Hindu country': it saves space in newspaper columns and seems accurate enough in some sense.

It also attracts academics who can perhaps be described as 'intellectual simplifiers'. For example, in his famous book, *The Clash of Civilizations and the Remaking of World Order*,[11] Samuel Huntington places India firmly in the category of 'the Hindu civilization'. In taking this peculiarly reductionist view, Huntington's perspective has to downplay the fact that India has many more Muslims (more than 140 million – larger than the entire British and French populations put together) than any other country in the world with the exception of Indonesia and, marginally, Pakistan, and that nearly every country in Huntington's definition of 'the Islamic civilization' has far fewer Muslims than India has. Something goes wrong here with the number-based assessment. But perhaps the difficulties in using the statistical argument lie in the nature of the argument itself.

The first difficulty is that a secular democracy which gives equal room to every citizen irrespective of religious background cannot be fairly defined in terms of the majority religion of the country. There is a difference between a constitutionally secular nation with a majority Hindu population and a theocratic Hindu state that might see Hinduism as its official religion (Nepal comes closer to the latter description than does India). Furthermore, no matter what the official standing of any community as a group may be, the status of individual citizens cannot be compromised by the smallness (if that is the case) of the group to which he or she belongs.*

To make a comparison, when the United States declared independence in 1776 the different religious communities were quite diverse in size: the new polity could have been described as being a 'largely Christian country' in the way India is seen by some as a 'mainly Hindu country'. But this did not derail the need for the US constitution to take a neutral view of the specific beliefs of the members of the different communities – non-Christian as well as Christian – irrespective of group dimensions. The respective sizes of the different religious

*The insecurities to which some minorities (particularly Muslims) have recently been subjected clearly violate the right to equal treatment that all Indian citizens have reason to expect. That basic human right was shamefully violated in the recent barbarities, in 2002, in Gujarat. The underlying issues are insightfully discussed by Rafiq Zakaria, *Communal Rage in Secular India* (Mumbai: Popular Prakashan, 2002).

communities should not be allowed to disrupt the rights, including the sense of belonging, that every citizen should be able to enjoy.

The second difficulty is conceptually deeper. What is seen as a majority depends critically on what principle of classification is used. The people of India can be classified on the basis of different criteria, of which religion is only one. It is, for example, also possible to categorize Indians according to class, or language, or literature, or political beliefs, to mention just a few. What counts as an 'Indian majority' depends therefore on the categories into which the nation is classified. There is no unique way of categorizing people.

For example, the status of being a majority in India can be attributed, among other groups, to

(1) the category of low- or middle-income people (say, the bottom 60 per cent of the population);
(2) the class of non-owners of much capital;
(3) the group of rural Indians;
(4) the people who do not work in the organized industrial sector; and
(5) Indians who are against religious persecution.

Each group thus identified is in fact a majority in its respective system of categorization, and their common characteristics can be taken to be important, depending on the context. In order to attach immense significance to the fact that Hindus constitute a majority group in Indian society in one particular system of classification, the priority of that religion-based categorization over other systems of classification would have to be established first.

It is possible to argue that the way a person is to be categorized must be, ultimately, for him or her to determine, rather than everyone being forced into a unique and pre-selected classification that ignores other principles of grouping. The fact that considerably less than a third of the Hindu population in India vote for the parties that belong to the Hindutva family would suggest that the religious identity of Hindutva is not seen as being of primary political importance by a large majority of Indian Hindus.

There is, in fact, nothing particularly odd in this dissociation. When, for example, people from what was then East Pakistan sought – and achieved – separation and independence as Bangladesh, they were not arguing that their principal religious identity was different from what characterized the people of West Pakistan: the vast majority of people in both East and West Pakistan shared the same religious identity. The Easterners wanted separation for reasons that linked firmly with language and literature (particularly the place of their mother tongue, Bengali) and also with political – including secular – priorities. While the statistics of Hindu majority are indeed correct, the use of the statistical argument for seeing India as a pre-eminently Hindu country is based on a conceptual confusion: our religion is not our only identity, nor necessarily the identity to which we attach the greatest importance.*

History and Indian Culture

Is the historical reasoning behind seeing India as a mainly Hindu country less problematic and more convincing than the statistical argument? Certainly, the ancientness of the Hindu tradition cannot be disputed. However, other religions, too, have had a long history in India, which has been, for a very long time indeed, a multi-religious country, making room for many different faiths and beliefs. Aside from the obvious and prominent presence of Muslims in India for well over a millennium (Muslim Arab traders settled in India from the eighth century), India was not a 'Hindu country' even before the arrival of Islam. Buddhism was the dominant religion in India for nearly a millennium. Indeed, Chinese scholars regularly described India as 'the Buddhist kingdom'.†

In fact, Buddhism is arguably as much an inheritor of the earlier Indian traditions of the Vedas and the Upaniṣads as Hinduism is, since both the religious traditions drew on these classics. Scholars in China, Japan, Korea, Thailand and other countries to which Buddhism went

*The far-reaching role of plurality and choice in the idea of 'identity' is discussed in my Romanes Lecture at Oxford University, published as *Reason before Identity* (Oxford: Oxford University Press, 1999), and my book on identity to be published by Norton, New York.

†See Essay 8, and also my paper 'Passage to China', in *New York Review of Books*, 2 Dec. 2004.

were introduced to the Upaniṣads mainly through their studies of Buddhism. Jainism, too, has had a similarly long history and in fact has a large presence in India today.

Also, as was discussed in Essay 1, there has been a very long and substantial tradition of atheism and agnosticism in India, which was already well developed in the first millennium BCE. And to this has to be added the early presence, also discussed in Essay 1, of Christians, Jews and Parsees from the first millennium CE, and the late – but vigorous – emergence of Sikhism in India as a universalist conviction that drew on both the Hindu and Islamic traditions but developed a new religious understanding. The high ground of history is certainly not comfortable for a Hindu sectarian outlook, which is one reason why there has been such a flurry of attempts by political fanatics to rewrite Indian history, which has produced much drama and some farce (to which I shall return later on in this essay).

No less importantly, it would be futile to try to have an understanding of the nature and range of Indian art, literature, music, architecture, cinema, theatre or food without seeing the contributions of constructive efforts that have defied the alleged barriers of religious communities.* Indeed, interactions in everyday living, or in cultural activities, are not segregated along communal lines. For example, Ravi Shankar, the magnificent musician and sitarist, may be contrasted with Ali Akbar Khan, the great sarod player, on the basis of their particular mastery over different forms of Indian music, but never as a 'Hindu musician' or a 'Muslim musician' respectively (though one does happen to be a Hindu and the other a Muslim). The same applies to other fields of cultural creativity, not excluding Bollywood – that great ingredient of Indian mass culture. India's cultural life does indeed bear the mark of the past, but the mark is that of its interactive and multi-religious history.

*There is a connection here with the general point that Shashi Tharoor makes powerfully that 'the only possible idea of India is that of a nation greater than the sum of its parts' (*India: Midnight to the Millennium*, New York: Arcade, 1997, p. 5).

Hindus and Muslims in History

Even though Indian history may, in general, be a difficult battle-ground for the Hindutva view, much more specialized success has been achieved by the Hindutva movement through agitation and propaganda that build on what is trumpeted as a historical 'guilt' of the Muslim conquerors who overran India. Indeed, the main political moves to undermine Indian secularism have tended to focus, not on discussing the broad current of India's social, cultural or intellectual history, but rather on arbitrarily highlighting specially chosen episodes or anecdotes of Muslim maltreatment of Hindus, evidently aimed at generating the desired anti-Muslim and anti-secular sentiments.

These accounts draw on history, but work through motivated selection and purposefully designed emphases as well as frequent exaggeration. It is certainly true that, from the eleventh century, early Muslim invaders did demolish – or mutilate – a remarkable number of temples, at the same time causing general devastation and bloodshed. For example, Sultan Mahmud of Ghazni, coming from Afghanistan, repeatedly invaded north and west India in the eleventh century, devastated several cities and ruined many temples, including particularly famous ones in Mathura, Kanauj, and what is now Kathiawar (where the wonderful Somnath temple had been widely renowned for its treasures). Alberuni, the Arab-Iranian traveller and distinguished mathematician, who would later learn Sanskrit and write a great book about India, saw the atrocities and wrote about the nastiness of Mahmud's barbaric behaviour.[12]

The 'slash and burn' culture of the Muslim invaders, making bloody excursions into India, did, however, gradually give way to immigration into India and to settling in the country, leading to Indianization of Muslim rulers. It would be as silly to deny the barbarities of the invasive history as it would be to see this savagery as the main historical feature of the Muslim presence in India. Recounting the destructions caused by Mahmud of Ghazni and other invaders cannot make us forget the long history of religious tolerance in India, and the fact that the conquering Muslim rulers, despite a fiery and brutal entry, soon developed – with a few prominent exceptions – basically tolerant attitudes.

Muslim rulers in India, such as the Moghals, could hardly be generally characterized as destroyers rather than as builders. Hindutva accounts of Muslim rulers tend to take such a partisan view that they end up being very like the reading of Indian history that Rabindranath Tagore had ridiculed as 'foreigner's history'. In an essay written more than a century ago (in 1902), he wrote:

> The history of India that we read in schools and memorize to pass examinations is the account of a horrible dream – a nightmare through which India has passed. It tells of unknown people from no one knows where entering India; bloody wars breaking out; father killing son and brother killing brother to snatch at the throne; one set of marauders passing away with another coming in to take its place; Pathan and Mughal, Portuguese, French and English – all helping to add to the nightmarish confusion.[13]

The history of India does indeed contain many nightmarish elements, but it also includes conversations and discussions, and extensive joint efforts in literature, music, painting, architecture, jurisprudence and a great many other creative activities. And it has included ways and means of allowing people of dissimilar convictions to live peacefully together rather than going constantly for each other's jugular.

Some Muslim rulers, in particular, were extremely keen on celebrating diversity and on protecting the rights of each religious group to pursue their own beliefs and traditions. Reference has already been made to the great emperor Akbar, who reigned from 1556 to 1605, and who was deeply interested in Hindu philosophy and culture along with other religious traditions (such as Christianity and Zoroastrianism). As was discussed in the earlier essays, Akbar tried also to initiate, not with great success, a synthetic religion (the 'Din-ilahi'), drawing on the different faiths in India. Akbar's court was filled with Hindu as well as Muslim artists, musicians, painters, scholars and writers, and his pronouncements on tolerance were quite magnificent then and remain rather remarkable, even today. Indeed, Akbar was a major theorist in the direction of toleration, and was a pioneering leader in the world in arranging inter-faith dialogues involving scholars from different religious backgrounds.

Many of the other essays of this volume go into the different ways in which Hindus and Muslims have interacted with each other in cultural, scientific and other creative pursuits. However, since the ancient epics the *Rāmāyaṇa* and the *Mahābhārata* have already figured a certain amount in this book, it would perhaps be interesting to mention that the very successful and extremely popular Bengali translations of these epics owed much to the efforts of the Muslim Pathan kings of Bengal. Dinesh Chandra Sen's authoritative account of the history of Bengali literature describes the events thus:

> The Pathans occupied Bengal early in the thirteenth century. . . . The Pathan Emperors learned Bengali and lived in close touch with the teeming Hindu population. . . . The Emperors heard of the far-reaching fame of the Sanskrit epics, the Ramayana and the Mahabharata, and observed the wonderful influence they exercised in moulding the religious and domestic lives of the Hindus, and they naturally felt the desire to be acquainted with the contents of those poems. . . . They appointed scholars to translate the works into Bengali which they now spoke and understood. The first Bengali translation of the Mahabharata of which we hear was undertaken at the order of Nasira Saha, the Emperor of Gauda [in Bengal] who ruled for 40 years till 1325 A.D. . . . The name of the Emperor of Gauda who appointed Krittivasa to translate the Ramayana is not known with certainty. He might be Raja-Kamsanaryana or a Moslem Emperor, but even if he was a Hindu king, there are abundant proofs to show that his court was stamped with Muslim influence.[14]

Hindutva critics have sometimes focused particularly on the intolerance of Aurangzeb, a later Moghal emperor who ruled from 1658 to 1707. Indeed, some Hindutva sectarians see historical justice in discriminating against Muslims precisely because Aurangzeb is supposed to have done the opposite – discriminating against Hindus – in the late seventeenth century. However, even if Aurangzeb had been the only Muslim ruler in India (he was, of course, one of a great many), the idea of a historical retribution would be exceptionally silly: it is a proposal for matching a historical folly by creating a new folly, penalizing people for 'sins' that they did not themselves commit. But also, Aurangzeb clearly was the least tolerant of the long line of Moghal rulers.*

As it happens, Aurangzeb was preceded and followed by other Muslim members of the royalty who took a very different view of religious tolerance, and he himself was surrounded by people who did not share his intolerance. Aurangzeb's son, also called Akbar, rebelled against his father in 1681, and joined the Hindu Rajput kings to fight his father. As the Rajputs were subdued by Aurangzeb's army, Aurangzeb's son continued his battle against his father by joining another Hindu king, Raja Sambhaji, the son of Shivaji who fought the Moghals and who is much revered by contemporary Hindu activists (even the name of the Hindu extremist party 'Shiv Sena' commemorates Shivaji, who gets much adoration from militant Hindus of today).†

Aurangzeb's elder brother, Dara Shikoh, the legitimate heir to the throne of his father, Shah Jahan (the creator of the Taj Mahal), whom Aurangzeb had killed on the way to the Moghal throne, had learned Sanskrit and studied Hindu philosophy extensively. In fact, the heir to the Moghal throne had himself translated into Persian some significant parts of the Upaniṣads, the ancient Hindu scriptures, and compared them – not unfavourably – with the Koran. It is this translation, which Dara did with the assistance of Hindu pundits, that gave many people in West Asia and Europe their first glimpse of Hindu philosophy.‡ To take Aurangzeb as the 'typical' Moghal monarch, or as the quintessential Muslim ruler of India, would be an extremely strange historical judgement, aside from the fact that the proposal for matching the intolerance of Aurangzeb by a similar asymmetry today would be remarkably peculiar jurisprudence.

*Even though Aurangzeb certainly had much intolerance, it is interesting to note that he too had Hindu scholars and musicians in his court in positions of importance.

†These historical connections are discussed more fully in Essay 14.

‡In fact, Sir William Jones, the founder of the Royal Asiatic Society of Bengal in 1784, who did so much to expand Sanskrit scholarship in India and to spread it abroad, was first introduced, as a Persian scholar, to the Upaniṣads, by Dara Shikoh's translation.

On Inventing the Past

History is an active field of intellectual engagement for the Hindutva movement, and parts of that movement have been very involved in the rewriting of history. Even though it is not surprising, given the nature of the Hindutva creed, that Indian history must play some part in the arguments presented by the movement, it is still worth enquiring precisely why these issues are taken to be so central, as a result of which Indian history has become such a battleground. What is its specific relevance in contemporary Indian politics, and why is Hindutva politics so keen on redescribing the past? I would argue that the answer lies in two specific features of contemporary Hindu politics.

The first is the need for the Hindutva movement to keep together its diverse components and to generate fresh loyalty from potential recruits. The Hindutva movement reaps considerable strategic benefit from the variety of styles and modes of operation that the diversity of organizations within the Parivar allows. As a modern political party in a multi-party functioning democracy, the BJP itself is committed to parliamentary rule, and does, by and large, listen to the views of others. But it can, at the same time, draw on support – sometimes violent support – from other members of the Hindutva family who can stray from the BJP's cultivated urbanity and provide a harsher force. The 'two nation' theory, which – it must be emphasized – is not a part of the BJP doctrine, is championed quite crudely by several sections of the Parivar.

The solidarity of the diverse members of the Sangh Parivar is greatly helped by taking a united view of India's history as essentially a 'Hindu civilization' (it is convenient for them that even a cultural theorist like Samuel Huntington has described India in exactly those terms, as was discussed earlier). The rewriting of India's history in line with the message of Hindutva is extremely important for the cohesion of different elements in the Sangh Parivar. They can differ on political means and tactics – varying from soft-spoken advocacy to hard-headed violence – but still agree on a grand Hindu vision of India.

The second reason for focusing on India's past is the large support for the Hindutva movement that comes from the Indian diaspora abroad, particularly in North America and Europe, for whom it is quite important to be able to retain their general Indian nationalist attachment while embracing any other loyalty they may be persuaded to have (such as Hindutva).* The two can be harnessed together by a narrowly Hinduized view of Indian history, which fosters the congruence of a Hindu identity with a more general Indian identity.

The rewriting of India's history serves the dual purpose of playing a role in providing a common basis for the diverse membership of the Sangh Parivar, and of helping to get fresh recruits to Hindu political activism, especially from the diaspora. It has thus become a major priority in the politics of Hindutva in contemporary India. Following the electoral victory of coalitions led by the BJP in 1998 and 1999, various arms of the government of India were mobilized in the task of arranging 'appropriate' rewritings of Indian history. Even though this adventure of inventing a past is no longer 'official' (because of the defeat of the BJP-led coalition in the general elections in the spring of 2004), that highly charged episode is worth recollecting both because of what it tells us about the abuse of temporal power and also because of the light it throws on the intellectual underpinning of the Hindutva movement.[15]

The rapidly reorganized National Council of Educational Research and Training (NCERT) became busy, from shortly after the BJP's assumption of office, not only in producing fresh textbooks for Indian school children, but also in deleting sections from books produced earlier by NCERT itself (under pre-BJP management), written by reputed Indian historians. The 'reorganization' of NCERT was accompanied by an 'overhaul' of the Indian Council of Historical Research (ICHR), with new officers being appointed and a new agenda chosen for both, mainly in line with the priorities of the Hindutva movement.[16]

The speed of the attempted textbook revision had to be so fast that the newly reconstituted NCERT evidently had some difficulty in finding historians to do this task who would be both reasonably distinguished and adequately compliant. In the early school textbooks that emanated from the NCERT, there was not only the predictable

*The importance of the identity issue for the diaspora is discussed in Essay 4.

sectarian bias in the direction of the politics of 'Hindutva', but also numerous factual mistakes of a fairly straightforward kind. School children were to be taught, in one of the textbooks, that Madagascar was 'an island in the Arabian sea' and that Lancashire had been 'a fast-growing industrial town'. The newly devised history of India in the new textbooks prepared by the Government of India received sharp criticism in the media and in public discussions that followed. The reviews in the major newspapers were almost uniformly disparaging. 'Bloomers Galore in the NCERT Texts', was the news headline in the *Hindusthan Times*.[17]

The BJP-led NCERT admitted some factual errors and promised to correct them (Madagascar, it was promised, would be returned to the Indian ocean). But there was no assurance on correcting the political slant imposed through selective omissions and chosen emphases to play up the Hindutva view of India. That, of course, belongs to the heart of the attempt to rewrite Indian history. The *Hindu*, a leading daily, put the gravity of the problem in perspective when it pointed to 'the havoc that indifferent scholarship combining with a distorted ideology could cause in school education'.[18]

Indeed, in addition to the plethora of innocuous confusions and silly mistakes, there were also serious omissions and lapses in the government-sponsored Indian history. For example, one of the textbooks that was meant to teach Indian school children about the events surrounding India's independence failed to mention the assassination of Mahatma Gandhi by Nathuram Godse, the Hindu political fanatic who had links with the activist RSS (the Rashtriya Swayam Sevak Sangh) – an omission of very considerable moment. More generally, the accounts given in these textbooks of the fight for India's independence were powerfully prejudiced in the direction of the politics of Hindutva.[19]

Many Indians felt greatly alarmed at that time that the Hindutva movement would stop at nothing short of alienating India from its own past through their control over schools and textbooks. There was certainly a good case (based both on respect for history and on treasuring the inclusive character of Indian society) for taking the threat seriously, and the need to be alive to these issues remains strong today. There are many outstanding historians in India and they clearly have a protective role to play here; this is best done if the defence of history comes from a genuine commitment to history, not just from political opposition to the Hindutva view. As it happens, many well-established and respected Indian historians did question, with reasoned justification, the accuracy and authenticity of the claims made by Hindutva ideologues.

Despite the understandable panic, it was never easy to see how the Hindutva movement could succeed in making Indians accept a 're-invented past', no matter how much control they might have had over educational policies in New Delhi. The redrawing of India's history using the Hindutva lens suffers from some deep empirical problems as well as conceptual tensions. The nature of the problem that the BJP faced in trying to change India's past can be illustrated with a simple example.

Given the priorities of Hindutva, the rewriting of India's history tends to favour internal and external isolation, in the form of separating out the celebration of Hindu achievements from the non-Hindu parts of its past and also from intellectual and cultural developments outside India. But an 'isolationist' programme is particularly difficult to sustain, given the importance of extensive interactions throughout India's history, both internally within the country and externally with the rest of the world. Thus, the isolationist perspective runs into severe conflict with many well-known aspects of India's history.

The problem starts with the account of the very beginning of India's history. The 'Indus valley civilization', dating from the third millennium BCE, flourished well before the timing of the earliest Hindu literature, the Vedas, which are typically dated in the middle of the second millennium BCE. The Indus civilization, or the Harappa civilization as it is sometimes called (in honour of its most famous site), covered much of the north-west of the undivided subcontinent (including what are today Punjab, Haryana, Sindh, Baluchistan, western Uttar Pradesh, Rajasthan and Gujarat) – a much larger area than Mesopotamia and Egypt, which flourished at about the same time.[20] It had many special achievements, including remarkable town planning, organized storage (of grain in particular), and extraordinary drainage systems (unequalled, if I am any judge, in the subcontinent in the following four thousand years).

There is obvious material here for national or civilizational pride of Indians. But this poses an immediate problem for the Hindutva view of India's history, since an ancient civilization that is clearly pre-Sanskritic and pre-Hindu deeply weakens the possibility of seeing Indian history in pre-eminently and constitutively Hindu terms.

Furthermore, there is a second challenge associated with India's ancient past, which relates to the arrival of the Indo-Europeans (sometimes called Aryans) from the West, most likely in the second millennium BCE, riding horses (unknown in the Indus valley civilization), and speaking a variant of early Sanskrit (the Vedic Sanskrit, as it is now called). The Hindutva view of history, which traces the origin of Indian civilization to the Vedas has, therefore, the double 'difficulty' of (1) having to accept that the foundational basis of Hindu culture came originally from outside India, and (2) being unable to place Hinduism at the beginning of Indian cultural history and its urban heritage.

The Hindutva enthusiasts have also been great champions of so-called 'Vedic mathematics' and 'Vedic sciences', allegedly developed in splendid isolation in exceedingly ancient India. As it happens, despite the richness of the Vedas in many other respects, there is no sophisticated mathematics in them, nor anything that can be called rigorous science.[21] There was, however, much of both in India in the first millennium CE (as was discussed in the first essay of this volume). These contributions were early enough in the history of mathematics and science to demand respectful attention, but the BJP-created proposed history textbooks tried, with little reason and even less evidence, to place the origin of some of these contributions in the much earlier, Vedic period.[22]

Thus, in the Hindutva theory, much hangs on the genesis of the Vedas. In particular: who composed them (it would be best for Hindutva theory if they were native Indians, settled in India for thousands of years, rather than Indo-Europeans coming from abroad)? Were they composed later than the Indus valley civilization (it would be best if they were not later, in sharp contrast with the accepted knowledge)? How ancient were the alleged Vedic sciences and mathematics (could they not be earlier than Greek and Babylonial contributions, putting Hindu India ahead of them)? There were, therefore, attempts by the Hindutva champions to rewrite Indian history in such a way that these disparate difficulties are simultaneously removed through the simple device of 'making' the Sanskrit-speaking composers of the Vedas also the very same people who created the Indus valley civilization!

The Indus valley civilization was accordingly renamed 'the Indus–Saraswati civilization', in honour of a non-observable river called the Sarasvatī which is referred to in the Vedas. The intellectual origins of Hindu philosophy as well as of the concocted Vedic science and Vedic mathematics are thus put solidly into the third millennium BCE, if not earlier. Indian school children were then made to read about this highly theoretical 'Indus–Saraswati civilization' in their new history textbooks, making Hindu culture – and Hindu science – more ancient, more urban, more indigenous, and comfortably omnipresent throughout India's civilizational history.

The problem with this account is, of course, its obvious falsity, going against all the available evidence based on archaeology and literature.* To meet that difficulty, 'new' archaeological evidence had to be marshalled. This was done – or claimed to be done – in a much-publicized book by Natwar Jha and N. S. Rajaram called *The Deciphered Indus Script*, published in 2000.[23] The authors claim that they have deciphered the as-yet-undeciphered script used in the Indus valley, which they attribute to the mid-fourth millennium BCE – stretching the 'history' unilaterally back by a further thousand years or so. They also claim that the tablets found there refer to *Rigveda*'s Sarasvatī river (in the indirect form of 'Ila surrounds the blessed land'). Further, they produced a picture of a terracotta seal with a

*For the sake of clarity, we have to distinguish between three distinct errors that are conflated together in this invented history: (1) the spurious claim of the indigenous origin of Sanskrit and the Vedas (denying their Indo-European roots); (2) the absurd belief in the Sanskrit-based nature of the Indus civilization (despite all evidence to the contrary); and (3) the manifestly false affirmation that the Vedas contain much sophisticated mathematics and many scientific discoveries (even though non-partisan readers cannot find them there). The third claim, by the way, also has the effect of implicitly asserting that Āryabhaṭa or Varāhamihira or Brahmagupta were not original in the fifth to the seventh centuries: their far-reaching scientific ideas and mathematical results had been, it was implied, known all along from ancient Vedic times, for more than two thousand years.

horse on it, which was meant to be further proof of the Vedic – and Aryan – identity of the Indus civilization. The Vedas are full of references to horses, whereas the Indus remains have plenty of bulls but – so it was hitherto thought – no horses.

The alleged discovery and decipherment led to a vigorous debate about the claims, and the upshot was the demonstration that there was, in fact, no decipherment whatever, and that the horse seal is the result of a simple fraud based on a computerized distortion of a broken seal of a unicorn bull, which was known earlier. The alleged horse seal was a distinct product of the late twentieth century, the credit for the creation of which has to go to the Hindutva activists. The definitive demonstration of the fraud came from Michael Witzel, Professor of Sanskrit at Harvard University, in a joint essay with Steve Farmer.[24] The demonstration did not, however, end references in official school textbooks (produced by the NCERT during the BJP-led rule, ending only in May 2004) to 'terracotta figurines' of horses in the 'Indus–Saraswati civilization'.

It is difficult to understand fully why a movement that began with pride in Hindu values, in which the pursuit of truth plays such a big part, should produce activists who would try to have their way not only through falsity but through carefully crafted fraud. Even though Marco Polo was not as impressed with what he saw in thirteenth-century south India as he was with central China, he did put on record, in a statement that is of some interest (even after discounting for the obvious exaggeration in it), his admiration for the commitment to truth that he found among the Indians he met: 'They would not tell a lie for anything in the world and do not utter a word that is not true.'[25] If that was indeed what Polo found, things have clearly moved on radically since then, with political inspiration playing an energetic part.

In a thrilling passage in the *Chāndogya Upaniṣad* from the first millennium BCE, young Śvetaketu's father tells Śvetaketu about the manifestation of God in all beings (including Śvetaketu himself): 'It is the True. It is the Self, and thou, O Śvetaketu, art it.' That exchange has been much discussed in post-Upaniṣad Hindu philosophy. It would be rather sad to have to complete Śvetaketu's education by adding to it a new postscript: 'And just in case thou art not all that, we will fix it with a bit of cleverness in reconstructing reality!' In trying to invent Indian history to suit the prejudices of Hindutva, the movement took on a profoundly contrary task. The task is particularly hard to achieve given what is known about India's long history. The unadorned truth does not favour the Hindutva view, and the adorned falsity does not survive critical scrutiny.

The Miniaturization of India

The size of Indian religious literature and the manifest presence of a profusion of religious practices across the country have to be balanced, as was discussed in the last essay, against the vigour and persistence of sceptical thought throughout Indian history. I have already discussed, in Essay 1, the historical relevance of the sceptical tradition both judged as a part of India's intellectual world, and also for its relevance to the development of science and mathematics as well as the politics of tolerance and secularism in India.

However, scepticism about religion need not always take the combative form of resisting religious pronouncements. It can also find expression as deep-seated doubts about the social relevance and political significance of differences in the religious beliefs of different persons. Despite the veritable flood of religious practices in India, there is also a resilient undercurrent of conviction across the country that religious beliefs, while personally significant, are socially unimportant and should be politically inconsequential. Ignoring the importance – and reach – of this underlying conviction has the effect of systematically overestimating the role of religion in Indian society.*

This claim might seem peculiarly implausible for a country in which allegedly religious conflicts have been extremely prominent in the recent past, and in which they seem to influence a good part of contemporary politics as well. We have to distinguish, however, between (1) evident *societal* tensions that we may see between pugnacious spokesmen of communities identified by different religious

*Also, as discussed in Essay 1, the Indian understanding of secularism, which has emerged mainly from its history of tolerant pluralism, is inclined towards favouring neutrality of the state between members of different religious communities.

ancestries (often led by sectarian activists), and (2) actual *religious* tensions in which the contents of religious beliefs are themselves material. Indeed, even when the enthusiasts for religious politics in India have been successful in playing up religious differences, they have worked mainly through generating societal frictions in which the demographic correlates of religion have been used to separate out the communities for selective roguery (as happened, to a great extent, in Gujarat in 2002). In this, the finery of religious beliefs has typically played little or no part.* It is important to appreciate the distinction between religious strifes, on the one hand, and political discords based on utilizing communal demography, on the other.[26]

It is possible that even the process of exploiting the classificatory divisiveness of religious demography, including the violence associated with it, is running into substantial resistance in contemporary India. The use of militant 'Hindutva' may have worked well in the state elections in December 2002 in strife-torn Gujarat, with whipped-up hysteria (much as the frenzy of pre-partition riots had 'communalized' Hindus, Muslims and Sikhs in the 1940s). But as the delirium quietened, the excitement of Hindutva activism delivered very little to sectarian politics in the four state elections held a few months later, in February 2003. After four successive defeats, including losing control of the state of Himachal Pradesh, a versatile – and revamped – BJP changed its tactics and went on to win handsomely at the polls in three out of four state elections in November 2003, mainly by prominently shifting the focus of its campaign to developmental issues (in particular 'roads, electricity and water'), with religious demography taking, by and large, a back seat.

However, the issue of divisiveness had not gone away, and surfaced again, in a big way, in the Indian general elections in May 2004. There is considerable evidence that the sectarian as well as economic divisiveness of the BJP did cost it considerable support across the country. Much has been written about the fact that the BJP's slogan 'India shining!' (which tried to take credit for the elevated growth rate and other economic buoyancy in India) backfired, since large groups of

*It is particularly important in this context to see the distinction, well analysed by Ayesha Jalal, between 'religion as faith' and 'religion as identity'; see her *Self and Sovereignty* (London: Routledge, 2000).

people, especially many among the poor, particularly the rural poor, had not received much of a share of the prosperity that the urban rich had enjoyed. But in addition to that economic infraction, it was possible for Congress and other parties outside the BJP-led alliance to make good electoral use of the anxiety and revulsion generated by the BJP through its cultivation of sectarianism and the targeting of minorities, which made the BJP look like a very divisive force in India.

Any set of election results, especially in a country as large as India, would tend to carry the impact of many different types of influences, and there cannot be any single-factor explanation of the different electoral outcomes. But looking through the nature of the electoral reverses of the BJP and its allies in the recent elections, including the total – or near-total – demise of the 'secular' parties in alliance with the BJP, it is difficult to miss a general sense of grievance about the neglect of secular concerns by parties which were not formally signed up for the Hindutva agenda. Not only were the voters keen on bringing down the BJP itself a notch or two, but it looks as if the 'secular' support that the BJP allies delivered to the BJP-led alliance was particularly imperilled by the Hindutva movement's aggressive – and sometimes violent – undermining of a secular India and the complete failure of the BJP's allies to resist the extremism of Hindutva.

In particular, the violence in Gujarat, especially aimed at Muslims, left a lasting mark on the BJP's image, and received much attention across the country. The concession by the former Prime Minister Atal Bihari Vajpayee, the leader of the defeated BJP, that the Gujarat killings had been a major influence in the BJP's defeat, seemed to be saying what was obvious to many.* But – not surprisingly – the less moderate part of the Hindutva leadership has reacted to this concession with unconcealed venom, making Vajpayee swallow most of his words of concession.

It is important to understand the hold of the sceptical tradition in India, despite the manifest presence of religions all across the country. In responding to the exploitation of religious demography in the

*Vajpayee is reported to have said: 'It is very difficult to say what all the reasons are for the defeat [of the BJP] in the elections but one impact of the violence was we lost the elections' (see 'Gujarat bloodbath cost us dearly: Vajpayee', *Times of India*, 12 June 2004).

politics of Hindutva, the defenders of secular politics often take for granted that the Indian population would want religious politics in one form or another. This has led to the political temptation to use 'soft Hindutva' as a compromise response by secularists to the politics of 'hard Hindutva'. But that tactical approach, which certainly has not given the anti-BJP parties any dividend so far, is foundationally mistaken. It profoundly ignores the strength of scepticism in India, which extends to religions as well, particularly in the form of doubting the relevance of religious beliefs in political affairs. Indeed, the tolerance of heterodoxy, and acceptance of variations of religious beliefs and customs, is deep rooted in India.

Rabindranath Tagore thought that the 'idea of India' itself militates 'against the intense consciousness of the separateness of one's own people from others'.[27] Through their attempts to encourage and exploit separatism, the Hindutva movement has entered into a confrontation with the idea of India itself. This is nothing short of a sustained effort to miniaturize the broad idea of a large India – proud of its heterodox past and its pluralist present – and to replace it by the stamp of a small India, bundled around a drastically downsized version of Hinduism. In the confrontation between a large and a small India, the broader understanding can certainly win. But the battle for the broad idea of India cannot be won unless those fighting for the larger conception know what they are fighting for. The reach of Indian traditions, including heterodoxy and the celebration of plurality and scepticism, requires a comprehensive recognition. Cognizance of India's past is important for an adequate understanding of the capacious idea of India.

4

The Diaspora and the World

An Issue of Identity

The nature of the Indian identity is significant for those who live in India.* But it is also important for the very large Indian diaspora across the world – estimated to be 20 million or more in number. They see, rightly, no contradiction between being loyal citizens of the country in which they are settled and where they are socially and politically integrated (Britain or the United States or Malaysia or Kenya or wherever), and still retaining a sense of affiliation and companionship with India and Indians. As is frequently the case with emigrants in general, the Indian diaspora is also keen on taking pride – some self-respect and dignity – in the culture and traditions of their original homeland. This frequently takes the form of some kind of 'national' or 'civilizational' appreciation of being Indian in origin. However, there is often some lack of clarity on the appropriate grounds for dignity: what should the Indian diaspora be proud of?

This is not a hard question to answer, given the breadth and richness of Indian civilization. Nevertheless, this subject has become something of a battleground in recent years. Indeed, the rather combative line of exclusionary thinking that the Hindutva movement has sponsored and championed has made strong inroads into the perceptions of the Indian diaspora. There has been a systematic effort to encourage non-resident Indians of Hindu background to identify themselves, not primarily as 'Indians', but particularly as 'Hindus' (or, at least, to see themselves as Indians within a Hinduized conception).

*Some general issues of identity are discussed in Essay 16 below.

The campaign has worked effectively over parts of the diaspora, and the Sangh Parivar – including its more aggressive components – receives large remittances from Indians overseas.

As it happens, sectarian and fundamentalist ideas of different religions often do get enthusiastic support from emigrants, who aggressively play up the value of what they identify as their 'own traditions' as they find themselves engulfed in a dominant foreign culture abroad. This tendency gave strength to Sikh political militancy in North America and Europe that was very powerful in the 1980s. It also continues to add to the vigour of Islamic fundamentalism in the world today. The Hindutva movement, too, has been busy recruiting its foreign legion with much vigour and considerable success.

Yet many expatriate Indians, irrespective of their religious background, find it hard to see themselves in such divisive terms, and are also worried about the use of brutalities and bloodshed associated with the extremist wing of the Hindutva movement; for example, in the riots in Gujarat in 2002: voices were even raised at the otherwise smooth meeting of 'Pravasi Bharatiya' (Indians living abroad), arranged with much fanfare by the government of India in New Delhi in January 2003 (to which 2,000 members of the diaspora came from sixty-three different countries), about the deep shame that many overseas Indians felt about the organized sectarian violence in Gujarat. There is a desire for national or cultural pride, but some uncertainty about what to take pride in.

Tradition and Pride

In this context, it is particularly important to look at the traditions of India in all their spaciousness – not artificially narrowed in sectarian lines. Indeed, within the Hindu tradition itself, there is surely much reason for pride in the reach and open-mindedness of the broad and capacious reading of the Hindu perspective, without a confrontational approach to other faiths. That perspective (as discussed in Essay 3) is radically different from the drastically downsized Hinduism that tends to receive the patronage of the Hindutva movement.

Even though the programme of identifying with a 'small India' is vigorously pushed (no Buddha, please, nor Ashoka or Akbar or Kabir or Nanak), there is a 'large India' too, available to the diaspora as much as to Indians in India. It is important to appreciate that the historical achievements in India in critical reasoning, public deliberation and analytical scrutiny, as well as in science and mathematics, architecture, medicine, painting and music, are products of Indian society – involving both Hindus and non-Hindus, and including the sceptical as well as the religious. Indians of any background should have reason enough to celebrate their historical or cultural association with (to consider a variety of examples) Nāgārjuna's penetrating philosophical arguments, Harṣa's philanthropic leadership, Maitreyī's or Gārgī's searching questions, Cārvāka's reasoned scepticism, Āryabhaṭa's astronomical and mathematical departures, Kālidāsa's dazzling poetry, Śūdraka's subversive drama, Abul Fazl's astounding scholarship, Shah Jahan's aesthetic vision, Ramanujan's mathematics, or Ravi Shankar's and Ali Akbar Khan's music, without first having to check the religious background of each.

In that large tradition, there is indeed much to be proud of, including some ideas for which India gets far less credit than it could plausibly expect. Consider, for example, the tradition of public reasoning. Even though the importance of dialogue and discussion has been emphasized in the history of many countries in the world, the fact that the Indian subcontinent has a particularly strong tradition in recognizing and pursuing a dialogic commitment is certainly worth noting, especially in the darkening world – with violence and terrorism – in which we live. It is indeed good to remember that some of the earliest open public deliberations in the world were hosted in India to discuss different points of views, with a particularly large meeting arranged by Ashoka in the third century BCE. It is good to remember also that Akbar championed – even that was four hundred years ago – the necessity of public dialogues and backed up his conviction by arranging actual dialogues between members of different faiths. The importance of such recollections does not lie merely in the celebration of history, but also in understanding the continuing relevance of these early departures in theory and practice.

It is at this time rather common in Western political discussions to assume that tolerance and the use of reason are quintessential – possibly unique – features of 'Occidental values': for example, Samuel Huntington has insisted that the 'West was West long before it was modern' and that the 'sense of individualism and a tradition of individual rights and liberties' to be found in the West are 'unique among civilized societies'.[1] Given the fair degree of ubiquity that such perceptions have in the modern West, it is perhaps worth noting that issues of individual rights and liberties have figured in discussions elsewhere as well, not least in the context of emphasizing the importance of the individual's right of decision-making, for example about one's religion.

There has been support as well as denial of such rights in the history of both Europe and India, and it is hard to see that the Western experience in support of these rights is peculiarly 'unique among civilized societies'. For example, when Akbar was issuing his legal order that 'no man should be interfered with on account of religion, and anyone is to be allowed to go over to a religion that pleases him',[2] and was busy arranging dialogues between Hindus, Muslims, Christians, Jains, Parsees, Jews and even atheists, Giordano Bruno was being burnt at the stake in Rome for heresy, in the public space of Campo dei Fiori.

Perhaps the most impressive aspect of Akbar's defence of a tolerant pluralist society is his focus on the role of reasoning in choosing this approach. Even in deciding on one's faith, one should be, Akbar argued, guided by 'the path of reason' (*rahi aql*), rather than led by 'blind faith'. Reason cannot but be supreme, since even when disputing reason, we would have to give reason for that disputation.[3] In the first two essays of this book, I have tried to comment on the long history of reasoning – and arguing – in India, and its connection with accomplishments in such fields as science, mathematics, epistemology, public ethics and in the politics of participation and secularism.

There is, I would argue, much in this tradition that should receive systematic attention from Indians today, including the diaspora, irrespective of whether the leadership comes from Hindus or Muslims or Buddhists or Christians or Sikhs or Parsees or Jains or Jews. Indeed, the importance of fuller knowledge about India's traditions is hard to overemphasize at the present time. It is not only relevant for the understanding of the 'large India', but also important for appreciating the variations and freedoms that a broad Indian identity allows – indeed, celebrates.

Colonial Dominance and Self-respect

One of the reasons for seeking a clearer view of the intellectual accomplishments in India's past relates to a bias in self-perception that is associated with India's colonial history. This is not the occasion to try to look at many other features of colonial relations that radically influenced attitudes and perceptions in India, but since I am focusing on something quite specific, I should warn about the slender nature of the programme of investigation here.[4]

The colonial experience of India not only had the effect of undermining the intellectual self-confidence of Indians, it has also been especially hard on the type of recognition that Indians may standardly have given to the country's scientific and critical traditions. The comparative judgement that Macaulay made popular in the early nineteenth century ('a single shelf of a good European library was worth the whole native literature of India and Arabia') was seen to apply particularly to Indian *analytical* work (as will be more fully discussed in Essay 7).[5]

Even though early colonial administrators in the late eighteenth century – Warren Hastings among them – took a very broad interest in India's intellectual past, the narrowing of the imperial mind was quite rapid once the empire settled in.[6] Coercion and dominance demanded the kind of distancing that could sustain the 'autocracy set up and sustained in the East by the foremost democracy in the Western world' (as Ranajit Guha has insightfully described colonial India).[7] India's religions and mystical thoughts did not threaten to undermine that imperial intellectual distance. There was no great difficulty in providing encouragement and assistance to those who gathered and translated 'the sacred books of the east' (as Max Müller did, with support from the East India Company, commissioned in 1847, resulting in a 50-volume collection).[8] But in the standard fields of pure and practical reason, the propensity to see a gigantic intellectual gap between India and the West – stretching far back into history – was certainly quite strong.*

Let me illustrate. Consider, for example, the originality of Āryabhaṭa's work, completed in 499 CE, on the diurnal motion of the earth (disputing the earlier understanding of an orbiting sun) and the related proposal that there was a force of gravity which prevented material objects from being thrown away as the earth rotated (described in Essay 1). The most influential colonial historian of British India, James Mill, took these claims to be straightforward fabrication. It was clear to Mill that the Indian 'pundits had become acquainted with the ideas of European philosophers respecting the system of the universe', and had then proceeded to claim that 'those ideas were contained in their own books'.[9] Mill's Indian history, which Macaulay described as 'on the whole the greatest historical work which has appeared in our language since that of Gibbon',[10] was tremendously influential in the intellectual world of the British Raj.[11]

As it happens, however, the scientific ideas in dispute were well reported, not just in Indian books, but also in the accounts of outside observers. In particular, they received careful and detailed description (as did other early Indian works in astronomy and mathematics) from Arab and Iranian mathematicians, who also translated and extensively used (with generous acknowledgement) some of the relevant Sanskrit books.† For example, the Iranian mathematician Alberuni commented specifically on this particular work of Āryabhaṭa (which Mill took to be the result of nineteenth-century fabrication) in an Arabic book on India (*Ta'rikh al-hind*), written in the early eleventh century:

*See the discussion of 'the magisterial view' in Essay 7 below.

†One of the oddities of the intellectually underinformed world of the Hindutva movement is the chastisement that it offers to the Arab world. The international head of the Vishwa Hindu Parishad, Praveen Togadia, whose knowledge of science cannot far exceed his political wisdom, is even on record asking 'Indian Muslims to get their genetics tested', to rule out the possibility that 'the blood of Arabia' may 'flow in their blood' ('Togadia Said It, and He's Proud of It', *Indian Express*, 21 Oct. 2002). The grossness of this gratuitous counsel is particularly galling, not just because of its moral crudity and scientific stupidity, but also because of Togadia's evident ignorance of the generosity and fairness with which the Arab authors have, historically, tended to treat the creative works of Hindu intellectuals (on this see Essay 7 below). In fact, Hindu mathematics became known in the Christian West mainly through the efforts of Muslim Arabs.

Brahmagupta says in another place of the same book: 'The followers of Āryabhaṭa maintain that the earth is moving and heaven resting. People have tried to refute them by saying that, if such were the case, stones and trees would fall from the earth.' But Brahmagupta does not agree with them, and says that that would not necessarily follow from their theory, apparently because he thought that all heavy things are attracted towards the centre of the earth.[12]

James Mill's comprehensive denial of Indian intellectual originality evidently sprang from his general belief that Indians had taken only 'a few of the earliest steps in the progress to civilization'.[13] Mill's conviction that Indian scholars were fabricating things would have received some help from his other general belief: 'Our ancestors, though rough, were sincere; but under the glosing exterior of the Hindu, lies a general disposition to deceit and perfidy.'[14] Mill was quite even-handed in dismissing all other claims of achievement of Indian science and mathematics as well, for example the development and use of the decimal system (Mill offered the enticing view that the Indian decimal notations were 'really hieroglyphics').*

Perhaps I should in fairness note the mitigating circumstance that Mill made a conscious decision to write his history of India without learning any Indian language and without ever visiting India. Mill declared these facts with some apparent pride in the Preface to his book – he evidently did not want to be biased by closeness to the subject matter. Alberuni, the Iranian mathematician, who mastered Sanskrit and roamed around in India for a great many years before writing his own history of India, eight hundred years before Mill, would have been a little puzzled by the research methodology of the leading British historian of India of the nineteenth century. Mill's work set the tone for many of the discussions on colonial policy of the day, including the educational arrangements instituted in British India, in which Macaulay in particular, citing Mill very often, played a big part.

Colonial undermining of self-confidence had the effect of driving many Indians to look for sources of dignity and pride in some special achievements in which there was less powerful opposition – and also

*These and other Millian diagnoses are more fully discussed in Essay 7 below.

less competition – from the imperial West, including India's alleged excellence in spirituality and the outstanding importance of her specific religious practices.[15] By creating their 'own domain of sovereignty' (as Partha Chatterjee has described it),[16] the Indians – like other people dominated by colonialism – have often sought their self-respect in unusual fields and special interests. This has been associated with an extraordinary neglect of Indian works on reasoning, science, mathematics and other so-called 'Western spheres of success'. There is certainly a need for some emendation here.

History and Public Reason

There is a need for a somewhat similar corrective regarding Indian traditions in public reasoning and tolerant communication, and more generally in what can be called the precursors of democratic practice (discussed in Essay 1). Imperial leaders in Britain, such as Winston Churchill, were not only sceptical of the ability of Indians to govern themselves, they found little reason to take an interest in the history of ideas on civil administration or participatory governance or public reasoning in India. In contrast, when India became independent in 1947 the political discussions that led to a fully democratic constitution, making India the largest democracy in the twentieth century, not only included references to Western experiences in democracy, but also recalled its own participatory traditions.

Jawaharlal Nehru, India's first Prime Minister, put particular emphasis on the toleration of heterodoxy and pluralism in Indian history.[17] The Chair of the Drafting Committee of the Indian constitution, Dr B. R. Ambedkar, a distinguished scholar and political leader from the community of Dalits (formerly, 'untouchables'), also went in some detail into the history of local democratic governance in India to assess whether it could fruitfully serve as a model for modern Indian democracy. Ambedkar eventually saw little merit in drawing on local democratic experience, since localism, he argued, generated 'narrow-mindedness and communalism' (speaking personally, Ambedkar even asserted that 'these village republics have been the ruination of India').[18] But Ambedkar also pointed to the general relevance of the history of public reasoning in India, and particularly emphasized the expression of heterodox views.[19]

Despite those early deliberations in independent India, the intellectual agendas related to national politics have tended to move firmly in other directions since then, influenced by, among other factors, the sectarianism of the Hindutva movement and the cultural ignorance of many of the globalizing modernizers. Yet the historical roots of democracy and secularism in India, no less than the reach of its scientific and mathematical heritage, demand serious attention in contemporary India. Indeed, public discussion – in addition to balloting and elections – is part of the very core of democratic arrangements. Just as the tradition of balloting (going back to the practice in Athens in the sixth century BCE) is rightly acclaimed in the history of democracy, there is a similar case for celebrating the development, across the world, of the tradition of open public discussion as an essential aspect of the roots of democracy. If Akbar was well ahead of his time in arranging state-organized inter-faith dialogues (possibly the first in the world), Ashoka must also be regarded as remarkable in his interest and involvement, in the third century BCE, in the rules of discussion and confrontation that should govern arguments between holders of diverse beliefs.

That connection has global relevance too, since Ashoka was critically important for the spread of Buddhism and its social values in the world beyond India. It is interesting to note that attaching special importance to discussions and dialogue moved with other Buddhist principles, wherever Buddhism went.* For example, in early seventh-century Japan, the influential Buddhist Prince Shotoku, who was regent to his mother, Empress Suiko, introduced a relatively liberal constitution or *kempo* (known as 'the constitution of seventeen articles') in 604 CE, which included the insistence (in the spirit of the Magna Carta to be signed six centuries later, in 1215): 'Decisions on

*Buddhism also had the effect, typically, of enhancing the social importance of general literacy. The continuing influence of this can, to a considerable extent, be seen in the relatively high levels of literacy in countries in which Buddhism has survived, from Japan and Korea, to Thailand and Sri Lanka, and even in an otherwise miserable Burma. The Buddhist commitment clearly gave way to other priorities in the thousand years after its effective exit from India.

important matters should not be made by one person alone. They should be discussed with many.' Shotoku also argued: 'Nor let us be resentful when others differ from us. For all men have hearts, and each heart has its own leanings. Their right is our wrong, and our right is their wrong.'[20] Indeed, some commentators have seen, in this seventh-century Buddhism-inspired constitution, Japan's 'first step of gradual development toward democracy'.[21]

Another major Buddhist achievement – not unrelated in fact to the interest in public communication – is that nearly every attempt at early printing in the world, in particular in China, Korea and Japan, was undertaken by Buddhist technologists, with an interest in expanding public communication.* The first ever printed book (or, more exactly, the first printed book that is actually dated) was the Chinese translation of an Indian Sanskrit treatise (*Vajracchedikaprajñāpāramitā*), the so-called 'Diamond Sutra'. This was translated into Chinese by Kumārajīva (a half-Indian, half-Turkish Buddhist scholar) in 402 CE and this manuscript was printed in 868.[22] The introductory note that went with the volume explicitly explained that it was made for 'universal free distribution'.[23]

I should also note here that the achievements that are linked to Buddhism include not just the focus on public reasoning and printing, but also accomplishments in mathematics, astronomy, literature, painting, sculpture and even in the practice of public health care – a subject in which Buddhists were particularly involved and which greatly interested Chinese visitors to India such as Faxian in the early fifth century and Yi Jing in the seventh.† Also Ashoka, the Buddhist emperor, was a pioneer in creating hospitals for public use in the third century BCE. There is also a statement in one of the Edicts that Ashoka had established hospitals in the Hellenistic kingdoms – a claim that

*There were early attempts at printing by Indian Buddhists also, but with far less success. Yi Jing, a Chinese scholar who visited India in the seventh century, talks of Buddhist images on silk and paper in India. On this and other early attempts at printing, see Essay 8 below, and the illuminating assessment of the different attempts by Joseph Needham, *Science and Civilization in China* (Cambridge: Cambridge University Press, 1985), vol. V, part i, pp. 148–50.

†The influences going in both directions between these two countries are discussed in Essay 8 below, and also in 'Passage to China', *New York Review of Books*, 2 Dec. 2004.

may sound implausible but has been plausibly defended on the basis of available evidence by Thomas McEvilley.[24]

One of the sad features of a narrowly Hinduized view of India's past is that the justifiable pride Indians can take in the achievements of non-Hindu as well as Hindu accomplishments in India is drowned in the sectarianism of seeing India as mainly a vehicle for Hindu thought and practice. That, combined with an astonishingly narrow and intolerant view of the Hindu tradition itself, amounts to denying a good deal of Indian history that Indians have reason to remember and to celebrate.

Global Connections

Since the 1980s there has been a gradual opening up of the Indian economy, with a big shift in 1992, under the leadership of Manmohan Singh (the present Prime Minister of India) who was then the Finance Minister in the Congress government led by Narasimha Rao.* That government gave way to others, but the reduction of the autarky of closed economic policies has continued. Significantly, when the BJP-led government came to office in 1998, and was consolidated in 1999, it did take a fairly broad view of India's global economic connections. The focus may have been geared particularly to some specific sectors, but the overall interest in global trade was strong. The parochialism manifest in the BJP's cultural agenda did not manage to overwhelm the BJP government's policies on international trade. The growth rate of the Indian economy was also fairly fast over those years.

However, even though the BJP's cultural prejudices did not manage to overpower the outward-looking economic programme of the Indian government, the cultural agenda itself – closely linked to its sectarian politics – maintained its parochial priorities. Indeed, the rewriting of India's past that the Hindutva movement offered is closely linked (as was discussed in Essay 3) with relating India's

*The relevance of these changes and the tasks that remain to be urgently taken up are discussed in Jean Drèze and Amartya Sen, *India: Development and Participation* (Delhi and Oxford: Oxford University Press, 2002); see also Essay 9 below.

civilizational accomplishments to constructive work done single-handedly at home, in splendid isolation.

This segregationist programme runs contrary to the fact that sustained interactions across the borders can be seen throughout India's long history. It is not so much that there was no deprecation of foreigners in Indian traditionalist thinking. Indeed, quite the contrary. But, as Alberuni, the Iranian historian of India, noted nearly a thousand years ago (in a statement with remarkable anthropological vision), 'depreciation of foreigners not only prevails among us and the Indians, but is common to all nations towards each other'.[25] Despite this scepticism of foreign people, there were interactions with outsiders throughout Indian history.

India's recent achievements in science and technology (including information technology), or in world literature, or in international business, have all involved a good deal of global interaction. The important point to note in the present context is that these interactions are not unprecedented in Indian history. Indeed, interactions have been part and parcel of the Indian civilization, from very early days. Consider Sanskrit – a splendid language with a rich literature – which has been one of the robust pillars of Indian civilization. Despite its quintessential 'Indianness', there is a general understanding that, in an early form, Sanskrit came to India from abroad in the second millennium BCE, with the migration of Indo-Europeans, and then it developed further and flourished magnificently in India. It is also interesting to note that the greatest grammarian in Sanskrit (indeed possibly in any language), namely Pāṇini, who systematized and transformed Sanskrit grammar and phonetics around the fourth century BCE, was of Afghan origin (he describes his village on the banks of the river Kabul). These foreign connections have not diminished the pride of classically minded Indians in that great language, nor in the exceptional achievements of the literature, culture and science that found its expression in Sanskrit.*

*I had initially hoped that, despite all its transgressions, the Hindutva movement would have the good effect of enhancing the study of Sanskrit in India, on which there were many declarations of intent. This expectation has not, however, been substantially realized, perhaps because so few of the Hindutva advocates seem to know Sanskrit, but also because many enthusiasts for 'Hindu traditions' evidently prefer to rely on garbled 'summaries' of the Vedas and the *Rāmāyaṇa*, combined with 'rewritten' Indian history, rather than looking for the classical documents themselves.

Indeed, interactions have enriched as well as spread Sanskrit beyond India's borders over many centuries.* The seventh-century Chinese scholar Yi Jing learned his Sanskrit in Java (in the city of Shri Vijaya) on his way from China to India. The influence of interactions is well reflected in languages and vocabularies throughout Asia from Thailand and Malaya to Indo-China, Indonesia, the Philippines, Korea and Japan. And this applies to China too, where scholarship in Sanskrit flourished greatly in the first millennium, aside from the influences that came via other countries in the region. It is not often realized that even the word 'Mandarin', standing as it does for a central concept in Chinese culture, is derived from a Sanskrit word, *Mantrī*, which went from India to China via Malaya.

Even though contemporary attacks on intellectual globalization tend to come not only from traditional isolationists but also from modern separatists, we have to recognize that our global civilization is a world heritage – not just a collection of disparate local cultures. The tendency of parts of the communitarian movement to push us in the direction of fragmented isolationism suffers, thus, from a serious epistemic weakness, in addition to whatever normative difficulties it might encounter vis-à-vis ethical universalism.

The need to resist colonial dominance is, of course, important, but it has to be seen as a fight against submissive compliance, rather than as a plea for segregation and localism. The so-called 'post-colonial critique' can be significantly constructive when it is dialectically engaged – and thus strongly interactive – rather than defensively withdrawn and barriered.† We can find a warning against isolationism in a parable about a well-frog – the 'kūpamaṇḍuka' – that persistently recurs in several old Sanskrit texts, such as *Ganapāṭha*, *Hitopadeśa*,

*On this and related issues, see especially Sheldon Pollock, 'India in the Vernacular Millennium: Literary Culture and Polity, 1000–1500', *Daedalus*, 127 (1998). Pollock discusses the vernacularization that occurred in the early centuries of the second millennium, following a long period of international dominance of Sanskrit, when 'Sanskrit literary texts circulated from Central Asia to Sri Lanka and from Afghanistan to Annam, and participating in such a literary culture meant participating in a vast ecumene' (p. 45).

†Gayatri Chakravorty Spivak's far-reaching work, for example, is at its productive best in its reactive mode. She writes, in a self-descriptive passage: 'I am viewed by the Marxists as too codic, by feminists as too male-dominated, by indigenous theorists as too committed to Western theory. I am *uneasily pleased* about this' (*The Post-Colonial*

Prasannarāghava and *Bhattikāvya*. The kūpamaṇḍuka is a frog that lives its whole life within a well, knows nothing else, and is suspicious of everything outside it. It talks to no one, and argues with no one on anything. It merely harbours the deepest suspicion of the outside world. The scientific, cultural and economic history of the world would have been very limited indeed had we lived like well-frogs.

Celebration of Indian civilization can go hand in hand with an affirmation of India's active role in the global world. The existence of a large diaspora abroad is itself a part of India's interactive presence. Ideas as well as people have moved across India's borders over thousands of years, enriching India as well as the rest of the world. Rabindranath Tagore put the rationale well, in a letter to C. F. Andrews: 'Whatever we understand and enjoy in human products instantly becomes ours, wherever they might have their origin.'*

Indians, including the diaspora, have reason to resist external isolation as well as internal miniaturization. Indeed, the openness of the argumentative tradition militates not only against exclusionary narrowness within the country, but also against the cultivated ignorance of the well-frog. We need not agree to be incarcerated in the dinginess of a much diminished India, no matter how hard the political advocates of smallness try to jostle us. There are serious choices to be made.

Critic: Interviews, Strategies, Dialogues, ed. Sarah Harasym, New York: Routledge, 1990, pp. 69–70; italics added). These arguments can indeed be interesting as well as constructive, and Gayatri Spivak, as the quintessential 'argumentative Indian' (if I may so describe a lifelong friend), need not be so 'uneasy' about her justified delight in these dialectics.

*I discuss Tagore's critique of intellectual isolation in Essay 5 below.

PART TWO

Culture and Communication

5

Tagore and His India*

Rabindranath Tagore, who died in 1941 at the age of 80, is a towering figure in the millennium-old literature of Bengal. Anyone who becomes familiar with this large and flourishing tradition will be impressed by the power of Tagore's presence in Bangladesh and in India. His poetry as well as his novels, short stories and essays are very widely read, and the songs he composed reverberate around the eastern part of India and throughout Bangladesh.

In contrast, in the rest of the world, especially in Europe and America, the excitement that Tagore's writings created in the early years of the twentieth century has largely vanished. The enthusiasm with which his work was once greeted was quite remarkable. *Gitanjali*, a selection of his poetry for which he was awarded the Nobel Prize in literature in 1913, was published in English translation in London in March of that year and had been reprinted ten times by November, when the award was announced. But he is not much read now in the West, and already by 1937 Graham Greene was able to say: 'As for Rabindranath Tagore, I cannot believe that anyone but Mr Yeats can still take his poems very seriously.'

The contrast between Tagore's commanding presence in Bengali literature and culture and his near-total eclipse in the rest of the world

*The original publication of this essay in the *New York Review of Books*, on 26 June 1997, corresponded roughly with the fiftieth anniversary of Indian independence on 15 August 1947, and the occasion is referred to in the text. The essay is also included in Robert B. Silvers and Barbara Epstein (eds.), *India: A Mosaic* (New York: New York Review of Books, 2000). For helpful discussions I am most grateful to Akeel Bilgrami, Sissela Bok, Sugata Bose, Supratik Bose, Krishna Dutta, Rounaq Jahan, Salim Jahan, Marufi Khan, Andrew Robinson, Nandana Sen, Gayatri Chakravorty Spivak and Shashi Tharoor.

is perhaps less interesting than the distinction between the view of Tagore as a deeply relevant and many-sided contemporary thinker in Bangladesh and India, and his image in the West as a repetitive and remote spiritualist. Graham Greene had, in fact, gone on to explain that he associated Tagore 'with what Chesterton calls "the bright pebbly eyes" of the Theosophists'. Certainly, an air of mysticism played some part in the 'selling' of Rabindranath Tagore to the West by Yeats, Pound and his other early champions. Even Anna Akhmatova, one of Tagore's few later admirers (who translated his poems into Russian in the mid-1960s), talks of 'that mighty flow of poetry which takes its strength from Hinduism as from the Ganges, and is called Rabindranath Tagore'.

Rabindranath did come from a Hindu family – one of the landed gentry who owned estates mostly in what is now Bangladesh. But whatever wisdom there might be in Akhmatova's invoking of Hinduism and the Ganges, it did not prevent the largely Muslim citizens of Bangladesh from having a deep sense of identity with Tagore and his ideas. Nor did it stop the newly independent Bangladesh from choosing one of Tagore's songs ('Amar Sonar Bangla', which means 'my golden Bengal') as its national anthem. This must be very confusing to those who see the contemporary world as a 'clash of civilizations' – with 'the Muslim civilization', 'the Hindu civilization' and 'the Western civilization' each forcefully confronting the others.

They would also be confused by Rabindranath Tagore's own description of his Bengali family as the product of 'a confluence of three cultures, Hindu, Mohammedan and British'.[1] Rabindranath's grandfather, Dwarkanath, was well known for his command of Arabic and Persian, and Rabindranath grew up in a family atmosphere in which a deep knowledge of Sanskrit and ancient Hindu texts was combined with an understanding of Islamic traditions as well as Persian literature. It is not so much that Rabindranath tried to produce – or had an interest in producing – a 'synthesis' of the different religions (as the great Moghal emperor Akbar tried hard to achieve) as that his outlook was persistently nonsectarian, and his writings – some two hundred books – show the influence of different parts of the Indian cultural background as well as that of the rest of the world.[2] Most of his work was written at Santiniketan (Abode of Peace), the small town that grew around the school he founded in Bengal in 1901. He not only conceived there an imaginative and innovative system of education – to which I shall return – but, through his writings and his influence on students and teachers, he was able to use the school as a base from which he could take a major part in India's social, political and cultural movements.

The profoundly original writer whose elegant prose and magical poetry Bengali readers know well is not the sermonizing spiritual guru admired – and then rejected – in London. Tagore was not only an immensely versatile poet; he was also a great short-story writer, novelist, playwright, essayist and composer of songs, as well as a talented painter whose pictures, with their whimsical mixture of representation and abstraction, are only now beginning to receive the acclaim that they have long deserved. His essays, moreover, ranged over literature, politics, culture, social change, religious beliefs, philosophical analysis, international relations, and much else. The coincidence of the fiftieth anniversary of Indian independence with the publication of a selection of Tagore's letters by Cambridge University Press[3] is a good occasion to examine the nature of Tagore's ideas and reflections, and the kind of leadership in thought and understanding he provided in the subcontinent in the first half of the twentieth century.

Gandhi and Tagore

Since Rabindranath Tagore and Mohandas Gandhi were two leading Indian thinkers in the twentieth century, many commentators have tried to compare their ideas. On learning of Rabindranath's death, Jawaharlal Nehru, then incarcerated in a British jail in India, wrote in his prison diary for 7 August 1941:

> Gandhi and Tagore. Two types entirely different from each other, and yet both of them typical of India, both in the long line of India's great men. . . . It is not so much because of any single virtue but because of the *tout ensemble*, that I felt that among the world's great men today Gandhi and Tagore were supreme as human beings. What good fortune for me to have come into close contact with them.

Romain Rolland was fascinated by the contrast between them, and when he completed his book on Gandhi, he wrote to an Indian academic, in March 1923: 'I have finished my *Gandhi*, in which I pay tribute to your two great river-like souls, overflowing with divine spirit, Tagore and Gandhi.' The following month he recorded in his diary an account of some of the differences between Gandhi and Tagore written by Reverend C. F. Andrews, the English clergyman and public activist who was a close friend of both men (and whose important role in Gandhi's life in South Africa as well as India is well portrayed in Richard Attenborough's film *Gandhi*). Andrews described to Rolland a discussion between Tagore and Gandhi, at which he was present, on subjects that divided them:

> The first subject of discussion was idols; Gandhi defended them, believing the masses incapable of raising themselves immediately to abstract ideas. Tagore cannot bear to see the people eternally treated as a child. Gandhi quoted the great things achieved in Europe by the flag as an idol; Tagore found it easy to object, but Gandhi held his ground, contrasting European flags bearing eagles, etc., with his own, on which he has put a spinning wheel. The second point of discussion was nationalism, which Gandhi defended. He said that one must go through nationalism to reach internationalism, in the same way that one must go through war to reach peace.[4]

Tagore greatly admired Gandhi but he had many disagreements with him on a variety of subjects, including nationalism, patriotism, the importance of cultural exchange, the role of rationality and of science, and the nature of economic and social development. These differences, I shall argue, have a clear and consistent pattern, with Tagore pressing for more room for reasoning, and for a less traditionalist view, a greater interest in the rest of the world, and more respect for science and for objectivity generally.

Rabindranath knew that he could not have given India the political leadership that Gandhi provided, and he was never stingy in his praise for what Gandhi did for the nation (it was in fact Tagore who popularized the term 'Mahatma' – great soul – as a description of Gandhi). And yet each remained deeply critical of many things that the other stood for. That Mahatma Gandhi has received incomparably more attention outside India and also within much of India itself makes it important to understand 'Tagore's side' of the Gandhi–Tagore debates.

In his prison diary, Nehru wrote: 'Perhaps it is as well that [Tagore] died now and did not see the many horrors that are likely to descend in increasing measure on the world and on India. He had seen enough and he was infinitely sad and unhappy.' Towards the end of his life, Tagore was indeed becoming discouraged about the state of India, especially as its normal burden of problems, such as hunger and poverty, was being supplemented by politically organized incitement to 'communal' violence between Hindus and Muslims. This conflict would lead in 1947, six years after Tagore's death, to the widespread killing that took place during partition; but there was much gore already during his declining days. In December 1939 he wrote to his friend Leonard Elmhirst, the English philanthropist and social reformer who had worked closely with him on rural reconstruction in India (and who had gone on to found the Dartington Hall Trust in England and a progressive school at Dartington that explicitly invoked Rabindranath's educational ideals):[5]

> It does not need a defeatist to feel deeply anxious about the future of millions who with all their innate culture and their peaceful traditions are being simultaneously subjected to hunger, disease, exploitations foreign and indigenous, and the seething discontents of communalism.

How would Tagore have viewed the India of today, we may well ask on the fiftieth anniversary of its independence in 1947? Would he see progress there, or wasted opportunity, perhaps even a betrayal of its promise and conviction? And, on a wider subject, how would he react to the spread of cultural separatism in the contemporary world?

East and West

Given the vast range of his creative achievements, perhaps the most astonishing aspect of the image of Tagore in the West is its narrowness; he is recurrently viewed as 'the great mystic from the East', an image with a putative message for the West, which some would welcome, others dislike, and still others find deeply boring. To a great extent this Tagore was the West's own creation, part of its tradition of message-seeking from the East, particularly from India, which – as Hegel put it – had 'existed for millennia in the imagination of the Europeans'.* Friedrich Schlegel, Schelling, Herder and Schopenhauer were only a few of the thinkers who followed the same pattern. They theorized, at first, that India was the source of superior wisdom. Schopenhauer at one stage even argued that the New Testament 'must somehow be of Indian origin: this is attested by its completely Indian ethics, which transforms morals into asceticism, its pessimism, and its avatar', in 'the person of Christ'. But then they rejected their own theories with great vehemence, sometimes blaming India for not living up to their unfounded expectations.

We can imagine that Rabindranath's physical appearance – handsome, bearded, dressed in non-Western clothes – may, to some extent, have encouraged his being seen as a carrier of exotic wisdom. Yasunari Kawabata, the first Japanese Nobel laureate in literature, treasured memories from his middle-school days of 'this sage-like poet':

> His white hair flowed softly down both sides of his forehead; the tufts of hair under the temples also were long like two beards, and linking up with the hair on his cheeks, continued into his beard, so that he gave an impression, to the boy I was then, of some ancient Oriental wizard.[6]

That appearance would have been well suited to the selling of Tagore in the West as a quintessentially mystical poet, and it could have made it somewhat easier to pigeonhole him. Commenting on Rabindranath's appearance, Frances Cornford told William Rothenstein: 'I can now imagine a powerful and gentle Christ, which I never could before.' Beatrice Webb, who did not like Tagore and resented what she took to be his 'quite obvious dislike of all that the Webbs stand for' (there is, in fact, little evidence that Tagore had given much thought to this subject), said that he was 'beautiful to look at' and that 'his speech has the perfect intonation and slow chant-like moderation of the dramatic saint'.

Ezra Pound and W. B. Yeats, among others, first led the chorus of adoration in the Western appreciation of Tagore, and then soon moved

*I have tried to analyse these 'exotic' approaches to India (along with other Western approaches) in 'India and the West', *New Republic*, 7 June 1993, and in Essay 7 below.

to neglect and even shrill criticism. The contrast between Yeats's praise of his work in 1912 ('These lyrics . . . display in their thought a world I have dreamed of all my life long', 'the work of a supreme culture') and his denunciation in 1935 ('Damn Tagore') arose partly from the inability of Tagore's many-sided writings to fit into the narrow box in which Yeats wanted to place – and keep – him. Certainly, Tagore did write a huge amount, and published ceaselessly, even in English (sometimes in indifferent English translation), but Yeats was also bothered, it is clear, by the difficulty of fitting Tagore's later writings into the image Yeats had presented to the West. Tagore, he had said, was the product of 'a whole people, a whole civilization, immeasurably strange to us', and yet 'we have met our own image . . . or heard, perhaps for the first time in literature, our voice as in a dream'.[7]

Yeats did not totally reject his early admiration (as Ezra Pound and several others did), and he included some of Tagore's early poems in *The Oxford Book of Modern Verse*, which he edited in 1936. Yeats also had some favourable things to say about Tagore's prose writings. His censure of Tagore's later poems was reinforced by his dislike of Tagore's own English translations of his work ('Tagore does not know English, no Indian knows English,' Yeats explained), unlike the English version of *Gitanjali* which Yeats had himself helped to prepare. Poetry is, of course, notoriously difficult to translate, and anyone who knows Tagore's poems in their original Bengali cannot feel satisfied with any of the translations (made with or without Yeats's help). Even the translations of his prose works suffer, to some extent, from distortion. E. M. Forster noted, in a review of a translation of one of Tagore's great Bengali novels, *The Home and the World*, in 1919: 'The theme is so beautiful', but the charms have 'vanished in translation', or perhaps 'in an experiment that has not quite come off'.*

*Tagore himself vacillated over the years about the merits of his own translations. He told his friend Sir William Rothenstein, the artist: 'I am sure you remember with what reluctant hesitation I gave up to your hand my manuscript of *Gitanjali*, feeling sure that my English was of that amorphous kind for whose syntax a school-boy could be reprimanded.' These – and related – issues are discussed by Nabaneeta Dev Sen, 'The "Foreign Reincarnation" of Rabindranath Tagore', *Journal of Asian Studies*, 25 (1966), reprinted, along with other relevant papers, in her *Counterpoints: Essays in Comparative Literature* (Calcutta: Prajna, 1985).

Tagore himself played a somewhat bemused part in the boom and bust of his English reputation. He accepted the extravagant praise with much surprise as well as pleasure, and then received denunciations with even greater surprise, and barely concealed pain. Tagore was sensitive to criticism, and was hurt by even the most far-fetched accusations, such as the charge that he was getting credit for the work of Yeats, who had 'rewritten' *Gitanjali*. (This charge was made by a correspondent for *The Times*, Sir Valentine Chirol, whom E. M. Forster once described as 'an old Anglo-Indian reactionary hack'.) From time to time Tagore also protested at the crudity of some of his overexcited advocates. He wrote to C. F. Andrews in 1920: 'These people . . . are like drunkards who are afraid of their lucid intervals.'

God and Others

Yeats was not wrong to see a large religious element in Tagore's writings. He certainly had interesting and arresting things to say about life and death. Susan Owen, the mother of Wilfred Owen, wrote to Rabindranath in 1920, describing her last conversations with her son before he left for the war which would take his life. Wilfred said goodbye with 'those wonderful words of yours – beginning at "When I go from hence, let this be my parting word".' When Wilfred's pocket notebook was returned to his mother, she found 'these words written in his dear writing – with your name beneath'.

The idea of a direct, joyful and totally fearless relationship with God can be found in many of Tagore's religious writings, including the poems of *Gitanjali*. From India's diverse religious traditions he drew many ideas, both from ancient texts and from popular poetry. But 'the bright pebbly eyes of the Theosophists' do not stare out of his verses. Despite the archaic language of the original translation of *Gitanjali*, which did not, I believe, help to preserve the simplicity of the original, its elementary humanity comes through more clearly than any complex and intense spirituality:

Leave this chanting and singing and telling of beads! Whom dost
thou worship in this lonely dark corner of a temple with doors all
shut?
Open thine eyes and see thy God is not before thee!
He is there where the tiller is tilling the hard ground and where the
pathmaker is breaking stones.
He is with them in sun and in shower, and his garment is covered
with dust.

An ambiguity about religious experience is central to many of Tagore's devotional poems, and makes them appeal to readers irrespective of their beliefs; but excessively detailed interpretation can ruinously strip away that ambiguity.[8] This applies particularly to his many poems which combine images of human love and those of pious devotion. Tagore writes:

I have no sleep to-night. Ever and again I open my door and look
out on the darkness, my friend!
I can see nothing before me. I wonder where lies thy path!
By what dim shore of the ink-black river, by what far edge of the
frowning forest, through what mazy depth of gloom, art thou
threading thy course to come to see me, my friend?

I suppose it could be helpful to be told, as Yeats hastens to explain, that 'the servant or the bride awaiting the master's home-coming in the empty house' is 'among the images of the heart turning to God'. But in Yeats's considerate attempt to make sure that the reader does not miss the 'main point', something of the enigmatic beauty of the Bengali poem is lost – even what had survived the antiquated language of the English translation.

Tagore certainly had strongly held religious beliefs (of an unusually nondenominational kind), but he was interested in a great many other things as well and had many different things to say about them. Some of the ideas he tried to present were directly political, and they figure rather prominently in his letters and lectures. He had practical, plainly expressed views about nationalism, war and peace, cross-cultural education, freedom of the mind, the importance of rational criticism, the need for cultural openness, and so on. His admirers in the West, however, were tuned to the more other-worldly themes which had been emphasized by his first Western patrons. People came to his public lectures in Europe and America expecting ruminations on grand, transcendental themes; when they heard instead his views on the way public leaders should behave, there was some resentment, particularly (as E. P. Thompson reports) when he delivered political criticism 'at $700 a scold'.

Reasoning in Freedom

For Tagore it was of the highest importance that people be able to live, and reason, in freedom. His attitudes towards politics and culture, nationalism and internationalism, tradition and modernity, can all be seen in the light of this belief.* Nothing, perhaps, expresses his values as clearly as a poem in *Gitanjali*:

> Where the mind is without fear and the head is held high;
> Where knowledge is free;
> Where the world has not been broken up into fragments by narrow
> domestic walls; . . .
> Where the clear stream of reason has not lost its way into the dreary
> desert sand of dead habit; . . .
> Into that heaven of freedom, my Father, let my country awake.

Rabindranath's qualified support for nationalist movements – and his opposition to the unfreedom of alien rule – came from this commitment. So did his reservations about patriotism, which, he argued, can limit both the freedom to engage ideas from outside 'narrow domestic walls' and the freedom also to support the causes of people in other countries. Rabindranath's passion for freedom underlies his firm opposition to unreasoned traditionalism, which makes one a prisoner of the past (lost, as he put it, in 'the dreary desert sand of dead habit').

Tagore illustrates the tyranny of the past in his amusing yet deeply

*Satyajit Ray, the film director, has argued that, even in Tagore's paintings, 'the mood evoked . . . is one of a joyous freedom' (Ray, Foreword to Andrew Robinson, *The Art of Rabindranath Tagore*, London: André Deutsch, 1989).

serious parable 'Kartar Bhoot' ('The Ghost of the Leader'). As the respected leader of an imaginary land is about to die, his panic-stricken followers request him to stay on after his death to instruct them on what to do. He consents. But his followers find their lives are full of rituals and constraints on everyday behaviour and are not responsive to the world around them. Ultimately, they ask the ghost of the leader to relieve them of his domination, when he informs them that he exists only in their minds.

Tagore's deep aversion to any commitment to the past that could not be modified by contemporary reason extended even to the alleged virtue of invariably keeping past promises. On one occasion when Mahatma Gandhi visited Tagore's school at Santiniketan, a young woman got him to sign her autograph book. Gandhi wrote: 'Never make a promise in haste. Having once made it fulfil it at the cost of your life.' When he saw this entry, Tagore became agitated. He wrote in the same book a short poem in Bengali to the effect that no one can be made 'a prisoner forever with a chain of clay'. He went on to conclude in English, possibly so that Gandhi could read it too, 'Fling away your promise if it is found to be wrong.'[9]

Tagore had the greatest admiration for Mahatma Gandhi as a person and as a political leader, but he was also highly sceptical of Gandhiji's form of nationalism and his conservative instincts regarding the country's past traditions. He never criticized Gandhi personally. In the 1938 essay 'Gandhi the Man', he wrote:

> Great as he is as a politician, as an organizer, as a leader of men, as a moral reformer, he is greater than all these as a man, because none of these aspects and activities limits his humanity. They are rather inspired and sustained by it.

And yet there is a deep division between the two men. Tagore was explicit about his disagreement:

> We who often glorify our tendency to ignore reason, installing in its place blind faith, valuing it as spiritual, are ever paying for its cost with the obscuration of our mind and destiny. I blamed Mahatmaji for exploiting this irrational force of credulity in our people, which might have had a quick result [in creating] a superstructure, while sapping the foundation. Thus

Mahatma Gandhi with Rabindranath Tagore during a visit to Tagore's school at Santiniketan, 18 February 1940

began my estimate of Mahatmaji, as the guide of our nation, and it is fortunate for me that it did not end there.

But while it 'did not end there', that difference of vision was a powerful divider.

Tagore, for example, remained unconvinced of the merit of Gandhi's forceful advocacy that everyone should spin at home with the 'charka', the primitive spinning wheel. For Gandhi, this practice was an important part of India's self-realization. 'The spinning-wheel gradually became', as his biographer B. R. Nanda writes, 'the centre of rural uplift in the Gandhian scheme of Indian economics.'[10] Tagore found the alleged economic rationale for this scheme quite unrealistic. As Romain Rolland noted, Rabindranath 'never tires of criticizing the charka'. In this economic judgement, Tagore was probably right. Except for the rather small specialized market for high-quality spun cloth, it is hard to make economic sense of hand-spinning, even with wheels less primitive than Gandhi's charka. Hand-spinning as a widespread activity can survive only with the help of heavy government subsidies.[11]

However, Gandhi's advocacy of the charka was not based only on economics. He wanted everyone to spin for 'thirty minutes every day as a sacrifice', seeing this as a way for people who are better off to identify themselves with the less fortunate. He was impatient with Tagore's refusal to grasp this point:

> The poet lives for the morrow, and would have us do likewise. . . . 'Why should I, who have no need to work for food, spin?' may be the question asked. Because I am eating what does not belong to me. I am living on the spoliation of my countrymen. Trace the source of every coin that finds its way into your pocket, and you will realise the truth of what I write. Every one must spin. Let Tagore spin like the others. Let him burn his foreign clothes; that is the duty today. God will take care of the morrow.[12]

If Tagore had missed something in Gandhi's argument, so did Gandhi miss the point of Tagore's main criticism. It was not only that the charka made little economic sense, but also, Tagore thought, that it was not the way to make people reflect on anything: 'The charka does not require anyone to think; one simply turns the wheel of the antiquated invention endlessly, using the minimum of judgement and stamina.'

On Celibacy and Personal Life

Tagore and Gandhi's attitudes towards personal life were also quite different. Gandhi was keen on the virtues of celibacy, theorized about it, and, after some years of conjugal life, made a private commitment – publicly announced – to refrain from sleeping with his wife. Rabindranath's own attitude on this subject was very different, but he was gentle about their disagreements:

> [Gandhiji] condemns sexual life as inconsistent with the moral progress of man, and has a horror of sex as great as that of the author of *The Kreutzer*

Sonata, but, unlike Tolstoy, he betrays no abhorrence of the sex that tempts his kind. In fact, his tenderness for women is one of the noblest and most consistent traits of his character, and he counts among the women of his country some of his best and truest comrades in the great movement he is leading.

Tagore's personal life was, in many ways, an unhappy one. He married in 1883, lost his wife in 1902, and never remarried. He sought close companionship, which he did not always get (perhaps even during his married life – he wrote to his wife, Mrinalini: 'If you and I could be comrades in all our work and in all our thoughts it would be splendid, but we cannot attain all that we desire'). He maintained a warm friendship with, and a strong Platonic attachment to, the literature-loving wife, Kadambari, of his elder brother, Jyotirindranath. He dedicated some poems to her before his marriage, and several books afterwards, some after her death (she committed suicide, for reasons that are not fully understood, at the age of 25, four months after Rabindranath's wedding).

Much later in life, during his tour of Argentina in 1924–5, Rabindranath came to know the talented and beautiful Victoria Ocampo, who later became the publisher of the literary magazine *Sur*. They became close friends, but it appears that Rabindranath deflected the possibility of a passionate relationship into a confined intellectual one.[13] Leonard Elmhirst, who accompanied Rabindranath on his Argentine tour, wrote:

> Besides having a keen intellectual understanding of his books, she was in love with him – but instead of being content to build a friendship on the basis of intellect, she was in a hurry to establish that kind of proprietary right over him which he absolutely would not brook.

Ocampo and Elmhirst, while remaining friendly, were both quite rude in what they wrote about each other. Ocampo's book on Tagore (of which a Bengali translation was made from the Spanish by the distinguished poet and critic Shankha Ghosh) is primarily concerned with Tagore's writings but also discusses the pleasures and difficulties of their relationship, giving quite a different account from Elmhirst's, and never suggesting any sort of proprietary intentions.

Ocampo, however, makes it plain that she very much wanted to get physically closer to Rabindranath: 'Little by little he [Tagore] partially tamed the young animal, by turns wild and docile, who did not sleep, dog-like, on the floor outside his door, simply because it was not done.'[14] Rabindranath, too, was clearly very much attracted to her. He called her 'Vijaya' (the Sanskrit equivalent of Victoria), dedicated a book of poems to her, *Purabi* – an 'evening melody' – and expressed great admiration for her mind ('like a star that was distant'). In a letter to her he wrote, as if to explain his own reticence:

> When we were together, we mostly played with words and tried to laugh away our best opportunities to see each other clearly. . . . Whenever there is the least sign of the nest becoming a jealous rival of the sky[,] my mind, like a migrant bird, tries to take . . . flight to a distant shore.

Five years later, during Tagore's European tour in 1930, he sent her a cable: 'Will you not come and see me.' She did. But their relationship did not seem to go much beyond conversation, and their somewhat ambiguous correspondence continued over the years. Written in 1940, a year before his death at eighty, one of the poems in *Sesh Lekha* ('Last Writings'), seems to be about her: 'How I wish I could once again find my way to that foreign land where waits for me the message of love! / . . . Her language I knew not, but what her eyes said will forever remain eloquent in its anguish.'[15]

However indecisive, or confused, or awkward Rabindranath may have been, he certainly did not share Mahatma Gandhi's censorious views of sex. In fact, when it came to social policy, he advocated contraception and family planning while Gandhi preferred abstinence.

Science and the People

Gandhi and Tagore severely clashed over their totally different attitudes towards science. In January 1934 Bihar was struck by a devastating earthquake which killed thousands of people. Gandhi, who was then deeply involved in the fight against untouchability (the barbaric system inherited from India's divisive past, in which 'lowly people' were kept at a physical distance), extracted a positive lesson from the tragic event. 'A man like me', Gandhi argued, 'cannot but believe this earthquake is a divine chastisement sent by God for our sins' – in particular the sins of untouchability. 'For me there is a vital connection between the Bihar calamity and the untouchability campaign.'

Tagore, who equally abhorred untouchability and had joined Gandhi in the movements against it, protested against this interpretation of an event that had caused suffering and death to so many innocent people, including children and babies. He also hated the epistemology implicit in seeing an earthquake as caused by ethical failure. 'It is', he wrote, 'all the more unfortunate because this kind of unscientific view of [natural] phenomena is too readily accepted by a large section of our countrymen.'

The two remained deeply divided over their attitudes towards science. However, while Tagore believed that modern science was essential to understanding physical phenomena, his views on epistemology were interestingly heterodox. He did not take the simple 'realist' position often associated with modern science. The report of his conversation with Einstein, published in the *New York Times* in 1930, shows how insistent Tagore was on interpreting truth through observation and reflective concepts. To assert that something is true or untrue in the absence of anyone to observe or perceive its truth, or to form a conception of what it is, appeared to Tagore to be deeply questionable. When Einstein remarked, 'If there were no human beings any more, the Apollo Belvedere no longer would be beautiful?' Tagore simply replied, 'No.' Going further – and into much more interesting territory – Einstein said, 'I agree with regard to this conception of beauty, but not with regard to truth.' Tagore's response was: 'Why not? Truth is realized through men.'[16]

Tagore's epistemology, which he never pursued systematically, would seem to be searching for a line of reasoning that would later be elegantly developed by Hilary Putnam, who has argued: 'Truth depends on conceptual schemes and it is nonetheless "real truth".'[17] Tagore himself said little to explain his convictions, but it is important to take account of his heterodoxy, not only because his speculations were invariably interesting, but also because they illustrate how his support for any position, including his strong interest in science, was accompanied by critical scrutiny.

Nationalism and Colonialism

Tagore was predictably hostile to communal sectarianism (such as a Hindu orthodoxy that was antagonistic to Islamic, Christian or Sikh perspectives). But even nationalism seemed to him to be suspect. Isaiah Berlin summarizes well Tagore's complex position on Indian nationalism (even though he oversimplified Tagore's view of the origin of political liberty):

> Tagore stood fast on the narrow causeway, and did not betray his vision of the difficult truth. He condemned romantic overattachment to the past, what he called the tying of India to the past 'like a sacrificial goat tethered to a post', and he accused men who displayed it – they seemed to him reactionary – of not knowing what true political freedom was, pointing out that it is from English thinkers and English books that the very notion of political liberty was derived. But against cosmopolitanism he maintained that the English stood on their own feet, and so must Indians. In 1917 he once more denounced the danger of 'leaving everything to the unalterable will of the Master', be he brahmin or Englishman.[18]

The duality Berlin points to is well reflected also in Tagore's attitude towards cultural diversity. He wanted Indians to learn what was going on elsewhere, how others lived, what they valued, and so on, while remaining interested and involved in their own culture and heritage. Indeed, in his educational writings the need for synthesis is strongly stressed. It can also be found in his advice to Indian students abroad. In 1907 he wrote to his son-in-law Nagendranath Gangulee, who had gone to America to study agriculture:

> To get on familiar terms with the local people is a part of your education. To know only agriculture is not enough; you must know America too. Of course if, in the process of knowing America, one begins to lose one's identity and falls into the trap of becoming an Americanised person contemptuous of everything Indian, it is preferable to stay in a locked room.

Tagore was strongly involved in protest against the Raj on a number of occasions, most notably in the movement to resist the 1905 British proposal to split in two the province of Bengal, a plan that was eventually withdrawn following popular resistance. He was forthright in denouncing the brutality of British rule in India, never more so than after the Amritsar massacre of 13 April 1919, when 379 unarmed people at a peaceful meeting were gunned down by the army, and two thousand more were wounded. Between 23 and 26 April, Rabindranath wrote five agitated letters to C. F. Andrews, who himself was extremely disturbed, especially after he was told by a British civil servant in India that, thanks to this show of strength, the 'moral prestige' of the Raj had 'never been higher'.

A month after the massacre, Tagore wrote to the Viceroy of India, asking to be relieved of the knighthood he had accepted four years earlier:

> The disproportionate severity of the punishments inflicted upon the unfortunate people and the methods of carrying them out, we are convinced, are without parallel in the history of civilized governments, barring some conspicuous exceptions, recent and remote. Considering that such treatment has been meted out to a population, disarmed and resourceless, by a power which has the most terribly efficient organisation for destruction of human lives, we must strongly assert that it can claim no political expediency, far less moral justification. . . . The universal agony of indignation roused in the hearts of our people has been ignored by our rulers – possibly congratulating themselves for imparting what they imagine as salutary lessons. . . . I for my part want to stand, shorn of all special distinctions, by the side of those of my countrymen who for their so-called insignificance are liable to suffer a degradation not fit for human beings.

Both Gandhi and Nehru expressed their appreciation of the important part Tagore took in the national struggle. It is fitting that, after independence, India chose a song of Tagore's ('Jana Gana Mana Adhinayaka', which can be roughly translated as 'the leader of people's minds') as its national anthem. Since Bangladesh would later choose another song of Tagore's ('Amar Sonar Bangla') as its national anthem, he may be the only one ever to have written the national anthems of two different countries.

Tagore's criticism of the British administration of India was consistently strong and grew more intense over the years. This point is often missed, since he made a special effort to dissociate his criticism of the

Raj from any denigration of British – or Western – people and culture. Mahatma Gandhi's well-known quip in reply to a question, asked in England, on what he thought of Western civilization ('It would be a good idea') could not have come from Tagore's lips. He would understand the provocations to which Gandhi was responding – involving cultural conceit as well as imperial tyranny. D. H. Lawrence supplied a fine example of the former: 'I become more and more surprised to see how far higher, in reality, our European civilization stands than the East, Indian and Persian, ever dreamed of. . . . This fraud of looking up to them – this wretched worship-of-Tagore attitude – is disgusting.' But, unlike Gandhi, Tagore could not, even in jest, be dismissive of Western civilization.

Even in his powerful indictment of British rule in India in 1941, in a lecture which he gave on his last birthday, and which was later published as a pamphlet under the title *Crisis in Civilization*, he strains hard to maintain the distinction between opposing Western imperialism and rejecting Western civilization. While he saw India as having been 'smothered under the dead weight of British administration' (adding 'another great and ancient civilization for whose recent tragic history the British cannot disclaim responsibility is China'), Tagore recalls what India has gained from 'discussions centred upon Shakespeare's drama and Byron's poetry and above all . . . the large-hearted liberalism of nineteenth-century English politics'. The tragedy, as Tagore saw it, came from the fact that what 'was truly best in their own civilization, the upholding of dignity of human relationships, has no place in the British administration of this country.' 'If in its place they have established, baton in hand, a reign of "law and order", or in other words a policeman's rule, such a mockery of civilization can claim no respect from us.'

Critique of Patriotism

Rabindranath rebelled against the strongly nationalist form that the independence movement often took, and this made him refrain from taking a particularly active part in contemporary politics. He wanted to assert India's right to be independent without denying the importance of what India could learn – freely and profitably – from abroad. He was afraid that a rejection of the West in favour of an indigenous Indian tradition was not only limiting in itself; it could easily turn into hostility to other influences from abroad, including Christianity, which came to parts of India by the fourth century, Judaism, which came through Jewish immigration shortly after the fall of Jerusalem, as did Zoroastrianism through Parsee immigration later on (mainly in the eighth century), and, of course – and most importantly – Islam, which has had a very strong presence in India since the eighth century.

Tagore's criticism of patriotism is a persistent theme in his writings. As early as 1908, he put his position succinctly in a letter replying to the criticism of Abala Bose, the wife of a great Indian scientist, Jagadish Chandra Bose: 'Patriotism cannot be our final spiritual shelter; my refuge is humanity. I will not buy glass for the price of diamonds, and I will never allow patriotism to triumph over humanity as long as I live.' His novel *Ghare Baire* (*The Home and the World*) has much to say about this theme. In the novel, Nikhil, who is keen on social reform, including women's liberation, but cool towards nationalism, gradually loses the esteem of his spirited wife, Bimala, because of his failure to be enthusiastic about anti-British agitations, which she sees as a lack of patriotic commitment. Bimala becomes fascinated with Nikhil's nationalist friend Sandip, who speaks brilliantly and acts with patriotic militancy, and she falls in love with him. Nikhil refuses to change his views: 'I am willing to serve my country; but my worship I reserve for Right which is far greater than my country. To worship my country as a god is to bring a curse upon it.'*

As the story unfolds, Sandip becomes angry with some of his countrymen for their failure to join the struggle as readily as he thinks they should ('Some Mohammedan traders are still obdurate'). He arranges to deal with the recalcitrants by burning their meagre trading stocks and physically attacking them. Bimala has to acknowledge the connection between Sandip's rousing nationalistic sentiments and his sectarian – and ultimately violent – actions. The dramatic events that

*Martha Nussbaum initiates her wide-ranging critique of patriotism (in a debate that is joined by many others) by quoting this passage from *The Home and the World* (in Martha C. Nussbaum *et al.*, *For Love of Country*, ed. Joshua Cohen, Boston: Beacon Press, 1996, pp. 3–4).

follow (Nikhil attempts to help the victims, risking his life) include the end of Bimala's political romance.

This is a difficult subject, and Satyajit Ray's beautiful film of *The Home and the World* brilliantly brings out the novel's tensions, along with the human affections and disaffections of the story. Not surprisingly, the story has had many detractors, not just among dedicated nationalists in India. Georg Lukács found Tagore's novel to be 'a petit bourgeois yarn of the shoddiest kind', 'at the intellectual service of the British police', and 'a contemptible caricature of Gandhi'. It would, of course, be absurd to think of Sandip as Gandhi, but the novel gives a 'strong and gentle' warning, as Bertolt Brecht noted in his diary, of the corruptibility of nationalism, since it is not even-handed. Hatred of one group can lead to hatred of others, no matter how far such feeling may be from the minds of humane nationalist leaders like Mahatma Gandhi.

Admiration and Criticism of Japan

Tagore's reaction to nationalism in Japan is particularly telling. As in the case of India, he saw the need to build the self-confidence of a defeated and humiliated people, of people left behind by developments elsewhere, as was the case in Japan before its emergence during the nineteenth century. At the beginning of one of his lectures in Japan in 1916 ('Nationalism in Japan'), he observed that 'the worst form of bondage is the bondage of dejection, which keeps men hopelessly chained in loss of faith in themselves'. Tagore shared the admiration for Japan widespread in Asia for demonstrating the ability of an Asian nation to rival the West in industrial development and economic progress. He noted with great satisfaction that Japan had 'in giant strides left centuries of inaction behind, overtaking the present time in its foremost achievement'. For other nations outside the West, he said, Japan 'has broken the spell under which we lay in torpor for ages, taking it to be the normal condition of certain races living in certain geographical limits'.

But then Tagore went on to criticize the rise of a strong nationalism in Japan, and its emergence as an imperialist nation. Tagore's outspoken criticisms did not please Japanese audiences and, as E. P. Thompson wrote, 'the welcome given to him on his first arrival soon cooled'.[19] Twenty-two years later, in 1937, during the Japanese war on China, Tagore received a letter from Rash Behari Bose, an anti-British Indian revolutionary then living in Japan, who sought Tagore's approval for his efforts there on behalf of Indian independence, in which he had the support of the Japanese government. Tagore replied:

> Your cable has caused me many restless hours, for it hurts me very much to have to ignore your appeal. I wish you had asked for my cooperation in a cause against which my spirit did not protest. I know, in making this appeal, you counted on my great regard for the Japanese for I, along with the rest of Asia, did once admire and look up to Japan and did once fondly hope that in Japan Asia had at last discovered its challenge to the West, that Japan's new strength would be consecrated in safeguarding the culture of the East against alien interests. But Japan has not taken long to betray that rising hope and repudiate all that seemed significant in her wonderful, and to us symbolic, awakening, and has now become itself a worse menace to the defenceless peoples of the East.

How to view Japan's position in the Second World War was a divisive issue in India. After the war, when Japanese political leaders were tried for war crimes, the sole dissenting voice among the judges came from the Indian judge, Radhabinod Pal, a distinguished jurist. Pal dissented on various grounds, among them that no fair trial was possible in view of the asymmetry of power between the victor and the defeated. Ambivalent feelings in India towards the Japanese military aggression, given the unacceptable nature of British imperialism, possibly had a part in predisposing Pal to consider a perspective different from that of the other judges.

More tellingly, Subhas Chandra Bose (no relation of Rash Behari Bose), a leading nationalist, made his way to Japan during the war via Italy and Germany after escaping from a British prison; he helped the Japanese to form units of Indian soldiers, who had earlier surrendered to the advancing Japanese army, to fight on the Japanese side as the 'Indian National Army'. Rabindranath had formerly entertained great admiration for Subhas Bose as a dedicated nonsectarian fighter for Indian independence.[20] But their ways would have parted when Bose's political activities took this turn, although Tagore was dead by the time Bose reached Japan.

Tagore saw Japanese militarism as illustrating the way nationalism can mislead even a nation of great achievement and promise. In 1938 Yone Noguchi, the distinguished poet and friend of Tagore (as well as of Yeats and Pound), wrote to Tagore, pleading with him to change his mind about Japan. Rabindranath's reply, written on 12 September 1938, was altogether uncompromising:

> It seems to me that it is futile for either of us to try to convince the other, since your faith in the infallible right of Japan to bully other Asiatic nations into line with your Government's policy is not shared by me. . . . Believe me, it is sorrow and shame, not anger, that prompt me to write to you. I suffer intensely not only because the reports of Chinese suffering batter against my heart, but because I can no longer point out with pride the example of a great Japan.

He would have been much happier with the post-war emergence of Japan as a peaceful power. Then, too, since he was not free of egotism, he would also have been pleased by the attention paid to his ideas by the novelist Yasunari Kawabata and others.[21]

International Concerns

Tagore was not invariably well-informed about international politics. He allowed himself to be entertained by Mussolini in a short visit to Italy in May–June 1926, a visit arranged by Carlo Formichi, professor of Sanskrit at the University of Rome. When he asked to meet Benedetto Croce, Formichi said, 'Impossible! Impossible!' Mussolini told him that Croce was 'not in Rome'. When Tagore said he would go 'wherever he is', Mussolini assured him that Croce's whereabouts were unknown.

Such incidents, as well as warnings from Romain Rolland and other friends, should have ended Tagore's flirtation with Mussolini more quickly than it did. But only after he received graphic accounts of the brutality of Italian fascism from two exiles, Gaetano Salvemini and Gaetano Salvadori, and learned more of what was happening in

Italy, did he publicly denounce the regime, publishing a letter to the *Manchester Guardian* in August. The next month, *Popolo d'Italia*, the magazine edited by Benito Mussolini's brother, replied: 'Who cares? Italy laughs at Tagore and those who brought this unctuous and insupportable fellow in our midst.'

With his high expectations of Britain, Tagore continued to be surprised by what he took to be a lack of official sympathy for international victims of aggression. He returned to this theme in the lecture he gave on his last birthday, in 1941:

> While Japan was quietly devouring North China, her act of wanton aggression was ignored as a minor incident by the veterans of British diplomacy. We have also witnessed from this distance how actively the British statesmen acquiesced in the destruction of the Spanish Republic.

But distinguishing between the British government and the British people, Rabindranath went on to note 'with admiration how a band of valiant Englishmen laid down their lives for Spain'.

Tagore's view of the Soviet Union has been a subject of much discussion. He was widely read in Russia. In 1917 several Russian translations of *Gitanjali* (one edited by Ivan Bunin, later the first Russian Nobel laureate in literature) were available, and by the late 1920s many of the English versions of his work had been rendered into Russian by several distinguished translators. Russian versions of his work continued to appear: Boris Pasternak translated him in the 1950s and 1960s.

When Tagore visited Russia in 1930, he was much impressed by its development efforts and by what he saw as a real commitment to eliminate poverty and economic inequality. But what impressed him most was the expansion of basic education across the old Russian empire. In *Letters from Russia*, written in Bengali and published in 1931, he unfavourably compares the acceptance of widespread illiteracy in India by the British administration with Russian efforts to expand education:

> In stepping on the soil of Russia, the first thing that caught my eye was that in education, at any rate, the peasant and the working classes have made

such enormous progress in these few years that nothing comparable has happened even to our highest classes in the course of the last hundred and fifty years . . . The people here are not at all afraid of giving complete education even to Turcomans of distant Asia; on the contrary, they are utterly in earnest about it.[22]

When parts of the book were translated into English in 1934, the under-secretary for India stated in Parliament that it was 'calculated by distortion of the facts to bring the British Administration in India into contempt and disrepute', and the book was then promptly banned. The English version would not be published until after independence.

Education and Freedom

The British Indian administrators were not, however, alone in trying to suppress Tagore's reflections on Russia. They were joined by Soviet officials. In an interview with *Izvestia* in 1930, Tagore sharply criticized the lack of freedom that he observed in Russia:

I must ask you: Are you doing your ideal a service by arousing in the minds of those under your training anger, class-hatred, and revengefulness against those whom you consider to be your enemies? . . . Freedom of mind is needed for the reception of truth; terror hopelessly kills it. . . . For the sake of humanity I hope you may never create a vicious force of violence, which will go on weaving an interminable chain of violence and cruelty. . . . You have tried to destroy many of the other evils of [the tsarist] period. Why not try to destroy this one also?

The interview was not published in *Izvestia* until 1988 – nearly sixty years later.*

Tagore's reaction to the Russia of 1930 arose from two of his strongest commitments: his uncompromising belief in the importance of 'freedom of mind' (the source of his criticism of the Soviet

*It was, however, published in the *Manchester Guardian* shortly after it was meant to be published in *Izvestia*. On this see Krishna Dutta and Andrew Robinson, *Rabindranath Tagore: The Myriad-Minded Man* (New York: St Martin's Press, 1995), p. 297.

Union), and his conviction that the expansion of basic education is central to social progress (the source of his praise, particularly in contrast to British-run India). He identified the lack of basic education as the fundamental cause of many of India's social and economic afflictions:

> In my view the imposing tower of misery which today rests on the heart of India has its sole foundation in the absence of education. Caste divisions, religious conflicts, aversion to work, precarious economic conditions – all centre on this single factor.

It was on education (and on the reflection, dialogue and communication that are associated with it), rather than on, say, spinning 'as a sacrifice' ('the charka does not require anyone to think'), that the future of India would depend.

Tagore was concerned not only that there be wider opportunities for education across the country (especially in rural areas where schools were few), but also that the schools themselves be more lively and enjoyable. He himself had dropped out of school early, largely out of boredom, and had never bothered to earn a diploma. He wrote extensively on how schools should be made more attractive to boys and girls and thus more productive. His own co-educational school at Santiniketan had many progressive features. The emphasis here was on self-motivation rather than on discipline, and on fostering intellectual curiosity rather than competitive excellence.

Much of Rabindranath's life was spent in developing the school at Santiniketan. The school never had much money, since the fees were very low. His lecture honoraria, '$700 a scold', went to support it, as well as most of his Nobel Prize money. The school received no support from the government, but did get help from private citizens – even Mahatma Gandhi raised money for it.

The dispute with Mahatma Gandhi on the Bihar earthquake touched on a subject that was very important to Tagore: the need for education in science as well as in literature and the humanities. At Santiniketan, there were strong 'local' elements in its emphasis on Indian traditions, including the classics, and in the use of Bengali rather than English as the language of instruction. At the same time there were courses on a great variety of cultures, and study programmes devoted to China, Japan and the Middle East. Many foreigners came to Santiniketan to study or teach, and the fusion of studies seemed to work.

I am partial to seeing Tagore as an educator, having myself been educated at Santiniketan. The school was unusual in many different ways, such as the oddity that classes, excepting those requiring a laboratory, were held outdoors (whenever the weather permitted). No matter what we thought of Rabindranath's belief that one gains from being in a natural setting while learning (some of us argued about this theory), we typically found the experience of outdoor schooling extremely attractive and pleasant. Academically, our school was not particularly exacting (often we did not have any examinations at all), and it could not, by the usual academic standards, compete with some of the better schools in Calcutta. But there was something remarkable about the ease with which class discussions could move from Indian traditional literature to contemporary as well as classical Western thought, and then to the culture of China or Japan or elsewhere. The school's celebration of variety was also in sharp contrast with the cultural conservatism and separatism that has tended to grip India from time to time.

The cultural give and take of Tagore's vision of the contemporary world has close parallels with the vision of Satyajit Ray, also an alumnus of Santiniketan, who made several films based on Tagore's stories.[23] Ray's words about Santiniketan in 1991 would have greatly pleased Rabindranath:

> I consider the three years I spent in Santiniketan as the most fruitful of my life. . . . Santiniketan opened my eyes for the first time to the splendours of Indian and Far Eastern art. Until then I was completely under the sway of Western art, music and literature. Santiniketan made me the combined product of East and West that I am.[24]

Fifty Years after Independence

What India has or has not achieved in its half century of independence is becoming a subject of considerable interest: 'What has been the story of those first fifty years?' (as Shashi Tharoor asks in his balanced, informative and highly readable account of *India: From Midnight to the Millennium*).[25] If Tagore were to see the India of today, half a century after independence, nothing perhaps would shock him so much as the continued illiteracy of the masses. He would see this as a total betrayal of what the nationalist leaders had promised during the struggle for independence – a promise that had figured even in Nehru's rousing speech on the eve of independence in August 1947 (on India's 'tryst with destiny').

In view of his interest in childhood education, Tagore would not be consoled by the extraordinary expansion of university education, in which India sends to its universities six times as many people per unit of population as does China. Rather, he would be stunned that, in contrast to East and South East Asia, including China, half the adult population and two-thirds of Indian women remain unable to read or write. Statistically reliable surveys indicate that even in the late 1980s nearly half of the rural girls between the ages of 12 and 14 did not attend any school for a single day of their lives.[26]

This state of affairs is the result of the continuation of British imperial neglect of mass education, which has been reinforced by India's traditional elitism, as well as upper-class-dominated contemporary politics (except in parts of India, such as Kerala, where anti-upper-caste movements have tended to concentrate on education as a great leveller). Tagore would see illiteracy and the neglect of education not only as the main source of India's continued social backwardness, but also as a great constraint that restricts the possibility and reach of economic development in India (as his writings on rural development forcefully make clear). Tagore would also have strongly felt the need for a greater commitment – and a greater sense of urgency – in removing endemic poverty.

At the same time, Tagore would undoubtedly find some satisfaction in the survival of democracy in India, in its relatively free press, and in general in the 'freedom of mind' that post-independence Indian politics has, on the whole, managed to maintain. He would also be pleased by the observation made by E. P. Thompson (whose father Edward Thompson had written one of the first major biographies of Tagore[27]):

All the convergent influences of the world run through this society: Hindu, Moslem, Christian, secular; Stalinist, liberal, Maoist, democratic socialist, Gandhian. There is not a thought that is being thought in the West or East that is not active in some Indian mind.[28]

Tagore would have been happy also to see that the one governmental attempt to dispense generally with basic liberties and political and civil rights in India, in the 1970s, when Prime Minister Indira Gandhi (ironically, herself a former student at Santiniketan) declared an 'emergency', was overwhelmingly rejected by the Indian voters, leading to the precipitate fall of her government.

Rabindranath would also see that the changes in policy that have eliminated famine since independence had much to do with the freedom to be heard in a democratic India. In Tagore's play *Raja O Rani* ('The King and the Queen'), the sympathetic queen eventually rebels against the callousness of state policy towards the hungry. She begins by enquiring about the ugly sounds outside the palace, only to be told that the noise is coming from 'the coarse, clamorous crowd who howl unashamedly for food and disturb the sweet peace of the palace'. The viceregal office in India could have taken a similarly callous view of Indian famines, right up to the easily preventable Bengal famine of 1943, just before independence, which killed between two and three million people. But a government in a multi-party democracy, with elections and free newspapers, cannot any longer dismiss the noise from 'the coarse, clamorous crowd'.*

Unlike Gandhiji, Rabindranath would not resent the development of modern industries in India, or the acceleration of technical progress, since he did not want India to be shackled to the turning of 'the wheel of an antiquated invention'. Tagore was concerned that people not be dominated by machines, but he was not opposed to making good use of modern technology. 'The mastery over the machine,' he wrote in *Crisis in Civilization*, 'by which the British have

*I have tried to discuss the linkage between democracy, political incentives and prevention of disasters in *Resources, Values and Development* (Cambridge, Mass.: Harvard University Press, 1984, repr. 1997), ch. 19, and in my presidential address to the American Economic Association, 'Rationality and Social Choice', *American Economic Review*, 85 (1995).

consolidated their sovereignty over their vast empire, has been kept a sealed book, to which due access has been denied to this helpless country.' Rabindranath had a deep interest in the environment – he was particularly concerned about deforestation and initiated a 'festival of tree-planting' (*vriksha-ropana*) as early as 1928. He would want increased private and government commitments to environmentalism; but he would not derive from this position a general case against modern industry and technology.

On Cultural Separatism

Rabindranath would be shocked by the growth of cultural separatism in India, as elsewhere. The 'openness' that he valued so much is certainly under great strain right now – in many countries. Religious fundamentalism still has a relatively small following in India; but various factions seem to be doing their best to increase their numbers. Certainly religious sectarianism has had much success in some parts of India (particularly in the west and the north). Tagore would see the expansion of religious sectarianism as being closely associated with an artificially separatist view of culture.

He would have strongly resisted defining India in specifically Hindu terms, rather than as a 'confluence' of many cultures. Even after the partition of 1947, India is still the third-largest Muslim country in the world, with more Muslims than in Bangladesh, and nearly as many as in Pakistan. Only Indonesia has substantially more followers of Islam. Indeed, by pointing to the immense heterogeneousness of India's cultural background and its richly diverse history, Tagore had argued that the 'idea of India' itself militated against a culturally separatist view – 'against the intense consciousness of the separateness of one's own people from others'.

Tagore would also oppose the cultural nationalism that has recently been gaining some ground in India, along with an exaggerated fear of the influence of the West. He was uncompromising in his belief that human beings could absorb quite different cultures in constructive ways:

Whatever we understand and enjoy in human products instantly becomes ours, wherever they might have their origin. I am proud of my humanity when I can acknowledge the poets and artists of other countries as my own. Let me feel with unalloyed gladness that all the great glories of man are mine. Therefore it hurts me deeply when the cry of rejection rings loud against the West in my country with the clamour that Western education can only injure us.

In this context, it is important to emphasize that Rabindranath was not short of pride in India's own heritage, and often spoke about it. He lectured at Oxford, with evident satisfaction, on the importance of India's religious ideas – quoting both from ancient texts and from popular poetry (such as the verses of the sixteenth-century Muslim poet Kabir). In 1940, when he was given an honorary doctorate by Oxford University, in a ceremony arranged at his own educational establishment in Santiniketan ('In Gangem Defluit Isis', Oxford helpfully explained), to the predictable 'volley of Latin' Tagore responded 'by a volley of Sanskrit', as Marjorie Sykes, a Quaker friend of Rabindranath, reports. Her cheerful summary of the match, 'India held its own', was not out of line with Tagore's pride in Indian culture. His welcoming attitude to Western civilization was reinforced by this confidence: he did not see India's culture as fragile and in need of 'protection' from Western influence.

In India, he wrote, 'circumstances almost compel us to learn English, and this lucky accident has given us the opportunity of access into the richest of all poetical literatures of the world.' There seems to me much force in Rabindranath's argument for clearly distinguishing between the injustice of a serious asymmetry of power (colonialism being a prime example of this) and the importance nevertheless of appraising Western culture in an open-minded way, in colonial and post-colonial territories, in order to see what uses could be made of it.

Rabindranath insisted on open debate on every issue, and distrusted conclusions based on a mechanical formula, no matter how attractive that formula might seem in isolation (such as 'This was forced on us by our colonial masters – we must reject it', 'This is our tradition – we must follow it', 'We have promised to do this – we must fulfil that promise', and so on). The question he persistently asks is whether we have reason enough to want what is being proposed, taking everything into account. Important as history is, reasoning has to go beyond the past. It is in the sovereignty of reasoning – fearless reasoning in freedom – that we can find Rabindranath Tagore's lasting voice.

6

Our Culture, Their Culture*

The works of Satyajit Ray (1921–92) present a perceptive understanding of the relation between different cultures, and his ideas remain pertinent to the major cultural debates in the contemporary world – not least in India. In Ray's films and in his writings, we see explorations of at least three general themes on cultures and their interrelations: the importance of *distinctions* between different local cultures and their respective individualities, the necessity to understand the deeply *heterogeneous* character of each local culture (even that of a community, not to mention a region or a country), and the great need for inter-cultural *communication* while recognizing the difficulties of such intercourse.

A deep respect for distinctiveness is combined in Ray's vision with an appreciation of the importance of inter-cultural communication and also the recognition of much internal diversity within each culture. In emphasizing the need to respect the individuality of each culture, Ray saw no reason for closing the doors to the outside world. Indeed, opening doors of communication was an important priority in Ray's work. In this respect his attitude contrasts sharply with the increasing tendency to see Indian culture (or cultures) in highly conservative terms – wanting it to be preserved from the 'pollution' of Western ideas and thought. Ray was always willing to enjoy and learn from ideas, art forms and lifestyles from anywhere – within India or abroad.

*This essay is an abridged version of the text of the Satyajit Ray Lecture, given at Nandan in Calcutta on 22 December 1995, and published as *Our Culture, Their Culture* (Calcutta: Nandan, 1996). Another version of the text, also abridged, was published in *New Republic*, 1 April 1996.

Ray appreciated the importance of heterogeneity within local communities. This insight contrasts sharply with the tendency of many communitarians – religious and otherwise – who are willing to break up the nation into some communities and then stop dead exactly there: 'thus far and no further'. The great film-maker's eagerness to seek the larger unit (ultimately, his ability to talk to the whole world) combined well with his enthusiasm for understanding the smallest of the small: the individuality of each person.

Distinctions and Communications

There can be little doubt about the importance that Ray attached to the distinctiveness of different cultures. He also discussed the problems that these divisions create in the possibility of communication across cultural boundaries. In his book *Our Films Their Films*, he noted the important fact that films acquire 'colour from all manner of indigenous factors such as habits of speech and behaviour, deep-seated social practices, past traditions, present influences and so on'. He went on to ask: 'How much of this can a foreigner – with no more than a cursory knowledge of the factors involved – feel and respond to?' He observed that 'there are certain basic similarities in human behaviour all over the world' (such as 'expressions of joy and sorrow, love and hate, anger, surprise and fear'), but 'even they can exhibit minute local variations which can only puzzle and perturb – and consequently warp the judgement of – the uninitiated foreigner'.[1]

The presence of such cultural divides raises many interesting problems. The possibility of communication is only one of them. There is the more basic issue of the individuality of each culture, and questions about whether and how this individuality can be respected and valued even though the world grows steadily smaller and more uniform. We live at a time when ideas and practices spread across boundaries of countries and regions with great rapidity, and the possibility that something extremely important is being lost in this process of integration has aroused understandable concern. And yet cultural interactions, even in a world of deep inequalities, can also create space for creative innovations, which combine construction with vulnerability.[2]

The individuality of cultures is a big subject nowadays, and the tendency towards homogenization of cultures, particularly in some uniform Western mode, or in the deceptive form of 'modernity', has been strongly challenged. Questions of this kind have been taken up in different forms in recent cultural studies, especially in high-profile intellectual circles influential in the West (from Paris to San Francisco). While these questions are being asked with increasing frequency in contemporary India as well, there is perhaps some irony in the fact that so much of the Third World critique of 'Western modernity' has been inspired and influenced by Western writings.

Engaging arguments on this subject have recently been presented by a number of Indian authors, including Partha Chatterjee.[3] These arguments often display a well-articulated 'anti-modernism', rejecting what is seen as the tyranny of 'modern' society (particularly of 'Western' forms of modernization). Among the diverse Indian critiques, there are some arguments, amidst others, in which the defiance of Western cultural modes is combined with enunciations of the unique importance of Indian culture and of the traditions of its local communities.

At the broader level of 'Asia' rather than India, the separateness of 'Asian values' and their distinction from Western norms has often been asserted, particularly in east Asia – from Singapore and Malaysia to China and Japan. The invoking of Asian values has sometimes occurred in rather dubious political circumstances. For example, it has been used to justify authoritarianism (and harsh penalties for alleged transgressions) in some east Asian countries. In the Vienna conference on human rights in 1993, the Foreign Minister of Singapore, citing differences between Asian and European traditions, argued that 'universal recognition of the ideal of human rights can be harmful if universalism is used to deny or mask the reality of *diversity*'.[4] The championing of 'Asian values' has typically come from government spokesmen rather than from individuals at a distance from established regimes. Still, the general issue is important enough to deserve our attention and scrutiny.

Critical Openness

Even though he emphasized the difficulties of inter-cultural communication, Ray did not, in fact, take cross-cultural comprehension to be impossible. He saw the difficulties as challenges to be encountered, rather than as strict boundaries that could not be breached. His was not a thesis of basic 'incommunicability' across cultural boundaries, merely one of the need to recognize the difficulties that may arise. On the larger subject of preserving traditions against foreign influence, Ray was not a cultural conservative. He did not give systematic priority to conserving inherited practices.

Indeed, I find no evidence in his work and writings that the fear of being too influenced by outsiders disturbed his equilibrium as an 'Indian' artist. He wanted to take full note of the importance of one's cultural background without denying what there is to learn from elsewhere. There is, I think, much wisdom in what we can call his 'critical openness', including the valuing of a dynamic, adaptable world, rather than one that is constantly 'policing' external influences and fearing 'invasion' of ideas from elsewhere.

The difficulties of understanding each other across the boundaries of culture are undoubtedly great. This applies to the cinema, but also to other art forms as well, including literature. For example, the inability of most foreigners – sometimes even other Indians – to see the astonishing beauty of Rabindranath Tagore's poetry (a failure that we Bengalis find so exasperating) is a good illustration of just such a problem. Indeed, the thought that these non-appreciating foreigners are being wilfully contrary and obdurate (rather than merely unable to appreciate across the barrier of languages and translations) is a frequently aired suspicion.

The problem is perhaps less extreme in films, in so far as the cinema is less dependent on language, since people can be informed even by gestures and actions. But our day-to-day experiences generate certain patterns of reaction and non-reaction that can be mystifying for foreign viewers who have not had those experiences. The gestures – and non-gestures – that are quite standard within the country (and understandable as 'perfectly ordinary') may appear altogether remarkable when seen by others.

Words, too, have a function that goes well beyond the information they directly convey; much is communicated by the sound of the language and special choice of words to convey a meaning, or to create a particular effect. As Ray has noted, 'in a sound film, words are expected to perform not only a narrative but a plastic function', and 'much will be missed unless one knows the language, and knows it well'.

Indeed, even the narrative may be inescapably transformed because of language barriers, especially the difficulty of conveying nuance through translation. I was reminded of Ray's remark the other day, when I saw *Tin Kanya* again, in Cambridge, Massachusetts, where a festival of Satyajit Ray's films (based on the wonderful reissues produced by the Merchant–Ivory enterprises) was being held. When obdurate Paglee – in the sparkling form of Aparna Sen (then Dasgupta) – decides to write, at last, a letter to her spurned husband, she conveys her new sense of intimacy by addressing him in the familiar form 'tumi' (as he had requested), rather than the formal and overly respectful 'apni'. This could not, of course, be caught in the English subtitle. So the translation had to show her as signing the letter as 'your wife' (to convey her new sense of intimacy). But the Bengali original in which she still signs as 'Paglee' but addresses him in the familiar form 'tumi' is infinitely more subtle.

The Audience and the Eavesdropper

Such difficulties and barriers cannot be avoided. Ray did not want to aim his movies at a foreign audience, and Ray fans abroad who rush to see his films know that they are, in a sense, eavesdropping. I believe this relationship of the creator and the eavesdropper is by now very well established among the millions of Ray fans across the world. There is no expectation that his films are anything other than the work of an Indian – and a Bengali – director made for a local audience, and the attempt to understand what is going on is a decision to engage in a self-consciously 'receptive' activity.

In this sense, Ray has triumphed – on his own terms – and this vindication, despite all the barriers, tells us something about possible communication and understanding across cultural boundaries. It may be hard, but it can be done, and the eagerness with which viewers with much experience of Western cinema flock to see Ray's films (despite the occasional obscurities of a presentation originally tailored for an entirely different audience) indicates what is possible when there is a willingness to go beyond the bounds of one's own culture.

Satyajit Ray makes an important distinction on what is or is not sensible in trying to speak across a cultural divide, especially between the West and India. In 1958 – two years after *Pather Panchali* won the Special Award in Cannes, and one year after the Grand Prix at Venice for *Aparajito* – he wrote the following in an essay called 'Problems of a Bengali Film Maker':

> There is no reason why we should not cash in on the foreigners' curiosity about the Orient. But this must not mean pandering to their love of the false-exotic. A great many notions about our country and our people have to be dispelled, even though it may be easier and – from a film point of view – more paying to sustain the existing myths than to demolish them.[5]

Ray was not, of course, unique in following this approach. A number of other great film directors from India have followed a similar route as Ray. As an old resident of Calcutta, I am proud of the fact that some of the particularly distinguished directors have come, like Ray, from this very city (I think of course of Mrinal Sen, Ritwik Ghatak, Aparna Sen and others). But what Ray calls pandering to the 'love of the false-exotic' has clearly tempted many other directors. Many Indian films that can fairly be called 'entertainment movies' have achieved great success abroad, including in the Middle East and Africa in addition to Europe and, increasingly, America, and Bombay has been a big influence on the cinematographic world in many countries.

It is not obvious whether the imaginary scenes of archaic splendour shown in such 'entertainment movies' should be seen as misdescriptions of the India in which they are allegedly set, or as excellent portrayals of some non-existent 'never-never land' (not to be confused with any real country). As Ray notes in another context, quite a few of these traditional Indian films, which attract large audiences, 'do away wholly with [the] bothersome aspect of social identification' and 'present a synthetic, non-existent society, and one can speak of credibility only within the norms of this make-belief world'.[6] Ray suggests that this feature 'accounts for their country-wide acceptance', in a country with such diversity. This is so, but this make-believe feature also contributes greatly to the appeal of these films to many foreign audiences, happy to see lavish entertainment in an imagined land. This is, of course, an understandable 'success' story, since acceptance abroad brings with it both reputation and revenue.

In fact, the exploitation of the biases and vulnerabilities of the foreign audience need not be concerned specifically with the 'love of the false-exotic'. Exploitation can take other forms – not necessarily false, nor especially exotic. There is, for example, nothing false about Indian poverty, nor about the fact – remarkable to others – that Indians have learned to live normal lives while taking little notice of the surrounding misery.

The graphic portrayal of extreme wretchedness, and the heartlessness of others towards the downtrodden, can itself be skilfully exploited, especially when supplemented by a goodly supply of vicious villains. At a sophisticated and elegant level, such exploitative use can be seen even in that extremely successful film *Salaam Bombay!* by the wonderfully talented director Meera Nair. That film has received much acclaim, as it should, since it is very powerfully constructed, beautifully absorbing and deeply moving. And yet it mercilessly exploits not only the viewers' raw sympathy, but also their interest in identifying 'the villain of the piece' who could be blamed for all this.*

Since *Salaam Bombay!* is full of villains and also of people totally lacking in sympathy and any sense of justice, the causes of the misery and suffering portrayed in the film begin to look easily understandable even to distant foreigners. I should add that this feature of reliance on villains is largely avoided in Meera Nair's next film, *Mississippi*

*As a postscript, I can express much happiness that the extraordinary talents of Meera Nair – which were absolutely clear even in *Salaam Bombay!*, despite what I thought was a serious flaw – have since then found predictable expression in her later films, which have established Meera Nair as one of the leading directors of our time.

Masala – another great film – which raises some interesting and important issues about identity and intermixing, in this case, involving ex-Ugandans of Indian origin. The underlying philosophy in *Salaam Bombay!* takes the viewer straight to the comforting question: given the lack of humanity of people around the victims, what else could you expect? The exploitative form draws at once on the knowledge – common in the West – that India has much poverty and suffering, and also on the comfort – for which there is some demand – of seeing the faces of the 'baddies' who are causing all this trouble (as in, say, American gangster movies). At a more mundane level, Roland Joffé's *The City of Joy* does the same with Calcutta, with clearly identified villains who have to be confronted.

By contrast, even when Ray's films deal with problems that are just as intense (such as the coming of the Bengal famine of 1943 in *Ashani Sanket*), the comfort of the ready explanation through the prominent presence of menacing villains is altogether avoided. Indeed, villains are remarkably rare – almost completely absent – in Satyajit Ray's films. When terrible things happen, there may be nobody clearly responsible for the evil. Even when someone is clearly responsible, as Dayamoyee's father-in-law most definitely is for her predicament, and indirectly for her death, in the film *Devi*, he too is a victim – of his misguided beliefs – and by no means devoid of humane features. If *Salaam Bombay!* and *The City of Joy* are, ultimately, in the 'cops and robbers' tradition (except that there are no 'good cops' in *Salaam Bombay!*), the Ray films have neither cops nor robbers, well illustrated, for example, by Ray's *Mahanagar* (The Great City), set in Calcutta, with many distressing events among joyous moments, leading to a deep tragedy, but with no villains on whom responsibility can be immediately pinned. One result of this absence is that Ray manages to convey something of the complexity of societal situations that lead to such tragedies, rather than seeking speedy explanations in the greed, cupidity and cruelty of some very bad people. In eschewing the easy communicability of films in which nasty people cause nasty events, Ray provides social visions that are both complex and illuminating.

Heterogeneity and External Contacts

While Satyajit Ray insists on retaining the real cultural features of the society that he portrays, his view of India – indeed, even of Bengal – recognizes a complex reality, with immense heterogeneity at every level. It is not the picture of a stylized East meeting a stereotypical West, the stock in trade of so many recent cultural writings critical of 'Westernization' and 'modernity'. Ray points out that the people who 'inhabit' his films are both complicated and extremely diverse:

Take a single province: Bengal. Or, better still, take the city of Calcutta where I live and work. Accents here vary between one neighbourhood and another. Every educated Bengali peppers his native speech with a sprinkling of English words and phrases. Dress is not standardized. Although women generally prefer the sari, men wear clothes which reflect the style of the thirteenth century or conform to the directives of the latest *Esquire*. The contrast between the rich and the poor is proverbial. Teenagers do the twist and drink Coke, while the devout Brahmin takes a dip in the Ganges and chants his *mantras* to the rising sun.[7]

One important thing to note immediately here is that the native culture which Ray emphasizes is not some pure vision of a tradition-bound society, but the heterogeneous lives and commitments of contemporary India. The Indian who does the 'twist' is as much there as the one who chants his mantras by the Ganges.

The recognition of this heterogeneity makes it immediately clear why Satyajit Ray's focus on local culture cannot be readily seen as an 'anti-modern' move. 'Our culture' can draw on 'their culture' as well, as 'their culture' can draw on 'ours'. The acknowledgement and emphasis on the culture of the people who inhabit Ray's films is in no way a denial of the legitimacy of seeking interest in ideas and practices originating elsewhere. Indeed, Ray recollects with evident joy the time when Calcutta was full of Western – including American – troops in the winter of 1942:

Calcutta now being a base of operations of the war, Chowringhee was chock-a-block with GIs. The pavement book stalls displayed wafer-thin editions of *Life* and *Time*, and the jam-packed cinema showed the very latest films from

Hollywood. While I sat at my office desk . . . my mind buzzed with the thoughts of the films I had been seeing. I never ceased to regret that while I had stood in the scorching summer sun in the wilds of Santiniketan sketching *simul* and *palash* in full bloom, *Citizen Kane* had come and gone, playing for just three days in the newest and biggest cinema in Calcutta.[8]

Ray's interest in things from elsewhere had begun a lot earlier. His engagement with Western classical music went back to his youth, but his fascination with films preceded his involvement with music. In his posthumously published book *My Years with Apu: A Memoir*, Ray recollects:

I became a film fan while still at school. I avidly read *Picturegoer* and *Photoplay*, neglected my studies and gorged myself on Hollywood gossip purveyed by Hedda Hopper and Louella Parsons. Deanna Durbin became a favourite not only because of her looks and her obvious gifts as an actress, but because of her lovely soprano voice. Also firm favourites were Fred Astaire and Ginger Rogers, all of whose films I saw several times just to learn the Irving Berlin and Jerome Kern tunes by heart.[9]

Ray's willingness to enjoy and learn from things happening elsewhere is plentifully clear in how he chose to live and what he chose to do.[10] When Ray describes what he learned as a student at Santiniketan – the distinguished centre of education started by Rabindranath Tagore where Ray studied fine arts – the elements from home and abroad are well mixed together. He learned a great deal about India's 'artistic and musical heritage' (he got involved in Indian classical music, apart from being trained to paint in traditional Indian ways), but also immersed himself in 'far-eastern calligraphy' (and particularly in the use of 'minimum brush strokes applied with maximum discipline'). When his teacher, Professor Nandalal Bose, a great artist and the leading light of the 'Bengal school', taught Ray how to draw a tree ('Not from the top downwards. A tree grows up, not down. The strokes must be from the base upwards . . .'), Bose was being at once critical of some Western conventions, while introducing Ray to the styles and traditions in two other countries, China and Japan (who did, among other things, get the tree right, Bose thought).

Ray did not hesitate to indicate how strongly his *Pather Panchali* – the profound movie that immediately made him a front-ranking film-maker in the world – was directly influenced by Vittorio De Sica's *Bicycle Thieves*. He notes that not only had he seen *Bicycle Thieves* within three days of arriving in London, but also the following: 'I knew immediately that if I ever made *Pather Panchali* – and the idea had been at the back of my mind for some time – I would make it in the same way, using natural locations and unknown actors.'[11] Despite this influence, *Pather Panchali* is a quintessentially Indian film, both in subject matter and in the style of presentation, and yet a major inspiration for its exact organization came directly from an Italian film. The Italian influence did not make *Pather Panchali* anything other than an Indian film – it simply helped it to become a *great* Indian film.

External Sources and Modernity

The growing tendency in contemporary India to champion the need for an indigenous culture that has 'resisted' external influences lacks credibility as well as cogency. It has become quite common to cite the foreign origin of an idea or a tradition as an argument against its use, and this has been linked up with an anti-modernist priority. Even as acute and perceptive a social analyst as Partha Chatterjee finds it possible to dismiss Benedict Anderson's thesis linking nationalism and 'imagined communities', by referring to the Western origin of that 'modular' form: 'I have one central objection to Anderson's argument. If nationalisms in the rest of the world have to choose their imagined community from certain "modular" forms already made available to them by Europe and the Americas, what do they have left to imagine?'[12] The conceptual form of the nation as an 'imagined community' which Anderson pursues might or might not have much to commend it (I personally think that it does – but this is a different issue), but the fear that its Western origin would leave us without a model that is our 'own' is a peculiarly parochial anxiety.

Indian culture, as it has evolved, has always been prepared to absorb material and ideas from elsewhere. Satyajit Ray's heterodoxy is not, in any sense, out of line with our tradition. Even in matters of day-to-day living, the fact that the chili, a basic ingredient of traditional Indian cooking, was brought to India by the Portuguese from the 'new world', does not make current Indian cooking any less Indian. Chili has now become an 'Indian' spice. Cultural influences are, of course, a two-way process, and India has borrowed from abroad, just as we have also given the world outside the benefits of our cooking traditions. For example, while tandoori came from the Middle East to India, it is from India that tandoori has become a staple British diet. Last summer I heard in London a quintessential Englishwoman being described as being 'as English as daffodils or chicken tikka massala'.[13]

Given the cultural and intellectual interconnections, the question of what is 'Western' and what is 'Eastern' (or 'Indian') is often hard to decide, and the issue can be discussed only in more dialectical terms. The diagnosis of a thought as 'purely Western' or 'purely Indian' can be very illusory. The origin of ideas is not the kind of thing to which 'purity' happens easily.

Science, History and Modernity

This issue has some practical importance at the moment, given the political developments of the last decade, including the increase in the strength of political parties focusing on Indian – and particularly Hindu – heritage. There is an important aspect of anti-modernism which tends to question – explicitly or by implication – the emphasis to be placed on what is called 'Western science'. If and when the challenges from traditional conservatism grow, this can become quite a threat to scientific education in India, affecting what young Indians are encouraged to learn.

The reasoning behind this anti-foreign attitude is flawed in several distinct ways. First, so-called 'Western science' is not the special possession of Europe and America. Certainly, since the Renaissance, the Industrial Revolution and the Enlightenment of the eighteenth century, most of the scientific progress has actually occurred in the West. But these scientific developments drew substantially on earlier work in mathematics and science done by the Arabs, the Chinese, the Indians and others. The term 'Western science' is misleading in this respect, and quite misguided in its tendency to establish a distance between non-Western peoples and the pursuit of mathematics and science.

Second, irrespective of where the discoveries and inventions took place, the methods of reasoning used in science and mathematics give them some independence of local geography and cultural history. There are, of course, important issues of local knowledge and of varying perspectives regarding what is or is not important, but much of substance is still shared in methods of argument, demonstration and the scrutiny of evidence. The term 'Western science' is misleading in this respect also.

Third, our decisions about the future need not be parasitic on the type of past we have experienced. Even if there were no Asian or Indian component in the evolution of contemporary mathematics and science (this is not the case, but even if it had been true), its importance in contemporary India need not be undermined for that reason.

There is a similar issue, to which I referred earlier, about the role of 'modernity' in contemporary India. Contemporary attacks on modernity (especially on a 'modernity' that is seen as coming to India from the West) draw greatly on the literature on 'post-modernism' and other related approaches, which have been quite influential in Western literary and cultural circles (and later on, somewhat derivatively, in India too). There is perhaps something of interest in this dual role of the West: the colonial metropolis supplying ideas and ammunition to post-colonial intellectuals to attack the influence of the colonial metropolis! But of course there is no contradiction there. What it does suggest, however, is that mere identification of Western connections of an idea could not be enough to damn it.

The critics of 'modernism' often share with the self-conscious advocates of 'modernism' the belief that being 'modern' is a well-defined concept – the only dividing point being whether you are 'for' modernity, or 'against' it. But the diagnosis of modernity is not particularly easy, given the historical roots – often very long roots – of recent – or 'modern' – thoughts and intellectual development, and given the mixture of origins in the genesis of ideas and techniques that are typically taken to characterize modernism.

The point is not at all that modern things must be somehow judged to be good, or that there are no reasons to doubt the wisdom of many developments which are justified in the name of a needed modernity. Rather, the point is that there is no escape from the necessity to scrutinize and assess ideas and proposals no matter whether they are seen as pro-modern or anti-modern. For example, if we have to decide what policies to support in education, health care or social security, the modernity or non-modernity of any proposal is neither here nor there. The relevant question is how these policies would affect the lives of people, and that enquiry is not the same as the investigation of the modernity or non-modernity of the policies in question. Similarly, if, faced with communal tensions in contemporary India, we suggest that there is much to be gained from reading the tolerant poems of Kabir (from the fifteenth century) or studying the political priorities of Akbar (dating from the sixteenth century), in contrast with, say, the intolerant approach of an Aurangzeb (in the seventeenth), that discrimination has to be done in terms of the worth of their respective positions, and not on the basis of some claim that Kabir or Akbar was 'more modern' or 'less modern' than Aurangzeb. Modernity is not only a befuddling notion, it is also basically irrelevant as a pointer of merit or demerit in assessing contemporary priorities.

The Elusive 'Asian Values'

What about the specialness of 'Asian values' on which so much is now being said by the authorities in a number of East Asian countries? These arguments, developed particularly in Singapore, Malaysia and China, appeal to the differences between 'Asian' and 'Western' values to dispute the importance of civil rights, particularly freedom of expression (including press freedoms) in Asian countries. The resistance to Western hegemony – a perfectly respectable cause in itself – takes the form, under this interpretation, of justifying suppression of journalistic freedoms and the violations of elementary political and civil rights on grounds of the alleged unimportance of these freedoms in the hierarchy of what are claimed to be 'Asian values'.

There are two basic problems with this mode of reasoning. First, even if it were shown that freedoms of this kind have been less important in Asian thoughts and traditions than in the West, that would still be an unconvincing way of justifying the violation of these freedoms in Asia. To see the conflict over human rights as a battle between Western liberalism on one side and Asian reluctance on the other is to cast the debate in a form that distracts attention from the central question: what would make sense in contemporary Asia? The history of ideas – in Asia and in the West – cannot settle this issue.

Second, it is by no means clear that, historically, greater importance has been systematically attached to freedom and tolerance in the West than in Asia. Certainly, individual liberty, in its contemporary form, is a relatively new notion both in Asia and in the West, and while the West did get to these ideas rather earlier (through developments such as the Renaissance, the European Enlightenment, the Industrial Revolution and so on), the divergence is relatively recent. In answer to the question, 'at what date, in what circumstances, the notion of individual liberty . . . first became explicit in the West', Isaiah Berlin has noted: 'I have found no convincing evidence of any clear formulation of it in the ancient world.'[14]

This view has been disputed by Orlando Patterson.[15] Patterson's historical arguments are indeed interesting. But his thesis of a freedom-centred tradition in the West in contrast with what happened elsewhere seems to depend on attaching significance to particular components of Western thought without looking adequately for similar components in non-Western intellectual traditions; for example, in the fairly extensive literatures on politics and participatory governance in Sanskrit, Pali, Chinese, Arabic and other languages.[16]

In the reading that sees the Western tradition as the natural habitat of individual freedom and political democracy, there is a substantial tendency to extrapolate backwards from the present. Values that the European Enlightenment and other relatively recent developments have made common and widespread can scarcely be seen as part of the long-term Western heritage – experienced in the West over millennia. There has, of course, been championing of freedom and tolerance in specific contexts in the Western classical tradition, but much the same can be said of many parts of the Asian tradition as well – not least in India, with the articulations associated for example with Ashoka's inscriptions, Śūdraka's drama, Akbar's pronouncements or Dadu's poetry, to name just a few examples.

It is true that tolerance has not been advocated by all in the Asian traditions. Nor has that advocacy typically covered everyone (though some, such as Ashoka, in the third century BCE, did indeed insist on completely universal coverage, without any exception). But much the same can be said about Western traditions as well. There is little evidence that Plato or St Augustine were more tolerant and less authoritarian than Confucius. While Aristotle certainly did write on the importance of freedom, women and slaves were excluded from the domain of this concern (an exclusion that, as it happens, Ashoka did not make around roughly the same time). The claim that the basic ideas underlying freedom and tolerance have been central to Western culture over the millennia and are somehow alien to Asia is, I believe, entirely rejectable.

The allegedly sharp contrast between Western and Asian traditions on the subject of freedom and tolerance is based on very poor history. The authoritarian argument based on the special nature of Asian values is particularly dubious. This supplements the more basic argument, presented earlier, that even if it had been the case that the values championed in Asia's past have been more authoritarian, this historical point would not be grounds enough to reject the importance of tolerance and liberties in contemporary Asia.

Over-aggregation and Heterogeneity

Discussion of Asian values draws attention to an important issue underlying attempts at generalizations about cultural contrasts between the West and the East, or between Europe and India, and so on. There are indeed many differences between Europe and India, but there are sharp differences also within India itself, or within Europe. And there are also great differences between different parts of the Indian intellectual and historical traditions. One of the things that goes deeply wrong with grand contrasts between 'our culture' and 'their culture' is the tremendous variety within each of these cultures. My old teacher Joan Robinson used to say: 'Whatever you can rightly say about India, the opposite is also true.' It is not that cultural differences are of no importance, but the contrasts do not come in the tailor-made form of some immense opposition between, say, the West and India, with relative homogeneity inside each.

The problem is, of course, even larger when there are attempts at generalization about 'Asian' values. Asia is where about 60 per cent of the world's entire population live. There are no quintessential values that apply to this immensely large and heterogeneous population which separate them out as a group from people in the rest of the world. Those who have written on the importance of cultural divisions have been right to point to them, and yet the attempt to see these divisions in the over-aggregated form of East–West contrasts hides more than it reveals.

Indeed, generalizations even about an individual religious community within India (such as the Hindus or the Muslims) or about a language group (such as the Bengalis or Gujaratis or Tamils) can be very deeply misleading. Depending on the context, there may be more significant similarity between groups of people in different parts of the country who come from the same class, have the same political convictions, or pursue the same profession or work. Such similarity can hold across national boundaries as well. People can be classified in terms of many different criteria, and the recent tendency to emphasize some contrasts (such as religion or community), while overlooking others, has ignored important differences even as it has capitalized on others.

'Ours' and 'Theirs'

The difficulties of communication across cultures are real, as are the judgemental issues raised by the importance of cultural differences. But these recognitions do not lead us to accept the standard distinctions between 'our culture' and 'their culture'. Nor do they give us cause to overlook the demands of practical reason and of political and social relevance in contemporary India, in favour of faithfulness to some alleged historical contrasts. I have tried to show that the contrasts are often not quite as they are depicted, and the lessons to be drawn are hardly the ones that the vigorous champions of 'our culture' claim them to be.

There is much to be learned in all this from Satyajit Ray's appreciation of cultural divides, along with his pursuit of communication across these divides. He never fashioned his creation to cater to what the West may expect from India, but nor did he refuse to enjoy and learn from what Western and other cultures offered. And when it came to the recognition of cultural diversity within India, Ray's delicate portrayal of the varieties of people that make us what we are as a nation cannot be outmatched. While reflecting on what to focus on in his films, he put the problem beautifully:

> What should you put in your films? What can you leave out? Would you leave the city behind and go to the village where cows graze in the endless fields and the shepherd plays the flute? You can make a film here that would be pure and fresh and have the delicate rhythm of a boatman's song.
>
> Or would you rather go back in time – way back to the Epics, where the gods and the demons took sides in the great battle where brother killed brother and Lord Krishna revivified a desolate prince with the words of the *Gita*? One could do exciting things here, using the great mimetic tradition of the *Kathakali*, as the Japanese use their Noh and Kabuki.
>
> Or would you rather stay where you are, right in the present, in the heart of this monstrous, teeming, bewildering city, and try to orchestrate its dizzying contrasts of sight and sound and milieu?

The celebration of these differences – the 'dizzying contrasts' – is far from what can be found in the laboured generalizations about 'our culture', and the vigorous pleas, increasingly vocal, to keep 'our culture', 'our modernity' distinctly unique and immune from the influence of 'their culture', 'their modernity'. In our heterogeneity and in our openness lies our pride, not our disgrace. Satyajit Ray taught us this, and that lesson is profoundly important for India. And for Asia, and for the world.

7

Indian Traditions and the Western Imagination*

The self-images (or 'internal identities') of Indians have been much affected by colonialism over the past centuries and are influenced – both collaterally and dialectically – by the impact of outside imagery (what we may call 'external identity'). However, the direction of the influence of Western images on internal Indian identities is not altogether straightforward. In recent years, separatist resistance to Western cultural hegemony has led to the creation of significant intellectual movements in many post-colonial societies – not least in India. This has particularly drawn attention to the important fact that the self-identity of post-colonial societies is deeply affected by the power of the colonial cultures and their forms of thought and classification. Those who prefer to pursue a more 'indigenous' approach often opt for a characterization of Indian culture and society that is rather self-consciously 'distant' from Western traditions. There is much interest in 'recovering' a distinctly Indian focus in Indian culture.

I would argue that this stance does not take adequate note of the dialectical aspects of the relationship between India and the West and, in particular, tends to disregard the fact that the external images of India in the West have often tended to emphasize (rather than downplay) the differences – real or imagined – between India and the West. Indeed, I propose that there are reasons why there has been a considerable Western inclination in the direction of 'distancing' Indian

*This essay draws on an earlier article entitled 'India and the West', *New Republic*, 7 June 1993. For helpful discussions, I am grateful to Akeel Bilgrami, Sugata Bose, Barun De, Jean Drèze, Ayesha Jalal, Dharma Kumar, V. K. Ramachandran, Tapan Raychaudhuri, Emma Rothschild, Lloyd Rudolph, Suzanne Rudolph, Ashutosh Varshney, Myron Weiner, Leon Wieseltier and Nur Yalman.

culture from the mainstream of Western traditions. The contemporary reinterpretations of India (including the specifically 'Hindu' renditions) which emphasize Indian particularism join forces in this respect with the 'external' imaging of India (in accentuating the distinctiveness of Indian culture). Indeed, it can be argued that there is much in common between James Mill's imperialist history of India and the Hindu nationalist picturing of India's past, even though the former image is that of a grotesquely primitive culture whereas the latter representation is dazzlingly glorious.

The special characteristics of Western approaches to India have encouraged a disposition to focus particularly on the religious and spiritual elements in Indian culture. There has also been a tendency to emphasize the contrast between what is taken to be 'Western rationality' and the cultivation of what 'Westerners' would see as 'irrational' in Indian intellectual traditions. While Western critics may find 'anti-rationalism' defective and crude, and Indian cultural separatists may find it cogent and penetrating (and perhaps even 'rational' in some deeper sense), they nevertheless agree on the existence of a simple and sharp contrast between the two heritages. The issue that has to be scrutinized is whether such a bipolar contrast is at all present in that form.

I will discuss these questions and argue that focusing on India's 'specialness' misses, in important ways, crucial aspects of Indian culture and traditions. The deep-seated heterogeneity of Indian traditions is neglected in these homogenized interpretations (even though the interpretations themselves are of different kinds). My focus will be particularly on images of Indian intellectual traditions, rather than on its creative arts and other features of social life. After distinguishing between three of the dominant approaches in Western interpretations of Indian intellectual traditions, I shall consider what may appear to be the overall consequence of these approaches in Western images of India and its impact on both external and internal identities.

Western Approaches to India: Three Categories

A dissimilarity of perceptions has been an important characteristic of Western interpretations of India, and several different and competing conceptions of that large and complex culture have been influential in the West. The diverse interpretations of India in the West have tended to work to a considerable extent in the same direction (that of accentuating India's spirituality) and have reinforced each other in their effects on internal identities of Indians. This is not because the distinct approaches to India are not fundamentally different; they certainly are very disparate. The similarity lies more in their impact – given the special circumstances and the dialectical processes – than in their content.

The analysis to be pursued here would undoubtedly invite comparison and contrast with Edward Said's justly famous analysis of 'Orientalism'. Said analyses the construction of the 'Orient' in Western imagination. As he puts it: 'The Orient is an idea that has a history and a tradition of thought, imagery, and vocabulary that have given it reality and presence *in and for the West*.'[1] This essay has a much narrower focus than Said's, but there is clearly an overlap of subject matter since India is a part of the 'Orient'. The main difference is at the thematic level. Said focuses on uniformity and consistency in a particularly influential Western characterization of the Orient, whereas I shall be dealing with several contrasting and conflicting Western approaches to understanding India.

Said explains that his work 'deals principally not with a correspondence between Orientalism and Orient, but with the internal consistency of Orientalism and its ideas about the Orient'.[2] I would argue that, unless one chooses to focus on the evolution of a specific conceptual tradition (as Said, in effect, does), 'internal consistency' is precisely the thing that is terribly hard to find in the variety of Western conceptions of India. There are several fundamentally contrary ideas and images of India, and they have quite distinct roles in the Western understanding of the country and also in influencing the self-perception of Indians.

Attempts from outside India to understand and interpret the country's traditions can be put into at least three distinct categories, which I shall call *exoticist* approaches, *magisterial* approaches and *curatorial* approaches.[3] The first (exoticist) category concentrates on the wondrous aspects of India. The focus here is on what is different, what is strange in the country that, as Hegel put it, 'has existed for millennia in the imagination of the Europeans'.

The second (magisterial) category strongly relates to the exercise of imperial power and sees India as a subject territory from the point of view of its British governors. This outlook assimilates a sense of superiority and guardianhood needed to deal with a country that James Mill defined as 'that great scene of British action'. While a great many British observers did not fall into this category (and some non-British ones did), it is hard to dissociate this category from the task of governing the Raj.

The third (curatorial) category is the most catholic of the three and includes various attempts at noting, classifying and exhibiting diverse aspects of Indian culture. Unlike the exoticist approaches, a curatorial approach does not look only for the strange (even though the 'different' must have more 'exhibit value'), and unlike the magisterial approaches, it is not weighed down by the impact of the ruler's priorities (even though the magisterial connection would be hard to avoid altogether when the authors are also members of the ruling imperial elite, as they sometimes were). For these reasons, there is more freedom from preconceptions in this third category. On the other hand, the curatorial approaches have inclinations of their own, with a general interest in seeing the object – in this case, India – as very special and extraordinarily interesting.

Other categories can be proposed that are not covered by any of the three. Also, the established approaches can be reclassified according to some *other* organizing principle. I am not claiming any grand definitive status of this way of seeing the more prominent Western approaches to India. However, for the purpose of this essay, I believe this threefold categorization is useful.

Curiosity, Power and Curatorial Approaches

I shall begin by considering the curatorial approaches. But first I must deal with a methodological issue; in particular, the prevalent doubts in contemporary social theory about the status of intellectual curiosity as a motivation for knowledge. In particular, there is much scepticism about the possibility of any approach to learning that is innocent of power. That scepticism is justified to some extent since the motivational issues underlying any investigation may well relate to power relations, even when that connection is not immediately visible.

Yet people seek knowledge for many different reasons, and curiosity about unfamiliar things is certainly among the possible reasons. It need not be seen as a figment of the deluded scientist's imagination, nor as a tactical excuse for some other, ulterior preoccupation. Nor does the pervasive relevance of different types of motivation have the effect of making all the different observational findings equally arbitrary. There are real lines to be drawn between inferences dominated by rigid preconceptions (for example, in the 'magisterial' approaches, to be discussed presently) and those that are not so dominated, despite the possibility that they too may have biases of their own.

There is an interesting methodological history here. The fact that knowledge is often associated with power is a recognition that had received far too little attention in traditional social theories of knowledge. But in recent social studies, the remedying of that methodological neglect has been so comprehensive that we are now in some danger of ignoring other motivations altogether that may not link directly with the seeking of power. While it is true that any useful knowledge gives its possessor some power in one form or another, this may not be the most remarkable aspect of that knowledge, nor the primary reason for which this knowledge is sought. Indeed, the process of learning can accommodate considerable motivational variations without becoming a functionalist enterprise of some grosser kind. An epistemic methodology that sees the pursuit of knowledge as entirely congruent with the search for power is a great deal more cunning than wise. It can needlessly undermine the value of knowledge in satisfying curiosity and interest; it significantly weakens one of the profound characteristics of human beings.

The curatorial approach relates to systematic curiosity. People are interested in other cultures and different lands, and investigations of a country and its traditions have been vigorously pursued throughout human history. Indeed, the development of civilization would have been very different had this not been the case. The exact motivation for these investigations can vary, but the enquiries need not be hopelessly bound by some overarching motivational constraint (such as those associated with the exoticist or magisterial approaches). Rather, the pursuit may be driven primarily by intellectual interests and concerns. This is not to deny that the effects of these investigative pursuits may go well beyond the motivating interests and concerns, nor that there could be mixed motivations of various kinds, in which power relations play a collateral role. But to deny the role of curiosity and interest as powerful motivational features in their own right would be to miss something rather important. For the curatorial approaches, that connection is quite central.

Curatorial Approaches in Early Arabic and European Studies

A fine example of a curatorial approach to understanding India can be found in Alberuni's *Ta'rikh al-hind* ('The History of India'), written in Arabic in the early eleventh century.[4] Alberuni, an Iranian born in Central Asia in 973 CE, first came to India accompanying the marauding troops of Mahmud of Ghazni. He became very involved with India and mastered Sanskrit; studied Indian texts on mathematics, natural sciences, literature, philosophy and religion; conversed with as many experts as he could find; and investigated social conventions and practices. His book on India presents a remarkable account of the intellectual traditions and social customs of early eleventh-century India.

Even though Alberuni's was almost certainly the most impressive of these investigations, there are a great many examples of serious Arabic studies of Indian intellectual traditions around that time.[5] Brahmagupta's pioneering Sanskrit treatise on astronomy had first been translated into Arabic in the eighth century (Alberuni retranslated it three centuries later), and several works on medicine, science and philosophy had an Arabic rendering by the ninth century. It was through the Arabs that the Indian decimal system and numerals reached Europe, as did Indian writings in mathematics, science and literature.

In the concluding chapter of his book on India, Alberuni describes the motivation behind his work thus: 'We think now that what we have related in this book will be sufficient for any one who wants to converse with [the Indians], and to discuss with them questions of religion, science, or literature, on the very basis of their own civilization.'[6] He is particularly aware of the difficulties of achieving an understanding of a foreign land and people, and specifically warns the reader about it:

> In all manners and usages, [the Indians] differ from us to such a degree as to frighten their children with us, with our dress, and our ways and customs, and as to declare us to be devil's breed, and our doings as the very opposite of all that is good and proper. By the bye, we must confess, in order to be just, that a similar depreciation of foreigners not only prevails among us and [the Indians], but is common to all nations towards each other.[7]

While Arab scholarship on India provides plentiful examples of curatorial approaches in the external depiction of India, it is not, of course, unique in this respect. The Chinese travellers Faxian (Fa-Hsien) and Xuanzang (Hiuan-tsang), who spent many years in India in the fifth and seventh centuries CE respectively, provided extensive accounts of what they saw. While they had gone to India for Buddhist studies, their reports cover a variety of Indian subjects, described with much care and interest.

Quite a few of the early European studies of India must also be put in this general category. A good example is the Italian Jesuit Roberto Nobili, who went to south India in the early seventeenth century, and whose remarkable scholarship in Sanskrit and Tamil permitted him to produce fairly authoritative books on Indian intellectual discussions, in Latin as well as in Tamil. Another Jesuit, Father Pons from France, produced a grammar of Sanskrit in Latin in the early eighteenth century and also sent a collection of original manuscripts to Europe (happily for him, the Bombay customs authorities were not yet in existence).

However, the real eruption of European interest in India took place a little later, in direct response to British – rather than Italian or French – scholarship on India. A towering figure in this intellectual transmission is the redoubtable William Jones, the legal scholar and officer of the East India Company, who went to India in 1783 and by the following year had established the Royal Asiatic Society of Bengal with the active patronage of Warren Hastings. In collaboration with scholars such as Charles Wilkins and Thomas Colebrooke, Jones and the Asiatic Society did a remarkable job in translating a number of Indian classics – religious documents (such as the *Gītā*) as well as legal treatises (particularly, *Manusmriti*) and literary works (such as Kālidāsa's *Śakuntalā*).

Jones was obsessed with India and declared his ambition 'to know India better than any other European ever knew it'. His description of his selected fields of study included the following modest list:

> the Laws of the Hindus and the Mohamedans, Modern Politics and Geography of Hindustan, Best Mode of Governing Bengal, Arithmetic and Geometry, and Mixed Sciences of the Asiaticks, Medicine, Chemistry, Surgery, and Anatomy of the Indians, Natural Productions of India, Poetry, Rhetoric, and Morality of Asia, Music of the Eastern Nations, Trade, Manufacture, Agriculture, and Commerce of India.[8]

One can find many other examples of dedicated scholarship among British officers in the East India Company, and there can be little doubt that the Western perceptions of India were profoundly influenced by these investigations. Not surprisingly, the focus here is quite often on those things that are distinctive in India. Specialists on India pointed to the uncommon aspects of Indian culture and its intellectual traditions, which were obviously more interesting given the perspective and motivation of the observers.[9] As a result, the curatorial approaches could not escape being somewhat slanted in their focus. I shall come back to this issue later.

The Magisterial Burden

I turn now to the second category, the magisterial approaches. The task of ruling a foreign country is not an easy one when its subjects are seen as equals. In this context, it is quite remarkable that the early British administrators in India, even the controversial Warren Hastings, were as respectful of the Indian traditions as they clearly were. The empire was still in its infancy and was being gradually acquired, rather tentatively.

A good example of a magisterial approach to India is the classic book on India written by James Mill, published in 1817, on the strength of which he was appointed as an official of the East India Company. Mill's *The History of British India* played a major role in introducing the British governors of India to a particular characterization of the country. Mill disputed and dismissed practically every claim ever made on behalf of Indian culture and its intellectual traditions, concluding that it was totally primitive and rude. This diagnosis went well with Mill's general attitude, which supported the idea of bringing a rather barbaric nation under the benign and reformist administration of the British Empire. Consistent with his beliefs, Mill was an expansionist in dealing with the remaining independent states in the subcontinent. The obvious policy to pursue, he explained, was 'to make war on those states and subdue them'.[10]

Mill chastised early British administrators (like William Jones) for having taken 'Hindus to be a people of high civilization, while they have in reality made but a few of the earliest steps in the progress to civilization'.[11] At the end of a comprehensive attack on all fronts, he came to the conclusion that Indian civilization was on a par with other inferior ones known to Mill – 'very nearly the same with that of the Chinese, the Persians, and the Arabians'; he also put in this category, for good measure, 'subordinate nations, the Japanese, Cochinchinese, Siamese, Burmans, and even Malays and Tibetans'.[12]

How well informed was Mill in dealing with his subject matter?* Mill wrote his book without ever having visited India. He knew no Sanskrit, nor any Persian or Arabic, had practically no knowledge of any of the modern Indian languages, and thus his reading of Indian material was of necessity most limited. There is another feature of Mill that clearly influenced his investigations, his inclination to distrust anything stated by native scholars, since they appeared to him to have 'a general disposition to deceit and perfidy'.[13]

Perhaps some examples of Mill's treatment of particular claims of achievement may be useful to illustrate the nature of his extremely influential approach. The invention of the decimal system with place values and the placed use of zero, now used everywhere, as well as

*The assessment of Mill's analysis of Indian works on science and mathematics that follows here corresponds to the discussion of Mill's critique, in Essay 4, though the focus here is on the nature of external evaluation from the 'magisterial' perspective, rather than on the impact of Mill's characterization on Indian self-identification.

the so-called Arabic numerals, are generally known to be Indian developments. In fact, Alberuni had already mentioned this in his eleventh-century book on India,[14] and many European as well as Arab scholars had written on this subject.[15] Mill dismisses the claim altogether on the grounds that 'the invention of numerical characters must have been very ancient' and 'whether the signs used by the Hindus are so peculiar as to render it probable that they invented them, or whether it is still more probable that they borrowed them, are questions which, for the purpose of ascertaining their progress in civilization, are not worth resolving'.

Mill proceeds then to explain that the Arabic numerals 'are really hieroglyphics' and that the claim on behalf of the Indians and the Arabs reflects the confounding of 'the origin of cyphers or numerical characters' with 'that of hieroglyphic writing'.[16] At one level Mill's rather elementary error lies in not knowing what a decimal or a place-value system is, but his ignorant smugness cannot be understood except in terms of his implicit unwillingness to believe that a very sophisticated invention could have been managed by such primitive people.

Another interesting example concerns Mill's reaction to Indian astronomy and specifically the argument for a rotating earth and a model of gravitational attraction (proposed by Āryabhaṭa, who was born in 476 CE, and investigated by, among others, Varāhamihira and Brahmagupta in the sixth and seventh centuries). These works were well known in the Arab world; as was mentioned earlier, Brahmagupta's book was translated into Arabic in the eighth century and retranslated by Alberuni in the eleventh. William Jones had been told about these works in India, and he in turn reported that statement. Mill expresses total astonishment at Jones's gullibility.[17] After ridiculing the absurdity of this attribution and commenting on the 'pretensions and interests' of Jones's Indian informants, Mill concludes that it was 'extremely natural that Sir William Jones, whose pundits had become acquainted with the ideas of European philosophers respecting the system of the universe, should hear from them that those ideas were contained in their own books'.[18]

For purposes of comparison it is useful to examine Alberuni's discussion of the same issue nearly eight hundred years earlier, concerning the postulation of a rotating earth and gravitational attraction in the still earlier writings of Āryabhaṭa and Brahmagupta:

> Brahmagupta says in another place of the same book: 'The followers of Aryabhata maintain that the earth is moving and heaven resting. People have tried to refute them by saying that, if such were the case, stones and trees would fall from the earth.' But Brahmagupta does not agree with them, and says that that would not necessarily follow from their theory, apparently because he thought that all heavy things are attracted towards the center of the earth.[19]

Alberuni himself proceeded to dispute this model, raised a technical question about one of Brahmagupta's mathematical calculations, referred to a different book of his own arguing against the proposed view, and pointed out that the relative character of movements makes this issue less central than one might first think: 'The rotation of the earth does in no way impair the value of astronomy, as all appearances of an astronomic character can quite as well be explained according to this theory as to the other.'[20] Here, as elsewhere, while arguing against an opponent's views, Alberuni tries to present such views with great involvement and care. The contrast between Alberuni's curatorial approach and James Mill's magisterial pronouncements could not be sharper.

There are plenty of other examples of 'magisterial' readings of India in Mill's history. This is of some practical importance, since the book was extremely influential in the British administration and widely praised, for example by Macaulay ('the greatest historical work . . . since that of Gibbon'). Macaulay's own approach and inclinations echoed James Mill's (as was discussed in Essay 4).

This view of the poverty of Indian intellectual traditions played a major part in educational reform in British India, as is readily seen from the 1835 'Minute on Indian Education', written by Macaulay himself. The priorities in Indian education were determined, henceforth, by a different emphasis – by the need, as Macaulay argued, for a class of English-educated Indians who could 'be interpreters between us and the millions whom we govern'.

The impact of the magisterial views of India was not confined to Britain and India. Modern documents in the same tradition have been influential elsewhere, including in the United States. In a series of long conversations on India and China conducted by Harold Isaacs in 1958 with 181 Americans – academics, professionals in mass media, government officials, missionaries and church officials, and officials of foundations, voluntary social-service groups, and political organizations – Isaacs found that the two most widely read literary sources on India were Rudyard Kipling and Katherine Mayo, the author of the extremely derogatory *Mother India*.[21] Of these, Kipling's writings would be more readily recognized as having something of the 'magisterial' approach to them. Lloyd Rudolph describes Mayo's *Mother India* thus:

> First published in 1927, *Mother India* was written in the context of official and unofficial British efforts to generate support in America for British rule in India. It added contemporary and lurid detail to the image of Hindu India as irredeemably and hopelessly impoverished, degraded, depraved, and corrupt. Mayo's *Mother India* echoed not only the views of men like Alexander Duff, Charles Grant, and John Stuart Mill but also those of Theodore Roosevelt, who glorified in bearing the white man's burden in Asia and celebrated the accomplishments of imperialism.[22]

Mahatma Gandhi, while describing Mayo's book as 'a drain inspector's report', had added that every Indian should read it and seemed to imply, as Ashis Nandy notes, that it is possible 'to put her criticism to internal use' (as an over-stern drain inspector's report certainly can be).[23] Gandhi himself was severely attacked in the book, but, given his campaign against caste and untouchability, he might have actually welcomed even her exaggerations because of its usefully lurid portrayal of caste inequities. But while Gandhi may have been right to value external criticism as a way of inducing people to be self-critical, the impact of the 'magisterial approach' certainly gives American perceptions of India a very clear slant.[24]

Exoticist Readings of India

I turn now to the 'exoticist' approaches to India. Interest in India has often been stimulated by the observation of exotic ideas and views there. Arrian's and Strabo's accounts of Alexander the Great's spirited conversations with various sages of north-west India may or may not be authentic, but ancient Greek literature is full of uncommon happenings and thoughts attributed to India.

Megasthenes' *Indika*, describing India in the early third century BCE, can claim to be the first outsider's book on India; it created much Greek interest, as can be seen from the plentiful references to it, for example, in the writings of Diodorus, Strabo and Arrian. Megasthenes had ample opportunity to observe India since, as the envoy of Seleucus Nicator to the court of Candragupta Maurya, he spent nearly a decade (between 302 and 291 BCE) in Pāṭaliputra (the site of modern Patna), the capital city of the Mauryan empire. But his superlatively admiring book is also so full of accounts of fantastic objects and achievements in India that it is hard to be sure what is imagined and what is really being observed.

There are various other accounts of exotic Indian travels by ancient Greeks. The biography of Apollonius of Tyana by Flavius Philostratus in the third century CE is a good example. In his search for what was out of the ordinary, Apollonius was, we are assured, richly rewarded in India: 'I have seen men living upon the earth and not upon it; defended without walls, having nothing, and yet possessing all things.'[25] How such contradictory things can be seen by the same person from the same observational position may not be obvious, but the bewitching charm of all this for the seeker of the exotic can hardly be doubted.

Exotic interests in India can be seen again and again, from its early history to the present day. From Alexander listening to the gymnosophists' lectures to contemporary devotees hearing the sermons of Maharishi Mahesh Yogi and Shri Rajneesh, there is a crowded lineage. Perhaps the most important example of intellectual exoticism related to India can be seen in the European philosophical discussions in the eighteenth and early nineteenth centuries, among the Romantics in particular.

Important figures in the Romantic movement, including the Schlegel brothers, Schelling and others, were profoundly influenced by rather magnified readings of Indian culture. From Herder, the

German philosopher and a critic of the rationalism of the European Enlightenment, we get the magnificent news that 'the Hindus are the gentlest branch of humanity' and that 'moderation and calm, a soft feeling and a silent depth of the soul characterize their work and their pleasure, their morals and mythology, their arts'.[26] Friedrich Schlegel not only pioneered studies of Indo-European linguistics (later pursued particularly by Max Müller) but also brought India fully into his critique of the contemporary West. While in the West 'man himself has almost become a machine' and 'cannot sink any deeper', Schlegel recommended learning from the Orient, especially India. He also guaranteed that 'the Persian and German languages and cultures, as well as the Greek and the old Roman, may all be traced back to the Indian'.[27] To this list, Schopenhauer added the New Testament, informing us that, in contrast with the Old, the New Testament 'must somehow be of Indian origin: this is attested by its completely Indian ethics, which transforms morals into asceticism, its pessimism, and its *avatar* (i.e., the person of Christ)'.[28]

Not surprisingly, many of the early enthusiasts were soon disappointed in not finding in Indian thought what they had themselves put there, and many of them went into a phase of withdrawal and criticism. Some of the stalwarts, Schlegel in particular, recanted vigorously. Others, including Hegel, outlined fairly negative views of Indian traditions and presented loud denials of the claim of pre-eminence of Indian culture – a claim that was of distinctly European origin. When Coleridge asked: 'What are / These potentates of inmost Ind?'[29] he was really asking a question about Europe, rather than about India.[30]

In addition to veridical weakness, the exoticist approach to India has an inescapable fragility and transience that can be seen again and again. A wonderful thing is imagined about India and sent into a high orbit, and then it is brought crashing down. All this need not be such a tragedy when the act of launching is done by (or with the active cooperation of) the putative star. Not many would weep, for example, for Maharishi Mahesh Yogi when the Beatles stopped lionizing him and left suddenly; in answer to the Maharishi's question of why they were leaving, John Lennon said: 'You are the cosmic one; you ought to know.'[31]

But it is a different matter altogether when both the boom and the bust are thrust upon the victim. One of the most discouraging episodes in literary reception occurred early in this century, when Ezra Pound, W. B. Yeats and others led a chorus of adoration at the lyrical spirituality of Rabindranath Tagore's poetry but followed it soon afterwards with a thorough disregard and firm denunciation. Tagore was a Bengali poet of tremendous creativity and range (even though his poetry does not translate easily – not even the spiritual ones that were so applauded) and also a great storyteller, novelist and essayist; he remains a dominant literary figure in Bangladesh and India. The versatile and innovative writer that the Bengalis know well is not the sermonizing spiritual guru put together in London; nor did he fit any better the caricature of 'Stupendranath Begorr' to be found in Bernard Shaw's 'A Glimpse of the Domesticity of Franklyn Barnabas'.

Interactions and Reinforcements

These different approaches have had very diverse impacts on the understanding of Indian intellectual traditions in the West. The exoticist and magisterial approaches have bemused and befuddled that understanding even as they have drawn attention to India in the West. The curatorial approaches have been less guilty of this, and indeed historically have played a major part in bringing out and drawing attention to the different aspects of Indian culture, including its nonmystical and nonexotic features. Nevertheless, given the nature of the curatorial enterprise, the focus inevitably leans towards that which is different in India, rather than what is similar to the West. In emphasizing the distinctiveness of India, even the curatorial approaches have sometimes contributed to the accentuation of contrasts rather than commonalities with Western traditions, though not in the rather extreme form found in the exoticist and magisterial approaches.

The magisterial approaches played quite a vigorous role in the running of the British Empire. Even though the Raj is dead and gone, the impact of the associated images survives, not least in the United States (as discussed earlier). To some extent, the magisterial authors also reacted against the admiration of India that can be seen in the writings of curatorial observers of India. For example, both Mill and Macaulay were vigorously critical of the writings of authors such as William Jones, and there are some important dialectics here. The respectful curatorial approaches painted a picture of Indian intellectual traditions that was much too favourable for the imperial culture of the nineteenth century, and contributed to the vehemence of the magisterial denunciations of those traditions. By the time Mill and Macaulay were writing, the British Indian empire was well established as a lasting and extensive enterprise, and the 'irresponsibility' of admiring the native intellectual traditions – permissible in the previous century for early servants of the East India Company – was hard to sustain as the favoured reading of India in the consolidated empire.

The outbursts of fascinated wonder in the exoticist approaches bring India into Western awareness in big tides of bewildering attention. But then they ebb, leaving only a trickle of hardened exoticists holding forth. There may well be, after a while, another tide. In describing the rise and decline of Rabindranath Tagore in London's literary circles, E. M. Forster remarked that London was a city of 'boom and bust', but that description applies more generally (that is, not confined only to literary circles in London) to the Western appreciation of exotic aspects of Eastern cultures.

The tides, while they last, can be hard work, though. I remember feeling quite sad for a dejected racist whom I saw, some years ago, near the Aldwych station in London, viewing with disgust a thousand posters pasted everywhere carrying pictures of the obese – and holy – physique of Guru Maharajji (then a great rage in London). Our dedicated racist was busy writing 'fat wog' diligently under each of the pictures. In a short while that particular wog would be gone, but I do not doubt that the 'disgusted of Aldwych' would scribble 'lean wog' or 'medium-sized wog' under other posters now.

It might be thought that since the exoticist approaches give credit where it may not be due and the magisterial approaches withhold credit where it may well be due, the two might neutralize each other nicely. But they work in very asymmetrical ways. Magisterial critiques tend to blast the rationalist and humanist aspects of India with the greatest force (this is as true of James Mill as of Katharine Mayo), whereas exoticist admirations tend to build up the mystical and extra-rational aspects with particular care (this has been so from Apollonius of Tyana down to the Hare Krishna activists of today). The result of the two taken together is to wrest the understanding of Indian culture forcefully away from its rationalist aspects. Indian traditions in mathematics, logic, science, medicine, linguistics or epistemology may be well known to the Western specialist, but they play little part in the general Western understanding of India.[32] Mysticism and exoticism, in contrast, have a more hallowed position in that understanding.

The Dialectics of Internal and External Identity

Western perceptions and characterizations of India have had considerable influence on the self-perception of Indians themselves. This is clearly connected to India's colonial past and continued deference to what is valued in the West.[33] However, the relationship need not take the form of simple acceptance – it sometimes includes strategic responses to the variety of Western perceptions of India that suit the interests of internal imaging. We have to distinguish between some distinct aspects of the influence that Western images have had on Indian internal identities.

First, the European exoticists' interpretations and praise found in India a veritable army of appreciative listeners, who were particularly welcoming given the badly damaged self-confidence resulting from colonial domination. The admiring statements were quoted again and again, and the negative remarks by the same authors (Herder, Schlegel, Goethe and others) were systematically overlooked.

In his *Discovery of India*, Jawaharlal Nehru comments on this phenomenon: 'There is a tendency on the part of Indian writers, to which I have also partly succumbed, to give selected extracts and quotations from the writings of European scholars in praise of old Indian literature and philosophy. It would be equally easy, indeed much easier, to give other extracts giving an exactly opposite viewpoint.'[34] In the process of accepting the exoticist praise, the Indian interpretation of the past has extensively focused on the objects of exoticist praise, concentrating more on the mystical and the antirationalist for which many in the West have such admiration.[35]

Second, the process fitted into the politics of elitist nationalism in colonial India and fed the craving for a strong intellectual ground to stand on to confront the imperial rulers. Partha Chatterjee discusses the emergence of this attitude very well:

> Anticolonial nationalism creates its own domain of sovereignty within colonial society well before its political battle with the imperial power. It does this by dividing the world of social institutions and practices into two domains – the material and the spiritual. The material is the domain of the 'outside,' of the economy and of statecraft, of science and technology, a domain where the West had proved its superiority and the East had succumbed. In this domain, then, Western superiority had to be acknowledged and its accomplishments carefully studied and replicated. The spiritual, on the other hand, is an 'inner' domain bearing the 'essential' marks of cultural identity. The greater one's success in imitating Western skills in the material domain, therefore, the greater the need to preserve the distinctiveness of one's spiritual culture. This formula is, I think, a fundamental feature of anticolonial nationalisms in Asia and Africa.[36]

There was indeed such an attempt to present what was perceived to be the 'strong aspects' of Indian culture, distinguished from the domain, as Chatterjee puts it, 'where the West had proved its superiority and the East had succumbed'.

Chatterjee's analysis can be supplemented by taking further note of the dialectics of the relationship between Indian internal identity and its external images. The diagnosis of strength in that non-materialist domain was as much helped by the exoticist admiration for Indian spirituality as the acceptance of India's weakness in the domain of science, technology and mathematics was reinforced by the magisterial dismissals of India's materialist and rationalist traditions. The emphases on internal identity that emerged in colonial India bear powerful marks of dialectical encounters with Western perceptions.

Third, as the focus has shifted in recent decades from elitist colonial history to the role of the non-elite, the concentration on the intellectual traditions of the elite has weakened. Here we run into one of the most exciting developments in historiography in India. There has been a significant shift of attention from the elite to the underdogs in the writing of colonial history, focusing more on the rural masses and the exploited plebeians – a broad group often identified by the capacious term 'subalterns'.[37] The move is entirely appropriate in its context (in fact, much overdue), and in understanding colonial history, this is a very important corrective.

While this shift in focus rejects the emphasis on elitist intellectual traditions in general (both of the materialist and the non-materialist kind), it is in many ways easier to relate the religious and spiritual traditions of the elite to the practices and beliefs of the non-elite. In contrast, the cutting edge of science and mathematics is inevitably related to formal education and preparation. In this context, the immense backwardness of India in mass education (an inheritance from the British period but not adequately remedied yet) compounds the dissociation of elite science and mathematics from the lives of the non-elite. Acceptance of the achievements of Indian spirituality tends to look less 'alienated' from the masses than the achievements in fields that demand more exacting formal education. Thus, the exoticists' praise of India is more easily accepted by those who are particularly careful not to see India in elitist terms.

The fact remains, however, that illiteracy is a deprivation. The issue of inter-class justice cannot be a matter only of recognizing the real role of the subalterns in history (for example, in anti-colonial national movements), important though it is. It is also a matter of remedying the immense inequalities in educational and other opportunities that severely limit, even today, the actual lives of the subalterns.

Interestingly enough, even by the eleventh century the seriousness of this loss was noted by Alberuni himself (one of the major curatorial authors whose work was referred to earlier). Alberuni spoke of the real deprivation of 'those castes who are not allowed to occupy themselves with science'.[38] This substantive deprivation remains largely unremedied even today (except in particular regions such as Kerala). In understanding the nature of Indian cultures and traditions, focusing mainly on the achievements – rather than deprivations – of the Indian subaltern can yield a deceptive contrast.*

*Indeed, in conceptualizing 'the good life' even from the perspective of the deprived underdog, it would be a mistake to ignore altogether the intellectual achievements of the elite, since part of the deprivation of the exploited lies precisely in being denied participation in these achievements. While Marx might have exaggerated a little in his

This shift in emphasis has also, to some extent, pushed the interpretation of India's past away from those achievements that require considerable formal training. While this move makes sense in some contexts, a comparison of a self-consciously non-elitist history of India with the typically classical understanding of the intellectual heritage of the West produces a false contrast between the respective intellectual traditions. In comparing Western thoughts and creations with those in India, the appropriate counterpoints of Aristotelian or Stoic or Euclidian analyses are not the traditional beliefs of the Indian rural masses or of the local wise men but the comparably analytical writings of, say, Kauṭilya or Nāgārjuna or Āryabhaṭa. 'Socrates meets the Indian peasant' is not a good way to contrast the respective intellectual traditions.

Concluding Remarks

The internal identities of Indians draw on different parts of India's diverse traditions. The observational leanings of Western approaches have had quite a major impact – positively and negatively – on what contributes to the Indian self-image that emerged in the colonial period and survives today. The relationship has several dialectical aspects, connected to the sensitivity towards selective admirations and dismissals from the cosmopolitan West as well as to the mechanics of colonial confrontations.

The differences between the curatorial, magisterial and exoticist approaches to Western understanding of Indian intellectual traditions lie, to a great extent, in the varying observational positions from which India has been examined and its overall images drawn. The dependence on perspective is not a special characteristic of the imaging of India alone. It is, in fact, a pervasive general feature in description and identification.[39] 'What is India really like?' is a good question

eloquence about 'the idiocy of the village life', there is nevertheless a substantial point here in identifying the nature of social deprivation. There is, in fact, no basic contradiction in choosing the subaltern perspective of history and taking systematic note of the scholarly accomplishments of the elite.

for a foreign tourist's handbook precisely because the description there may sensibly be presented from the particular position of being a foreign tourist in India. But there are other positions, other contexts, other concerns.

The three approaches investigated here have produced quite distinct views of Indian intellectual history, but their overall impact has been to exaggerate the non-material and arcane aspects of Indian traditions compared to its more rationalistic and analytical elements. While the curatorial approaches have been less guilty of this, their focus on what is really different in India has, to some extent, also contributed to it. But the bulk of the contribution has come from the exoticist admiration of India (particularly of its spiritual wonders) and the magisterial dismissals (particularly of its claims in mathematics, science and analytical pursuits).

The nature of these slanted emphases has tended to undermine an adequately pluralist understanding of Indian intellectual traditions. While India has certainly inherited a vast religious literature, a large wealth of mystical poetry, grand speculation on transcendental issues, and so on, there is also a huge – and often pioneering – literature, stretching over two and a half millennia, on mathematics, logic, epistemology, astronomy, physiology, linguistics, phonetics, economics, political science and psychology, among other subjects concerned with the here and now.[40]

Even on religious subjects, the only world religion that is firmly agnostic (Buddhism) is of Indian origin, and, furthermore, the atheistic schools of Cārvāka and Lokāyata have generated extensive arguments that have been seriously studied by Indian religious scholars themselves.[41] Heterodoxy runs throughout the early documents, and even the ancient epic *Rāmāyaṇa*, which is often cited by contemporary Hindu activists as the holy book of the divine Rama's life, contains dissenting characters. For example, Rama is lectured to by a worldly pundit called Jāvāli on the folly of his religious beliefs: 'O Rama, be wise, there exists no world but this, that is certain! Enjoy that which is present and cast behind thee that which is unpleasant.'[42]

What is in dispute here is not the recognition of mysticism and religious initiatives in India, which are certainly plentiful, but the overlooking of all the other intellectual activities that are also abundantly present. In fact, despite the grave sobriety of Indian religious preoccupations, it would not be erroneous to say that India is a country of fun and games in which chess was probably invented, badminton originated, polo emerged, and the ancient *Kāmasūtra* told people how to have joy in sex.* Indeed, Georges Ifrah quotes a medieval Arab poet from Baghdad called al-Sabhadi, who said that there were 'three things on which the Indian nation prided itself: its method of reckoning, the game of chess, and the book titled *Kalila wa Dimna* (a collection of legends and fables).'[43] This is not altogether a different list from Voltaire's catalogue of the important things to come from India: 'our numbers, our backgammon, our chess, our first principles of geometry, and the fables which have become our own.'[44] These selections would not fit the mainstream Western image of Indian traditions, focused on religion or spirituality.

Nor would they fit the way many Indians perceive themselves and their intellectual past, especially those who have come to take a 'separatist' position on the nature of Indian culture. I have tried to discuss how that disparity has come about and how it is sustained. I have also tried to speculate about how the selective alienation of India from a very substantial part of its past has been nourished by the asymmetrical relationship between India and the West. It is, oddly enough, the rationalist part of India's tradition that has been affected most by this dialectical alienation.

*Gita Mehta makes excellent use of the Indian game of snakes and ladders to help interpret modern India (*Snakes and Ladders: Glimpses of Modern India*, New York: Anchor Books, 1998).

8

China and India*

'Is there anyone in any part of India who does not admire China?' asked Yi Jing in the seventh century, on returning from India to China.[1] Yi Jing may have fallen a little for exaggerated rhetoric, but there was certainly much intellectual interest about China in India at that time, as there was about India in China. Yi Jing had just spent ten years at the institute of higher learning, Nālandā, which attracted many scholars from outside India, in addition to domestic students.

Yi Jing, who studied medicine in Nālandā (in particular, 'Ayurveda' or 'the science of longevity') in addition to Buddhist philosophy and practice, was one of many Chinese scholars who visited India in the first millennium to study Buddhism and other subjects (and also to collect Sanskrit documents), and many of them spent a decade or more in India.† In the other direction, hundreds of Indian scholars went to China and worked there between the first century and the eleventh. They were engaged in a variety of work, which included translating Sanskrit documents into Chinese (mostly Buddhist writings), but also other activities, such as the pursuit of mathematics and science. Several Indian mathematicians and astronomers held high positions in China's scientific establishment, and an Indian scientist called Gautama Siddhārtha (Qutan Xida, in Chinese) even

*For many useful comments and suggestions, I am extremely grateful to Patricia Mirrlees, Sugata Bose, Geoffrey Lloyd, David McMullen, Emma Rothschild, Roel Sterckx, Sun Shuyun and Rosie Vaughan. A shorter version of this paper was published in the *New York Review of Books*, 2 Dec. 2004.

†There are accounts of more than 200 Chinese scholars who spent extensive periods of time in India in this period; see Tan Yun-Shan, *Sino-Indian Culture* (Calcutta: Visva-Bharati, 1998).

Xuanzang (Hiuan-tsang) returning to China with Sanskrit manuscripts from India in 645 AD

became the president of the official Board of Astronomy in China in the eighth century.

Intellectual links between China and India, stretching over much of the first millennium and beyond, were important in the history of the two countries. And yet they are hardly remembered today. What little notice they do get tends to come from those interested in religious history, particularly Buddhism. But religion is only one part of a much bigger story of Sino-Indian connections over the first millennium, and there is need for a broader understanding of the reach of these relations. This is important for a fuller appreciation not only of the history of a third of the world's population, but also for the continuing relevance of these connections, linked as they are with contemporary political and social concerns.

It is certainly correct to see religion as a major reason for the historical closeness of China and India, and to appreciate the central role of Buddhism in initiating the movement of people and ideas between the two countries. However, even though Buddhism served as a critically important influence, the intellectual interactions between the two countries initiated by Buddhism were not confined to religion only. The non-religious (or what, in current terminology, may be called 'secular') consequences of these relations stretched well into science, mathematics, literature, linguistics, architecture, medicine and music. We know from the elaborate accounts left by a number of Chinese visitors to India, such as Faxian in the fifth century and Xuanzang and Yi Jing in the seventh,[2] that their interest was by no means restricted to religious theory and practices only. Similarly, the Indian scholars who went to China, especially in the seventh and eighth centuries, included not only religious experts, but also other professionals, such as astronomers and mathematicians.

It is not, however, easy to rescue the variety and reach of early Sino-Indian intellectual relations from their interpretational confinement in the religious basket. Indeed, religious reductionism has been reinforced in recent years by the contemporary obsession with classifying the world population into distinct 'civilizations' defined principally by religion (well illustrated, for example, by Samuel Huntington's partitioning of the world into such categories as 'Western civilization', 'Islamic civilization', 'Buddhist civilization', 'Hindu civilization').

There is, as a result, a tendency to see people mainly – or even entirely – in terms of their religion, even though that attribution of a singular identity can miss out on much that is important. This segregation has already done significant harm to the understanding of other parts of the global history of ideas and commitments, for example through the confusion it generates between the history of Muslim people in general and Islamic history in particular, ignoring the flowering of science, mathematics and literature pursued by Muslim intellectuals, particularly between the eighth and the thirteenth centuries.*

There is, in fact, another factor that influences this interpretational bias. There is an odd dichotomy in the way in which Western and non-Western ideas and scholarship are currently comprehended, with a tendency to attribute a predominant role to religiosity in interpreting the works of non-Western intellectuals who had secular interests along with strong religious beliefs. It is, for example, not assumed that, say, Isaac Newton's scientific work must be understood in primarily Christian terms (even though he did have Christian beliefs), nor presumed that his contributions to worldly knowledge must somehow be interpreted in the light of his deep interest in mysticism (important as mystical speculations evidently were to Newton himself and even perhaps for some of the motivation for his efforts). In contrast, when it comes to non-Western cultures, religious reductionism tends to exert a gripping influence. For example, there is a widespread tendency to presume that none of the general intellectual works of Buddhist scholars or of Tantric practitioners in India or China could be 'properly understood' except in the special light of their religious beliefs and practices.

The extensive contacts that were generated between India and China through Buddhist connections were not confined to the subject

*If the disaffected Arab activist today is induced to take pride only in the purity of Islam, rather than in the many-sided richness of Arab history, the unique prioritization of religion has certainly played a big part in that interpretational enclosure. There is an increased tendency also to see the broad civilization of India as just 'Hindu civilization' – to use the monothematic phrase favoured both by cultural classifiers like Samuel Huntington and by Hindu political activists (on this see Essay 1 above). The narrowing effects of some types of identity-based thinking, including the privileging of a singular identity, are discussed in my forthcoming book, *Identity and Violence: The Illusion of Destiny*, to be published by Norton, New York.

matter of Buddhism only. They had significant effects in other fields as well, including science, mathematics, literature, linguistics, medicine and music. They also broadened, in a general way, the intellectual horizons of people in the two countries, and even helped to make each of them less insular. This essay is concerned specifically with Sino-Indian historical relations in the first millennium that went beyond the confines of religious interactions. A particular focus of attention is the catalytic role that the connections inspired by Buddhism, and fostered by Buddhist contacts, played in advancing what can be broadly described as secular pursuits.

Trade, Religion and Beyond

As it happens, Buddhism was not the only vehicle of Sino-Indian relations, which began almost certainly with trade. Indian traders were engaged in importing goods from China for re-export to Central Asia more than two thousand years ago. Zhang Qian, an early Han emissary to Bactriana in the second century BCE, was surprised to find, in the local markets, Chinese goods from Yunnan (mainly cotton and bamboo products), and on enquiry he learned that they had been brought there by Indian caravans through India and Afghanistan.[3] Indian intermediation in trade between China and the west of Asia continued over the centuries, though the commodity pattern went on changing. Silk was very important initially, but 'by the eleventh century . . . porcelain had already replaced silk as the leading Chinese commodity transshipped through India'.[4]

In India itself, consumption habits, particularly of rich Indians, were radically influenced a couple of thousand years ago by innovations made in China. Kauṭilya's Sanskrit treatise on economics and politics, *Arthaśāstra*, first written in the fourth century BCE though revised and finalized a few centuries later, gives a special place to 'silk and silk-cloth from the land of China' among 'precious articles' and 'objects of value'. There are references in the ancient epic the *Mahābhārata* to Chinese fabric or silk (*cīnaṃśuka*) being given as gifts, and there are similar references also in the ancient *Laws of Manu*.[5]

The exotic nature of Chinese products was captured in many literary works in the early part of the first millennium. In a critical moment in the great fifth-century play *Śakuntalā* by Kālidāsa (perhaps the greatest poet and dramatist in classical Sanskrit literature), when King Duṣyanta sees, in the middle of a hunting expedition, the stunning hermit-girl Śakuntalā, and is altogether stricken by her beauty, the lovesick king explains the state of his transfixation by comparing himself with the way a banner made of Chinese silk flutters in the wind: 'My body goes forward, / But my reluctant mind runs back / Like Chinese silk on a banner / Trembling against the wind.' In *Harṣacarita* by Bāṇa, written in the seventh century, the celebrated wedding of the beautiful Rājyaśrī is made particularly resplendent by her decision to be clothed in elegant Chinese silk. There are also plentiful references in the Sanskrit literature in this period to many Chinese products other than silk that made their way into India, varying from camphor (*cīnaka*), fennel (*cīnāka*), vermilion (*cīnapiṣṭa*) and high-quality leather (*cīnasi*) to pear (*cīnarājaputra*) and peach (*cīnani*).[6]

If China was enriching the material world of India two thousand years ago, India was busy, it appears, exporting Buddhism to China. That often-recollected process is certainly a part of history, and this straightforward story requires acknowledgement first, before more complex correlates of those relations are examined. The first firm record of the arrival of Indian monks in China goes back to the first century CE, when Dharmarakṣa and Kāśyapa Mātaṅga came at the invitation of Emperor Mingdi of the Han dynasty. According to legend, the emperor had seen Gautama Buddha in his dream (there must have been some knowledge already of Buddhism in China for the central character in the royal dream to be recognized as Gautama), and he dispatched a search team to fetch Buddhist experts from India. Dharmarakṣa and Mātaṅga, the two Indian monks, arrived with masses of texts and relics on a white horse, whereupon the Chinese built for them the 'White Horse Monastery', *Baima si*, where the two apparently spent the rest of their lives.

From then on, Indian scholars and monks kept coming to China in an unbroken stream, and this went on until the eleventh century. There are records of the lives and works of hundreds of such scholars and translators, who produced Chinese versions of thousands of Sanskrit documents. Even as the flow came to an end in the eleventh century (no further arrivals are recorded in the Chinese chronicles after 1036), the translations were going on with astonishing rapidity (we learn that 201 further Sanskrit volumes were translated between 982 and 1011). But by then Buddhism was in long-term decline in China with the growing dominance of Neo-Confucianism. It had also, by this time, declined in the country of its origin (the last Buddhist dynasty in India, the Pālas of Bengal, petered out in the twelfth century).[7]

There was a similar – though somewhat smaller – flow in the opposite direction, from China to India. The reports that the Chinese visitors wrote about India covered its intellectual pursuits as well as religious practices, living styles and social systems. Yi Jing, quoted earlier, went to India in 675, on the sea route via Śrīvijaya, a flourishing coastal city in seventh-century Sumatra, which had strong Indian influences (and was where Yi Jing acquired his Sanskrit). He studied at the institute of higher learning, at Nālandā, located close to Pāṭaliputra (now Patna), the ancient capital of Maurya India (the first all-India state, established in the fourth century BCE). Yi Jing wrote a detailed account, completed in 691, on what he saw and assimilated in his decade in India.[8] His investigation of what to learn from India concentrated, as one would expect, on Buddhist philosophy and practice in particular, but it also included other fields of study such as procedures of health care and medicine – a subject of special interest to him, to which Yi Jing devoted three chapters of his book. I shall return later to Yi Jing's observations on this subject.

The first Chinese scholar to leave a serious account of his visit to India was Faxian, a Buddhist scholar from western China who wanted to go to India to seek some Sanskrit texts (such as *Vinaya*) and to make them available in China. He arrived in India almost three hundred years before Yi Jing, in 401. He undertook an arduous journey through the northern route via Khotan (which had a strong Buddhist presence), having started off from China in 399. After ten active years in India, Faxian returned by sea, sailing from the mouth of the Ganges or Hooghly (not far from present-day Calcutta), via Buddhist Sri Lanka, and finally Hindu Java. Faxian spent his time in

India travelling widely, visiting major cities and Buddhist sites, collecting documents (which he would later translate into Chinese), and talking – it would appear – with everyone around him. He wrote a highly illuminating account of India and Sri Lanka, *A Record of Buddhist Kingdoms*.[9] Faxian's years in Pāṭaliputra were devoted to studying language and literature, in addition to religious texts. However, with a somewhat similar interest in public health as Yi Jing would display later, Faxian also paid particular attention to the Indian arrangements for health care, and to this, too, I shall return.

The most famous visitor from China, Xuanzang, came in the seventh century under the later Tang dynasty. Xuanzang, who was a formidable scholar, collected a great many Sanskrit texts (again, he would translate many of them after his return to China), and travelled throughout India for sixteen years, including the years he spent (like Yi Jing who would follow him there) in the distinguished educational establishment at Nālandā. There Xuanzang studied medicine, philosophy, logic, mathematics, astronomy and grammar, in addition to Buddhism.[10] Xuanzang also met the Buddhist emperor of north India, King Harṣa, and had conversations with him on Sino-Indian relations.[11]

Xuanzang's visit was well remembered for many centuries, both in India and China. A Buddhist visitor to India from Japan in the ninth century noted with much interest the fact that, in a large number of Buddhist temples in 'middle India', Xuanzang was represented in paintings with his 'hemp shoes, spoon and chop-sticks mounted on multicoloured clouds'.[12] In China there were a great many legends about Xuanzang, which became quite popular by the tenth century and were frequently performed as plays on the Chinese stage later on. The best known and most popular of these semi-fictional accounts is a sixteenth-century allegorical novel, *Xi You Ji* ('The Journey to the West', also translated as *Monkey*), by Wu Cheng'en.[13]

Insularity and Openness

Despite the respect in which the India-returned Chinese scholars were viewed in their own country, including the royal patronage they often received, it is important not to overlook the resistance to Indian – particularly Buddhist – influence that was also widespread in China. The resistance to Buddhism in various periods of Chinese history contained, among other elements, a strong belief in China's sense of intellectual invulnerability, and in particular the persuasion that ideas generated outside China could not really be very important. Han Yu, an anti-Buddhist intellectual in the ninth century, who would be much championed later on by Confucians, put the issue starkly in his 'Memorial on Buddhism' written in 819:

> The Buddha was of barbarian origin. His language differed from Chinese speech; his clothes were of a different cut; his mouth did not pronounce the prescribed words of the Former Kings; his body was not clad in garments prescribed by the Former Kings. He did not recognize the relationship between prince and subject, nor the sentiments of father and son.

Han Yu even offered an illustrative proof of the wrongness of Buddhist ways:

> [Emperor Wu of the Liang] dedicated himself to the service of the Buddha. He refused to use animals in the sacrifices in his own ancestral temple. His single meal a day was limited to fruits and vegetables. In the end he was driven out and died of hunger. His dynasty likewise came to an untimely end. In serving the Buddha he was seeking good fortune, but the disaster that overtook him was only the greater. Viewed in the light of this, it is obvious that the Buddha is not worth serving.

Daoist (or Taoist) opposition to Buddhism also had a strong element of Chinese intellectual nationalism and a sense of superiority of Chinese ways. As it happens, Buddhism and Daoism have many similarities, but that only made the battle even harder, and the issue of temporal priority, too, figured in this conflict. For example, in the early fourth century a Daoist activist, named Wang Fu, wrote a book called *Laozi Hua Hu Jing* ('The Classic about Lao-tzu's

Civilizing the Barbarians'). In this account, Laozi (or Lao-tzu, to use the old but perhaps more familiar spelling), the founder of Daoism (who is normally placed in the third century BCE), was put on an imagined civilizing mission to India, especially to influence Gautama Buddha (who, as it happens, had died a few centuries before Laozi's alleged arrival). Charles Hucker has pithily described this intensely polemical work and the rather bizarre controversy it generated:

> [Wang Fu's] basic thesis is that Lao-tzu, on departing China, traveled across Central Asia into India and there either (1) magically transformed an accompanying disciple into the historic Buddha, (2) converted Buddha to Taoism, or (3) became Buddha himself, depending on which version of the text one reads. Buddhists fought this Taoist attack primarily by moving the life of the Buddha back to earlier and earlier times, and Taoists responded in kind by reassigning dates to Lao-tzu.[14]

As Leon Hurvitz and Tsai Heng-Ting have discussed, the question, 'Why should a Chinese allow himself to be influenced by Indian ways?' was, in fact, 'one of the objections most frequently raised by Confucians and Daoists once Buddhism had acquired a foothold on Chinese soil'.[15] The loss of the central position of China in the order of things in the world was among the concerns. The Buddhist response took varying forms, but helped to open up some issues of universalist ethics at least in some of the responses to anti-Buddhist polemic. Mouzi, a vigorous defender of Buddhism and of the compatibility of the Buddhist outlook with being a good Chinese, even asked the question in his combative *Lihao lun* ('Disposing of Error') whether the Chinese should claim to be uniquely central in the world, and articulated a strong claim in favour of Buddhist universalism:

> The commentary says, 'The north polar star is in the center of Heaven and to the north of man.' From this one can see that the land of China is not necessarily situated under the center of Heaven. According to the Buddhist scriptures, above, below, and all around, all beings containing blood belong to the Buddha-clan.[16]

One of the positive contributions Buddhist connections produced in China is the general sense that even the Chinese must, to some extent, look outwards. Indeed, not only did Buddhism suggest that there were sources of wisdom well outside China, but it also led to the tendency of many Chinese intellectuals to go abroad, in particular to India, in search of enlightenment and understanding. Furthermore, since these visitors to India came back with tales of wonderful things they had seen in India, it was difficult to take an entirely Sino-centric view of world civilization. There were also other admirable sites and achievements they could see on the way to India. For example, Xuanzang in the seventh century marvelled at the gigantic Bamiyan statues of the Buddha in Afghanistan, which he saw as he approached India from the West (on the circuitous route he had taken via Khotan).*

In fact, some Chinese commentators felt threatened not only by the dilution of China's centrality, but – worse – by the tendency of some Buddhists to take India to be actually more central than China.[17] Even though India was commonly referred to, at that time, as 'the Western kingdom' (giving China a more central position), the Buddhist perspective tended to favour placing India at the centre of things. For example, Faxian's fifth-century book on his travels described India as 'the Middle kingdom', with China as a frontier country.[18]

While all this was intensely irritating for believers in China's centrality, such heterodoxy did bring in a challenge to what would otherwise have been China's monolithic self-centredness. This was certainly a moderating influence on China's insularity, and might even have made an indirect contribution to the interest and enthusiasm with which Chinese mathematicians and astronomers greeted Indian works in these fields (to be discussed presently).

On the other side, Buddhist connections also helped to moderate Indian self-centredness and sense of civilizational exclusiveness. Suspicion of foreigners has been a continuing factor in parts of Indian thinking. Even as late as the eleventh century, Alberuni, the remarkable Iranian visitor, in his book *Ta'rikh al-hind* ('The History of India'), complained about the Indian attitude towards foreigners:

*These were the statues of Buddha that were destroyed recently by the Taliban, thirteen centuries after Xuanzang wrote eloquently about them.

On the whole, there is very little disputing about theological topics among themselves. . . . On the contrary all their fanaticism is directed against those who do not belong to them – against all foreigners. They call them *mleccha*, i.e., impure, and forbid having any connection with them, be it by intermarriage or any other kind of relationship, or by sitting, eating, and drinking with them.[19]

That attitude did receive a challenge from Buddhist universalism and from the fact that Indians became, for many centuries, closely linked to other people through the common bond of a shared religion.

As it happens, despite the spread of Buddhism beyond the borders of India, locally confined Indian Buddhists did not always recognize what a world religion Buddhism was becoming. In the early fifth century, Faxian noted that when he met some Buddhist monks at the Jetavana monastery in India, he was surprised by their sense of uniqueness. The account, in third person, recounts the experience of Faxian and Dao Jing, who had accompanied Faxian:

The crowd of monks came out, and asked them from what kingdom they were come. 'We are come,' they replied, 'from the land of Han.' 'Strange,' said the monks with a sigh, 'that men of a border country should be able to come here in search of our Law!' Then they said to one another, 'During all the time that we, preceptors and monks, have succeeded to one another, we have never seen men of Han, followers of our system, arrive here.'[20]

The reach of Buddhism and the presence of Chinese Buddhists in India would have done something to challenge the tendency to see the world in narrowly Indian terms.

Buddhist educational institutions, particularly that at Nālandā in east India, with many distinguished Chinese and other foreign students, provided a good basis for overcoming that mistrust. The conflicting attitudes came out very sharply at the point of Xuanzang's departure from Nālandā, in the seventh century. The Nālandā establishment greatly admired Xuanzang and wanted him to stay on, and they had offered him a leading position in the academic staff there. Xuanzang's disciple Hui Li reports the attempt by the Nālandā academic staff to give a plethora of reasons to persuade Xuanzang to make India his home:

The monks of Nālandā, when they heard of it [Xuanzang's plan to return to China], begged him to remain, saying: 'India is the land of Buddha's birth, and though he has left the world, there are many traces of him. . . . Why then do you wish to leave having come so far? Moreover, China is a country of *mlecchas*, of unimportant barbarians, who despise the religious and the Faith. That is why Buddha was not born there. The mind of the people is narrow, and their coarseness profound, hence neither saints nor sages go there. The climate is cold and the country rugged – you must think again.'[21]

To this Xuanzang replied with two counterarguments. The first disputed the syllogism by invoking Buddhist universalism without questioning the empirical premise: 'Buddha established his doctrine so that it might be diffused to all lands. Who would wish to enjoy it alone, and to forget those who are not yet enlightened?' Xuanzang's second argument disputed the empirical premise about China, in a spirit of national pride, without contradicting his own universalist outlook:

Besides, in my country the magistrates are clothed with dignity, and the laws are everywhere respected. The emperor is virtuous and the subjects loyal, parents are loving and sons obedient, humanity and justice are highly esteemed, and old men and sages are held in honour. . . . How then can you say that Buddha did not go to my country because of its insignificance?

Xuanzang returned to China in 645, but continued his communications with India. A few years afterwards he received a letter from his old friend, Prajñadeva, from Nālandā, who sent his regards along with those of other Indian friends of Xuanzang, and added:

The Upāsakas [students and trainees] always continue to offer their salutations to you. We are sending you a pair of white cloths to show that we are not forgetful. The road is long. So do not mind the smallness of the present. We wish you may accept it. As regards the Sūtras and the Śāstras [Sanskrit texts] which you may require, please send us a list. We will copy them and send them to you.

Xuanzang replied by first noting that he had heard the sad news of the death of one of his teachers in Nālandā, and then by taking up Prajñadeva's offer to help in sending useful documents from India:

I learnt from an ambassador who recently came back from India that the great teacher Śīlabhadra was no more. This news overwhelmed me with grief that knows no bounds. . . . I should let you know that while crossing the Indus I had lost a load of sacred texts. I now send you a list of the texts annexed to this letter. I request you to send them to me if you get a chance. I am sending some small articles as presents. Please accept them.

Through the normal sorrows and tragedies of human life, the borderless engagement in pursuing a common understanding continued. But the foreign contacts generated through Buddhism had, at least temporarily, shamed the self-centred arrogance of some of the leading Indian intellectuals of the time.

The broadening effects of Buddhist connections on the self-centredness of both Chinese and Indian intellectuals are among the significant secular consequences of these linkages. They added a psychological and perceptual dimension to the other – more palpable – secular consequences of Buddhist connections, over such diverse fields as mathematics, astronomy, literature, linguistics, music, fine arts, medicine and public health, which I take up now.

Transmission of Ideas: A Methodological Difficulty

Interactions between Indian and Chinese intellectuals in the first millennium were particularly strong in mathematics and science (especially astronomy). Before assessing these interactions, it would be useful to consider a serious methodological difficulty related to the procedure for diagnosing the movement of ideas from one country to another. Even though plausible connections are easy to point out, direct evidence of movement of ideas is often hard to find. 'In works on the Chinese sciences,' Jean-Claude Martzloff has noted in his history of Chinese mathematics, 'no question has been touched on more often than that of the circulation of ideas,' and yet 'we still know very little about the subject.'[22]

Joseph Needham has attempted to provide a list of mathematical ideas that 'radiated from China', particularly to India, and he has argued that many more ideas went from China to India than came in the opposite direction: 'India was the more receptive of the two cultures.'[23] Martzloff criticizes Needham's procedure 'because of its chronological and methodological imprecision', and goes on to provide some serious counterarguments to Needham's substantive conclusions.[24] In the absence of direct evidence of the movement of an idea, Needham presumes that the idea in question actually did move from the country where its known use is earlier to the country where the evidence of its first recorded use is at a later date. The procedure is, thus, essentially speculative, and can be faulted, among other problems, for ignoring the possible loss of an earlier record of use which could affect chronological priority, and not acknowledging the possibility of an independent discovery.

The investigation of the movement of mathematical or scientific ideas between China and India is also seriously hampered by the fact that there is a substantial informational asymmetry between the preserved records in the two countries. The Chinese records are much more extensive and much better preserved than their Indian counterparts. It has become increasingly common to claim in recent Indian discussions that the Hindu and Buddhist records from the first millennium were substantially destroyed during and after the Muslim conquests in the following centuries. That did occur to some extent, particularly in north India, but, no less importantly, the general lack of enthusiasm in chronicling events and incidents in ancient India does contrast with Chinese meticulousness in wanting to produce – and keep – detailed records. John Kieschnick has drawn attention to another possible explanation of the paucity of Indian early documents: 'With the inscriptions on metal, clay, or stone, most writings in ancient India were inscribed on pieces of birch bark or palm leaves, which were then bound together. Few such manuscripts survive from ancient and medieval India, owing perhaps more to the ephemerality of palm leaves and birch bark than to disinterest in the medium.'[25]

Whatever the causes of this asymmetry of records (and we do not have to settle that larger issue here), it clearly has very substantial effects – as it happens in 'opposite' directions – on the methods that have been used, that is, the traditional reliance on direct evidence of movement, and Needham's technique of relying on chronological priority of records to presume a geographical transfer. As far as the reliance on direct evidence is concerned, the informational asymmetry makes it a lot easier to show that ideas moved from India to China, rather than the opposite, since the Chinese records of derivation from India are much fuller and much better preserved than the corresponding Indian records of Chinese influence. This tends to exaggerate China's receptivity, compared with India's. On the other hand, Needham's presumptive method of comparing the dates of first known use in each country tends to tilt the diagnoses in favour of movements from China to India, rather than the opposite, since Chinese records of early use of particular ideas are much fuller and much better kept than the corresponding Indian records. Indeed, given the asymmetry of records, there would seem to be no obvious way of avoiding bias in one direction or the other.

It is indeed hard to settle Needham's enquiry into what can be called the 'balance of trade' in the movement of new ideas between India and China. But we don't really have to resolve that rather esoteric issue. What is important to note here is that ideas in mathematics and science, and also in other non-religious subjects, moved plentifully in both directions. Both countries can to a considerable extent be absolved from the charge of abiding intellectual insularity.

Mathematics and Science

One of the connections on which evidence of intellectual connections is plentiful is the impact of Buddhists in general, and of adherents of Tantric Buddhism in particular, on Chinese mathematics and astronomy in the seventh and eighth centuries, in the Tang period. Yi Jing, with whose rhetorical question this essay began, was one of many translators of Tantric texts from Sanskrit into Chinese. He was in India in the last quarter of the seventh century, at a time when Tantrism was beginning to generate a lot of interest in China. Tantrism became a major force in China in the seventh and eighth centuries, and had followers among Chinese intellectuals of the highest standing. Since many Tantric scholars had a deep interest in mathematics (perhaps connected, at least initially, with the Tantric fascination with numbers), Tantric mathematicians had a significant influence on Chinese mathematics as well.

Indeed, as Needham notes, 'the most important Tantrist was I-Hsing (+672 to +717), the greatest Chinese astronomer and mathematician of his time'. Needham goes on to remark that 'this fact alone should give us pause, since it offers a clue to the possible significance of this form of Buddhism for all kinds of observational and experimental sciences'.[26] Though Tantrism is of Indian origin, the influences, as Needham points out, went in both directions.[27] Indeed, 'Cīnācāra' (or Chinese practice) figures prominently in parts of the Indian Tantric literature, as do Indian texts in Chinese Tantric writings.[28]

Yi Xing (or I-Hsing, to use Needham's spelling) was fluent in Sanskrit. As a Buddhist monk, he was familiar with Indian religious literature, but he had acquired a great expertise also on Indian writings on mathematics and astronomy. Despite his own religious connection, it would be a mistake to assume that Yi Xing's mathematical or scientific work must have been motivated by religious concerns. As a general mathematician who happened to be also a Tantrist, Yi Xing dealt with a variety of analytical and computational problems, many of which had no particular connection with Tantrism or Buddhism at all. The combinatorial problems tackled by Yi Xing included such classic ones as 'calculating the total number of possible situations in chess'. Yi Xing was particularly concerned with calendrical calculations, and even constructed, on imperial order, a new calendar for China.

Calendrical studies, in which Indian astronomers located in China in the eighth century, along with Yi Xing, were particularly involved, made good use of the progress of trigonometry that had already occurred in India by then (going much beyond the original Greek roots of Indian trigonometry). The movement east of Indian trigonometry to China was part of a global exchange of ideas that also went west around that time. Indeed, this was also about the time when Indian trigonometry was having a major impact on the Arab world (with widely used Arabic translations of the works of Āryabhaṭa, Varāhamihira, Brahmagupta and others), which would later influence European mathematics as well, through the Arabs. Some verbal signposts to the global movement of ideas can be readily traced. A good example is the transformation of Āryabhaṭa's Sanskrit term *jya* for what we now call *sine*: *jya* was translated, through proximity of sound, into Arabic *jiba* (a meaningless word in Arabic) and later transformed into *jaib* (a bay or a cove in Arabic), and ultimately into the Latin word *sinus* (meaning a bay or a cove), from which the modern term 'sine' is derived. Āryabhaṭa's *jya* was translated in Chinese as *ming* and was used in such tables as *yue jianliang ming*, literally 'sine of lunar intervals'.[29]

There are detailed Chinese records of the fact that several Indian astronomers and mathematicians were employed in high positions in the Astronomical Bureau at the Chinese capital in this period. As was mentioned earlier, one of them, Gautama (Qutan Xida), became President of the Board of Astronomy in China. He produced the great Chinese compendium of astronomy *Kaiyvan Zhanjing* – an eighth-century scientific classic.[30] He was also engaged in adapting a number of Indian astronomical works into Chinese. For example, *Jiuzhi li*, which draws on a particular planetary calendar in India ('Navagraha' calendar), is clearly based on the classical *Pañcasiddhāntika*, produced around 550 CE by Varāhamihira. It is mainly an algorithmic guide to computation, estimating such things as the duration of eclipses based on the diameter of the moon and other relevant parameters. The techniques involved drew on methods that were established by Āryabhaṭa and then further developed by his followers in India such as Varāhamihira and Brahmagupta.

Yang Jingfeng, an eighth-century Chinese astronomer, described the mixed background of official Chinese astronomy thus:

> Those who wish to know the positions of the five planets adopt Indian calendrical methods. . . . So we have three clans of Indian calendar experts, Chiayeb (Kāśyapa), Chhüthan (Gautama), and Chümolo (Kumāra), all of whom hold office at the Bureau of Astronomy. But now most use is made of the calendrical methods of Master Chhüthan [Qutan], together with his 'Great Art', in the work which is carried out for the government.[31]

In scrutinizing these Sino-Indian connections in science, which were evidently important, we have to assess the role of Buddhism as a catalyst. Even though the Indian astronomers, such as Gautama, or

Kāśyapa or Kumāra, would not have been in China but for the relations generated by Buddhism, their work can hardly be seen primarily as contributions to Buddhism.

Creative Arts, Literature and Language

Turning from science and mathematics to the broader field of culture, the consequences of Buddhist connections on China and India were also extensive. The Chinese produced some of the finest Buddhist monuments, temples and monasteries, and among the greatest Buddhist sculpture and paintings in the world. While these must, at one level, be seen as religious achievements, one would have to be quite boorish to see in these works of art nothing other than graphic religiosity. And even though, as Kieschnick has illuminatingly argued, bridge-building has special connections with Buddhist ideas and theories,[32] the art and engineering of bridge-building, which received much encouragement from the spread of Buddhism, must be seen to be of considerable secular relevance, no matter what the initial religious inspiration might have been.

The same can be said of music, though the influences here are less immediate than in the visual arts and material construction. Buddhist chants as well as Indian music in various forms (such as *Tianzhu* music) penetrated into China in the Tang period, and the interactions continued over the centuries. In 1404 Emperor Chengzu, also known as the Yongluo emperor, of the Ming dynasty, is supposed to have compiled and edited 'Songs of Buddha', which had been popular in China from the Tang to Yuan dynasties (618 to 1368) and various versions of this song book can be found even today in China as well as in south-east Asia, for example in Vietnam and Burma.

That Buddhism had an impact on Chinese literature cannot come as a surprise. The use of religious and mythological themes for poetry, fiction and drama is standard practice around the world, and any new source of intellectual stimulation cannot but have its impact on what is written and read and enjoyed. There is also nothing astonishing in the fact that over time what began as a purely religious theme can become sufficiently detached – and 'secularized' – to be enjoyed irrespective of one's own religious persuasion. A Chinese audience enjoying Peking operas based on 'The Heavenly Girl Scattering Flowers' and 'Maudgyayana Saving His Mother' does not need expertise on the Indian Buddhist tradition to make sense of what is going on, and the same applies to the appreciation of the large volume of Chinese poetry and prose that was influenced by Buddhist ideas and its rich treasury of anecdotes.

What is more striking is the indication that thousands of new words and idioms were introduced into the Chinese language through translations from Sanskrit. While some of these Sanskrit words had religious connections, such as *dhyana* (meditation), which became *ch'an* in Chinese (and then *zen*), others did not. Indeed, even the word 'Mandarin' derives from the Sanskrit word *Mantrī* (an adviser or a minister: the Prime Minister of India is still the country's 'Pradhān Mantrī'), though that came much later – evidently via Malaya. Sanskrit, like classical Chinese, does have a rich vocabulary, and the immense volume of Sanskrit texts that were translated into Chinese provided the occasion for adding to China's already rich lexicon.

Another general area of considerable interaction was linguistics and grammar, on which Pāṇini, the Sanskritist, had made a major breakthrough in the fourth century BCE. In the seventh century, Xuanzang discusses the contributions of Pāṇini and his disciples. Within decades of that, Yi Jing separates out this field as one in which India and China had both made significant contributions to scholarly understanding in the whole world. 'How much more then', mused this India-returned Chinese scholar, 'should people of the Divine Land (China), as well as the Celestial Store House (India), teach the real rules of language!'[33] How deep these contributions were and how much the two cultures benefited from their interactions remain to be assessed, but this area too, like others already identified, demands investigation from the perspective of broader consequences of Buddhist connections.

Public Communication and Arguments

The movement of ideas and skills in mathematics and science remains particularly relevant in the contemporary world, and creativity based on give and take has immediate implications for global commerce and enterprise (involving, for example, the use and development of information technology or modern industrial methods). What may be perhaps less immediately obvious is the importance of learning from each other in the commitment to public communication and in the art of public health care. These were important in the intellectual relations between China and India in the first millennium and remain quite central even today.

Though Buddhism is a religion like any other, it began with at least two specific characteristics that were quite unusual, to wit, its foundational agnosticism and its commitment to public communication and discussion. The latter was responsible for the fact that some of the earliest open public meetings in the world, aimed specifically at settling disputes between different views, took place in India in elaborately organized Buddhist 'councils', where adherents of different points of view tried to argue out their differences, particularly on public practices as well as religious beliefs. As was discussed in Essay 1 above, these councils are of great importance for the history of public arguments. The host of the largest of these councils (the third), Ashoka, even tried to establish, in the third century BCE, good rules for productive debating to be followed by all, with 'restraint in regard to speech' and with the points of view of all being 'duly honoured in every way on all occasions'.

In so far as public reasoning is central to democracy (as political philosophers like John Stuart Mill, John Rawls and Juergen Habermas have argued), parts of the global roots of democracy can indeed be traced to the tradition of public discussion that received much encouragement in both India and China (and also in Japan, Korea and elsewhere), from the dialogic commitment of Buddhist organization. It is also significant that nearly every attempt at early printing in China, Korea and Japan was undertaken by Buddhist technologists.* As was mentioned in Essay 4, the first printed book in the world with a date (corresponding to 868 CE), which was the Chinese translation of a Sanskrit treatise, the so-called 'Diamond Sutra' (Kumārajīva had translated it in 402 CE), carried the remarkable motivational explanation: 'for universal free distribution'.†

John Kieschnick has noted that 'one of the reasons for the important place for books in the Chinese Buddhist tradition is the belief that one can gain merit by copying or printing Buddhist scriptures', and he has argued that 'the origins of this belief can be traced to India'.[34] There is some ground for that diagnosis, but aside from any belief in the merit of reproduction, there is surely a connection here also with the importance of public communication, emphasized by such Buddhist leaders as Ashoka, who covered India with stone tablets bearing inscriptions on good public behaviour, including rules on how to conduct an argument.

The development of printing was, of course, important in the long run for democracy as we know it, but even in the short run, it transformed the possibilities of public communication in general, with enormously important consequences for social and political life in China. Among other things, it also influenced neo-Confucian education, and, as Theodore de Bary has noted, 'women's education

*It appears that there were early attempts at printing by Indian Buddhists as well. Indeed, Yi Jing, the Chinese scholar who visited India in the seventh century, apparently encountered prints of Buddhist images on silk and paper in India, but these were probably rather primitive image blocks. A little earlier, Xuanzang is said to have printed pictures of an Indian scholar (Bhadra) as he returned to China from India. On this early history, see Joseph Needham, *Science and Civilization in China* (Cambridge: Cambridge University Press, 1985), vol. V, part i, pp. 148–9.

†Kumārajīva was a half-Indian and half-Kucian scholar (from east Turkestan), who studied in India but had a leading position at the Institute of Foreign Languages and Literatures in Xian [Changan], from 402 CE. Yao Xing, the king and the patron of Kumārajīva, bestowed on him the title 'the Teacher of the Nation'. The 'Diamond Sutra' was one of seventy or so Sanskrit books that Kumārajīva is reputed to have translated (of these, more than thirty have been authenticated), in addition to writing commentaries on Nāgārjuna, the Indian Buddhist philosopher, and on *Daode Jing* (also known as *Tao tö king*), the Taoist classic. The Diamond Sutra itself was translated into Chinese many – perhaps even a dozen – times. But it is the translation of this Sanskrit document by Kumārajīva that has the distinction of being the first dated printed book in the world.

achieved a new level of importance with the rise of the Song [dynasty] learning and its neo-Confucian extensions in the Ming, marked by the great spread of printing, literacy and schooling'.[35]

Health Care and Medicine

Aside from public communication, the inter-country connections in public health care are also of importance, and the two do interrelate with each other (this linkage will be presently discussed). As was mentioned earlier, Faxian, who arrived in India in 401 CE, took considerable interest in contemporary health arrangements in India. He was particularly impressed by the civic facilities for medical care in fifth-century Pāṭaliputra:

> All the poor and destitute in the country . . . and all who are diseased, go to these houses, and are provided with every kind of help, and doctors examine their diseases. They get the food and medicine which their cases require, and are made to feel at ease; and when they are better, they go away of themselves.[36]

Whether or not this description was over-flattering to early fifth-century Patna (which seems very likely), what is important is the involvement with which Faxian wanted to observe and learn from the arrangements for medical care in the country he visited for a decade.

Yi Jing too, two and a half centuries later, was very engaged in examining health care, to which he devoted three chapters of his book on India. He was more impressed with Indian health practice than with Indian medicine. While giving India credit for some medical treatments, mainly aimed at palliation (such as 'ghee, oil, honey, or syrups give one relief from cold'), he concluded: 'In the healing arts of acupuncture and cautery and the skill of feeling the pulse, China has never been surpassed [by India]; the medicament for prolonging life is only found in China.' On the other hand, there were things to learn from India on health behaviour, such as 'the Indians use fine white cloth for straining water and in China fine silk should be used', and: 'in China, people of the present time eat fish and vegetables mostly uncooked; no Indians do this.' While Yi Jing returned to China happy enough with his country of origin, he did not omit to discuss what China could nevertheless learn from India.

Public Health and Public Arguments

The extensive intellectual relations between China and India in the first millennium are of obvious narrative significance both for the history of a big part of humanity and for the relevance of these deliberations in the global history of ideas. The need to study these relations is made even stronger by the way this rich history has tended to be ignored in the contemporary understanding of our global past. Many of the concerns and interests that linked China and India in the first millennium (varying from mathematics and science to literature, arts and public communication), with interactions across the borders, have continued to exert their influence in the thousand years that have passed since the first millennium.

There are, however, additional questions of conjectural interest about the light that Sino-Indian intellectual engagements in the first millennium may throw on political, social and economic discussion in the world today. Is the old history of these cross-border interactions between China and India of any relevance to the present-day concerns in these countries, and more broadly, in the contemporary world? For example, does the overcoming of national or civilizational insularity have continuing interest? Is there any contemporary relevance in the traditions and practices in the two countries that, to varying extents, engaged both countries in the first millennium, such as 'the art of prolonging life' or the extent to which 'public arguments' are to be encouraged?

Public health is a subject in which learning from each other can indeed be extremely important, and this – as we saw earlier – was a subject of concentration in Sino-Indian relations even as early as the fifth century. While Chinese commentators were particularly engaged in asking what China could learn from India in the 'art of prolonging life', in the modern context it is much easier to see what India can learn from China, rather than the converse. The lessons for India from China will be a particular focus of attention in Essay 9. In fact, China has enjoyed a life expectancy that is significantly longer than India's over quite a few decades now (in fact, from shortly after the Chinese revolution and India's independence, respectively).

However, the history of progress in life expectancy in the two countries tells a much richer story than that overall summary comparison can reveal. Maoist China made an early start in widespread health care shortly after its revolution, in the form of some health insurance for all, delivered by the state or by the collectives or communes in the rural areas. There was nothing comparable in India at that time. By the time economic reforms were introduced in China in 1979, China had a lead of fourteen years over India in longevity. The Chinese life expectancy – around 68 years by 1979 – was almost a decade and a half longer than India's puny figure of 54 years, at the time of the Chinese economic reforms.

With the reforms of 1979, the Chinese economy surged ahead spectacularly and grew much faster than India's more modest performance (even though India's growth rate from the 1980s onwards was higher than her own past performance). However, despite China's much faster economic growth, the rate of extension of life expectancy in India has been about three times as fast, on the average, as that in China, since 1979. China's life expectancy, which is now just about 71 years, compares with India's figure of 64 years, so that the life-expectancy gap in favour of China, which was fourteen years in 1979 (at the time of the Chinese reforms), has now been halved to only seven years.

Indeed, China's life expectancy of 71 years is now significantly lower than that in parts of India, most notably in the state of Kerala. It is particularly instructive to look at Kerala, despite the fact that it is just one state within a large country. In fact, with its 30 million people, Kerala could have been a country on its own, but more importantly, Kerala's experience has been particularly distinguished in combining Indian style multi-party democracy with social intervention of the type in which pre-reform China was perhaps the world leader. The advantage of that combination shows itself not only in achievements in high life expectancy, but also in many other fields. For example, while the female–male ratio in the total population in China is only 0.94 and the Indian overall average is a little lower, namely 0.93,

Kerala's ratio is 1.06, exactly as it is in North America and Western Europe (reflecting the survival advantages of women in the absence of unequal treatment).* The fall in the fertility rate in Kerala has also been substantially faster than in China, despite the coercive birth-control policies used in the latter.†

At the time of the Chinese reforms in 1979, Kerala's life expectancy was slightly lower than China's. However, by 1995–9 (the last period for which firm figures for life expectancy in India are available), Kerala's life expectancy of seventy-four years was already significantly higher than China's last firm figure of seventy-one years for 2000.‡ Going further into specific points of concern, the infant-mortality rate in China has declined extremely slowly since the economic reforms, whereas it has continued to fall very quickly in Kerala. While Kerala had roughly the same infant-mortality rate as China – 37 per thousand – at the time of the Chinese reforms in 1979, Kerala's present rate, 10 per thousand, is a third of China's 30 per thousand (where it has stagnated over the last decade).

A couple of factors, both of which link to the issue of democracy, can help to explain the slackening of Chinese progress in the art of prolonging life, despite being helped by its extremely rapid economic growth. First, the reforms of 1979 led to the ending of free public health insurance, and it was now necessary to buy private health insurance at one's own cost (except when provided by the employer, which covers only a small minority of cases). This retrograde movement in the coverage of health care, with the withdrawal of a highly valued public facility, received little political resistance –

*I have discussed the causal factors underlying the phenomenon of 'missing women' in 'More Than 100 Million Women Are Missing', *New York Review of Books*, 20 Dec. 1990; 'Missing Women', *British Medical Journal*, 304 (7 Mar. 1992); 'Missing Women Revisited', *British Medical Journal*, 327 (6 Dec. 2003). See also Essay 11 in this volume.

†On this see my 'Population: Delusion and Reality', *New York Review of Books*, 22 Sept. 1994, and 'Fertility and Coercion', *University of Chicago Law Review*, 63 (Summer 1996). See also Essay 9, below.

‡See National Bureau of Statistics of China, *China Statistical Yearbook 2003* (Beijing: China Statistics Press, 2003), table 4.17, p. 118. Chinese big cities, in particular Shanghai and Beijing, outmatch the state of Kerala, but most Chinese provinces have life expectancy figures far lower than Kerala's.

as it undoubtedly would have met in any multi-party democracy.

Second, democracy also makes a direct contribution to health care by bringing social failures into public scrutiny.* India offers high-quality medical facilities to the Indian rich and to rich foreigners, but basic health services in India are quite bad, as we know from elaborate criticisms of these services in the Indian media. But the possibility of intense criticism is also a social opportunity to make amends. In fact, vigorous reporting of the deficiencies of Indian health services is, ultimately, a source of India's dynamic strength, which is partly reflected in the sharp reduction in the China–India gap in life expectancy and the better achievements of Kerala by combining democratic participation with a radical social commitment. The terrible effects of the secrecy surrounding the SARS epidemic, which surfaced in China in November 2002 but information about which was suppressed until the following spring, also bring out the link between public communication and health care.†

So while India has much to learn from China about health care (especially from the powerful public commitment of the early post-revolutionary period) and about economic policy making (from China's post-reform experience), the relevance of public communication, which is central to democracy, is a general lesson that India can

*This connection is similar to the more prominent observation that major famines do not occur in democracies, even when they are very poor, on which see my 'How Is India Doing?', *New York Review of Books*, Christmas Number 1982, and jointly with Jean Drèze, *Hunger and Public Action* (Oxford: Clarendon Press, 1989). Large famines, which continued to occur in British India right up to the end (the last – the Bengal famine of 1943 – was just four years before India's independence), disappeared abruptly with the establishment of a multi-party democracy in India. In contrast, China had the largest famine in recorded history during 1958–61, when nearly 30 million people, it is estimated, died.

†It is possible that the sharp increase of economic inequality in recent years in China may have also contributed to the slowing down of the progress in life expectancy. There has, in fact, been some increase in economic inequality in India as well, though nothing as sharp as in China. But it is interesting – and relevant to the role of democracy – that even that more moderate increase in inequality seems to have played a major part in the defeat of the ruling government in New Delhi in the elections held in May 2004. There were other factors, too, that contributed to the defeat, in particular the violation of the rights of the Muslim minority in the sectarian riots in Gujarat (it is, of course, to the credit of a deliberative democratic system that majority voting can respond to the plight of minorities and the need for less biased political priorities).

still offer to China. Interestingly, it is the tradition of irreverence and defiance of authority which came with Buddhism from India that was singled out for a particularly strong chastisement in early anti-Buddhist criticisms in China. Fu-yi, a powerful Confucian leader, submitted in the seventh century the following complaint about Buddhists to the Tang emperor (almost paralleling the contemporary ire of the Chinese authorities about the disorder generated by the present-day Falungong):

> Buddhism infiltrated into China from Central Asia, under a strange and barbarous form, and as such, it was then less dangerous. But since the Han period the Indian texts began to be translated into Chinese. Their publicity began to adversely affect the faith of the Princes and filial piety began to degenerate. The people began to shave their heads and refused to bow their heads to the Princes and their ancestors.[37]

Fu-yi proposed not only a ban on Buddhist preaching, but also quite a novel way of dealing with the 'tens of thousands' of activists rampaging around in China. 'I request you to get them married,' Fu-yi advised the Tang emperor, and 'then bring up [their] children to fill the ranks of your army'. The emperor, we learn, refused to undertake this imaginative programme of eliminating Buddhist defiance.

China has joined – and become a leader of – the world economy with stunning success, and from this India, like many other countries, has been learning a great deal, particularly in recent years. The insularity of the earlier Indian approach to economic development needed to be replaced and here the experience of China has been profoundly important. There are great lessons also from China's early move to universalized health care and basic education. But the role of democratic participation in India suggests that some learning and understanding may go in the other direction as well.

As it happens, India is the only country in the outside world to which scholars from ancient China went for education and training. The overcoming of cultural insularity that we can observe both in China and in India in the first millennium has continuing interest and practical usefulness in the world today. When Xuanzang put a profound rhetorical question about human knowledge to his teachers in Nālandā, 'Who would wish to enjoy it alone?', he was pointing to a foundational issue the relevance of which reaches far beyond Buddhist enlightenment in particular. Indeed, that concern and commitment remain as relevant today as they were in Xuanzang's world in the seventh century. India and China learned a lot from each other in the first millennium, but the significance of that epistemic process has not dried up even at the beginning of the third millennium.

PART THREE

Politics and Protest

9

Tryst with Destiny*

It was a thrilling moment. On 14 August 1947, on the eve of India's independence, we glued ourselves to the radio in our little school a hundred miles from Calcutta. It was almost exactly four years after the terrible famine we had seen as young children (with millions dying), which gave many of us, unaffected by the famine, the enduring thought that 'there, but for the grace of class divisions, go I'. Those were terrible days, but August 1947 was a different and a joyous time. In celebration of independence and in welcoming a democratic India, Jawaharlal Nehru's voice roared loud and clear over the radio, telling us about India's 'tryst with destiny'. The 'task ahead' included 'the ending of poverty and ignorance and disease and inequality of opportunity'. We heard with rapt attention and we felt powerfully inspired.

The Pledge and the Record

Rather more than half a century has passed since then, and it is not too soon to ask what came of that 'tryst' with destiny, and of the 'tasks ahead'. The answer is not altogether simple.[1] In line with Nehru's formulation, we can split the evaluation into three broad fields: (1) practice of democracy, (2) removal of social inequality and backwardness, and (3) achievement of economic progress and equity. We

*This is an extended and updated text of an essay published in the *Financial Times* on the occasion of the fiftieth anniversary of Indian independence, on 15 August 1997.

must also ask how the successes and failures in these different fields interconnect and relate to each other.

There are reasons for satisfaction in the first area.* While the correspondent of *The Times* in 1967 did report, with some sense of absolute certainty, that he had just witnessed 'the last general elections' in India (Indian democracy, he confided, could not but end very soon), the doom did not come as anticipated. Systematic elections have continued to happen with regularity and reasonable fairness.† Political parties have come into office after winning elections, and have left after losing them. The media have remained largely free, and the press has continued to report, scrutinize and protest. Civil rights have been taken seriously, and the courts have been fairly active in pursuing violations.‡ The military has stayed well inside the barracks.

This is largely a story of success. And yet the achievements of Indian democracy have been far from unblemished. While political movements have been very effective in dealing with some wrongs, other wrongs have not received anything like sufficient redress or even serious engagement. Since democracy is not only a blessing in itself, but can also be the most important means to pursue public ends, it is

*For an illuminating set of studies, see Atul Kohli (ed.), *The Success of India's Democracy* (Cambridge: Cambridge University Press, 2001). See also Granville Austin's meticulous investigation, *Working of a Democratic Constitution: The Indian Experience* (New Delhi and Oxford: Oxford University Press, 1999), along with his earlier book on the nature and history of the constitution of India, *Indian Constitution: The Cornerstone of a Nation* (New Delhi and Oxford: Oxford University Press, 1966). See also Judith M. Brown, *Modern India: The Origins of an Asian Democracy* (Delhi: Oxford University Press, 1984).

†Indira Gandhi's brief attempt in the 1970s at curtailing basic political and civil rights was firmly rejected by the voters, thereby electorally ending the proposal as well as her government. Even in that misguided initiative, there was, however, no attempt to replace elections, nor any proposal for ignoring the electoral verdict. Indira Gandhi took her defeat with good grace, and, after dropping her plans to prune political and civil rights, she returned to being Prime Minister with a victory in general elections within a few years with a strongly democratic platform.

‡Among the more recent efforts of the Supreme Court is its attempt to have a fair trial of the miscreants in Gujarat responsible for the killings – mostly of Muslims – in 2002. The Supreme Court found the acquittal of the accused in the judicial process in Gujarat to be lacking in due process, and has insisted that the accused be retried outside Gujarat, which is still ruled by the same state government which was in office during the uncontrolled riots in 2002.

not enough to make sure that Indian democracy survives. While we must give credit where it is due, Indian democracy has to be judged also by the strength and reach of public reasoning and its actual accomplishments. After discussing the other areas of concentration identified by Nehru, I shall come back to these concerns about democracy which are more complex than the mere survival of democracy.

The second field – that of social progress and equity – has fared much worse than democracy itself: not quite an immeasurable failure, but certainly a measurable underperformance.[2] Educational progress has been remarkably uneven. Even though India has many more university-educated persons than China has, China has made remarkable progress towards universal literacy, while India is still far behind. The proportion of literates among adult males is still below 75 per cent in India (in comparison with China's above 90), and only about half of Indian women are literate (compared with China's 80 per cent or more). Life expectancy at birth in India has climbed to around 64 years (from being near 30 at the time of independence), but it is still significantly below China's life expectancy of 71 years.* Further, mortality rates in India sharply differ between different states, and also between classes and between urban and rural areas. Many rural residents, especially the poorer villagers, are still far removed from decent medical attention.† Inequalities between women and men in economic and social opportunities, and often even in health care, remain quite large.[3]

What about the third field – that of economic progress? India's economic expansion was particularly slow before the 1980s, especially in comparison with the spectacular performance of Asian economies further east, such as South Korea or Taiwan. After the quickening of Indian economic growth from the 1980s, India has done comparatively better, not just in the aggregate movement of the

*This static comparison is, however, somewhat deceptive since the life expectancy gap between China and India has sharply declined after 1980, and some parts of India, notably Kerala, have overtaken China and gone considerably ahead of it. In this change over time, public reasoning and democracy in India have made, it would appear, a significant contribution. These issues are discussed in the last part of Essay 8, and also in my 'Passage to China', *New York Review of Books*, 2 Dec. 2004.

†A new problem that is clearly serious in India is the rapid spread of HIV infection and AIDS. Public efforts to confront this new hazard are still extremely inadequate.

gross national product (GNP) and gross domestic product (GDP), but also in terms of reduction of income poverty. The economic reforms introduced in 1992, led by Manmohan Singh (then the Finance Minister, and now the Prime Minister of India since the spring of 2004), have led to considerable liberalization and freeing of international trade, and to some replacement of what used to be called the 'licence Raj' (with pervasive bureaucratic control over private economic initiatives).[4] This has greatly added to business opportunities in India and has also helped to consolidate India's faster economic growth. Liberalization, which still has some distance to go, has helped to free Indian entrepreneurs to seek global trade, and the success has been especially large in specific sectors such as the development and use of information technology.[5] The overall performance of the economy may not have matched that of post-reform China (with its sustained growth rate of 8 to 10 per cent a year), but India's move from the rigid box of a 3 per cent growth rate to the 5 to 8 per cent arena is certainly not a negligible development.

The proportions of the Indian population with incomes below the standard poverty lines seem to have fallen over the 1980s and 1990s, even though there are disputes about the extent of this decline, and some doubts about the social reality that lies behind these statistical figures.[6] What is, however, clear enough is that India's reduction of poverty has been far less rapid than what has occurred in China since the economic reforms.

Poverty and Social Opportunity

There is indeed much about the process of economic growth and development that India can learn from the experience of China.* Making good use of global trade opportunities is among the lessons that China offers to India, and the lessons here can be critically important for India's economic progress. A similar message had already emerged from the economic success of other East Asian economies,

*In Essay 8, I also consider the converse, that is, what China may find useful in India's experiences. This issue is not taken up in the present essay.

including South Korea, but given China's size and the intensity of its pre-existing poverty, China's experiences are particularly relevant for India's economic policy-making. The general lesson that good use can be made of global opportunities of trade and commerce to enhance domestic income and to reduce poverty has emerged very clearly from the success of economies in East and South East Asia – led now by China.

It is, however, important to avoid the much-aired simplification that argues that all India needs to do to achieve fast economic growth and speedy reduction of poverty is greater reliance on the global market and on international trade. This reflects, in fact, a serious misreading of the variety of factors that have contributed to the kind of economic success achieved in China, South Korea, Thailand and other countries in East and South East Asia. These countries did emphasize international trade and made fine use of the global market mechanism. But they also made it possible to have broad-based public participation in economic expansion, through such policies as extensive schooling and high literacy, good health care, widespread land reforms, and some considerable fostering of gender equity (not least through female education and employment).

This is not to doubt that India can achieve reasonably high growth rates of aggregate GNP even with the rather limited social opportunities that exist in India. For one thing, it can continue to do extremely well in industries that make excellent use of India's accomplishments in higher education and technical training. New centres of technical excellence, like Bangalore and Hyderabad, can prosper and flourish, and India can even accelerate its progress along the lines that it has already established well. This will be a substantial achievement of considerable economic importance.

Yet even a hundred Bangalores and Hyderabads will not, on their own, solve India's tenacious poverty and deep-seated inequality. The very poor in India get a small – and basically indirect – share of the cake that information technology and related developments generate. The removal of poverty, particularly of extreme poverty, calls for more participatory growth on a wide basis, which is not easy to achieve across the barriers of illiteracy, ill health, uncompleted land reforms and other sources of severe societal inequality. The process of economic advance cannot be divorced from the cultivation and enhancement of social opportunities over a broad front.*

The products that China exports to the outside world include a great many that are made by not particularly highly skilled labour, but schooled and literate labour nevertheless. Their production generates much employment, with a great deal of income going to poorer sections of the community. Utilization of the world market for such exports requires production according to specification, quality control and an informed consciousness of the economic tasks involved. Good school education is central for these tasks. Similarly, good health is extremely important if productive effort and economic schedules are not to be affected by illnesses and intermittent absence.†

Basic education, good health and other human attainments are not only directly valuable as constituent elements of human capabilities and quality of life (these are the direct pay-offs of schooling, health care and other social arrangements), but these capabilities can also help in generating economic success of a more standard kind, which in turn can contribute to enhancing the quality of human life even more. If there is something that India can learn from China's *post-reform* experience in the 1980s onwards about making skilful use of global markets, there is also much that India can assimilate from China's *pre-reform* experience in rapidly expanding the delivery of basic education and elementary health care.

Political Voice and Social Opportunity

If social and economic tasks are so interrelated, what about links with the politics of democracy? While it has frequently been claimed that democracy is inimical to fast economic growth (India itself has been

*On this and related issues, see Jean Drèze and Amartya Sen, *India: Economic Development and Social Opportunity* (Delhi and Oxford: Oxford University Press, 1996), and the follow-up book: *India: Development and Participation* (Delhi and Oxford: Oxford University Press, 2002).

†In addition to traditional problems of ill-health, the new epidemic of HIV infection and AIDS will have devastating effects both on human lives and on economic and social operations unless they are adequately confronted without any further delay.

cited often enough to illustrate this specious thesis), there is little statistical evidence to confirm this. Indeed, even the limited success of India in recent years in raising economic growth shows that growth can profit more from a friendly economic climate than from a coercive political environment.*

India has certainly benefited from the protective role of democracy in giving the rulers excellent political incentive to act supportively when disasters threaten and when an immediate change in policy is imperative. India has successfully avoided famines since independence,† while China experienced a massive famine during the failure of the Great Leap Forward when faulty policies were not revised for three years while famine mortality took from 23 to 30 million lives. Even today India is, by and large, in a better position than China both to prevent abuse of coercive power and to make quicker emendations if and when policies go badly wrong (this issue is discussed, among other themes, in Essay 8).

Democracy gives an opportunity to the opposition to press for policy change even when the problem is chronic and has had a long history (rather than only when it is acute and sudden, as is the case with famines). The weakness of Indian social policies on education, health care, land reform and gender equity is as much a failure of the opposition parties as of the governments in office. In comparative terms, the political commitment of leaders of some of the less democratic countries has often led to more achievement in these fields than has been produced by the working of democracy in India. The educational and health achievements of Maoist China illustrate this well.‡ Indeed, post-reform China has made excellent use of China's pre-reform accomplishments

*This general issue is discussed in my *Development as Freedom* (New York: Knopf, and Oxford: Oxford University Press, 1999).

†The elimination of large famines in India must not, however, be seen as the removal of undernutrition and hunger. Indeed, India has a very high proportion of undernourished people, who are chronically hungry, to varying extents. The problem of persistent underfeeding is discussed in Essay 10.

‡We must, however, distinguish between cases of good results brought about by strong political commitment and any expectation that authoritarian leadership would, in general, produce such results. North Korea is authoritarian too, as was the Taliban's Afghanistan, Idi Amin's Uganda and Mobutu's Congo. The central point at issue concerns political vision rather than coercive power.

(particularly, in raising basic education and health levels across the country) to make its market-based expansion after 1979 draw widely on the capabilities of a better educated and healthier population.

Only in some parts of India have the failures of social achievement been adequately politicized. The state of Kerala is perhaps the clearest example, where the need for universal education, basic health care, elementary gender equity and land reforms has received effective political backing. The explanation involves both history and contemporary development: the educational orientation of Kerala's anti-upper-caste movements (of which the current left-wing politics of Kerala is a successor), the early initiatives of the native kingdoms of Travancore and Cochin (outside the British Raj), missionary activities in the spread of education (not confined only to Christians – a fifth of the population), and also a bigger voice for women in family decisions, partly linked to the presence and prominence of matrilineal property rights for a substantial and influential section – the Nairs – of the Hindu community. Over a very long time Kerala has made good use of political activism and voice to expand the range of social opportunities.

The contribution of modern and radical politics to Kerala's social progress is sometimes underestimated. At the time of Indian independence, in 1947, the proportion of literate people in Kerala, while higher than in the rest of India, was still quite low. The work for the achievement of literacy for all happened mostly in the second half of the twentieth century. Also, the state of Kerala was formed, on linguistic lines, at the time of independence by putting together two 'native states' – Travancore and Cochin – which were formally outside the British Raj and one area – Malabar – from old Madras in the Raj. At that time, Malabar's level of education was far lower than that of Travancore and Cochin. But today the three regions are very close together, practically indistinguishable from each other in terms of school education. The credit that is due to participatory and vocal politics should not all be given away to favourable past history.*

*Along with the positive achievements of radical left-wing politics, its problematic side should be recognized too. Kerala has been comparatively slow in reforming economic policies in a market-utilizing direction. While people from Kerala have easily earned good money working elsewhere (often abroad – much in the Gulf), the opportunity of taking economic initiatives at home has moved relatively slowly. This has not

The Use of Voice

It is hard to escape the general conclusion that economic performance, social opportunity and political voice are deeply interrelated. Despite the political facilities provided by India's democratic system, the weakness of voices of protest has helped to make the progress of social opportunities unnecessarily slow. That, in turn, has not only been a serious handicap in itself for the quality of life in India, it has also served as a major drag in the process of economic development, including the range and coverage of growth and the alleviation of economic poverty. As was discussed in Essay 2, political voice is extremely important for social equity, and to that recognition we have to add the connection between equitable expansion of social opportunities and the force, range and reach of the process of economic development.

In those fields in which there has recently been a more determined use of political and social voice, there are considerable signs of change. The issue of gender inequality has produced somewhat more political engagement in recent years (often led by women's movements in different fields), and this has added to determined political efforts at reducing gender asymmetry in social and economic fields. There is a long history in India of women's prominence in some particular areas, including in the sharing of leadership positions in politics.* While those achievements were themselves linked with the use of women's voice (helped by the opportunities of participatory politics in recent centuries), their reach was largely confined to relatively small segments of the population (often women members of the urban elite). An important aspect of the strengthening of women's voice in contemporary Indian public life is the broadening of this social coverage.

There is, however, still a long way to go in removing the unequal position of women in India, but the increasing political involvement

---

prevented Kerala from experiencing one of the fastest reductions of poverty in India, but the full economic potentials of its social advantages still remain partly unreaped. On this and related issues, see Drèze and Sen, *India: Development and Participation*.

*See Essay 1, section headed 'Gender, Caste and Voice', and Essay 2.

about women's social role has been an important and constructive development.* There is also some achievement through the increased politicization of educational inequalities in general and the neglect of basic health care, especially for the poor. These disparities receive more public attention today than they did earlier, and the effects of that favourable change can, to some extent, be already seen in the relative progress made in spreading medical attention and educational opportunities. Again, there is still a very long way to go, but positive developments demand acknowledgement, if only to overcome the persistent cynicism that often characterizes public perception about what democracy can or cannot do.

The possibilities of public agitation on issues of societal inequality and deprivation are now beginning to be more utilized than before. There has been much more action recently in organized movements based broadly on demands for human rights, such as the right to school education, the right to food (and, in particular, to midday school meals), the entitlement to basic health care, guarantees of environmental preservation, and the right of employment guarantee. These movements serve to focus attention on particular societal failures, partly as supplements to broad public discussions in the media, but they also provide a politically harder edge to socially important demands. The interdependences between economic, social and political freedoms gives a critically important role to the use of democratic opportunities and to the deployment of political voice.

The remedy for many of the central failures of Indian society is closely linked to broadening the force and range of political arguments and social demands.† The 'tryst with destiny' is thus partly an invitation to further engagement and encounter. What Nehru hoped would happen automatically with the independence of India may continue to be neglected unless it is demanded with an insistence that makes it politically critical in a democratic system. It is not enough to continue to have systematic elections, to safeguard political

*See Essay 11 on a general assessment of gender inequality in India and its changes over time.

†The inadequacy of steps taken so far to confront the growing epidemic of HIV infection and AIDS is also both a governmental failure (in the form of inaction) and a failure of political engagement (in the form of comparative silence).

liberties and civil rights, to guarantee free speech and an open media. Nor is it adequate to eliminate famine, or to reduce the lead of China in longevity and survival. A more vigorous – and vocal – use of democratic participation can do much more in India than it has already achieved.

10

Class in India*

In his speech on the 'tryst with destiny' delivered on 14 August 1947, with which the last essay began, Jawaharlal Nehru talked not just about freedom from British rule, but also about his grand vision of independent India.† Nehru was particularly determined to remove the barriers of class stratification and their far-reaching effects on inequality and deprivation in economic, political and social spheres. It was a thrilling image that could rival Alfred Tennyson's eloquence: 'For I dipt into the future, far as human eye could see, / Saw the Vision of the world, and all the wonder that would be.' It was good for free India to be told, at the defining moment of its birth, about the possibility of 'all the wonder that would be'.[1]

Nehru's vision was not fulfilled during his own lifetime. There is nothing surprising in that, since the vision was ambitious. What is, however, more distressing is the slowness of our progress in the direction to which Jawaharlal Nehru so firmly pointed. But that is not all. There is disturbing evidence that the battle against class divisions has very substantially weakened in India. In fact, there are clear indications that at different levels of economic, social and political policy, the debilitating role of class inequality now receives remarkably little attention. Furthermore, support for consolidation of class barriers comes not only from old vested interests, but also from new sources of privilege, and this makes the task much harder.

*This essay is based on my Nehru Lecture, given in New Delhi on 13 Nov. 2001.

†Jawaharlal Nehru's speech, delivered at the Constituent Assembly, New Delhi, is included in *Jawaharlal Nehru: An Anthology*, ed. Sarvepalli Gopal (Oxford and Delhi: Oxford University Press, 1983).

Diverse Disparities

This is a difficult subject to deal with, for two distinct reasons. First, class is not the only source of inequality, and interest in class as a source of disparity has to be placed within a bigger picture that includes other divisive influences: gender, caste, region, community and so on. For example, inequality between women and men is also a major contributor to inequity. This source of inequality used to be fairly comprehensively neglected in India even a few decades ago, and in this neglect the single-minded concern with class did play a role. Indeed, about three decades ago, in the early 1970s, when I first tried to work on gender inequality in India, I was struck by the fact that even those who were extremely sympathetic to the plight of the underdogs of society were reluctant to take a serious interest in the evil of gender discrimination. This was to a great extent because of the firmly established tradition of concentrating almost entirely on class divisions as a source of inequality. That single-mindedness is no longer dominant, and there is increasing recognition of the importance of causes of disparity other than class divisions, including inequality between women and men. Even though gender and other contributors to inequality still require, I would argue, more systematic attention, nevertheless there has been a considerable enrichment of the versatility and reach of public discussion in India.

There is, however, an interesting issue that goes beyond the 'whether' question to the 'how' question. Should these different sources of inequality be seen as primarily 'additive' to each other ('there is class and then there is also gender, and furthermore, caste, and so on'), or should they instead be treated together, making more explicit room for their extensive interdependences? These different sources of vulnerability are each significant, but no less importantly, we must see that they can strengthen the impact of each other because of their complementarity.

Class, in particular, has a very special role in the establishment and reach of social inequality, and it can make the influence of other sources of disparity (such as gender inequality) much sharper. The intellectual gain in broadening our comprehension of other types of inequity has to be followed with a more integrated understanding of the functioning of class in alliance with other causes of injustice. Or, to put it differently, class is not only important on its own, it can also magnify the impact of other contributors to inequality, enlarging the penalties imposed by them. The integration of class in a consolidated understanding of injustice is of paramount importance given the need to address, simultaneously, different sources of inequality, related to class, gender, community, caste and so on, and given the overwhelming role of class in the working of each of the other contributors to inequality.

A second source of complexity lies in the fact that some of the new social barriers reinforcing rather than weakening the hold of class divisions come – as it were – from the 'friendly' side of the dividing line; they can, in fact, be rooted in institutional devices that are intended to be among the remedial features against class division. For example, public programmes of intervention can protect vulnerable interests and thus serve as a good instrument in the battle against class-based inequality. However, they can also have regressive consequences if the battle lines are wrongly drawn, or if the remedies are wrongly devised.

In fact, what the armed forces call 'friendly fire' – whereby an army is hit by its own firing rather than by enemy shelling – is a concept that may have relevance not just in the military spheres but in social fields as well. The actual impact of supportive public institutions and public policies has to be constantly scrutinized. The operative impact of institutions and programmes that have been instituted as anti-inequality devices requires probing investigation in an open-minded – rather than in a fixed, formulaic – way.

I shall take up these two issues in turn: first, the need for an integrated understanding of the contribution of class in the combined impact of diverse sources of inequality; and second, the possibility of 'friendly fire', which requires us to rethink the old battle lines against inequality. In particular, the relevance of new barriers strongly suggests the need to re-examine the ways and means of confronting class inequality.

In this essay, I shall try to identify two specific issues to examine in trying to understand the far-reaching relevance of class in India: first, the 'integration issue' (to see the influence of class as not merely additive, but also as transformational), and second, the 'institutional issue', in particular the role of institutional features – new and old – in reinforcing and even strengthening class barriers.

Class, Gender, Caste and Community

The significant presence of non-class sources of inequality is an important recognition that can be combined with the acknowledgement that there is hardly any aspect of our lives that stays quite untouched by our place in the class stratification. Class does not act alone in creating and reinforcing inequality, and yet no other source of inequality is fully independent of class.[2]

Consider gender. South Asian countries have a terrible record in gender inequality, which is manifest in the unusual morbidity and mortality rates of women, compared with what is seen in regions that do not neglect women's health care and nutrition so badly. At the same time, women from the upper classes are often more prominent in South Asia than elsewhere. Indeed, India, Pakistan, Bangladesh and Sri Lanka have all had, or currently have, women Prime Ministers – something that the United States (along with France, Italy, Germany and Japan) has never had and does not seem poised to have in the near future (if I am any judge).

Belonging to a privileged class can help women to overcome barriers that obstruct women from less thriving classes. Gender is certainly an additional contributor to societal inequality, but it does not act independently of class. Indeed, a congruence of class deprivation and gender discrimination can blight the lives of poorer women very severely indeed. It is the interactive presence of these two features of deprivation – being low class and being female – that can massively impoverish women from the less privileged classes.

Similarly, turning to caste, even though being lower caste is undoubtedly a separate cause of disparity, its impact is all the greater when the lower-caste families also happen to be very poor. The blighting of the lives of Dalits or people from other disadvantaged castes, or of members of the Scheduled Tribes, is particularly severe when the caste or tribal adversities are further magnified by abject penury. Even the violence associated with caste-related conflicts tends to involve a great deal more than just caste.

For example, the Ranveer Sena in Bihar may be a private army that draws its sustenance from the upper (in this case, Bhumihar and Rajput) castes, and the victims of brutality may typically be low-caste Dalits, yet the predicament of the potential victims cannot be adequately grasped if we do not take note of the poverty and landlessness of Dalits, or place the conflicts in a broad social and economic background. This recognition does not suggest that caste is unimportant (quite the contrary), but it does make it necessary to place caste-related violence in a broader context in which class, *inter alia*, belongs. The basic issue is complementarity and interrelation rather than the independent functioning of different disparities that work in seclusion (like ships passing at night). Given the wide reach and generic relevance of class, related to poverty and wealth, ownership and indigence, work and employment, and so on, it is not surprising that it tends to rear its ugly head in a great many conflicts that have other identifications and correlates.

In fact, there is also considerable evidence that affirmative action in favour of lower castes has tended to do much more for the economically less strained members of those castes than for those who are weighed down by the combined burden of extreme poverty and lowness of caste. For example, 'reserved' posts often go to relatively affluent members of disadvantaged castes. No policy of affirmative action aimed at caste disadvantage can be adequately effective without taking account of the class background of members of the lower castes. The impact of caste, like that of gender, is substantially swayed by class.

Or consider the deprivation that is generated by communal violence. Members of a minority community can indeed have reason for fear even when they come from a prosperous class. Yet the raw danger to which targeted communities are exposed is immensely magnified when the persons involved not only belong to those communities, but also come from poorer and less privileged families. This is brought out by the class distribution of victims of Hindu–Muslim riots around the time of independence and the partition of India. The easiest to kill among the members of a targeted community are those of that group who have to go out unprotected to work, who live in slums, and who lead, in one way or another, a thoroughly vulnerable life. Not surprisingly, they provide the overwhelming proportion of the victims in communal riots.

My own first exposure to murder, at the age of 11, occurred when I encountered a profusely bleeding Muslim daily labourer, Kader Mia, who had been knifed by Hindu assassins just outside our home in Dhaka (he died in the hospital to which my father took him). Almost his last words to me were that he knew he was taking a heavy risk in coming to a largely Hindu region of the city, but he had to do it in the hope of earning a little money from some work (he was on his way there when he was knifed). Kader Mia died as a victimized Muslim, but he also died as an unemployed labourer, looking desperately for a bit of work and money.

This was in 1944. The riots today are not any different in this respect. In the Hindu–Muslim riots in the 1940s, Hindu thugs killed the unprotected Muslims, while Muslim thugs assassinated the impoverished Hindu victims. Even though the community identity of the exterminated preys was quite different (Hindu and Muslim, respectively), their class identities were often extremely similar. The class dimension of sectarian violence tends to receive inadequate attention, even in newspaper accounts, because of unifocal reporting that concentrates on the divisive communal identity of the victims rather than on their unified class identity.

This remark would apply also to the recent communal killings and victimizations in India, for example the anti-Sikh riots that were organized in Delhi following Indira Gandhi's assassination, the anti-Muslim brutalities that accompanied the terrible days that followed the demolition of the Babri masjid, and so on. Class is an ever-present feature of communal and sectarian violence.

What we need, therefore, is some kind of a dual recognition of the role and reach of class that takes into account its non-uniqueness as well as its transformational function. We have to recognize, simultaneously, that

(1) there are many sources of disparity other than class: we must avoid the presumption that class encompasses all sources of disadvantage and handicap; and

(2) nevertheless, class disparities are not only important on their own, but they also tend to intensify the disadvantages related to the other forms of disparity.

Class is neither the only concern, nor an adequate proxy for other forms of inequality, and yet we do need class analysis to see the working and reach of other forms of inequality and differentiation.

Inequality, Concurrence and the Underdogs

Aside from the variety of factors that contribute to inequality, there is also the important issue of the form that inequality may take. Here, it may be thought, class speaks in many voices, with much discordance. There is truth in this recognition, but once again this may not weaken the overwhelming relevance of pre-eminent class divisions in understanding the plight of the underdogs of society. We have to see simultaneously the distinctions as well as the interconnections.

There are many different forms of deprivation: economic poverty, illiteracy, political disempowerment, absence of health care, and so on. These distinct dimensions of inequality are not entirely congruent in their incidence. Indeed, they can yield very different social rankings.[3] The tendency to see deprivation simply in terms of income poverty is often strong and can be quite misleading. And yet there are also powerfully uniting features in the manifestation of severe deprivation. This is partly because different types of handicap reinforce each other, but also because they often tend to go together at the extreme ends, dividing the general 'haves' from the comprehensive 'have-nots'. The absence of a conceptual congruence between different types of deprivation does not preclude their empirical proximity along a big dividing line, which is a central feature of classical class analysis.

Some Indians are rich; most are not. Some are very well educated; others are illiterate. Some lead easy lives of luxury; others toil hard for little reward. Some are politically powerful; others cannot influence anything. Some have great opportunities for advancement in life; others lack them altogether. Some are treated with respect by the police; others are treated like dirt. These are different kinds of inequality, and each of them requires serious attention. Yet often enough – and this is the central issue in the centrality of class analysis – the same people are poor in income and wealth, suffer from illiteracy, work hard for little remuneration, are uninfluential in politics, lack social and economic opportunities, and are treated with brutal callousness by the police. The dividing line of 'haves' and 'have-nots' is not just a rhetorical cliché, but also an important part of diagnostic analysis, pointing us towards a pre-eminent division that can deeply inform our social, economic and political understanding. This concurrence of deprivation adds to the overarching relevance of class as a source of inequality and disparity.

When I come to discuss the issue of what I called 'friendly fire', the role of such manifest concurrence in the lives of the extreme underdogs of society will become particularly relevant. Many of the distributional institutions that exist in India and elsewhere are designed to defend the interests of groups with some deprivation (or some vulnerability) but who are not by any means the absolute underdogs of society. There is an understandable rationale for seeing them as 'friendly' institutions in the battle against class divisions. Yet if they also have the effect of worsening the deal that the real underdogs get, at the bottom layers of society, the overall impact may be to strengthen class divisions rather than weaken them. This is the sense in which their effects can be seen as 'friendly fire', and I am afraid there is a great deal of this phenomenon in Indian public policy as it stands.

It is extremely important to study the issue of 'friendly fire', though not because it is the largest contributor to class divisions in India: traditional factors, such as massive inequality of wealth and assets, immense gaps in education and other social opportunities and so on, remain central to our understanding of the brute force of class divisions. Yet these traditional features are now supplemented by new barriers, some of which were created precisely to overcome the influence of class, but end up having the opposite effect.

I can illustrate the point with a great many examples. I shall, however, concentrate in this essay on exactly two paradigmatic illustrations, dealing respectively with food policy and elementary schooling, both of which have a major bearing on the lives of the most deprived among the Indian people, that is, the hungry and the illiterate.

Food Policy and Hunger

India's record in countering hunger and famine is strangely mixed. The rapid elimination of famine since independence is an achievement of great importance (the last real famine occurred in 1943 – four years *before* independence), and this is especially so in contrast to the failure of many other countries – most notably China – to prevent famine. Whenever a famine has threatened, the safeguards of a democratic process have come into operation, with rapidly arranged protective policies, including temporary public employment, which give the threatened destitutes the money to buy food. The mechanism of famine prevention in India has been discussed in my joint book with Jean Drèze, *Hunger and Public Action*.[4] It is a record, we argue, of considerable achievement.

And yet India's overall record in eliminating hunger and undernutrition is quite terrible. Not only is there persistent recurrence of severe hunger in particular regions, but there is also a dreadful prevalence of endemic hunger across much of India. Indeed, India does worse in this respect than even sub-Saharan Africa.[5] Calculations of general undernourishment – what is sometimes called 'protein-energy malnutrition' – show that it is nearly twice as high in India as in sub-Saharan Africa on the average. It is astonishing that despite the intermittent occurrence of famine there, Africa still manages to ensure a higher level of regular nourishment than does India. Judged in terms of the usual standards of retardation in weight for age, the proportion of undernourished children in Africa is 20 to 40 per cent, whereas the percentage of undernourished Indian children is a gigantic 40 to 60 per cent.[6] About half of all Indian children are, it appears, chronically undernourished, and more than half of all adult women suffer from anaemia. In maternal undernourishment as well as the incidence of underweight babies, and also in the frequency of cardiovascular disease in later life (to which adults are particularly prone if nutritionally deprived in the womb), India's record is among the very worst in the world.[7]

A striking feature of the persistence of this dreadful situation is not only that it continues to exist, but that the little public attention it gets, when it gets any at all, is so badly divided.* Indeed, it is amazing to hear persistent repetition of the false belief that India has managed the challenge of hunger very well since independence. This is based on a profound confusion between famine prevention, which is a simple achievement, and the avoidance of endemic undernourishment and hunger, which is a much more complex task. India has done worse than nearly every country in the world in the latter respect.

In this context, it is particularly remarkable that India has continued to amass extraordinarily large stocks of food grain in the central government's reserve, without finding good use for them. In 1998 the stock was around 18 million tonnes – close to the official 'buffer stock' norms. It has climbed and climbed since then, firmly surpassing 62 million tonnes at the time this essay was written (as a Nehru Lecture in 2001). To take Jean Drèze's graphic description, if all the sacks of grain were laid up in a row, this would stretch more than a million kilometres, taking us to the moon and back. To see it in another way, the stocks substantially exceeded one tonne of food grain for every family below the poverty line.

The counterintuitiveness – not to mention the inequity – of the history of this development is so gross that it is hard to explain it by the presumption of mere insensitivity – it looks more and more like insanity. What could be the perceived rationale of all this? What could explain the simultaneous presence of the worst undernourishment and the largest unused food stocks in the world (with the stocks being constantly augmented at extremely heavy cost)?

The immediate explanation is not hard to find. The accumulation of stocks results from the government's commitment to high minimum support prices for food grain – for wheat and rice in particular. But a regime of high prices in general (despite a gap between procurement prices and consumers' retail prices) both expands procurement and depresses demand. The bonanza for food producers and sellers is matched by the privation of food consumers. Since the biological

*We discuss the role of inadequacy of public discussion in the formulation and persistence of faulty public policy in our joint book, Drèze and Sen, *India: Economic Development and Social Opportunity* (Delhi and Oxford: Oxford University Press, 1996), and in the follow-up monograph, *India: Development and Participation* (Delhi and Oxford: Oxford University Press, 2002).

need for food is not the same thing as the economic entitlement to food (what people can afford to buy given their economic circumstances and the prices), the large stocks procured are hard to get rid of, despite rampant undernourishment across the country. The very price system that generated a massive supply kept the hands – and the mouths – of the poorer consumers away from food.

But does not the government automatically remedy this problem through subsidizing food prices compared with the procurement prices – surely that should keep food prices low to consumers? Not quite. The issues involved are discussed more fully in my joint book with Jean Drèze, *India: Development and Participation* (2002), but one big part of the story is simply the fact that much of the subsidy does in fact go to pay for the cost of *maintaining* a massively large stock of food grain, with a mammoth and unwieldy food administration (including the Food Corporation of India). Also, since the cutting edge of the price subsidy is to subsidize farmers to produce more and earn more, rather than to sell existing stocks to consumers at lower prices (that happens too, but only to a limited extent and to restricted groups), the overall effect of the subsidy is more spectacular in transferring money to medium and large farmers with food to sell, than in giving food to the undernourished consumers.

If there were ever a case for radical class analysis, in which 'the left' could take 'the right' to the cleaners, one would have thought that this would be it. To some extent, we do see such criticism, but not nearly enough. The dog that does not bark is the expectable howl of criticism from the perspective of class analysis.

Why? This is where the diagnosis of 'friendly fire' becomes relevant. When the policy of food procurement was introduced and the case for purchasing food from farmers at high prices was established, various benefits were foreseen, and they were not altogether pointless, nor without some claim to equity. First, building up stocks up to a certain point is useful for food security – necessary even for the prevention of famines. That would make it a good thing to have a large stock up to some limit – in today's conditions, perhaps even a stock of 20 million tonnes or so. The idea that since it is good to build up stocks as needed, it must be even better to build up even more stocks, is not only mistaken, but also leads to shooting oneself in the foot.

I must also examine a second line of reasoning in defence of high food prices, which also comes in as a good idea and then turns counterproductive. Those who suffer from low food prices include some who are not affluent – the small farmer or peasant who sells a part of his crop. The interests of this group are mixed up with those of big farmers, and this produces a lethal confusion of food politics. While the powerful lobby of privileged farmers presses for higher procurement prices and pushes for public funds to be spent to keep them high, the interests of poorer farmers, who also benefit from the high prices, is championed by political groups that represent these non-affluent beneficiaries. Stories of hardship among these people play a powerful part not only in the rhetoric in defence of high food prices, but also in the genuine conviction of many equity-oriented activists that this would help some very badly off people. And so it would, but of course it would help the rich farmers much more, and cater to their pressure groups, while the interests of the much larger number of people who buy food rather than sell it would be badly sacrificed.

There is a need for more explicit analysis of the effects of these policies on the different classes, and in particular on the extreme underdogs of society who, along with their other deprivations (already discussed), are also remarkably underfed and undernourished. For casual labourers, slum dwellers, poor urban employees, migrant workers, rural artisans, rural non-farm workers, even farm workers who are paid cash wages, high food prices bite into what they can eat. The overall effect of high food prices is to hit many of the worst-off members of society extremely hard. And while they do help some of the farm-based poor, the net effect is quite regressive on distribution. There is, of course, relentless political pressure in the direction of high food prices coming from farmers' lobbies, and the slightly muddied picture of benefiting some farm-based poor makes the policy issues sufficiently befuddled to allow the confusion that high food prices are a pro-poor stance, when in overall effect they are very far from that. It is said that a little knowledge is a dangerous thing. So unfortunately is a little bit of equity when its championing coincides with massive injustice to vast numbers of people. It is, again, a case of 'friendly fire', even though the involvement of the rich farmers' pressure groups thickens the plot.

Elementary Education

For my second example, I turn to primary education in India. It suffers, of course, from many deficiencies.[8] The paucity of financial resources is obviously a principal problem: there are not enough schools and the facilities available in the ones that exist are often very limited. But there are several other problems as well. A major difficulty lies in the weak institutional structure of primary schools in much of India, which are often inefficiently run. A further problem concerns inequity of schooling arrangements, and the challenge of bringing first-generation school attenders into a sympathetic and just system of primary education.[9]

I have had the opportunity of getting a sample of the problems involved through a small study conducted on this subject by the Pratichi Trust, which I was privileged to set up in 1999 with the help of the proceeds of my Nobel award.* We investigated the working of a number of elementary schools from three districts in West Bengal initially (but later the study was extended to six districts in West Bengal and one from the neighbouring state of Jharkhand). The overall picture that emerges from these investigations is very depressing. A significant proportion of teachers were absent from school on the days we visited them unannounced. Teacher absenteeism was very much greater in schools where the bulk of the pupils come from Scheduled Caste or Scheduled Tribe families; indeed, 75 per cent of those schools in our list had serious problems of teacher absenteeism – much higher than in schools in which the pupils come from less disadvantaged families. A very large proportion of the children rely on private tuition as a supplement to what they get from the schools, and those who do not are evidently prevented from doing so because of penury, rather than because of being satisfied with the teaching the children get in the school. Indeed, of the pupils in Classes 3 and 4 we could test, the vast majority of those who did not get private tuition could not even sign their names.

*The investigation cited was carried out by Kumar Rana, Abdur Rafique and Amrita Sengupta, working with me. Our first Education Report presents the main findings from the first part of the study: *The Delivery of Public Education: A Study in West Bengal* (New Delhi: Pratichi Trust, 2002).

Effective elementary education has in practice ceased to be free in substantial parts of the country, which of course is a violation of a basic right. All this seems to be reinforced by a sharp class division between teachers and the poorer families. Yet the teachers' unions – related to the respective parties – sometimes vie with each other in championing the immunity of teachers from discipline. The parents from disadvantaged families have little voice in the running of schools, and the official inspectors seem too scared to discipline the delinquent teachers, especially when the parents come from the bottom layer of society. The teachers' unions have, of course, had quite a positive role in the past in defending the interests of teachers, when they used to be paid very little and were thoroughly exploited. The teachers' unions then served as an important part of the institutional support in favour of more justice. Now, however, these institutions of justice seem to work largely against justice through their inaction – or worse – when faced with teacher absenteeism and other irresponsibilities.

The problem is, in some ways, compounded by the fact that school teachers are now comparatively well paid – no longer the recipients of miserably exploitative wages. The recent boost in the salary of public servants in India (leaving far behind those who are served by the public servants, such as agricultural and industrial labourers) has led to a very substantial rise in the remuneration of school teachers (as public servants), all over India. The primary school teachers in West Bengal, where our study was conducted, now tend to get between Rs. 5,000 and 10,000 per month, in the form of salary and allowances, which compares with the total salary of teachers in the alternative schools – called Sishu Siksha Kendras – of Rs. 1,000 per month.

The salary of teachers in regular schools has gone up dramatically over recent years, even in real terms, that is, after correcting for price changes. This is an obvious cause for celebration at one level (indeed, I remember being personally involved, as a student at Presidency College fifty years ago, in agitations to raise the desperately low prevailing salaries of school teachers). But the situation is now very different. The big salary increases in recent years have not only made school education vastly more expensive (making it much harder to offer regular school education to those who are still excluded from it), but have also tended to draw the school teachers as a group further away from the families of children, especially those from disadvantaged backgrounds. There is considerable evidence that the class barrier that deeply impairs the delivery of school education to the worst-off members of society is now further reinforced by the increase in economic and social distance between the teachers and the poorer (and less privileged) children.

A Concluding Remark

Nehru's hope of overcoming class divisions in the economic, social and political progress of the country remains largely unfulfilled. The barriers to progress come not only from old dividing lines, but also from new ones. Sometimes the very institutions that were created to overcome disparities and barriers have tended to act as reactionary influences in reinforcing inequity. There are many examples of such 'friendly fire', of which I have discussed two particular cases.

The terrible combination that we have in India of immense food mountains on the one hand and the largest conglomeration of undernourished population in the world on the other is one example of this. The positive hopes of equity through high support prices of food and payment of subsidies have, to a considerable extent, tended to produce exactly the opposite effect. Another example relates to the institutional features of delivery of primary education. The teachers' unions, which have a very positive role to play in protecting the interests of teachers and have played that part well in the past, are often turning into an influence that reinforces the neglect of the interests of children from desperately underprivileged families. There is evidence of a hardening of class barriers that separate the newly affluent teachers from the impoverished rural poor.

I do not want to end on a note of pessimism. The point of diagnosing a problem is to use it to remedy the identified deficiencies. In the two cases considered, possible lines of reform are not hard to see. On the latter, the report of the Pratichi Trust makes a number of policy suggestions, which include emphasizing the need to strengthen the voice of parents, especially of those from the underprivileged sections, in school management. This would require a restructuring of the administration of primary education, though making room for effective parent–teacher committees for individual schools, with legal authority. With the help of the countervailing power of the interest group most directly involved – that is, parents – the role of teachers' unions can be made more constructive. Similarly, on the former problem, the food mountains can be turned into assets rather than liabilities, with an appropriate focus on the interests of the worst-off members of the society (for example through use in school meals).*

These and other policy changes call for urgent action and consideration. That process can be facilitated by clear analysis of the exact effects of actual and possible public policies. It is important to prevent 'friendly fire' as well as to press for policies that can make a real difference to the inequalities of class division in India. It is crucial to scrutinize the benefits to be obtained and the losses to be sustained by the different classes and occupation groups, resulting from each policy proposal. The ubiquitous role of class divisions influences social arrangements in remarkably diverse ways and deserves a fuller recognition than it has tended to get in the making of Indian public policy. There is something serious to argue about here.

*The recent initiative of the Indian government (in late 2004) to help provide cooked midday meals in schools across the country is a very positive move that has emerged since the Nehru Lecture was given in 2001. This initiative, which followed directly from the Indian Supreme Court's visionary decision to cover this right among the entitlements of children, has favourable potential in simultaneously addressing the twin problems of child undernourishment and school absenteeism. It has had much success in states (such as Tamil Nadu) where it has been in use for many years, and it is beginning to have positive effects where it is just being introduced. Investigations by the Pratichi Trust team in West Bengal record higher school attendance and a high level of satisfaction from the poorer families.

11

Women and Men*

Many Faces of Gender Inequality

Inequality between women and men can appear in many different forms – it has many faces.[1] Gender disparity is, in fact, not one affliction but a multitude of problems. Sometimes the different asymmetries are quite unrelated to each other. Indeed, there may be no significant inequality in one sphere but a great deal of inequality in another. For example, Japan has no particular gender bias in nutrition or health care or school education, but men do seem to have considerable relative advantage in securing high leadership positions in administration or business.

However, in other cases, gender inequality of one type tends to encourage and sustain gender inequality of other kinds. Consequential analysis can then be critically important even within the large corpus of gender relations in general, in order to examine and scrutinize how the different aspects of gender inequality relate to each other. For while gender inequality has many faces, these are not independent (like those in the austere image of Brahma in early Indian iconography). Rather, they speak to each other and sometimes strongly encourage one another. For example, when women lack decisional power within the family, which amounts to a deprivation of women's effective agency, this can also adversely affect their own well-being.

*This essay is based on the text for the Sunanda Bhandare Memorial Lecture I gave in Delhi (titled 'The Nature and Consequences of Gender Inequality') on 14 Nov. 2001. Sunanda Bhandare was an outstanding Indian judge and a leading social and legal thinker, and it was a great privilege for me to join in the celebration of her memory. I am also grateful for helpful discussions with Bina Agarwal, Satish Agnihotri, Jean Drèze, Devaki Jain and V. K. Ramachandran.

The two kinds of deprivation may not only move together – be 'covariant' – but they may be linked with each other through causal connections.

Well-being and Agency

It is useful to relate the topic of this essay to the general distinction between two features of human life, to wit, 'well-being' and 'agency', which I have explored elsewhere.[2] This distinction corresponds to the old dichotomy, much used in medieval European literature, between 'the patient' and 'the agent'. The distinction is not only important in itself, it also has a very substantial bearing on the causal connections related to gender relations.*

The agency aspect refers to the pursuit of goals and objectives that a person has reason to value and advance, whether or not they are connected with the person's own well-being. People may actively choose to pursue other objectives (that is, other than personal well-being), which could, quite possibly, be very broad, such as independence of one's country, the elimination of famines and epidemics, or (related to the present context) the removal of gender inequality in general. Even though there may be some overlap between different objectives, nevertheless as a general rule in championing these broader ends people may not be primarily influenced by the extent to which these general objectives affect their own quality of life or welfare.

The distinction between 'agency' and 'well-being' is conceptually rich, since they refer to two distinct ways in which a person's values, ends, ambitions, freedoms and achievements can be understood, using two different perspectives of assessment. As it happens, the distinction is of substantial relevance, in general, in interpreting practical policies and activities, and, in particular, in understanding the priorities of social movements, including the increasingly powerful 'women's movements' in many parts of the world.

*The role of agency, in addition to that of well-being, is quite central to the process of development, as I have tried to discuss in *Development as Freedom* (New York: Knopf, and Oxford: Oxford University Press, 1999).

Indeed, until recently the activities of these movements were typically aimed, at least to a great extent, at working towards achieving better treatment for women, in particular a more 'square deal'. This involved a focus on women's well-being in particular. The choice of this focus has, of course, an obvious rationale, given the way women's interests and well-being have been neglected in the past and continue to be neglected even today. But in the course of the evolution of women's movements, their objectives have gradually broadened from this narrowly 'welfarist' focus towards incorporating and emphasizing the active role of women as agents in doing things, assessing priorities, scrutinizing values, formulating policies and carrying out programmes.

Women are, in this broadened perspective, not passive recipients of welfare-enhancing help brought about by society, but are active promoters and facilitators of social transformations. Such transformations influence, of course, the lives and well-being of women, but also those of men and all children – boys as well as girls. This is a momentous enrichment of the reach of women's movements.

Interconnections and Reach

As far as women's own well-being is concerned, it is also important to take note of the extensive interconnections between the agency aspect and the well-being aspect of women's lives. It is obvious that the active agency of women cannot ignore the urgency of rectifying many social influences that blight the well-being of women and subject them to deprivations of various kinds. Thus the agency role must be deeply concerned *inter alia* with women's well-being as well. Similarly, to consider the link from the other direction, it is not only the case that a woman whose agency is severely restricted will – for that reason and to that extent – be handicapped in well-being as well, but also, any practical attempt at enhancing the well-being of women cannot ignore the agency of women themselves in bringing about such a change. So the well-being aspect and the agency aspect of women's movements inevitably have substantial interconnections.

Despite these connections, however, agency and well-being are two quite different perspectives, since the role of a person as an 'agent' is fundamentally different from the role of the same person as a 'patient'. It is, of course, true that agents may have to see themselves, at least to some extent, as patients as well. For example, the old admonition, 'physician, heal thyself', is an invitation to the physician to be both an agent and a patient. But this does not alter the additional modalities and responsibilities that are inescapably associated with the agency of a person. An agent has an active role in pursuing valuable goals, and while these goals would typically include, among other objects, the person's own well-being, they can be, at the same time, far more spacious and extensive in their coverage. The agency role can, thus, be much broader than the promotion of self welfare.

The changing focus of women's movements towards the agency aspect is, thus, a crucial broadening of the scope and reach of these movements, and involves substantial additions to older concerns (without denying the continuing relevance of those concerns). The earlier concentration on the well-being of women, or to be more exact, on the 'ill-being' of women and the deprivations that yield that ill-being, was not, of course, silly or mistaken. Deprivations in the well-being of women were certainly serious – sometimes atrocious – and their removal is clearly important for social justice. There are excellent reasons for bringing these deprivations of women's well-being to light, and to fight for the removal of these iniquities. But nevertheless, conceptualizing women's deprivation basically in terms of well-being, and thus concentrating on the 'patient' aspect of women, cannot but miss out something extraordinarily important about women as active agents of change, which can transform their own lives and the lives of other women, and indeed the lives of everyone in society – women, men and children. Women's movements as well as the growing volume of feminist literature have both been involved, in recent decades, in this broadening of focus. As a consequence, the new agenda has tended to transcend the view of women as patient solicitors of social equity, and see women as harbingers of major social change, in making the world a more liveable place for all. The focus on voice in this book fits well particularly with the agency aspect of gender relations.

Distinct Faces of Gender Inequality

The difference between well-being and agency has remarkable analytical reach, and I shall draw again on this conceptual distinction later on in this essay. But before that I would like to discuss the wide range of variations between the different 'faces' of gender inequality.[3]

I shall examine the distinct phenomena under the following headings:

(1) survival inequality;
(2) natality inequality;
(3) unequal facilities;
(4) ownership inequality;
(5) unequal sharing of household benefits and chores; and
(6) domestic violence and physical victimization.

Given the demographic and social complexity in identifying and understanding the first two categories, I shall concentrate on them in particular, and refer to the others only rather rapidly.

Survival Inequality

In many parts of the world, gender inequality takes the savage form of unusually high mortality rates of women and a consequent preponderance of men in the total population. This contrasts particularly sharply with the preponderance of women found in societies with little or no gender bias in health care and nutrition. It has been widely observed that, given similar health care and nutrition, women tend typically to have lower age-specific mortality rates than men. It is interesting that even female fetuses tend to have a lower probability of miscarriage than male fetuses. Even though, everywhere in the world, more male babies are born than female babies (and an even higher proportion of male fetuses are conceived than female fetuses), in those places in which men and women receive similar health care and attention, the overabundance of men is gradually reduced and then reversed. So the populations of Europe and North America have about 105 or more females per

100 males, and this higher female–male ratio (of about 1.05 or 1.06) comes about as a result of the greater survival chance of females in different age groups.

In contrast with this pattern, in many regions of the world, women receive less – sometimes far less – care than men, and in particular, girls often receive very much less support than boys. As a result of this gender bias in health care and social attention, mortality rates of females are unusually high compared with what may be expected from the local male mortality rates. Indeed, quite often female mortality rates actually exceed the male rates, in total contrast with what is biologically expected and what is actually observed in the pattern of mortality in Europe and North America.

The concept of 'missing women' was devised to give some idea of the enormity of this phenomenon by focusing on the women who are simply not there, primarily due to unusually high mortality compared with normal female–male mortality ratios. The methodology involves finding some way – unavoidably rather rough – of estimating the quantitative difference between the actual number of women in these countries, and the number we could expect to see had the gender ratio in survival been similar, in these countries, to that in other regions of the world where there is not such a significant anti-female bias in health care and other social influences relevant for survival.*

For example, if we take the ratio of women to men in sub-Saharan Africa as the standard (on the grounds that there is relatively little bias against women in health care, social status and mortality rates in sub-Saharan Africa, even though the absolute mortality rates are very high for both men and women), then its female–male ratio of 1.022 can be used to calculate the number of missing women in women-short countries. With India's female–male ratio of 0.93, there is a 'relative deficit' of women of 9 per cent of the Indian male population between that ratio and the standard used for comparison, that is, 1.02 (based on the sub-Saharan African ratio). This already

*I have discussed the methodology involved in estimating the number of missing women and the principal results in 'Missing Women', *British Medical Journal*, 304 (7 Mar. 1992), and 'Missing Women Revisited', *British Medical Journal*, 327 (6 Dec. 2003). See also my joint book with Jean Drèze, *Hunger and Public Action* (Oxford: Clarendon Press, 1989).

yields a figure of 37 million missing women in India in 1986 (when I first did the estimation).[4] Similarly, the use of the same 'standard' of 1.02 (based on the sub-Saharan African ratio) produces a figure of 44 million for missing women in China at the same point of time. By adding these country estimates together, it soon emerges that for the world as a whole the magnitude of shortfall of women easily exceeds 100 million, already 'missing' in 1986 (since then the numbers have grown with the growth of absolute size of the respective populations).[5] Other standards and different demographic procedures can also be used, as has been done by Ansley Coale and Stephan Klasen. These procedures yield somewhat different numbers, but invariably very large ones. For example, Klasen's total number for the earlier period (as in the estimates by Coale and Sen) was about 80 million missing women. For more recent years, Stephan Klasen's method yields numbers that are larger than 100 million.[6] Anti-female bias in care and mortality imposes a massive penalty across the world against the survival of women.

Natality Inequality and an Indian Divide

Even within the demographic domain, gender inequality can manifest itself not just in the old form of mortality asymmetry, but also in the new form of sex-specific abortions aimed at eliminating female fetuses. This 'natality inequality' reflects the fact that many parents want the newborn to be a boy rather than a girl, given a general preference for boys in many male-dominated societies. The availability of modern techniques to determine the gender of the fetus has made such sex-selective abortion possible and easy, and it has become very common in many societies. It is particularly prevalent in east Asia, in China and South Korea in particular, but there is evidence that it also occurs to a statistically identifiable extent in Singapore and Taiwan. It is beginning to emerge as a significant phenomenon in India and south Asia as well.

This 'high-tech sexism' has changed – and is continuing to change – the female–male ratios at birth. Compared with the biologically determined standard ratio of about 95 girls being born per 100 boys (which is the ratio we observe in Europe and North America since sex-specific abortion does not exist as a significant phenomenon there), Singapore and Taiwan have 92, South Korea 88, and China a mere 86 girls born per 100 boys.

Given the incompleteness of birth registration in India, it is not easy to get exactly comparable female–male ratios at birth, but the ratio of females to males among children can serve, *inter alia*, as a guide to the natality bias as well, even though differences in child mortality rates of females and males can also influence these statistics. Indeed, both these phenomena (sex-selective abortions and female disadvantage in mortality of children) reflect anti-female bias, and they can certainly work together. As far as Indian statistics are concerned overall, even though mortality rates of boys and girls are now very close to each other, nevertheless the female–male ratio of the population under age 6 has fallen from 94.5 girls per 100 boys in 1991 (which was thus much in line with the ratio in Europe and North America) to 92.7 girls per 100 boys in 2001. This drop basically reflects the spread of sex-selective abortions and natality inequality, rather than any rise in the mortality of female children relative to male children.

There is a remarkable regional pattern associated with this new phenomenon in India. There has been, in fact, little (or no) decline in some parts of the country, mainly in the east and south, but it has fallen sharply in other regions, mainly in the north and west of India. There have been, for example, extremely sharp declines in the female–male ratios of children in Punjab, Haryana, Gujarat and Maharashtra, and significantly low ratios can be observed in most other states in the north and west of the country.

Because of the legitimate fear that sex-selective abortions might occur in India and serve as a new vehicle of India's traditional anti-female bias, some years ago the Indian parliament banned the use of sex determination techniques for fetuses, except when as a by-product of some necessary medical investigation. But it appears that the enforcement of this law has been comprehensively neglected.

Consolation might be sought in the fact that even the latest ratio of females to males among Indian children (93 girls per 100 boys), while lower than the figure ten years ago, is still much higher than South Korea's female–male ratio among children of 88 girls and China's 86 girls per 100 boys.[7] There are, however, additional grounds for concern, which require us to go beyond the current all-India average of female–male ratio of children. First, there are big variations within India, and the all-India average hides the fact that there are several states – in the north and west of India – where the female–male ratio for children is very much lower than the Indian average, and lower even than the Chinese and Korean numbers. Second, it must be asked whether these are 'early days' and whether – as the technology of sex determination becomes more widely available across India – the Indian ratio will continue to fall, catching up with – and perhaps even going below – the Korean and Chinese numbers.

There appears to be something of a social divide at this time running right across India and splitting the country effectively into two contiguous halves, in the extent of anti-female bias in natality and post-natality mortality. Since more boys than girls are born everywhere in the world for biological reasons, we must use as our comparative standard not a one-to-one ratio, but the proportions that can be observed in advanced industrial countries (in Europe and North America, for example), where sex-selective abortion is not a significant phenomenon. The female–male ratio for the 0–5 age group is 94.8 in Germany, 95.0 in the United Kingdom, and 95.7 in the United States, and perhaps we can sensibly pick the German ratio of 94.8 as the 'cut-off point' below which significant anti-female intervention can be suspected.

This dividing line produces a remarkable geographical split of the country. There are states in the north and west, led by Punjab, Haryana, Delhi and Gujarat, where the female–male ratio of children is very substantially below the benchmark figure (with ratios between 79.3 and 87.8). Other states in these regions also have ratios significantly below the dividing line of 94.8 girls per 100 boys, such as Himachal Pradesh, Madhya Pradesh, Rajasthan, Uttar Pradesh, Maharashtra, Jammu and Kashmir, and Bihar.[8] On the other side of the divide, the states in the east and south of India tend to have female–male ratios that are above the benchmark line (that is, 94.8 girls per 100 boys, taken as our cut-off standard): with Kerala, Andhra Pradesh, West Bengal and Assam (each between 96.3 and 96.6 girls), and also Orissa, Karnataka and the north-eastern states to the east of Bangladesh (Meghalaya, Mizoram, Manipur, Nagaland,

Arunachal Pradesh). The country looks split in the middle, falling neatly into two divergent segments.[9]

A partial exception to this sharp pattern of twofold regional split is provided by the southern state of Tamil Nadu, where the female–male ratio is just below 94. As it happens, Tamil Nadu's female-child ratio is still higher than the ratio of any state in the north and west, which form the 'deficit list', but nevertheless Tamil Nadu's ratio is somewhat below the German cut-off point. However, the astonishing finding is not that one particular state seems to provide a marginal misfit, but that the vast majority of Indian states fall firmly into two contiguous halves, classified broadly into the north and west on one side and the south and east on the other. Indeed – and this is quite remarkable – every state in the north and west[10] has a strictly lower female–male ratio of children than every state in the east and south (even Tamil Nadu fits into this classification), and the country stands firmly and sharply divided.

It may be asked whether the female–male ratio in child mortality is also similarly divisive. There is a statistical connection there, but nevertheless the pattern of female–male ratio of the number of children (which incorporates the impact of sex-specific abortion) produces a much sharper regional classification than does the female–male ratio of mortality of children, even though the two are also fairly strongly correlated. The female–male ratio in child mortality varies between, at one end, 0.91 in West Bengal and 0.93 in Kerala (in favour of girls) in the southern and eastern regions, on one side, to 1.3 in Punjab, Haryana and Uttar Pradesh, at the other, with high ratios (against girls) also in Gujarat, Bihar and Rajasthan, in the northern and western regions.

The empirical contrasts make it difficult to escape the conclusion that the north and west have clear characteristics of anti-female bias, influencing the composition of children, in a way that is not quite present – at least, not yet – in most of the east and south. Also, the incidence of sex-specific abortions cannot be explained by the availability of medical resources for determining the sex of the fetus, that is, by the presumption that the states that have more sex-selective abortions are the ones in which medical facilities are more developed and thus usable for this purpose. For example, Kerala and West

Bengal in the non-deficit list, both with a ratio of 96.3 girls to 100 boys (comfortably higher than the benchmark cut-off of 94.8), have at least as many medical facilities as exist in such low-female-ratio states as Madhya Pradesh or Rajasthan. So the availability of medical opportunities cannot provide an adequate explanation – quite the contrary – and we have to look at factors that go beyond the supply side of medical technology. If facilities specifically for sex identification and subsequent abortion have been more extensively developed in some states than in others, the explanation has to be sought largely on the demand side, and not in terms of general development of medical opportunities.

Furthermore, the contrast does not seem to have any immediate and clearly explicable economic connection. The states with strong anti-female bias include rich ones (Punjab and Haryana) as well as poor (Madhya Pradesh and Uttar Pradesh), and fast-growing states (Gujarat and Maharashtra) as well as growth failures (Bihar and Uttar Pradesh). It is thus clear that we have to look beyond material prosperity or economic success or GNP growth into broadly cultural and social influences.

A variety of potential connections must be considered here, and there is a need for fresh research to explain the link between these demographic features and the subject matter of social anthropology and cultural studies.[11] There is, of course, a wealth of substantial social anthropological studies, undertaken in the past, that have examined regional contrasts within India.[12] These would certainly prove useful, though they must be further extended, especially since the regional division of India appears rather different in the new light of natality inequality. Indeed, the division between the north and west on the one hand and the east and south on the other is essentially different from the well-known traditional division between the broad north and the broad south that has received much attention already in Indian social anthropology, at least since Irawati Karve's pioneering work, *Kinship Organization in India*.

However, before I end this section of my essay, I must also sound two notes of caution, concerning the temptation to take the observable pattern of regional contrast to be something bigger and sharper than it, quite conceivably, might eventually prove to be. First, any cultural resistance in the east and south to selective abortion against girls might not be immutable, and we must at least consider the possibility that, while the east and south seem more egalitarian in this respect at present, there can be a gradual spread of new practices – slower than in the north and west, but ultimately similarly pervasive. These are, of course, really pessimistic fears, but it is important to avoid complacency about the future of gender equity in the eastern and southern regions of India even as far as natality asymmetry is concerned. If counteracting measures are to be used, they must be considered even for those areas of India which seem relatively secure at the moment.

Having said that, however, it is certainly appropriate to note the observed regional division, from the gender perspective, between the north and west on one side and the east and south on the other. The causal antecedents of this division undoubtedly deserve investigative attention. This is also broadly, though not exactly, in line with the relatively lower relative mortality of female children vis-à-vis male children, in the east and south, compared with the north and west. The female–male ratio in child mortality varies, as was noted earlier, from as low as 0.91 in West Bengal and 0.93 in Kerala, on one side, all the way to 1.30 in Punjab, Haryana and Uttar Pradesh, on the other.

Second, even in the eastern and southern states in which the overall female–male ratio is still within the European range, there are signs that urban centres have, by and large, a somewhat lower ratio than rural parts of those very states. For example, the female-children ratio per 100 boys is 93.7 in urban Orissa as opposed to the ratio for rural Orissa of 95.4. Karnataka's urban ratio is 93.9, compared with its rural ratio of 95.4. West Bengal's urban ratio of 94.8, while much the same as the German cut-off line, is still below its rural ratio of 96.7. There may be some evidence here of the use of sex-selective abortions in the urban areas of the east and south as well, even though they seem far less frequent than in the north and west. Indeed, while the eastern and southern urban ratios of girls to boys (such as 93.7 in Orissa, 93.9 in Kerala and 94.8 in West Bengal) are typically lower than the corresponding rural ratios, they are still close to – or even similar to – the international benchmark (94.8) and very much higher than the urban ratios in the north and west, such as 86.6 in Delhi, 84.4 in Chandigarh, 82.7 in Gujarat, 80.9 in Haryana and 78.9 in Punjab.

It is not easy to settle, without further scrutiny, how deep these regional or cultural influences are. But the remarkable geographical division of India into two halves in terms of female–male ratio among children (reflecting the combined influence of the inequality generated by sex-specific abortions and differential post-natal mortality) does call for acknowledgement and further analysis. It will also be extremely important to keep a close watch on whether the incidence of sex-specific abortions significantly increases in the states in the east and south, where they are at this time relatively uncommon.

Unequal Facilities

Natality inequality and survival disparity both have important demographic features, which means that gender bias can be identified, in these cases, on the basis of demographic statistics. However, even when the statistics of life and death do not show much – or any – anti-female bias, there are other ways in which women can have less than a square deal. For example, there are many countries in Asia and Africa, and in parts of Latin America, where girls have far less opportunity for schooling than boys. This is certainly true of most parts of India, and even more so in Pakistan, though the situation in Bangladesh, while still quite unequal, seems to be changing fairly rapidly. Inequality in schooling has far-reaching consequences for the fabric of society and it can profoundly influence many different aspects of gender inequality and also deprivation in general for men as well as women (on which more presently).

There are also other basic facilities that are often asymmetrically distributed. For example, the opportunity to enter politics or commerce may be particularly restricted for women. There are inequalities also in social participation, especially when women are confined to their homes and incarcerated within traditional family lives. These can impose significant handicaps for both the well-being and the agency of women, and they can, as I shall argue presently, have far-reaching social consequences – well beyond the immediate deprivation they directly reflect. Furthermore, even when there is relatively little difference in basic facilities including schooling, the opportunities of special facilities, such as higher education or technical training, may be far fewer for young women than for young men.

Traditionally, this type of asymmetry has been linked to the superficially innocuous idea that the respective 'provinces' of men and women are different. This thesis has been championed in different forms over the centuries, and has had much implicit as well as explicit following. It was presented with particular directness in England by the Reverend James Fordyce in his *Sermons to Young Women* (1766), a book which, as Mary Wollstonecraft noted in her *A Vindication of the Rights of Women* (1792), had been 'long made a part of woman's library'. Fordyce warned the young women to whom his sermons were addressed against 'those masculine women that would plead for your sharing any part of their province with us', identifying the province of men as including not only 'war', but also 'commerce, politics, exercises of strength and dexterity, abstract philosophy and all the abstruser sciences'.[13]

Even though such clear-cut beliefs about the 'provinces' of men and women are now rather rare (or at least, expressing such beliefs has become quite unfashionable), nevertheless the presence of extensive gender asymmetry can be seen in many areas of education, training and professional work even in the advanced industrial countries, for example in Europe and North America. If India has gender inequality in basic education in a way, say, that Europe or North America does not, the latter has not yet been able to overcome entirely the inequality of educational facilities in general.

There is a similarity here with professional inequality as well. In terms of employment as well as promotion in work and occupation, women often face much greater handicap than men. This remains a problem even in the West. Indeed, if I may indulge in a bit of a personal reminiscence, as I worked sequentially at Delhi University, Oxford University and Harvard University, the proportion of women among my tenured colleagues steadily declined.

Since so much of this essay is based on probing in some detail such elementary manifestations of gender inequality as asymmetry in mortality and natality, in which many developing countries (including India) do very badly but which do not affect lives in the more economically advanced countries, it is particularly important to remember that the absence of one kind of gender inequality does not entail immunity from other types of gender inequality. A country like Japan may be quite egalitarian in matters of demography or basic facilities, and even, to a great extent, in higher education, and yet there is evidence to indicate that progress to senior levels of employment and occupation can be much more problematic for Japanese women than for Japanese men.

In this essay I am paying particular attention to the experience of gender inequality in the subcontinent and India in particular, but I must warn against the temptation to think that the United States or Western Europe or Japan is in general free from gender bias simply because some of the empirical evidence of gender inequality that is readily observable in the subcontinent cannot be found, in that form, in these economically advanced societies.

In fact, sometimes the picture may be quite contrary. For example, India, Bangladesh, Pakistan and Sri Lanka all have – or have had – female heads of government, which the United States has not yet had (and does not, if I am any judge, seem very likely to have in the immediate future).* Indeed, in the case of Bangladesh, where both the Prime Minister and the leader of the Opposition are women, one might begin to wonder whether any Bangladeshi man could, in the near future, plausibly aspire to rise to the top political leadership there. Given the many faces of gender inequality, much would depend on which face we choose to look at.

Ownership Inequality

Turning now to a different type of disparity, inequality in the ownership of property is a classic category of social inequality. This is, of course, the primary factor behind class divisions. While ownership differences between classes and their far-reaching implications have

*Also, as was discussed in Essay 1, there has been a higher involvement of women in leadership positions in the Indian struggle for independence than in the Russian or Chinese revolutionary movements, and the Congress Party had women Presidents fifty years earlier than any major British political party. On the other hand, the ratio of women members of the Indian parliament is at this time significantly lower than in Britain. There is a strong move in India to find ways and means of making sure that a third of the parliamentary members are women, but there is much disagreement on how to bring this about.

received considerable attention (for example from Marx, who was particularly concerned with the class-based inequality in the ownership of 'means of production'), gender divisions in ownership can also be a source of much social inequality. In many societies the ownership of property, even that of basic assets (such as homes and land), tends to be very asymmetrically divided between men and women. The absence of claims to property can not only reduce the voice of women, it can also make it harder for women to enter and flourish in commercial, economic and social activities. Bina Agarwal has provided a far-reaching investigation of the disempowering effects of landlessness of women in many societies.[14]

Ownership inequality between women and men is not a newly emerging inequality, in contrast with natality inequality, for example. It has existed in most parts of the world for a very long time. However, there are also important local variations in the prevalence of this inequality. For example, even though traditional property rights tend to favour men over women in most parts of India, nevertheless in the state of Kerala, over a long period of history there has been matrilineal inheritance for an influential part of the community, most notably the Nayars, who constitute about a fifth of the total population of Kerala and who have long been influential in the governance and politics of Kerala. In the exceptional nature of Kerala's social achievements, the greater voice of women seems to have been an important factor, and in this the long tradition of matrilineal inheritance on the part of an influential segment of the society has played a significant role.

Unequal Sharing of Household Benefits and Chores

The common family tradition in many parts of the world by which men tend to own much of the assets of the household can also be an important factor in the inequality of power within the family. But household inequality has other causes as well, and this is an important subject which has only recently started to receive the attention it deserves. There are, often enough, basic inequalities in gender relations within the family or the household, which can take many different forms, involving variables I have already discussed, such as health and nutritional attention or the opportunity of schooling and of post-school education.

Even in the cases in which there are no overt signs of crude anti-female bias in the form, say, of survival inequality, family arrangements can still be quite unequal in terms of sharing the burden of housework and child care. It is, for example, quite common in many societies to take for granted that while men will naturally work outside the home, it is acceptable for women to do this if and only if they could engage in such work in addition to their inescapable – and unequally shared – household duties.* This is sometimes called 'division of labour', though it may be more descriptive to see it as the 'accumulation of labour' on women.

The entrenched tradition of such 'division' of labour can also have far-reaching effects on the knowledge and understanding of different types of work in professional circles. When I first started working on gender inequality, in the 1970s, I remember being struck by the fact that the much-used *Handbook of Human Nutrition Requirement*, in presenting 'calorie requirements' for different categories of people, chose to classify household work as 'sedentary activity', requiring little deployment of energy.[15] The influential *Handbook* was based on the report of a high-level Expert Committee jointly appointed by the WHO (World Health Organization) and FAO (Food and Agriculture Organization). It was hard not to think that the lack of experience of household work on the part of the patrician members of that august committee might have had a role in the remarkable diagnosis that household work was 'sedentary'.

Domestic Violence and Physical Victimization

One of the most brutal features of gender inequality takes the form of physical violence against women. The incidence of such violence is

* I have tried to discuss this issue in my 'Gender and Cooperative Conflict', in Irene Tinker (ed.), *Persistent Inequalities* (New York: Oxford University Press, 1990); see also the extensive literature on household inequalities cited there. See also Nancy Folbre, 'Hearts and Spades: Paradigms of Household Economics', *World Development*, 14 (1986), and Marianne A. Ferber and Julie A. Nelson (eds.), *Beyond Economic Man* (Chicago: Chicago University Press, 1993).

remarkably high, not only in poorer and less developed economies, but also in wealthy and modern societies. Indeed, the frequency of battering of women even in the richest and the most developed economies is astonishingly high. Some studies have suggested that there are as many as 1.5 million cases per year of rape and physical assault on women in the United States alone.

Turning to India, it must be acknowledged first that the frequency of assault on women is high in the country. To that terrible general recognition has to be added the special role of violence connected with particular social features, such as dowry and economic settlements. Even though the numbers involved in violent deaths are dwarfed by the larger numbers that perish from neglect of health care and social attention, the crude and brutal nature of this form of gender inequality makes it a particularly severe manifestation of the deprivation of women.

This inequality has been traced by some commentators to the physical asymmetry of women and men, with men having greater immediate power in the gross bodily sense. Undoubtedly, this asymmetry does have a substantial role in the prevalence and survival of this terrible state of affairs, made worse by periods of particular vulnerability for women, such as pregnancy and early post-natal phases. But in addition to the physical aspects of this inequality, attitudinal factors cannot but be major influences. The possibility of physical violence can actually be used (to settle a dispute or to gain an advantage) only when the permissibility of such behaviour is accepted, explicitly or by implication. While physical differences can be countered to a limited extent (training in self-defence rightly receives attention in this context), attitudinal factors can be more comprehensively targeted in any programme of social reform addressed to physical violence against women. Educational, cultural and political movements have roles to play in this transformation.

Free Agency and the Role of Critical Scrutiny

I return now to a subject introduced earlier, the role of women's agency, and the interdependence between the 'agency' aspect and the 'well-being' aspect of women's disadvantage. Perhaps the most immediate argument for focusing on women's agency is precisely the role that agency can play in removing the iniquities that depress the well-being of women. Recent empirical work has brought out very clearly how the relative respect and regard for women's well-being is strongly influenced by such variables as women's ability to earn an independent income, to find employment outside the home, to have ownership rights, and to have literacy and be educated participants in decisions within and outside the family. Indeed, even the survival disadvantage of women compared with men in developing countries seems to decrease sharply – and may even be eliminated – as progress is made in these agency aspects.

The differences between such distinct characteristics as women's earning power, economic role outside the family, literacy and education, property rights and so on may at first sight appear to be quite disparate and not linked with each other. What they all have in common, however, is the positive contribution of each in adding force to women's agency – through making women more independent and empowered. For example, empirical investigations have brought out the way in which women's working outside the home and earning an independent income tends to have a powerful impact on enhancing women's standing and voice in decision-making within the household and more broadly in society.[16] The contribution of female members of the family to its prosperity, which is often ignored when women's work – typically very hard – is inside the home, becomes much more difficult to neglect when women work outside the home. Women tend, as a result, to have more 'say', both because of enhanced standing and also because of reduced financial dependence on men. Furthermore, outside employment often has useful 'educational' effects, in terms of exposure to the world outside the household, making a woman's agency better informed and more effective. Similarly, female education strengthens women's agency and also tends to make it better informed and functionally more powerful. The ownership of property can also add to the influence and power of women in decisions within the family and beyond.

The diverse variables that enhance women's social capability and effectiveness thus have empowering roles, both individually and jointly. Their combined operation has to be related to the understanding that women's power – economic independence as well as social emancipation – can have far-reaching effects on the forces and organizing principles that govern divisions within the family, and can, in particular, influence what are implicitly accepted as women's 'entitlements'. From the crude barbarity of physical violence to the complex instrumentality of health neglect, the deprivation of women is ultimately linked not only to the lower status of women, but also to the fact that women often lack the power to influence the behaviour of other members of society and the operation of social institutions.

It is important in this context to understand the constructive role not only of information and knowledge, but also that of courage and temerity to think differently, in giving women's agency the independence and power to overturn iniquitous but entrenched practices and societal arrangements that are often accepted as part and parcel of an assumed 'natural order'. For example, in China or South Korea the standard routes to women's empowerment, such as female literacy and female economic independence (in which both Korea and China have had major achievements and which have done much for these countries in removing some standard forms of gender inequality, such as survival asymmetry), have not been able to stem the tide of natality inequality working through sex-specific abortions which specially target female fetuses. In India, too, even as women's increased empowerment has contributed to the reduction of excess female mortality, the tendency to use new technology to abort female fetuses has grown, in many parts of the country.

Indeed, there is some evidence that the immediate agency for taking decisions on sex-selective abortions is often that of the mothers themselves.* This raises important issues as to how to interpret the agency of women and its social influence. It is important to see the concept of agency as stretching beyond immediate

*In her insightful reports on India in the *New York Times* in 2001, Celia Dugger noted that the officials in charge of enforcing the ban on sex determination of fetuses frequently cited difficulties in achieving successful prosecution due to the reluctance of mothers to give evidence for the use of such techniques, which are often requested specifically by the mothers involved.

'control' over decisions. The fuller sense of 'agency' must, *inter alia*, involve the freedom to question established values and traditional priorities.*

Agency freedom must, in fact, include the freedom to think freely, without being severely restrained by pressured conformism or by the ignorance of how the prevailing practices in the rest of the world differ from what can be observed locally. For example, what is particularly critical in remedying the terrible biases in natality discrimination is the role of women's informed and independent agency, including the power of women to overcome unquestioningly inherited values and attitudes. What may make a real difference in dealing with this new – and 'high-tech' – face of gender disparity, is the willingness, ability and courage to reassess critically the dominance of received and entrenched norms. When anti-female bias in action reflects the hold of traditional masculinist values from which mothers themselves may not be immune, what is crucial is not just freedom of action but also freedom of thought.[17] Informed and critical agency is important in combating inequality of every kind, and gender inequality is no exception.

Inequality within Families as Cooperative Conflicts

A particular field in which these interdependences are especially strong and blatant concerns inequality between women and men within the household. To understand the process more fully, we can start by noting the fact that women and men have both congruent and conflicting interests affecting family life. Because of the extensive areas of congruence of interest, decision-making in the family tends to take the form of the pursuit of cooperation, with some agreed solution – usually implicit – of the conflicting aspects. Each of the parties has much to lose if cooperation were to break down, and yet there are various

*On this, see my 'Well-being, Agency and Freedom: The Dewey Lecture 1984', *Journal of Philosophy*, 83 (Apr. 1985); 'Open and Closed Impartiality', *Journal of Philosophy*, 99 (Sept. 2002); and *Rationality and Freedom* (Cambridge, Mass.: Harvard University Press, 2002).

alternative 'cooperative solutions', each of which is better for both the parties than no cooperation at all, but which respectively give different – possibly extremely different – relative gains to the two parties.

The formal nature of this type of relationship with partial congruence of interest along with substantial conflicts was outlined by the mathematician John Nash in a classic paper, called 'The Bargaining Problem' (though he was not particularly concerned with family arrangements).* The nature of the problem is very general and arises also in many other real-life contexts, including trade bargaining, labour relations, political treaties, and even in understanding the nature of the gains and losses from the contemporary globalization.† Nash's formulation and related ones also help to provide a basic understanding of what is involved in assessing the fairness of family division – of both chores and benefits. The simultaneous presence of cooperation and conflict is indeed a major feature of family arrangements which demand both predictive and normative scrutiny, even though, as I have argued elsewhere, the ethics and the politics of the problem have to be seen somewhat differently from the way Nash himself characterized it.‡

Exactly how does a problem of interactive relations involve both cooperation and conflict? Both the parties have a strong interest in having some cooperative solution rather than none, and yet they rank the different cooperative solutions in quite dissimilar ways – indeed, typically in opposite directions. For example, between two cooperative solutions *A* and *B* (the former more favourable to the first person and the latter to the second), each party is better off with either *A* or *B* than no cooperation at all, but while the first person's interests are better served by *A* than by *B*, the second gets a significantly better deal in *B* than in *A*. The first person has a self-interested reason to work towards the joint acceptance of *A*, whereas the second person has a similar reason for trying to get to *B*. There is,

*Published in *Econometrica*, 1950. This was among the papers cited by the Royal Swedish Academy in awarding Nash the Nobel Prize in economics in 1994.

†On the last, see my 'How to Judge Globalism', *American Prospect*, Jan. 2002.

‡On this, see my *Collective Choice and Social Welfare* (San Francisco: Holden-Day, 1970; repr. Amsterdam: North-Holland, 1979), chs. 8 and 8*, and also 'Gender and Cooperative Conflict', in Tinker (ed.), *Persistent Inequalities*.

therefore, the simultaneous presence of cooperation as well as conflict in relationships of this kind.

Family arrangements are quintessential examples of such cooperative conflict. The choice of one cooperative arrangement from the set of many alternative possibilities leads to a particular distribution of joint benefits. Some of these divisions are particularly unfavourable to women, and if cooperation is arranged through such a division, it can yield tremendous gender inequality. The structure of 'cooperative conflict' is a general feature of many group relations, and a better understanding of the nature and effects of cooperative conflicts can help to identify the influences that operate on the 'deal' that women get in family divisions.[18] Conflicts between partially disparate interests within family living are typically resolved through implicitly agreed patterns of behaviour that may or may not be particularly egalitarian. The special nature of family life – leading joint lives and sharing a home – requires that the elements of conflict must not be explicitly emphasized. Indeed, dwelling on conflicts rather than the family's 'unity' tends to be seen as aberrant behaviour. Sometimes the deprived woman may not only be silent, she may not even have a clear assessment of the extent of her relative deprivation.

The perception of who is doing how much 'productive' work, or who is 'contributing' how much to the family's prosperity, can be, in this context, very influential, even though the underlying 'theory' regarding how 'contributions' or 'productivity' are to be assessed may rarely be discussed explicitly.[19] The interpretation of individual contributions and appropriate entitlements of women and men plays a major role in the division of the family's joint benefits between men and women. As a result, the circumstances that influence these perceptions of contributions and appropriate entitlements (such as women's ability to earn an independent income, to work outside the home, to be educated, to own property) can have a crucial bearing on these divisions. The impact of greater empowerment and independent agency of women thus includes the correction of the iniquities that blight the lives and well-being of women vis-à-vis men. The lives that women save through more powerful agency certainly include their own.

Women's Agency and the Survival of Children

I have been concentrating so far on the impact of women's agency on the well-being and freedom of women themselves. That is not the whole story, however. Other lives – men's and children's – are also involved. So the consequences of gender asymmetry, beyond the domain of gender inequality in all its forms, must also be considered. To illustrate, it is particularly important to see the role of women's agency in reducing child mortality and restraining fertility. Both relate to concerns that are central to the process of development, and while they clearly do influence the well-being of women as well, their relevance is undoubtedly very much wider.

Recent empirical work has brought out the influence of women's agency and women's empowerment in reducing child mortality. The influence works through many channels, but, perhaps most immediately, it works through the importance that mothers typically attach to the welfare of their children, and the opportunity they have, when their agency is respected and empowered, to influence family decisions in that direction. This has been a matter of particular interest in empirical studies in India.[20]

There is, however, an interesting difference between distinct channels through which women's agency may be enhanced, for example the distinction between women's gainful employment in the labour force and women's literacy and education. It is natural to expect that the impact of female literacy and education must be entirely positive, and that is exactly what is observed. However, in the case of women's labour force participation, there are factors working in different directions. First, involvement in gainful employment has many positive effects on a woman's agency roles, and this, in turn, may entail increased emphasis being placed on child care and also a greater ability of women to emphasize the interests of children in joint family decisions. Second, since men typically show great reluctance to share domestic chores, the greater inclination towards more priority on child care (resulting from a larger voice of women in family decisions) may not be easy to execute when women are saddled with the 'double burden' of household work and outside employment. The net effect could thus go in either direction. Not surprisingly, therefore, in the important comparison of inter-district data in India by Mamta Murthi, Anne-Catherine Guio and Jean Drèze, we do not get a clear-cut and statistically significant result in either direction for the impact of female employment on child mortality.[21]

In contrast, female literacy and education are found to have an unambiguously powerful and statistically significant impact in reducing under-5 mortality, even after controlling for male literacy. This is consistent with growing evidence of a close relationship between female literacy and child survival in many other countries as well.[22]

It is in this context also interesting to examine the impact of these agency variables on gender bias in child survival (as opposed to total child mortality and survival). For this particular variable, it turns out that both female labour force participation and female literacy have very strong ameliorating effects on the extent of female disadvantage in child survival, so that higher levels of female literacy and labour force participation are strongly associated with lower levels of relative female disadvantage in child survival. By contrast, variables that relate to the general level of economic development and modernization turn out, in these statistical studies, to have no significant effect on gender bias in child survival, and can sometimes – when not accompanied by empowerment of women – even strengthen, rather than weaken, the gender bias in child survival. This applies *inter alia* to urbanization, male literacy, the availability of medical facilities, and the level of poverty (with lower levels of poverty being sometimes associated with *lower* female–male ratios).[23] In so far as a positive connection does exist in India between the level of development and reduced gender bias in survival, it seems to work mainly through variables that are directly related to women's agency, such as female literacy and female labour force participation.

Emancipation, Agency and Fertility Reduction

To examine another causal connection, we can scrutinize the agency role of women in the reduction of fertility rates. The adverse effects of very high birth rates include the denial of women's freedom to do other things – through persistent bearing and rearing of children – routinely imposed on many Asian and African women. It is thus not surprising that reductions in birth rates have often followed the enhancement of women's status and power. The lives that are most constrained by over-frequent bearing and rearing of children are those of young women, and any social change that increases their voice and influence on fertility decisions can be expected to have the effect of reducing the frequency of births.

This expectation is indeed confirmed in investigations of inter-district variations of the total fertility rate in India. In fact, among all the variables included in the comparative empirical analysis presented by Drèze, Guio and Murthi, the only ones that have a statistically significant effect in reducing fertility are female literacy and female labour force participation. Once again, the importance of women's agency emerges forcefully from this analysis, especially in comparison with the weaker effects of variables relating to general economic progress, such as a rise in per capita real income.

The link between female literacy and fertility is particularly clear. This connection has been widely observed in other countries also, and it is not surprising that it should emerge in India, too. The unwillingness of educated women to be shackled to continuous child-rearing clearly plays a role in bringing about this change. Education also helps to broaden the horizon of vision, and, at a more mundane level, assists in disseminating knowledge of family planning. And of course educated women tend to have greater freedom to exercise their agency in family decisions, including in matters of fertility and childbirth.

The case of Kerala, the most socially advanced state in India, is also worth noting here, because of its particular success in fertility reduction based on women's agency. While the total fertility rate for India as a whole is still as high as 3.0, that rate in Kerala has now fallen well below the 'replacement level' of 2.1 to 1.7 (even lower than China's fertility rate). Female agency and literacy are important also in the reduction of mortality rates, and this is another – more indirect – consequential route through which women's agency (including female literacy) may have helped to reduce birth rates, since there is some evidence that a reduction of death rates, especially of children, tends to contribute to the reduction of fertility rates. Kerala has also had other favourable features for women's empowerment and agency, including a greater recognition of women's property rights for a substantial and influential part of the community.*

Recently, there has been a good deal of discussion on the imperative need to reduce birth rates in the world. The issue has figured in the context of India in particular, and it has been predicted that India will overtake China in population size in a few decades. China's achievement in cutting down birth rates over a short period through rather draconian measures has suggested to many the need for countries such as India to emulate China in this respect. These coercive methods do involve many social costs, including the direct one of the loss of the effective freedom of people – in particular of women – to take decisions on matters that are clearly rather personal.

It is perhaps worth noting in this context that compulsion has not produced a lower birth rate in China compared with what Kerala has already achieved entirely through voluntary channels, relying on the educated agency of women. When China introduced its 'one child policy' and other coercive measures, China had a fertility rate of 2.8 while Kerala's fertility rate was somewhat higher, at 3.0. By the early 1990s, China's fertility rate was down from 2.8 to 2.0, whereas Kerala's had fallen from 3.0 to 1.9. Kerala has remained ahead of China as fertility rates have continued to fall both in Kerala and in China. Some other Indian states, such as Tamil Nadu and Himachal Pradesh, have also experienced faster fertility decline than China has had with its coercive measures. The fertility decline in the successful Indian states has been closely linked with women's empowerment, particularly through female education, economic independence and involvement in remunerative work outside the household.

In fact, it is not quite clear exactly how much extra reduction in its birth rate China has been able to achieve by resorting to coercive methods. China has brought about many social and economic changes that have enhanced the power of women (for example, through raising

*On these and related general issues, see my 'Population: Delusion and Reality', *New York Review of Books*, 22 Sept. 1994; 'Fertility and Coercion', *University of Chicago Law Review*, 63 (Summer 1996); *Development as Freedom*, chs. 6, 8 and 9.

female literacy rates and expanding female participation rates in the labour force), and these changes have made conditions more favourable to fertility reduction through voluntary channels. These factors would themselves have reduced the birth rates (well below that of the Indian average, for example). While China seems to get too much credit for its coercive and brutal measures, it gets far too little credit for its supportive and facilitating policies that have actually helped it to cut its birth rate.

Kerala's low birth rate – lower than China's – also suggests that the consequential effects of these supportive developments may be effective enough to render compulsion largely redundant, even if it were acceptable otherwise. It so happens that Kerala not only has a much higher level of female literacy than India as a whole, it is also well ahead of China's female literacy rate (and higher indeed than every province of China).[24] The fact that the ranking of female literacy is exactly the same as that of birth rates is in line with other evidence for the close connection between the two. There is a 'virtuous circle' that deserves more attention than it tends to get.

Gender Inequality and Adult Diseases

I turn finally to an 'external' consequence of gender inequality that is only now beginning to receive serious attention. From English data, David Barker, and others working on a similar line, have found that low birth weight is often closely associated with higher incidence – many decades later – of a number of adult diseases, including hypertension, glucose intolerance and other cardiovascular hazards.[25] The 'Barker thesis', if further confirmed, will offer a possibility of identifying different empirical regularities that have been observed as prominent health-related phenomena in South Asia:

(1) high rate of maternal undernourishment;
(2) high incidence of underweight births;
(3) widespread prevalence of undernourished children; and
(4) high incidence of cardiovascular diseases.

If the Barker thesis gets further confirmation (the debate on this subject is quite intense at this moment), it would offer the 'missing link' in a chain of causal connections that have much policy importance in India and South Asia. Indeed, in understanding the different – and apparently disparate – empirical observations (1) to (4) above, social and medical relations have to be examined together and linked up.[26] There is much plausibility in seeing a causal pattern that goes from the nutritional neglect of women to maternal undernourishment, and from there to fetal growth retardation and underweight babies, thence to greater child undernourishment and – through the Barker connection – to a higher incidence of cardiovascular afflictions much later in adult life. What begins as a neglect of the interests of women ends up causing adversities in the health and survival of all – even at advanced ages.

At one level this finding is not surprising. Given the unique role of women in the reproductive process, it would be hard to imagine that the deprivation to which women are subjected would not have some adverse impact on the lives of all human beings who are 'born of a woman' (as the Book of Job describes every person, not particularly daringly). Interestingly enough, since men suffer disproportionately more from cardiovascular diseases than women, the suffering of women (particularly in the form of maternal undernourishment) ultimately hits men even harder than women (through heart disease and premature deaths). The extensive penalties of neglecting women's interests rebounds, it appears, on men with a vengeance.

It is clear from these biological connections that the consequences of neglecting women's interests extend far beyond the well-being of women only. Biology is not, however, the only consequential link. There are other, non-biological, connections that operate through women's conscious agency. The expansion of women's capabilities not only enhances women's own freedom and well-being, but also has many other effects on the lives of all.* Active agency of women can, in many circumstances, contribute substantially to the lives of all

*On the extensive role and reach of capabilities of women, see particularly Martha Nussbaum, *Women and Human Development: The Capabilities Approach* (Cambridge: Cambridge University Press, 2000).

people – men as well as women, children as well as adults. Indeed, the effects, discussed earlier, of the impact of women's emancipation on child mortality and fertility already illustrate these broader – more conscious and less biological – connections.

There is also new evidence that the functioning of women in other areas, including in economic and political fields, makes a radical difference to the social outcome. Substantial links between women's agency and social achievements have been noted in many different countries. There is, for example, plenty of evidence that whenever social and economic arrangements depart from the standard practice of male ownership, women can seize business and economic initiative with much success. It is also clear that the result of women's participation is not merely to generate income for women, but also to provide many other social benefits that come from women's enhanced status, enterprise and independence. The remarkable success in Bangladesh of organizations like the Grameen Bank and BRAC, directed particularly at the economic and social roles of women, illustrate how women's agency can help to transform the lives of all human beings. Indeed, in the gradual transformation of Bangladesh, which was seen not long ago as a 'basket case', into a country with significant economic and social success and much promise, the agency role of women is playing a critically important part. The precipitate fall of the total fertility rate in Bangladesh from 6.1 to 2.9 in the course of two decades (perhaps the fastest decline in the world) is merely one illustration of the dynamic power of women's agency and the consequential correlates of gender equity.

A Concluding Remark

When Queen Victoria wrote to Sir Theodore Martin complaining about 'this mad, wicked folly of "Woman's Rights"', she may have underrated the reach of that 'wicked folly', which can actually influence the lives of all, women, men and children. However, Victoria herself could not have been, I venture to say, unaware of the fact that women – indeed, even one woman – could make a difference to the lives of many. While hostility to women's rights, to which the formidable queen-empress gave expression, has substantially weakened since that indictment was expressed (in 1870), the fact that women's reasoned agency has far-reaching consequences on the lives of all deserves a larger recognition than it tends to get, even today. Despite various achievements of Indian women, the need for a general recognition of this basic point remains strong.

I end with two final points, based on the conceptual and empirical discussions already presented. First, the importance of women's agency and voice reflects itself in nearly every field of social life. Even though for many purposes such simple indicators as women's education, employment and land ownership have much predictive power, there are broader influences on women's agency that also need consideration. For example, the parts of the country where there is extensive use of sex-specific abortion include some regions in which the simple characteristics of women's education and employment are not exceptionally low. A social and cultural climate in which mothers may themselves seek sons rather than daughters may require a more radical departure than mere schooling or outside employment can provide (even though they too would, to some limited extent, help). The issue of agency has to be broadened to focus particularly on deliberative agency. The social and political understanding that can make a crucial difference demands broad public discussion and informed agitation. The argumentative route has something to offer here, but it requires a very broad engagement indeed.

Second, it is necessary to widen the focus of attention from women's well-being, seen on its own, to women's agency (including, *inter alia*, its association with women's well-being but taking on, along with it, very many other aspects of society). We need a fuller cognizance of the power and reach of women's enlightened and constructive agency and an adequate appreciation of the fact that women's power and initiative can uplift the lives of all human beings – women, men and children. Gender inequality is a far-reaching societal impairment, not merely a special deprivation of women. That social understanding is urgent as well as momentous.

12

India and the Bomb*

Weapons of mass destruction have a peculiar fascination. They can generate a warm glow of strength and power carefully divorced from the brutality and genocide on which the potency of the weapons depends. The great epics – from the *Iliad* and *Rāmāyaṇa* to the *Kalevala* and *Nibelungenlied* – provide thrilling accounts of the might of special weapons, which are not only powerful in themselves, but also greatly empower their possessors. As India, along with Pakistan, goes down the route of cultivating nuclear weapons, the imagined radiance of perceived power is hard to miss.

The Moral and the Prudential

Perceptions can deceive. It has to be asked whether powerful weapons in general and nuclear armaments in particular can be expected – invariably or even typically – to strengthen and empower their possessor. An important prudential issue is involved here. There is, of course, also the question of ethics, and in particular the rightness or wrongness of a nuclear policy. That important issue can be distinguished from the question of practical benefit or loss to a nation from a particular policy. We have good grounds to be interested in both the questions – the prudential and the ethical – but also reason enough

*This essay is based on the first Dorothy Hodgkin Lecture at the Annual Pugwash Conference in Cambridge, England, on 8 August 2000. For helpful comments, I am grateful to Jean Drèze, Ayesha Jalal, V. K. Ramachandran and Emma Rothschild. A considerably shortened version of this essay was published earlier in the *New Republic*, 25 Sept. 2000.

not to see the two issues as disparate and totally unconnected to each other. Our behaviour towards each other cannot be divorced from what we make of the ethics of one another's pursuits, and the reasons of morality have, as a result, prudential importance as well.* It is in this light that I want to examine the challenges of nuclear policy in the subcontinent in general and in India in particular.

Whether, or to what extent, powerful weapons empower a nation is not a new question. Indeed, well before the age of nuclear armament began, Rabindranath Tagore had expressed a general doubt about the fortifying effects of military strength. If 'in his eagerness for power', Tagore had argued in 1917, a nation 'multiplies his weapons at the cost of his soul, then it is he who is in much greater danger than his enemies'.† Tagore was not as uncompromisingly pacifist as Mahatma Gandhi, and his warning against the dangers of alleged strength through more and bigger weapons related to the need for ethically scrutinizing the functions of these weapons and the exact uses to which they are to be put, as well as the practical importance of the reactions and counteractions of others. The 'soul' to which Tagore referred includes, as he explained, the need for humanity and understanding in international relations.

Tagore was not merely making a moral point, but also one of pragmatic importance, taking into account the responses from others that would be generated by one's pursuit of military might. His immediate concern in the quoted statement was with Japan and its move towards extensive nationalism. Tagore was a great admirer of Japan and the Japanese, but felt very disturbed by its shift from economic and social development to aggressive militarization. The heavy sacrifices that were forced on Japan later on, through military defeat and nuclear devastation, Tagore did not live to see (he died in 1941), but they would have only added to Tagore's intense sorrow. But the conundrum that he invoked, about the weakening effects of military power,

*I have tried to explore the connections between the two sets of questions in the analysis of economic problems in my 'Rational Fools: A Critique of the Behavioral Foundations of Economic Theory', *Philosophy and Public Affairs*, 6 (1977), and *On Ethics and Economics* (Oxford: Blackwell, 1987).

†Rabindranath Tagore, *Nationalism* (London: Macmillan, 1917; new edn. with an Introduction by E. P. Thompson, 1991).

has remained active in the writings of contemporary Japanese writers, perhaps most notably Kenzaburo Oe.*

Science, Politics and Nationalism

The leading architect of India's ballistic missile programme and a key figure in the development of nuclear weapons is Dr Abdul Kalam, a scientist of much distinction.† Dr Kalam, who comes from a Muslim family and is a researcher of great achievement, has a very strong commitment to Indian nationalism. He is also an extremely amiable person (as I had discovered when I had the privilege of his company at an honorary degree ceremony at Jadavpur University in Calcutta in 1990). Kalam's philanthropic concerns are very strong, and he has a record of helping in welfare-related causes, such as charitable work for mentally impaired children in India.

Kalam recorded his proud reaction as he watched the Indian nuclear explosions in Pokhran, on the edge of the Thar desert in Rajasthan, in May 1998: 'I heard the earth thundering below our feet and rising ahead of us in terror. It was a beautiful sight.'[1] It is rather remarkable that the admiration for sheer force should be so strong in the reactions of even such a kind-hearted person, but perhaps the power of nationalism played a role here, along with the general fascination that mighty weapons seem to generate. The intensity of Kalam's strong nationalism may be well concealed by the mildness of his manners, but it was evident enough in his statements after the blasts ('for 2,500 years India has never invaded anybody'), no less than his joy at India's achievement ('a triumph of Indian science and technology').

This was, in fact, the second round of nuclear explosions in the same site, in Pokhran; the first was under Indira Gandhi's Prime Ministership in 1974. But at that time the whole event was kept under a shroud of secrecy, partly in line with the government's ambiguity

*Kenzaburo Oe, *Japan, the Ambiguous, and Myself* (Tokyo and New York: Kodansha International, 1995).

†*Postscript*: since this essay was written for the 2000 Pugwash conference, Dr Kalam has been elected as the President of the Republic of India.

about the correctness of the nuclear weaponization of India. While China's nuclearization clearly had a strong influence in the decision of the Gandhi government to develop its own nuclear potential (between 1964 and 1974 China had conducted fifteen nuclear explosions), the official government position was that the 1974 explosion in Pokhran was strictly for 'peaceful purposes', and that India remained committed to doing without nuclear weapons. The first Pokhran tests were thus followed by numerous affirmations of India's rejection of the nuclear path, rather than any explicit savouring of the destructive power of nuclear energy.

It was very different in the summer of 1998 following the events that have come to be called Pokhran-II. By then there was strong support from various quarters. This included, of course, the Bharatiya Janata Party (or the BJP), which had included the development of nuclear weapons in its electoral manifesto, and which led the political coalition that came to office after the February elections in 1998. While some of the previous Indian governments had taken steps to make it easier to follow up the 1974 blast by new ones, they had stopped short of making fresh explosions, but with the new – more intensely nationalist – government the lid was lifted, and the blasts of Pokhran-II occurred within three months of its coming to power. The BJP, which has built up its base in recent years by capturing and to a great extent fanning Hindu nationalism, received in the elections only a modest minority of Hindu votes, and *a fortiori* a minority of total votes in the multi-religious country (India has nearly as many Muslims as Pakistan and many more Muslims than Bangladesh, and also of course Sikhs, Christians, Jains, Parsees and other communities). But even with a minority of parliamentary seats (182 out of 543 elected members), BJP could head an alliance – a fairly *ad hoc* alliance – of many different political factions, varying from strictly regional parties (such as AIDMK, PMK and MDMK of Tamil Nadu, Haryana Lok Dal and Haryana Vikas Party of Haryana, Biju Janata Dal of Orissa, Trinamool Congress of West Bengal) to specific community-based parties (including the Akali Dal, the party of Sikh nationalism), and some breakaway factions of other parties. As the largest group within the coalition, the BJP was the dominant force in the 1998 Indian government (as it was again after the 1999 general elections), which gives it much more authority than a minority party could otherwise expect to get in Indian politics.

The BJP's interest in following up the 1974 blast by further tests and by actually developing nuclear weapons received strong support from an active pro-nuclear lobby, which includes many Indian scientists.[2] The advocacy by scientists and defence experts was quite important in making the idea of a nuclear India at least plausible to many, if not quite fully acceptable yet as a part of a reflective equilibrium of Indian thinking. As Praful Bidwai and Achin Vanaik put it in their well-researched and well-argued book: 'The most ardent advocates of nuclear weapons have constantly sought to invest these weapons with a religious-like authority and importance – to emphasize the awe and wonder rather than the revulsion and horror – to give them an accepted and respectable place in the mass popular culture of our times.'[3]

The Thrill of Power

Kalam's excitement at the power of nuclear explosions was not, of course, unusual as a reaction to the might of weapons. The excitement generated by destructive power, dissociated from any hint of potential genocide, has been a well-observed psychological state in the history of the world. Even the normally unruffled J. Robert Oppenheimer, the principal architect of the world's first nuclear explosion, was moved to quote the two-millennia-old *Bhagavad Gītā* (Oppenheimer knew Sanskrit well enough to get his *Gītā* right) as he watched the atmospheric explosion of the first atom bomb in a United States desert near the village of Oscuro on 16 July 1945: 'the radiance of a thousand suns . . . burst into the sky.'[4]

As was discussed in Essay 1, Oppenheimer went on to quote further from the *Bhagavad Gītā*: 'I am become death, the destroyer of worlds.' That image of death would show its naked and ruthless face next month in Hiroshima and Nagasaki (what Kenzaburo Oe has called 'the most terrifying monster lurking in the darkness of Hiroshima'[5]). As the consequences of nuclearization became clearer to Oppenheimer, he went on to campaign against nuclear arms, and with special fervour against the hydrogen bomb. But in July 1945, in the experimental station in the US desert, 'Jornala del Muerto' (translatable as 'Death Tract'), there was only sanitized abstractness firmly detached from any actual killing.

The thousand suns have now come home to the subcontinent to roost. The five Indian nuclear explosions in Pokhran on 11 and 13 May 1998 were quickly followed by six Pakistani blasts in the Chagai hills the following month. 'The whole mountain turned white', was the Pakistani government's charmed response. The subcontinent was by now caught in an overt nuclear confrontation, masquerading as further empowerment of each country.

These developments have received fairly uniform condemnation abroad, but considerable favour inside India and Pakistan, though we must be careful not to exaggerate the actual extent of domestic support. Pankaj Mishra did have reason enough to conclude, two weeks after the blasts, that 'the nuclear tests have been extremely popular, particularly among the urban middle class'.[6] But that was too soon to see the long-run effects on Indian public opinion. Furthermore, the enthusiasm of the celebrators is more easily pictured on television than are the deep doubts of the sceptics. Indeed, the euphoria that the television pictures captured on the Indian streets immediately following the blasts concentrated on the reaction of those who did celebrate and chose to come out and rejoice. It was accompanied by doubts and reproaches by a great many people who took no part in the festivities, who did not figure in the early television pictures, and whose doubts and opposition found increasingly vocal expression over time. As Amitav Ghosh, the novelist, noted in his extensive review of Indian public reactions to the bomb for the *New Yorker*, 'the tests have divided the country more deeply than ever'.[7]

It is also clear that the main political party that chose to escalate India's nuclear adventure, namely the BJP, did not get any substantial electoral benefit from the Pokhran blasts. In fact quite the contrary, as analyses of local voting since the 1998 blasts tend to show. By the time India went to the polls again, in September 1999, the BJP had learned the lesson sufficiently well to refrain from bragging about the nuclear tests in their campaign with the voters. And yet, as N. Ram (the political commentator and editor of *Frontline*) has cogently argued in his anti-nuclear book *Riding the Nuclear Tiger*, we 'must not make the mistake of assuming that since the Hindu Right has done badly out of Pokhran-II, the issue has been decisively won'.[8]

Indian attitudes towards nuclear weaponization are characterized not only by ambiguity and moral doubts, but also by some uncertainty as to what is involved in making gainful use of these weapons. It may be the case, as several opinion polls have indicated, that public opinion in India has a much smaller inclination, compared with Pakistani public opinion, to assume that nuclear weapons will ever be actually used in a subcontinental war.[9] But since the effectiveness of these weapons depends ultimately on the willingness to use them in some situations, there is an issue of coherence of thought that has to be addressed here. Implicitly or explicitly, an eventuality of actual use has to be among the possible scenarios that must be contemplated, if some benefit is to be obtained from the possession and deployment of nuclear weapons. To hold the belief that nuclear weapons are useful but must never be used lacks cogency and can indeed be seen to be a part of the odd phenomenon that Arundhati Roy (the author of *The God of Small Things*) has called 'the end of imagination'.[10]

As Roy has also brought out with much clarity, the nature and results of an actual all-out nuclear war are almost impossible to imagine in a really informed way. Arundhati Roy describes a likely scenario thus:

> Our cities and forests, our fields and villages will burn for days. Rivers will turn to poison. The air will become fire. The wind will spread the flames. When everything there is to burn has burned and the fires die, smoke will rise and shut out the sun.[11]

It is hard to think that the possibility of such an eventuality can be a part of a wise policy of national self-defence.

Established Nuclear Powers and Subcontinental Grumbles

One of the problems in getting things right arises from a perceived sense of inadequacy, prevalent in India, of any alternative policy that would be entirely satisfactory and would thus help to firm up a rejection of nuclear weapons through the transparent virtues of a resolutely non-nuclear path (as opposed to the horrors of the nuclear route). This is perhaps where the gap in perceptions is strongest between the discontent and disgust with which the subcontinental nuclear adventures are viewed in the West and the ambiguity that exists on this subject within India (not to mention the support of the nuclear route that comes from the government, the BJP and India's pro-nuclear lobby). It is difficult to understand what is going on in the subcontinent without placing it solidly in a global context.

Nuclear strategists in South Asia tend to resent deeply the international condemnation of Indian and Pakistani policies and decisions that does not take note of the nuclear situation in the world as a whole. They are surely justified in this resentment, and also right to question the censoriousness of Western critics of subcontinental nuclear adventures without adequately examining the ethics of their own nuclear policies, including preservation of an established and deeply unequal nuclear hegemony, with very little attempt to achieve global denuclearization. The Defence Minister of India, George Fernandes, told Amitav Ghosh: 'Why should the five nations that have nuclear weapons tell us how to behave and what weapons we should have?' This was matched by the remark of Qazi Hussain Ahmed, the leader of Jamaat-e-Islami (Pakistan's principal religious party), to Ghosh: 'we don't accept that five nations should have nuclear weapons and others shouldn't. We say, "Let the five also disarm."'[12]

The enquiry into the global context is indeed justified, but what we have to examine is whether the placing of the subcontinental substory within the general frame of a bigger global story really changes the assessment that we can reasonably make of what is going on in India and Pakistan. In particular, to argue that their nuclear policies are deeply mistaken does not require us to dismiss the widespread resentment in the subcontinent of the smugness of the dominant global order. These complaints, even if entirely justified and extremely momentous, do not establish the sagacity of a nuclear policy that dramatically increases uncertainties within the subcontinent without achieving anything to make each country more secure. Indeed, Bangladesh is probably now the safest country to live in, in the subcontinent.

Moral Resentment and Prudential Blunder

There are, I think, two distinct issues, which need to be carefully separated. First, the world nuclear order is extremely unbalanced and there are excellent reasons to complain about the military policies of the major powers, particularly the five that have a monopoly over official nuclear status as well as over permanent membership in the Security Council of the United Nations. The second issue concerns the choices that other countries – other than the big five – face, and this has to be properly scrutinized, rather than being hijacked by resentment of the oligopoly of the power to terrorize. The fact that other countries, including India and Pakistan, have grounds enough for grumbling about the nature of the world order, sponsored and supported by the established nuclear powers without any serious commitment to denuclearization, does not give them any reason to pursue a nuclear policy that worsens their own security and adds to the possibility of a dreadful holocaust. Moral resentment cannot justify a prudential blunder.

I have so far not commented on the economic and social costs of nuclearization and the general problem of allocation of resources. That issue is, of course, important, even though it is hard to find out exactly what the costs of the nuclear programmes are. The expenses of this are carefully hidden in both countries. Even though it is perhaps easier to estimate the necessary information in India (given a greater need for disclosure in the Indian polity), the estimates are bound to be quite rough.

Recently, C. Rammanohar Reddy, a distinguished commentator, has estimated that the cost of nuclearization is something around half of one per cent of the gross domestic product per year.[13] This might not sound like much, but it is large enough if we consider the alternative uses of these resources. For example, it has been estimated that the additional costs of providing elementary education for every child with neighbourhood schools at every location in the country would cost roughly the same amount of money.* The proportion of illiteracy

*The so-called PROBE report cites two distinct estimates made by two government committees, which came to roughly the same figure; see *Public Report on Basic Education in India* (Delhi: Oxford University Press, 1999).

in the Indian adult population is still about 40 per cent, and it is about 55 per cent in Pakistan. Furthermore, there are other costs and losses as well, such as the deflection of India's scientific talents to military-related research away from more productive lines of research and also from actual economic production. The prevalence of secretive military activities also restrains open discussions in the parliament and tends to subvert traditions of democracy and free speech.

Despite all this, the principal argument against nuclearization is not ultimately an economic one. It is rather the increased insecurity of human lives that constitutes the biggest penalty of the subcontinental nuclear adventures. That issue needs further scrutiny.

Does Nuclear Deterrence Work?

What of the argument that nuclear deterrence makes war between India and Pakistan less likely? Why would not the allegedly proven ability of nuclear balance, which is supposed to have kept peace in the world, be effective also in the subcontinent? I believe that this question can be answered from four different perspectives.

First, even if it were the case that the nuclearization of India and Pakistan reduces the probability of war between the two, there would be a trade-off here between a lower chance of conventional war against some chance of a nuclear holocaust. No sensible decision-making can concentrate only on the probability of war without taking note of the size of the penalties of war should it occur. Indeed, any significant probability of the scenario captured by Arundhati Roy's description of 'the end of imagination' can hardly fail to outweigh the greater probability, if any, of the comparatively milder penalties of conventional war.

Second, there is nothing to indicate that the likelihood of conventional war is, in fact, reduced by the nuclearization of India and Pakistan. Indeed, hot on the heels of the nuclear blasts, the two countries did undergo a major military confrontation in the Kargil district in Kashmir. The Kargil conflict, which occurred within a year of the nuclear blasts of India and Pakistan, was in fact the first military conflict between the two in nearly thirty years. Many Indian commentators have argued that the confrontation, which was provoked by separatist guerrillas coming across the line of control from Pakistan (in their view, joined by army regulars), was helped by Pakistan's understanding that India would not be able to use its massive superiority in conventional forces to launch a bigger war in retaliation, precisely because it would fear a nuclear holocaust. Whether or not this analysis is right, there is clearly substance in the general reasoning that the enemy's fear of nuclear annihilation can be an argument in favour of military adventurism without expectation of a fuller retaliation from the enemy. Be that as it may, the proof of the pudding is in the eating, and no matter what the explanation, nuclearization evidently has not prevented non-nuclear conflicts between India and Pakistan.

Third, the danger of accidental nuclear war is much greater in the subcontinent than it was in the cold war itself. This is not only because the checks and controls are much looser, but also because the distances involved are so small between India and Pakistan that there is little time for any conversation when a crisis might occur and a first strike were feared. Also, the much discussed hold of fundamentalist militants within the Pakistani military and the absence of democratic control add to the fear of a sudden flashpoint.

Fourth, there is a need also to assess whether the peace that the world enjoyed with nuclear deterrence during the global cold war was, in fact, predictable and causally robust. The argument for the balance of terror has been clear enough for a long time, and was most eloquently put by Winston Churchill in his last speech to the House of Commons on 1 March 1955. His ringing words on this ('safety will be the sturdy child of terror, and survival the twin brother of annihilation') have a mesmerizing effect, but Churchill himself did make exceptions to his rule, when he said that the logic of deterrence 'does not cover the case of lunatics or dictators in the mood of Hitler when he found himself in his final dug-out'.*

Dictators are not unknown in the world (even in the subcontinent), and at least part-lunatics can be found with some frequency in both the countries, judging by what some eloquent commentators seem to be

Winston S. Churchill: His Complete Speeches 1897–1963, ed. Robert Rhodes James (New York: R. R. Bowker, 1974), pp. 8629–30.

able to write on the nuclear issue itself. But perhaps more importantly, we have reason to note that risks have been taken also by people with impeccable credentials on sanity and lucidity. To give just one example (a rather prominent one), in choosing the path of confrontation in what has come to be called the Cuban Missile Crisis, President Kennedy evidently took some significant risks of annihilation on behalf of humanity. Indeed, Theodore C. Sorenson, Special Counsel to President Kennedy, put the facts thus (in a generally admiring passage):

> John Kennedy never lost sight of what either war or surrender would do to the whole human race. His UN Mission was preparing for a negotiated peace and his Joint Chiefs of Staff were preparing for war, and he intended to keep both on rein. . . . He could not afford to be hasty or hesitant, reckless or afraid. The odds that the Soviets would go all the way to war, he later said, seemed to him then 'somewhere between one out of three and even.'*

Well, a chance of annihilation between one-third and one-half is not an easy decision to be taken on behalf of the human race.

I think we have to recognize that the peace of nuclear confrontation in the cold war partly resulted from luck, and may not have been preordained. To take *post hoc* to be *propter hoc* is a luxury that can be quite costly for charting out future policies in the nuclear – or indeed any other – field. We have to take account not only of the fact that circumstances are rather different in the subcontinent compared with what obtained during the nuclear confrontation in the global cold war, but also that the world was actually rather fortunate to escape annihilation even in the cold war itself. And the dangers of extermination did not come only from lunatics or dictators.

So, to conclude this section, the nuclearization of the subcontinental confrontations need not reduce the risk of war (either in theory or in practice), and it escalates the penalty of war in a dramatic way. The unjust nature of the world military balance does not change this crucial prudential recognition.

*Theodore C. Sorenson, *Kennedy* (London: Hodder and Stoughton, 1965), p. 705. The 'Kennedy Tapes', too, bring out how close the world came to a nuclear annihilation.

Were the Indian Government's Goals Well Served?

I come now to a question of rather limited interest, but which is asked often enough, addressed particularly to India. Even if it is accepted that the subcontinent is less secure as a result of the tit-for-tat nuclear tests, it could be the case that India's own self-interest has been well served by the BJP-led government's nuclear policy. India has reason to grumble, it is argued, at not being taken as seriously as one of the largest countries in the world should be. There is unhappiness also at the attempt by some countries, certainly the United States in the past, to achieve some kind of a 'balance' between India and Pakistan, whereas India is nearly seven times as large as Pakistan and must not be taken to be at par with it. Rather, the comparison should be with China, and for this – along with other causes, such as getting India a permanent seat in the Security Council – India's nuclear accomplishment could be expected to make a contribution. The subcontinent may be less secure as a result of the nuclear developments, but, it is argued, India did get some benefit. How sound is this line of argument?

I have some difficulty in pursuing this exercise. Even though I am a citizen of India, I don't really think I can legitimately enquire only into the advantages that India alone may have received from a certain policy, excluding the interests of others who were also affected. However, it is possible to scrutinize the effects of a certain policy in terms of the given goals of the Indian government (including strategic advantages over Pakistan as well as enhancement of India's international standing), and ask the rather coldly 'scientific' question whether those goals have been well served by India's recent nuclear policy. We do not have to endorse these goals to examine whether they have actually been better promoted.

There are good reasons to doubt that these goals have indeed been better served by the sequence of events at Pokhran and Chagai. First, India had – and has – massive superiority over Pakistan in conventional military strength. That strategic advantage has become far less significant as a result of the new nuclear balance. Indeed, since Pakistan has explicitly refused to accept a 'no first use' agreement,

India's ability to count on conventional superiority is now, to a great extent, less effective (along with increasing the level of insecurity in both countries). In the Kargil confrontation, India could not even make use of its ability to cross into the Pakistani-administered Kashmir to attack the intruders from the rear, which military tacticians seem to think would have made much more sense than trying to encounter the intruders by climbing steeply up a high mountain from the Indian side to battle the occupants at the top. This not only made the Indian response less effective and rapid, it also led to more loss of Indian soldiers (1,300 lives, according to the government of India's estimate and 1,750 according to Pakistan's estimate) and added greatly to the expenses of the war conducted from an unfavoured position ($2.5 billion in direct expenses).[14] With the danger of a nuclear outburst, the Indian government's decision not to countercross the line of control in retaliation was clearly right, but it had no real option in this respect, given the strategic bind which it had itself helped to create.

Second, the fact that India can make nuclear weapons was well established before the present tit-for-tat nuclear tests were conducted. Pokhran-I in 1974 had already established the point, even though Indian official statements tried to play down the military uses of that blast a quarter of a century ago. After the 1998 tests, India's and Pakistan's positions seem to be much more even, at least in international public perception. As it happens, Pakistan was quite modest in its response. I remember thinking in the middle of May 1998, following the Indian tests, that surely Pakistan would now blast a larger number of bombs than India's five. I was agreeably impressed by Pakistan's moderation in blasting only six, which is the smallest whole number larger than five. The government of India may deeply dislike any perception of parity with Pakistan, but did its best, in effect, to alter a favourable situation of acknowledged asymmetry into one of perceived parity.

Third, aside from perceptions, in terms of the scientific requirement for testing, Pakistan clearly had a greater case for testing, never having conducted a nuclear test before 1998. This contrasted with India's experience of Pokhran-I in 1974. Also, with a much smaller community of nuclear scientists and a less extensive development of the possibilities of computerized simulation, the scientific need for an actual test may have been much greater in Pakistan than in India. While Pakistan was concerned about the condemnation of the world community should it have tested on its own, the Indian blasts in May 1998 created a situation in which Pakistan could go in that direction without being blamed for starting any nuclear adventure. Eric Arnett puts the issue thus:

> In contrast to its Indian counterparts, Pakistan's political elite is less abashed about the need for nuclear deterrence. Military fears that the Pakistani nuclear capability was not taken seriously in India combined with a feeling of growing military inferiority after being abandoned by the USA after the cold war to create an imperative to test that was resisted before May 1998 only because of the threat of sanctions. The Indian tests created a situation in which the Pakistani leadership saw an even greater need to test and a possible opening to justify the test as a response that was both politically and strategically understandable.[15]

The thesis, often articulated by India's pro-nuclear lobby, that India was in a greater danger of a first strike from Pakistan before the summer of 1998 lacks scientific as well as political credibility.

Fourth, there was not much success in getting recognition for India as being in the same league as China, or for its grumble that inadequate attention is internationally paid to the dangers India is supposed to face from China. Spokesmen of the Indian government were vocal on these issues. A week before the Pokhran tests in 1998, Indian Defence Minister George Fernandes said in a much quoted television interview: 'China is potential threat number one. . . . The potential threat from China is greater than that from Pakistan.'[16] In between the tests on 11 and 13 May, the Indian Prime Minister Vajpayee wrote to President Clinton to point to China as being related to the motivation for the tests. This letter, published in the *New York Times* (after being leaked) on 13 May, did not name China, but referred to it in very explicit terms:

> We have an overt nuclear weapon state on our borders, a state which committed armed aggression against India in 1962. Although our relations with that country have improved in the last decade or so, an atmosphere of

distrust persists mainly due to the unresolved border problem. To add to the distrust that country has materially helped another neighbour of ours to become a covert nuclear weapons state.[17]

However, as a result of the tit-for-tat nuclear tests by India and Pakistan, China could stand well above India's little grumbles, gently admonishing it for its criticism of China, and placing itself in the position of being a subcontinental peace-maker. When President Clinton visited China in June 1998, China and the United States released a joint statement declaring that the two countries would cooperate in non-proliferation efforts in the subcontinent.

Mark Frazier's assessment of the gap between the government of India's attempts and its achievement in this field captures the essence of this policy failure:

> Had it been India's intention to alert the world to its security concerns about China as a dangerous rising power, the tests managed to do just the opposite – they gave the Chinese officials the opportunity to present China as a cooperative member of the international community seeking to curb nuclear weapons proliferation. Far from looking like a revisionist state, China played the role of a status quo power, and a rather assertive one at that.[18]

Fifth, the blasts did not advance the cause of India's putative elevation to a permanent membership of the Security Council. If a country could blast its way into the Security Council, this would give an incentive to other countries to do the same. Furthermore, the new parity established between India and Pakistan after Pokhran-II and the Chagai hills also militates against the plausibility of that route to permanency in the Security Council, and this too could have been well predicted. I personally don't see why it is so important for India to be permanently on the Security Council (it may be in the interest of others for this to happen, given India's size and growing economic strength, but that is a different issue altogether). However, for the government of India, which clearly attached importance to this possibility, it would surely have been wiser to emphasize its restraint in not developing nuclear weapons, despite its proven ability to do so since 1974, and also use the pre-1998 asymmetry with Pakistan, in contrast with the symmetry that developed – following the Indian government's own initiative – after Pokhran-II and Chagai.

One of the interesting sidelights that emerge from a scrutiny of Indian official perceptions is the extent to which the government underestimated India's importance as a major country, a democratic polity, a rich multi-religious civilization, with a well-established tradition in science and technology (including the cutting edge of information technology), and with a fast-growing economy that could grow, with a little effort, even faster. The overestimation of the persuasive power of the bomb went with an underestimation of the political, cultural, scientific and economic strengths of the country. There might have been pleasure in official circles at the success of President Clinton's visit to India and the asymmetrically favoured treatment it got in that visit vis-à-vis Pakistan, but the tendency to attribute that asymmetry to Indian nuclear adventure, rather than to India's large size, democratic politics and its growing economy and technology, is difficult to understand.

On Separating the Issues

To conclude, it is extremely important to distinguish two distinct problems, both of which have a bearing on subcontinental nuclear policies. First, the world order on weapons needs a change and in particular requires an effective and rapid disarmament, particularly in nuclear arsenals. Second, the nuclear adventures of India and Pakistan cannot be justified on the ground of the unjustness of the world order, since the people whose lives are made insecure as a result of these adventures are primarily the residents of the subcontinent themselves. Resenting the obtuseness of others is not a good ground for shooting oneself in the foot.

This does not, of course, imply that India or Pakistan has reason to feel happy about the international balance of power that the world establishment seems keen on maintaining, with or without further developments, such as an attempted 'nuclear shield' for the United States. Indeed, it must also be said that there is an inadequate appreciation in the West of the extent to which the role of the big five arouses suspicion and resentment in the Third World, including the subcontinent. This applies not only to the monopoly over nuclear armament, but also, on the other side, to the 'pushing' of conventional, non-nuclear armaments in the world market for weapons.

For example, as the *Human Development Report 1994*, prepared under the leadership of that visionary Pakistani economist Mahbub ul Haq, pointed out, not only were the top five arms-exporting countries in the world precisely the five permanent members of the Security Council of the United Nations, but they were also, together, responsible for 86 per cent of all the conventional weapons exported during 1988–92.[19] Not surprisingly, the Security Council has not been able to take any serious initiative that would really restrain the merchants of death. It is not hard to understand the scepticism in India and Pakistan – and elsewhere – about the responsibility and leadership of the established nuclear powers.

As far as India is concerned, the two policies – of nuclear abstinence and demanding a change of world order – can be pursued simultaneously. Nuclear restraint strengthens rather than weakens India's voice. To demand that the Comprehensive Test Ban Treaty be redefined to include a dated programme of denuclearization may well be among the discussable alternatives. But making nuclear bombs, not to mention deploying them, and spending scarce resources on missiles and what is euphemistically called 'delivery', can hardly be seen as a sensible policy. The belief that subcontinental nuclearization would somehow help to bring about world nuclear disarmament is a wild dream that can only precede a nightmare. The moral folly in these policies is substantial, but what is also clear and decisive is the prudential mistake that has been committed. The moral and the prudential are, in fact, rather close in a world of interrelated interactions, for reasons that Rabindranath Tagore discussed around a hundred years ago.

Finally, on a more specific point, no country has as much stake as India in having a prosperous and civilian democracy in Pakistan. Even though the Nawaz Sharif government was clearly corrupt in many ways, India's interests are not well served by the undermining of civilian rule in Pakistan, to be replaced by activist military leaders. Also, the encouragement of cross-border terrorism, which India accuses Pakistan of, is likely to be dampened rather than encouraged by Pakistan's economic prosperity and civilian politics. It is particularly important in this context to point to the dangerousness of the argument, often heard in India, that the burden of public expenditure would be more unbearable for Pakistan, given its smaller size and relatively stagnant economy, than it is for India. This may well be the case, but the penalty that could visit India from an impoverished and desperate Pakistan, in the present situation of massive insecurity, could be quite catastrophic. Strengthening of Pakistan's stability and enhancement of its well-being has prudential importance for India, in addition to its obvious ethical significance. That central connection – between the moral and the prudential – must be urgently grasped.

PART FOUR

Reason and Identity

13

The Reach of Reason*

W. B. Yeats wrote on the margin of his copy of *The Genealogy of Morals*, 'But why does Nietzsche think the night has no stars, nothing but bats and owls and the insane moon?' Nietzsche outlined his scepticism of humanity and presented his chilling vision of the future just before the beginning of the last century – he died in 1900. The events of the century that followed, including world wars, holocausts, genocides and other atrocities that occurred with systematic brutality, give us reason enough to worry whether Nietzsche's sceptical view of humanity may not have been right.

Instinct and Humanity

Jonathan Glover, an Oxford philosopher, argues in his recent and enormously interesting 'moral history of the twentieth century' that we must not only reflect on what has happened in the last century, but also 'need to look hard and clearly at some monsters inside us' and to consider ways and means of 'caging and taming them'.[1] The end of a century – and of a millennium – is certainly a good moment to engage in critical examinations of this kind. Indeed, as the first millennium of the Islamic Hijri calendar came to an end in 1591–2 (a thousand lunar years – shorter than solar years – after Mohammed's epic journey from Mecca to Medina in 622 CE), Akbar, the Moghal emperor of India, engaged in just such a far-reaching scrutiny. He paid particular

*This essay was previously published in the *New York Review of Books*, 20 July 2000. For helpful suggestions, I am most grateful to Sissela Bok, Mozaffar Qizilbash, Emma Rothschild and Thomas Scanlon.

attention to relations among religious communities and to the need for peaceful coexistence in the already multicultural India.

Taking note of the denominational diversity of Indians (including Hindus, Muslims, Christians, Jains, Sikhs, Parsees, Jews and others), he laid the foundations of the secularism and religious neutrality of the state which he insisted must ensure that 'no man should be interfered with on account of religion, and anyone is to be allowed to go over to a religion that pleases him'.[2] Akbar's thesis that 'the pursuit of reason' rather than 'reliance on tradition' is the way to address difficult social problems is a view that has become all the more important for the world today.[3]

It is striking how little critical assessment of the experience of the millennium took place during its recent worldwide celebration.[4] As the century and the second Gregorian millennium came to an end, the memory of the dreadful events that Glover describes with devastating effect did not seem to stir people much; nor was there much detectable interest in the challenging questions that Glover asks. The lights of celebratory glory not only drowned the stars but also the bats and the owls and the insane moon.

Nietzsche's scepticism about ethical reasoning and his anticipation of difficulties to come were combined with an ambiguous approval of the annihilation of moral authority – 'the most terrible, the most questionable, and perhaps also the most hopeful of all spectacles', he wrote. Glover argues that we must respond to 'Nietzsche's challenge': 'The problem is how to accept [Nietzsche's] scepticism about a religious authority for morality while escaping from his appalling conclusions.' This issue is related to Akbar's thesis that morality can be guided by critical reasoning; in making moral judgements, Akbar argued, we must not make reasoning subordinate to religious command, nor rely on 'the marshy land of tradition'.

Interest in such questions was particularly strong during the European Enlightenment, which was optimistic about the reach of reason. The Enlightenment perspective has come under severe attack in recent years, and Glover adds his own powerful voice to this reproach.[5] He argues that 'the Enlightenment view of human psychology' has increasingly looked 'thin and mechanical', and 'Enlightenment hopes of social progress through the spread of humanitarianism and the scientific outlook' now appear rather 'naive'. Following an increasingly common tendency, Glover goes on to attribute many of the horrors of the twentieth century to the influence of the Enlightenment. He links modern tyranny with that perspective, noting not only that 'Stalin and his heirs were in thrall to the Enlightenment', but also that Pol Pot 'was indirectly influenced by it'. But since Glover does not wish to seek solutions through the authority of religion or of tradition (in this respect, he notes, 'we cannot escape the Enlightenment'), he concentrates his fire on other targets, such as reliance on strongly held beliefs. 'The crudity of Stalinism', he argues, 'had its origins in the beliefs [Stalin held].' This claim is plausible enough, as is Glover's reference to 'the role of ideology in Stalinism'.

However, why is this a criticism of the Enlightenment perspective? It seems a little unfair to put the blame for the blind beliefs of dictators on the Enlightenment tradition, since so many writers associated with the Enlightenment insisted that reasoned choice was superior to any reliance on blind belief. Surely 'the crudity of Stalinism' could be opposed, as it indeed was, through a reasoned demonstration of the huge gap between promise and practice, and by showing its brutality – a brutality that the authorities had to conceal through strict censorship. Indeed, one of the main points in favour of reason is that it helps us to transcend ideology and blind belief. Reason was not, in fact, Pol Pot's main ally. He and his gang of followers were driven by frenzy and badly reasoned belief and did not allow any questioning or scrutiny of their actions. Given the cogency of Glover's other arguments, there is something deeply puzzling about his willingness to join the fashionable chorus of attacks on the Enlightenment.

There is, however, an important question that emerges from Glover's discussion on this subject, too. Are we not better advised to rely on our instincts when we are not able to reason clearly because of some hard-to-remove impediments to our critical thinking? The question is well illustrated by Glover's remarks on a less harsh figure than Stalin or Pol Pot, namely Nikolai Bukharin, who, Glover notes, was not at all inclined to 'turn into wood'. Glover writes that Bukharin 'had to live with the tension between his human instincts and the hard beliefs he defended'. Bukharin was repelled by the actions of the regime, but the surrounding political climate, combined with his own formulaic thinking, prevented him from reasoning clearly enough about them. This, Glover writes, left him dithering between his 'human instincts' and his 'hard beliefs', with no 'clear victory for either side'. Glover is attracted by the idea – plausible enough in this case – that Bukharin would have done better to be guided by his instincts. Whether or not we see this as the basis of a general rule, Glover here poses an interesting argument about the need to take account of the situation in which reasoning takes place – and that argument deserves attention (no matter what we make of the alleged criminal tendencies of the Enlightenment).

Reason and Enlightenment

The possibility of reasoning is a strong source of hope and confidence in a world darkened by horrible deeds. It is easy to understand why this is so. Even when we find something immediately upsetting, or annoying, we are free to question that response and ask whether it is an appropriate reaction and whether we should really be guided by it. We can reason about the right way of perceiving and treating other people, other cultures, other claims, and examine different grounds for respect and tolerance. We can also reason about our own mistakes and try to learn not to repeat them. For example, the Japanese novelist and visionary social theorist Kenzaburo Oe argues powerfully that the Japanese nation, aided by an understanding of its own 'history of territorial invasion', has reason enough to remain committed to 'the idea of democracy and the determination never to wage a war again'.[6]

Intellectual enquiry, moreover, is needed to identify actions and policies that are not evidently injurious but which have that effect. For example, famines can remain unchecked on the mistaken presumption that they cannot be averted through immediate public policy. Starvation in famines results primarily from a severe reduction in the food-buying ability of a section of the population that has become destitute through unemployment, diminished markets, disruption of agricultural activities, or other economic calamities. The economic victims are forced into starvation whether or not there is also a diminution of the total supply of food. The unequal deprivation of such people can be immediately countered by providing employment at relatively low wages through emergency public programmes, which can help them to share the national food supply with others in the community.

Famine, like the devil, takes the hindmost (rarely more than 5 per cent of the population is affected – almost never more than 10 per cent), and reducing the relative deprivation of destitute people by augmenting their incomes can rapidly and dramatically reduce their absolute deprivation in the amount of food obtained by them. By encouraging critical public discussion of these issues, democracy and a free press can be extremely important in preventing famine. Otherwise, unreasoned pessimism, masquerading as composure based on realism and common sense, can serve to 'justify' disastrous inaction and an abdication of public responsibility.*

Similarly, environmental deterioration frequently arises not from any desire to damage the world but from thoughtlessness and lack of reasoned action – separate or joint – and this can end up producing dreadful results.[7] To prevent catastrophes caused by human negligence or obtuseness or callous obduracy, we need practical reason as well as sympathy and commitment.

Attacks on ethics based on reason have come recently from several different directions. Apart from the claim that 'the Enlightenment view of human psychology' neglects many human responses (as Glover argues), we also hear the claim that to rely primarily on reasoning in the ethics of human behaviour involves a neglect of culture-specific influences on values and conduct. People's thoughts and identities are fairly comprehensively determined, according to this claim, by the tradition and culture in which they are reared rather than by analytical reasoning, which is sometimes seen as a 'Western' practice. We must examine whether the reach of reasoning is really

*I have tried to discuss the causes of famines and the policy requirements for famine prevention in *Poverty and Famines: An Essay on Entitlement and Deprivation* (Oxford: Oxford University Press, 1981) and, jointly with Jean Drèze, in *Hunger and Public Action* (Oxford: Clarendon Press, 1989). Famine prevention requires diverse policies, among which income creation is immediately and crucially important (for example, through emergency employment in public works programmes); but, especially for the long term, they also include expansion of production in general and food production in particular.

compromised either by the undoubtedly powerful effects of human psychology, or by the pervasive influence of cultural diversity. Our hopes for the future and the ways and means of living in a decent world may greatly depend on how we assess these criticisms.

Jonathan Glover's arguments for the need for a 'new human psychology' take account of the ways that politics and psychology affect each other. People can indeed be expected to resist political barbarism if they instinctively react against atrocities. We have to be able to react spontaneously and resist inhumanity whenever it occurs. If this is to happen, the individual and social opportunities for developing and exercising moral imagination have to be expanded. We do have moral resources, including, as Glover writes, 'our sense of our own moral identity'. But to 'function as a restraint against atrocity, the sense of moral identity most of all needs to be rooted in the human responses'. Two responses, Glover argues, are particularly important: 'the tendency to respond to people with certain kinds of respect' and 'sympathy: caring about the miseries and the happiness of others'. Hope for the future lies in cultivating such responses, and this line of reasoning leads Glover to conclude: 'It is to psychology that we should now turn.'

Indeed, the importance of instinctive psychology and sympathetic response should be adequately recognized, and Glover is also right in believing that our hope for the future must, to a considerable extent, depend on the sympathy and respect with which we respond to things happening to others. For Glover, it is therefore critically important to replace 'the thin, mechanical psychology of the Enlightenment with something more complex, something closer to reality'.

While applauding the constructive features of this approach, we must also ask whether Glover is being quite fair to the Enlightenment (even without Pol Pot and assorted criminals blocking our vision). Glover does not refer to Adam Smith, but the author of *The Theory of Moral Sentiments* would, in fact, have greatly welcomed Glover's diagnosis of the central importance of emotions and psychological response. While it has become fashionable in modern economics to attribute to Smith a view of human behaviour that is devoid of all concerns except cool calculation of a narrowly defined personal interest, those who read his basic works know that this was not his position.[8]

Indeed, many issues in human psychology that Glover discusses (as part of the demands of 'humanity') were discussed by Smith as well. But Smith – no less than Diderot or Condorcet or Kant – was very much an 'Enlightenment author', whose arguments and analyses deeply influenced the thinking of his contemporaries.[9]

Smith may not have gone as far as another leader of the Enlightenment, David Hume, in asserting that 'reason and sentiment concur in almost all moral determinations and conclusions',[10] but both saw reasoning and feeling as deeply interrelated activities. In fact, Hume (to whom Glover also does not refer) is often seen as having precisely the opposite bias by giving precedence to passion over reason. Indeed, as Thomas Nagel puts it in his strongly argued defence of reason,

> Hume famously believed that because a 'passion' immune to rational assessment must underlie every motive, there can be no such thing as specifically practical reason, nor specifically moral reason either.[11]

The crucial issue is not whether sentiments and attitudes are seen as important (they were clearly so recognized by most of the writers whom we tend to think of as part of the Enlightenment), but whether – and to what extent – these sentiments and attitudes can be influenced and cultivated through reasoning.[12] Adam Smith argued that our 'first perceptions' of right and wrong 'cannot be the object of reason, but of immediate sense and feeling'. But even these instinctive reactions to particular conduct must, he argued, rely – if only implicitly – on our reasoned understanding of causal connections between conduct and consequences in 'a vast variety of instances'. Furthermore, our first perceptions may also change in response to critical examination, for example on the basis of empirical investigation that may show that a certain 'object is the means of obtaining some other'.[13]

Two pillars of Enlightenment thinking are sometimes wrongly merged and jointly criticized: the power of reasoning, and the perfectibility of human nature. Though closely linked in the writings of many Enlightenment authors, they are, in fact, quite distinct claims, and undermining one does not disestablish the other. For example, it might be argued that perfectibility is possible, but not primarily through reasoning. Or, alternatively, it can be the case that in so far as anything works, reasoning does, and yet there may be no hope of getting anywhere near what perfectibility demands. Glover, who gives a richly characterized account of human nature, does not argue for human perfectibility; but his own constructive hopes clearly draw on reasoning as an influence on psychology through 'the social and personal cultivation of the moral imagination'. Glover has more in common with at least some parts of the Enlightenment literature – Adam Smith in particular – than would be guessed from his stinging criticisms of the Enlightenment.

Cultural Contentions

What of the sceptical view that the scope of reasoning is limited by cultural differences? Two particular difficulties – related but separate – have been emphasized recently. There is, first, the view that reliance on reasoning and rationality is a particularly 'Western' way of approaching social issues. Members of non-Western civilizations do not, the argument runs, share some of the values, including liberty or tolerance, that are central to Western society and are the foundations of ideas of justice as developed by Western philosophers from Immanuel Kant to John Rawls. That centrality is not in dispute; indeed the long-awaited publication of Rawls's collected papers allows us to see, in a wonderfully integrated way, just how significant and pivotal 'the principles of toleration and liberty of conscience' are in the ethical and political analyses of the foremost moral philosopher of our own time.* Since it has been claimed that many non-Western societies have values that place little emphasis on liberty or tolerance (the recently championed 'Asian values' have been so described), this issue has to be addressed. Values such as tolerance, liberty and reciprocal respect have been described as 'culture-specific' and basically confined to Western civilization. I shall call this the claim of 'cultural boundary'.

*John Rawls, *Collected Papers*, ed. Samuel Freeman (Cambridge, Mass.: Harvard University Press, 1999).

The second difficulty concerns the possibility that people reared in different cultures may systematically lack basic sympathy and respect for one another. They may not even be able to understand one another, and could not possibly reason together. This could be called the claim of 'cultural disharmony'. Since atrocities and genocide are typically imposed by members of one community on members of another, the significance of understanding among communities can hardly be overstated. And yet such understanding might be difficult to achieve if cultures are fundamentally different from one another and are prone to conflict. Can Serbs and Albanians overcome their 'cultural animosities'? Can Hutus and Tutsis, or Hindus and Muslims, or Israeli Jews and Arabs? Even to ask these pessimistic questions may appear to be sceptical of the nature of humanity and the reach of human understanding; but we cannot ignore such doubts, since recent writings on cultural specificity (whether in the self-proclaimed 'realism' of the popular press or in the academic criticism of the folly of 'universalism') have given them such serious standing.

The issue of cultural disharmony is very much alive in many cultural and political investigations, which often sound as if they are reports from battle fronts, written by war correspondents with divergent loyalties: we hear of the 'clash of civilizations', the need to 'fight' Western cultural imperialism, the irresistible victory of 'Asian values', the challenge to Western civilization posed by the militancy of other cultures, and so on. The global confrontations have their reflections within the national frontiers as well, since most societies now have diverse cultures, which can appear to some to be very threatening. 'The preservation of the United States and the West requires', Samuel Huntington argues, 'the renewal of Western identity.'[14]

Walls in Theory

The subject of 'the reach of reason' is related to another theme, which has been important in the anthropological literature. I refer to what Clifford Geertz has called 'culture war', well illustrated by the much-discussed differences over the interpretation of Captain Cook's sad death in 1779 at the hands of club-wielding and knife-brandishing

Hawaiians.[15] In his article, Geertz contrasts the theories of two leading anthropologists: Marshall Sahlins, he writes, is 'a thoroughgoing advocate of the view that there are distinct cultures, each with a "total cultural system of human action", and they are to be understood along structuralist lines'. The other anthropologist, Gananath Obeyesekere, is 'a thoroughgoing advocate of the view that people's actions and beliefs have particular, practical functions in their lives and that those functions and beliefs should be understood along psychological lines'.

Whatever view we find persuasive, however, the question still should be asked whether the people involved must remain inescapably confined to their traditional modes of thought and behaviour (as cultural determinists argue). Neither Sahlins's nor Obeyesekere's approach rules out communication between cultures, even though this may be a more arduous task if we follow Sahlins's interpretation. But we have to ask what kind of reasoning the members of each culture can use to arrive at better understanding and perhaps even sympathy and respect. Indeed, this is one of the questions Glover poses when he advocates moral imagination as a solution to the brutality and ruthlessness with which groups treat one another. Moral imagination, he hopes, can be cultivated through mutual respect, tolerance and sympathy.

The central issue here is not how dissimilar distinct societies may be from one another, but what ability and opportunity the members of one society have – or can develop – to appreciate and understand how others function. This may not, of course, be an immediate way of resolving such conflicts. The killers of Captain Cook could not instantly revise their culture-bound view of him, nor could Cook acquire at once the comprehension or acumen needed to hold his pistol rather than fire it. Rather, the hope is that the reasoned cultivation of understanding and knowledge would eventually overcome such impulsive action.

The question that has to be faced here is whether such exercises of reasoning may require values that are not available in some cultures. This is where the 'cultural boundary' becomes a central issue. There have, for example, been frequent declarations that non-Western civilizations typically lack a tradition of analytical and sceptical reasoning, and are thus distant from what is sometimes called 'Western rationality'. Similar comments have been made about 'Western liberalism', 'Western ideas of right and justice' and generally about 'Western values'. Indeed, there are many supporters of the claim (articulated by Gertrude Himmelfarb with admirable explicitness) that ideas of 'justice', 'right', 'reason' and 'love of humanity' are 'predominantly, perhaps even uniquely, Western values'.[16]

This and similar beliefs figure implicitly in many discussions, even when the exponents shy away from stating them with such clarity. If the reasoning and values that can help in the cultivation of imagination, respect and sympathy needed for better understanding and appreciation of other people and other societies are fundamentally 'Western', then there would indeed be ground enough for pessimism. But are they?

It is, in fact, very difficult to investigate such questions without seeing the dominance of contemporary Western culture over our perceptions and readings. The force of that dominance is well illustrated by the recent millennial celebrations. The entire globe was transfixed by the end of the Gregorian millennium as if that were the only authentic calendar in the world, even though there are many flourishing calendars in the non-Western world (in China, India, Iran, Egypt and elsewhere) that are considerably older than the Gregorian calendar.* It is, of course, extremely useful for the technical, commercial and even cultural interrelations in the world that we can share a common calendar. But if that visible dominance reflects a tacit assumption that the Gregorian is the only 'internationally usable' calendar, then that dominance becomes the source of a significant misunderstanding, since several of the other calendars could be used in much the same way if they were jointly adopted in the way the Gregorian has been.

Western dominance has similar effects also on the understanding of other aspects of non-Western civilizations. Consider, for example, the idea of 'individual liberty', which is often seen as an integral part of 'Western liberalism'. Modern Europe and America, including the European Enlightenment, have certainly had a decisive part in the

*The different Indian calendars are discussed (both on their own and as ways of interpreting India's history and traditions) in my essay 'India through Its Calendars', *Little Magazine*, 1 (May 2000), Essay 15 below.

evolution of the concept of liberty and the many forms it has taken. These ideas have disseminated from one country to another within the West and also to countries elsewhere, in ways that are somewhat similar to the spread of industrial organization and modern technology. To see libertarian ideas as 'Western' in this limited and proximate sense does not, of course, threaten their being adopted in other regions. For example, to recognize that the form of Indian democracy is based on the British model does not undermine it in any way. In contrast, to take the view that there is something quintessentially 'Western' about these ideas and values, related specifically to the history of Europe, can have a dampening effect on their use elsewhere.

But is the historical claim correct? Is it indeed true (as claimed, for example, by Samuel Huntington) that 'the West was the West long before it was modern'?[17] The evidence for such claims is far from clear. When civilizations are categorized today, individual liberty is often used as a classificatory device and is seen as a part of the ancient heritage of the Western world, not to be found elsewhere. It is, of course, easy to find the advocacy of particular aspects of individual liberty in Western classical writings. For example, freedom and tolerance both get support from Aristotle (even though only for free men – not women and slaves). However, we can find championing of tolerance and freedom in non-Western authors as well. A good example is the emperor Ashoka in India, who during the third century BCE covered the country with inscriptions on stone tablets about good behaviour and wise governance, including a demand for basic freedoms for all – indeed, he did not exclude women and slaves as Aristotle did; he even insisted that these rights must be enjoyed also by 'the forest people' living in pre-agricultural communities distant from Indian cities.[18] Ashoka's championing of tolerance and freedom may not be at all well known in the contemporary world, but that is not dissimilar to the global unfamiliarity with calendars other than the Gregorian.

There are, to be sure, other Indian classical authors who emphasized discipline and order rather than tolerance and liberty, for example Kauṭilya in the fourth century BCE (in his book *Arthaśāstra* – translatable as 'Economics'). But Western classical writers such as Plato and St Augustine also gave priority to social discipline. In view of the diversity within each country, it may be sensible, when it comes to liberty and tolerance, to classify Aristotle and Ashoka on one side, and, on the other, Plato, Augustine and Kauṭilya. Such classifications based on the substance of ideas are, of course, radically different from those based on culture or region.

Even when beliefs and attitudes that are seen as 'Western' are largely a reflection of present-day circumstances in Europe and North America, there is a tendency – often implicit – to interpret them as age-old features of the 'Western tradition' or of 'Western civilization'. One consequence of Western dominance of the world today is that other cultures and traditions are often identified and defined by their contrasts with contemporary Western culture.

Different cultures are thus interpreted in ways that reinforce the political conviction that Western civilization is somehow the main, perhaps the only, source of rationalistic and liberal ideas – among them analytical scrutiny, open debate, political tolerance and agreement to differ. The West is seen, in effect, as having exclusive access to the values that lie at the foundation of rationality and reasoning, science and evidence, liberty and tolerance, and of course rights and justice.

Once established, this view of the West, seen in confrontation with the rest, tends to vindicate itself. Since each civilization contains diverse elements, a non-Western civilization can then be characterized by referring to those tendencies that are most distant from the identified 'Western' traditions and values. These selected elements are then taken to be more 'authentic' or more 'genuinely indigenous' than the elements that are relatively similar to what can be found also in the West.

For example, Indian religious literature such as the *Bhagavad Gītā* or the Tantric texts, which are identified as differing from secular writings seen as 'Western', elicits much greater interest in the West than do other Indian writing, including India's long history of heterodoxy. Sanskrit and Pāli have a larger atheistic and agnostic literature than exists in any other classical tradition. There is a similar neglect of Indian writing on non-religious subjects, from mathematics, epistemology and natural science to economics and linguistics. (The exception, I suppose, is the *Kāmasūtra*, in which Western readers have managed to cultivate an interest.) Through selective emphases that point up differences with the West, other civilizations can, in this way, be redefined in alien terms, which can be exotic and charming, or else bizarre and terrifying, or simply strange and engaging. When identity is thus 'defined by contrast', divergence with the West becomes central.

Take, for example, the case of 'Asian values', often contrasted with 'Western values'. Since many different value systems and many different styles of reasoning have flourished in Asia, it is possible to characterize 'Asian values' in many different ways, each with plentiful citations. By selective citations of Confucius, and by selective neglect of many other Asian authors, the view that Asian values emphasize discipline and order – rather than liberty and autonomy, as in the West – has been given apparent plausibility. This contrast, as I have discussed elsewhere,[19] is hard to sustain when one actually compares the respective literatures.

There is an interesting dialectic here. By concentrating on the authoritarian parts of Asia's multitude of traditions, many Western writers have been able to construct a seemingly neat picture of an Asian contrast with 'Western liberalism'. In response, rather than dispute the West's unique claim to liberal values, some Asians have responded with a pride in distance: 'Yes, we are very different – and a good thing too!' The practice of conferring identity by contrast has thus flourished, driven both by Western attempts to establish its exclusiveness and also by the Asian counter-attempt to establish its own contrary exclusiveness. Showing how other parts of the world differ from the West can be very effective and can shore up artificial distinctions. We may be left wondering why Gautama Buddha, or Laozi or Ashoka – or Gandhi or Sun Yat-sen – was not really an Asian.

Similarly, under this identity by contrast, the Western detractors of Islam as well as the new champions of Islamic heritage have little to say about Islam's tradition of tolerance, which has been at least as important historically as its record of intolerance. We are left wondering what could have led Maimonides, as he fled the persecution of Jews in Spain in the twelfth century, to seek shelter in Emperor Saladin's Egypt. And why did Maimonides, in fact, get support as well as an honoured position at the court of the Muslim emperor who fought valiantly for Islam in the Crusades?

Despite recent outbursts of intolerance in Africa, we can recall that in 1526, in an exchange of discourtesies between the kings of Congo and Portugal, it was the former not the latter, who argued that slavery was intolerable. King Nzinga Mbemba wrote to the Portuguese king that the slave trade must stop, 'because it is our will that in these kingdoms of Kongo there should not be any trade in slaves nor any market for slaves'.[20]

Of course, it is not being claimed here that all the different ideas relevant to the use of reasoning for social harmony and humanity have flourished equally in all civilizations of the world. That would not only be untrue; it would also be a stupid claim of mechanical uniformity. But once we recognize that many ideas that are taken to be quintessentially Western have also flourished in other civilizations, we also see that these ideas are not as culture-specific as is sometimes claimed. We need not begin with pessimism, at least on this ground, about the prospects of reasoned humanism in the world.

Tolerance and Reason

It is worth recalling that in Akbar's pronouncements of four hundred years ago on the need for religious neutrality on the part of the state, we can identify the foundations of a non-denominational, secular state which was yet to be born in India or for that matter anywhere else. Thus, Akbar's reasoned conclusions, codified during 1591 and 1592, had universal implications. Europe had just as much reason to listen to that message as India had. The Inquisition was still in force, and just when Akbar was writing on religious tolerance in Agra in 1592, Giordano Bruno was arrested for heresy, and ultimately, in 1600, burnt at the stake in the Campo dei Fiori in Rome.

For India in particular, the tradition of secularism can be traced to the trend of tolerant and pluralist thinking that had begun to take root well before Akbar, for example, in the writings of Amir Khusrau in the fourteenth century as well as in the non-sectarian devotional poetry of Kabir, Nanak, Chaitanya and others. But that tradition got its firmest official backing from Emperor Akbar himself. He also practised as he preached – abolishing discriminatory taxes imposed earlier on non-Muslims, inviting many Hindu intellectuals and artists into his court (including the great musician Tansen), and even trusting a Hindu general, Man Singh, to command his armed forces.

In some ways, Akbar was precisely codifying and consolidating the need for religious neutrality of the state that had been enunciated, in a general form, nearly two millennia before him by the Indian emperor Ashoka, whose ideas I have referred to earlier. While Ashoka ruled a long time ago, in the case of Akbar there is a continuity of legal scholarship and public memory linking his ideas and codifications with present-day India.

Indian secularism, which was strongly championed in the twentieth century by Gandhi, Nehru, Tagore and others, is often taken to be something of a reflection of Western ideas (despite the fact that Britain is a somewhat unlikely choice as a spearhead of secularism). In contrast, there are good reasons to link this aspect of modern India, including its constitutional secularism and judicially guaranteed multiculturalism (in contrast with, say, the privileged status of Islam in the constitution of the Islamic Republic of Pakistan), to earlier Indian writings and particularly to the ideas of this Muslim emperor of four hundred years ago.

Perhaps the most important point that Akbar made in his defence of a tolerant multiculturalism concerns the role of reasoning. Reason had to be supreme, since even in disputing the validity of reason we have to give reasons. Attacked by traditionalists who argued in favour of instinctive faith in the Islamic tradition, Akbar told his friend and trusted lieutenant Abul Fazl (a formidable scholar in Sanskrit as well as Arabic and Persian):

> The pursuit of reason and rejection of traditionalism are so brilliantly patent as to be above the need of argument. If traditionalism were proper, the prophets would merely have followed their own elders (and not come with new messages).[21]

Convinced that he had to take a serious interest in the religions and cultures of non-Muslims in India, Akbar arranged for discussions to take place involving not only mainstream Hindu and Muslim philosophers (Shia and Sunni as well as Sufi), but also involving Christians, Jews, Parsees, Jains and, according to Abul Fazl, even the followers of

Cārvāka – one of the Indian schools of atheistic thinking the roots of which can be traced to around the sixth century BCE.[22] Instead of taking an all-or-nothing view of a faith, Ashoka liked to reason about particular components of each multifaceted religion. For example, arguing with Jains, Akbar would remain sceptical of their rituals, and yet become convinced by their argument for vegetarianism and end up deploring the eating of all flesh. . .

All this caused irritation among those who preferred to base religious belief on faith rather than reasoning. There were several revolts against Akbar by orthodox Muslims, on one occasion joined by his eldest son, Prince Salim, with whom he later reconciled. But he stuck to what he called 'the path of reason' (*rahi aql*), and insisted on the need for open dialogue and free choice. At one stage, Akbar even tried, not very successfully, to launch a new religion, Din-ilahi (God's religion), combining what he took to be the good qualities of different faiths. When he died in 1605, the Islamic theologian Abdul Haq concluded with some satisfaction that, despite his 'innovations', Akbar had remained a good Muslim.[23] This was indeed so, but Akbar would have also added that his religious beliefs came from his own reason and choice, not from 'blind faith', or from 'the marshy land of tradition'.

Akbar's ideas remain relevant – and not just in the subcontinent. They have a bearing on many current debates in the West as well. They suggest the need for scrutiny of the fear of multiculturalism (for example, of Huntington's argument that 'multiculturalism at home threatens the United States and the West'). Similarly, in dealing with controversies in universities in the United States about confining core readings to the 'great books' of the Western world, Akbar's line of reasoning would suggest that the crucial weakness of this proposal is not so much that students from other backgrounds (say, African-American or Chinese) should not have to read Western classics, as that confining one's reading only to the books of one civilization reduces one's freedom to learn about and choose ideas from different cultures in the world.[24] And the counter-demand that the great Western books be banished from the reading list for students from other backgrounds would also be faulty, since that too would reduce the freedom to learn, reason and choose.

There are implications also for the 'communitarian' position, which argues that one's identity is a matter of 'discovery', not choice. As Michael Sandel presents this conception of community (one of several alternative conceptions he outlines): 'Community describes not just what they *have* as fellow citizens but also what they *are*, not a relationship they choose (as in a voluntary association) but an attachment they discover, not merely an attribute but a constituent of their identity.'[25] This view – that a person's identity is something he or she detects rather than determines – would have been resisted by Akbar on the ground that we do have a choice about our beliefs, associations and attitudes, and must take responsibility for what we actually choose (if only implicitly).

The notion that we 'discover' our identity is not only epistemologically limiting (we certainly can try to find out what choices – possibly extensive – we actually have), but it may also have disastrous implications for how we act and behave (well illustrated by Jonathan Glover's account of the role of unquestioning loyalty and belief in precipitating atrocities and horrors). Many of us still have vivid memories of what happened in the pre-partition riots in India just preceding independence in 1947, when the broadly tolerant subcontinentals of January rapidly and unquestioningly became the ruthless Hindus or the fierce Muslims of June.[26] The carnage that followed had much to do with the alleged 'discovery' of one's 'true' identity, unhampered by reasoned humanity.

Akbar's analyses of social problems illustrate the power of open reasoning and choice even in a clearly pre-modern society. Shirin Moosvi's wonderfully informative book *Episodes in the Life of Akbar: Contemporary Records and Reminiscences* gives interesting accounts of how Akbar arrived at social decisions – many of them defiant of tradition – through the use of reasoning.[27]

Akbar was, for example, opposed to child marriage, then a quite conventional custom. He argued that 'the object that is intended' in marriage 'is still remote, and there is immediate possibility of injury'. He went on to remark that 'in a religion that forbids the remarriage of the widow [Hinduism], the hardship is much greater'. On property division, he noted that 'in the Muslim religion, a smaller share of inheritance is allowed to the daughter, though owing to her weakness, she deserves to be given a larger share'. When his second son, Murad, who knew that his father was opposed to all religious rituals, asked him whether these rituals should be banned, Akbar immediately protested, on the grounds that 'preventing that insensitive simpleton, who considers body exercise to be divine worship, would amount to preventing him from remembering God [at all]'. Addressing a question on the motivation for doing a good deed (a question that still gets asked often enough), Akbar criticizes 'the Indian sages' for the suggestion that 'good works' be done to achieve a favourable outcome after death: 'To me it seems that in the pursuit of virtue, the idea of death should not be thought of, so that without any hope or fear, one should practice virtue simply because it is good.' In 1582 he resolved to release 'all the Imperial slaves', since 'it is beyond the realm of justice and good conduct' to benefit from 'force'.

Incidentally, the fact that reason may not be infallible, especially in the presence of uncertainty, is well illustrated by Akbar's reflections on the newly arrived practice of smoking tobacco. His doctor, Hakim Ali, argued against its use: 'It is not necessary for us to follow the Europeans, and adopt a custom, which is not sanctioned by our own wise men, without experiment or trial.' Akbar ignored this argument on the ground that 'we must not reject a thing that has been adopted by people of the world, merely because we cannot find it in our books; or how shall we progress?' Armed with that argument, Akbar tried smoking but happily for him he took an instant dislike of it, and never smoked again. Here instinct worked better than reason (in circumstances rather different from the case of Bukharin described by Glover). But reason worked often enough.

Millennial Insights

There was good sense in Akbar's insistence that a millennial occasion is not only for fun and festivities (of which there were plenty in Delhi and Agra as the first Hijri millennium was completed in 1591–2), but also for serious reflection on the joys and horrors and challenges of the world in which we live. Akbar's emphasis on reason and scrutiny serves as a reminder that 'cultural boundaries' are not as limiting as is sometimes alleged (as, for example, in the view, discussed earlier, that 'justice', 'right', 'reason', and 'love of humanity' are 'predominantly, perhaps even uniquely, Western values'). Indeed, many features of the European Enlightenment can be linked with questions that were raised earlier – not just in Europe but widely across the world.

As the second Gregorian millennium began, India was visited by an intellectual tourist in the form of Alberuni, an Iranian who was born in Central Asia in 973 CE and who wrote in Arabic. As a mathematician, Alberuni's primary interest was in Indian mathematics (he produced, among other writings, an improved Arabic translation of Brahmagupta's sixth-century Sanskrit treatise on astronomy and mathematics – first translated into Arabic in the eighth century). But he also studied Indian writings on science, philosophy, literature, linguistics, religion and other subjects, and wrote a highly informative book about India, called *Ta'rikh al-hind* ('The History of India'). In explaining why he wrote it, Alberuni argued that it is very important for people in one country to know how others elsewhere live, and how and what they think. Evil behaviour (of which Alberuni had seen plenty in the barbarity of his former patron, Sultan Mahmud of Ghazni, who had savagely raided India several times) can arise from a lack of understanding of – and familiarity with – other people:

> In all manners and usages, [the Indians] differ from us to such a degree as to frighten their children with us, with our dress, and our ways and customs, and as to declare us to be devil's breed, and our doings as the very opposite of all that is good and proper. By the bye, we must confess, in order to be just, that a similar depreciation of foreigners not only prevails among us and [the Indians], but is common to all nations towards each other.[28]

That insight from the beginning of the last millennium has remained pertinent a thousand years later.

In trying to go beyond what Adam Smith called our 'first perceptions', we need to transcend what Akbar saw as the 'marshy land' of unquestioned tradition and unreflected response. Reason has its reach – compromised neither by the importance of instinctive psychology nor by the presence of cultural diversity in the world. It has an especially important role to play in the cultivation of moral imagination. We need it in particular to face the bats and the owls and the insane moon.

14

Secularism and Its Discontents*

When India became independent more than half a century ago, much emphasis was placed on its secularism, and there were few voices dissenting from that priority. In contrast, there are now persistent pronouncements deeply critical of Indian secularism, and attacks have come from quite different quarters. Many of the barbed attacks on secularism in India have come from activists engaged in the Hindutva movement, including the BJP, which has been described as 'the principal political party representing the ideology of Hindu nationalism in the electoral arena'.†

However, intellectual scepticism about secularism is not confined to those actively engaged in politics. Indeed, eloquent expressions of this scepticism can also be found in the high theory of Indian culture and society.[1] Many of the attacks are quite removed from the BJP and other official organs of Hindu nationalism. In addressing the issue of Indian secularism it is important to take note of the range as well as the vigour of these critiques, and also the fact that they come from varying quarters and use quite distinct arguments. If today 'secular-

*This is a slightly revised version of an essay published in Kaushik Basu and Sanjay Subrahmanyam (eds.), *Unravelling the Nation: Sectarian Conflict and India's Secular Identity* (Delhi: Penguin, 1996). For helpful discussion I am grateful to Kaushik Basu, Sabyasachi Bhattacharya, Akeel Bilgrami, Sugata Bose, Emma Rothschild and Sanjay Subrahmanyam.

†Ashutosh Varshney, 'Contested Meanings: Indian National Unity, Hindu Nationalism, and the Politics of Anxiety', *Daedalus*, 122 (1993), p. 231. See also his later book, *Ethnic Conflict and Civic Life: Hindus and Muslims in India* (New Haven: Yale University Press, 2002). The various components of the Hindutva movement were described in Essay 2 above.

ism, the ideological mainstay of multi-religious India, looks pale and exhausted' (as Ashutosh Varshney describes it), the nature of that predicament would be misidentified – and somewhat minimized – if it were to be seen simply in terms of the politics of Hindu sectarianism. While the attacks on secularism have often come from exactly that quarter, there are other elements as well, and the subject calls for a wider analysis and response.

Despite this broad and forceful challenge, secularist intellectuals in India tend to be somewhat reluctant to debate this rather unattractive subject. Reliance is placed instead, usually implicitly, on the well-established and unquestioning tradition of seeing secularism as a good and solid political virtue for a pluralist democracy. As an unreformed secularist myself, I understand, and to some extent share, this reluctance, but also believe that addressing these criticisms is important. This is so not only because the condemnations have implications for political and intellectual life in contemporary India, but also because it is useful for secularists to face these issues explicitly – to scrutinize and re-examine habitually accepted priorities, and the reasoning behind them. There is much need for self-examination of beliefs – nowhere more so than in practical reason and political philosophy.* Hence this attempt at discussing some of the critical questions about secularism that have been forcefully raised.

Incompleteness and the Need for Supplementation

The nature of secularism as a principle calls for some clarification as well as scrutiny. Some of the choices considered under the heading of secularism lie, I would argue, beyond its immediate scope. Secularism in the political – as opposed to ecclesiastical – sense requires the separation of the state from any particular religious order. This can be interpreted in at least two different ways. The first view argues that secularism demands that the state be equidistant from all religions –

*In this context, see also Charles Taylor *et al.*, *Multiculturalism and 'The Politics of Recognition'* (Princeton: Princeton University Press, 1993).

refusing to take sides and having a neutral attitude towards them. The second – more severe – view insists that the state must not have any relation at all with any religion. The equidistance must take the form, then, of being altogether removed from each.

In both interpretations, secularism goes against giving any religion a privileged position in the activities of the state. In the broader interpretation (the first view), however, there is no demand that the state must stay clear of any association with any religious matter whatsoever. Rather, what is needed is to make sure that, in so far as the state has to deal with different religions and members of different religious communities, there must be a basic symmetry of treatment. In this view, there would be no violation of secularism for a state to protect everyone's right to worship as he or she chooses, even though in doing this the state has to work with – and for – religious communities. In the absence of asymmetric attention (such as protecting the rights of worship for one religious community, but not others), working hard for religious freedom does not breach the principle of secularism.

The important point to note here is that the requirement of symmetric treatment still leaves open the question as to what form that symmetry should take. To illustrate with an example, the state may decide that it must not offer financial or other support to any hospital with any religious connection. Alternatively, it can provide support to all hospitals, without in any way discriminating between their respective religious connections (or lack of them). While the former may appear to be, superficially, 'more secular' (as it certainly is in the 'associative' – the second – sense, since it shuns religious connections altogether), the latter is also politically quite secular in the sense that the state, in this case, supports hospitals irrespective of whether or not there are any religious connections (and if so, what), and through this neutrality, it keeps the state and the religions quite separate.

It is the broader view that has been the dominant approach to secularism in India.* But this, it must be recognized, is an incomplete specification. Secularism excludes some alternatives (those that favour

*The historical lineage of this interpretation of secularism and some of the implications of this broader approach have been discussed in Essay 1, section headed 'Understanding Secularism'.

some religions over others), but still allows several distinct options related to the unspecified distance at which the state should keep all religions, without discrimination. There is thus a need, in dealing with religions and religious communities, to take up questions that lie 'beyond' secularism. While this essay is concerned with scrutinizing attacks on secularism as a political requirement, the organizational issues that lie beyond secularism must also be characterized.* In analysing the role of secularism in India, note must be taken of its intrinsic 'incompleteness', including the problems that this incompleteness leads to, as well as the opportunities it offers.

Critical Arguments

Scepticism about Indian secularism takes many different forms. I shall consider in particular six distinct lines of argument. This may be enough for one essay, but I do not claim that all anti-secularist attacks are covered by the arguments considered here.

(1) The 'Non-existence' Critique

Perhaps the simplest version of scepticism about Indian secularism comes from those who see nothing much there, at least nothing of real significance. For example, Western journalists often regard Indian secularism as essentially non-existent, and their language tends to contrast 'Hindu India' (or 'mainly Hindu India') with 'Muslim Pakistan' (or 'mainly Muslim Pakistan'). Certainly, Indian secularism has never been a gripping thought in broad Western perceptions, and recent pictures of politically militant Hindus demolishing an old mosque in Ayodhya have not helped to change these perceptions. Indian protestations about secularism are often seen in the West as sanctimonious nonsense – hard to take seriously in weighty discourses on

*Some of the arguments presented here draw on an earlier paper (my Nehru Lecture at Trinity College, Cambridge, on 5 Feb. 1993), published under the title 'Threats to Indian Secularism', in the *New York Review of Books*, 8 Apr. 1993. See also Akeel Bilgrami, 'Two Concepts of Secularism', *Yale Journal of Criticism*, 7 (1994).

international affairs and in the making of foreign policy (by powerful and responsible Western states that dominate the world of contemporary international politics).

(2) The 'Favouritism' Critique

A second line of attack argues that, in the guise of secularism, the Indian constitution and political and legal traditions really favour the minority community of Muslims, giving them a privileged status not enjoyed by the majority community of Hindus. This 'favouritism' critique is popular with many of the leaders and supporters of the Hindu activist parties. The rhetoric of this attack can vary from wanting to 'reject' secularism to arguing against what is called 'pseudo-secularism' ('favouring the Muslims').

(3) The 'Prior Identity' Critique

A third line of critique is more intellectual than the first two. It sees the identity of being a Hindu, or a Muslim, or a Sikh, to be politically 'prior' to being an Indian. The Indian identity is 'built up' from the *constitutive* elements of separate identities. In one version of the identity argument, it is asserted that, given the preponderance of Hindus in the country, any Indian national identity cannot but be a function of some form or other of a largely Hindu identity. Another version would go further and aim at a homogeneous identity as a necessary basis of nationhood (in line with the picturesque analogy that 'a salad bowl does not produce cohesion; a melting pot does'[2]), and move on from that proposition to the claim that only a shared cultural outlook, which in India can only be a largely Hindu view, can produce such a cohesion. Even the unity of India derives, it is argued, from the 'cementing force' of Hinduism.

(4) The 'Muslim Sectarianism' Critique

In another line of critique, the proposed dominance of Hindu identity in 'Indianness' does not turn on the logic of numbers, but is 'forced on the Hindus', it is argued, by the 'failure' of the Muslims to see themselves as Indians first. This form of argument draws heavily on what is seen as the historical failure of Muslim rulers in India to identify themselves with others in the country, always seeing Muslims as a separate and preferred group. It is also claimed that Muslim kings systematically destroyed Hindu temples and religious sites whenever they had the chance to do so.

Jinnah's 'two-nation' theory, formulated before independence (and historically important in the partition of India), is seen as a continuation of the evident Muslim refusal to identify with other Indians. It is argued that, while the partition of India has provided a 'homeland' for the Muslims of the subcontinent, the Muslims left in India are unintegrated and are basically not 'loyal' to India. The 'evidential' part of this line of critique is thus supposed to include suspicions of Muslim disloyalty in contemporary India as well as particular readings of Indian history.

(5) The 'Anti-modernist' Critique

Contemporary intellectual trends, primarily in the West but also (somewhat derivatively) in India, give much room for assailing what is called 'modernism'. The fifth line of critique joins force with this assault by attacking secularism as a part of the folly of 'modernism'. While post-modernist criticisms of secularism can take many different forms, the more effective assaults on 'secularism as modernism' in India, at this time, combine general anti-modernism with some specific yearning for India's past when things are supposed to have been less problematic in this respect (particularly in terms of the peaceful coexistence of different religions). Elements of such understanding tend to form integral parts of the intellectual critiques of some contemporary social analysts.

Ashis Nandy notes that 'as India gets modernized, religious violence is increasing', and he expresses admiration for 'traditional ways of life [which] have, over the centuries, developed internal principles of tolerance'. The denunciation of secularism that follows from this line of reasoning is well captured in Nandy's sharp conclusion: 'To accept the ideology of secularism is to accept the ideologies of progress and modernity as the new justification of domination, and the use of violence to achieve and sustain ideologies as the new opiates of the masses.'[3]

(6) The 'Cultural' Critique

The sixth and last critique I shall consider takes the ambitiously 'foundational' view that India is, in essence, a 'Hindu country', and that as a result it would be culturally quite wrong to treat Hinduism as simply one of the various religions of India. It is Hinduism, in this view, that makes India what it is, and to require secularism, with its insistence on treating different religions symmetrically, must turn an epistemic error into a political blunder.

This line of criticism often draws on analogies with formally Christian states such as that of Britain, where the particular history of the country and the special role of its 'own religion' are 'fully acknowledged'. For example, the Archbishop of Canterbury conducts political ceremonies of the state at the highest level ('no nonsense about secularism there'). Similarly, British laws of blasphemy are specifically protective of Christianity and of no other religion (just as in Pakistan the domain of blasphemy laws penalizes 'insults' only to Islam). India, it is complained, denies its indigenous cultural commitment in not providing anything like a similarly privileged status to its 'own' tradition, to wit, the predominantly Hindu heritage.

I shall consider these half-dozen critiques in turn. As was stated before, other grounds for rejection of secularism have also been offered. Some of these critiques involve elaborate conceptual compositions and estimable intricacy of language, and are not breathtakingly easy to penetrate (even armed with a dictionary of neologisms on the one hand, and courage on the other). I shall confine myself only to these six lines of criticism of secularism, without pretending to be dealing with all the arguments against secularism that have actually been proposed.

On the 'Non-existence' Critique

Is the 'non-existence' critique to be taken seriously? Many Indian intellectuals tend to view this kind of opinion with some contempt, and are rather reluctant to respond to what they see as the obduracy (or worse) of Western observers. This is sometimes combined with a general theory that it does not really matter what 'others' think about India (at most, this is something for Indian embassies to worry about). This studied non-response is not only insular (ignoring the importance of international understanding in the contemporary world), it also overlooks how crucial outside perceptions have historically been to the identity of Indians themselves.* Even the composite conception of Hinduism as one religion includes the impact of the outsiders' view of the classificatory unity of the religious beliefs and practices in the country.

There is also the recent phenomenon of the support provided by opulent expatriates from the subcontinent to community-based political movements – of Sikhs, Muslims and Hindus – back at 'home'. And because of the relevance of what they read and react to, we can scarcely take foreign reporting on India as 'inconsequential' – even for immediate issues of internal politics in India.

The 'non-existence' critique certainly has to be addressed (even if the more informed reader would decide to switch off while that addressing takes place). Is India really the Hindu counterpart of Pakistan? When British India was partitioned, Pakistan chose to be an Islamic republic, whereas India chose a secular constitution.† Is that distinction significant? It is true that, in standard Western journalism, little significance is attached to the contrast, and those in India who would like the country to abandon its secularism often cite this 'forced parity' in Western vision as proof enough that there is something rather hopeless in India's

*I have touched on this question in my 'India and the West', *New Republic*, 7 June 1993. It is also discussed in Essay 7 above.

†The emergence of Pakistan as a 'Muslim state', under the leadership of Mohammad Ali Jinnah, has a complex – and circumstantially quite contingent – history, on which see particularly Ayesha Jalal, *The Sole Spokesman: Jinnah, the Muslim League and the Demand for Pakistan* (Cambridge: Cambridge University Press, 1985).

attempt at secularism when the new masters of global politics cannot even tell what on earth is being attempted in India.

Yet the distinction between a secular republic and a religion-based state is really rather important from the legal point of view, and its political implications are also quite extensive. This applies to different levels of social arrangements, including the operations of the courts, all the way up to the headship of the state. For example, unlike Pakistan, whose constitution requires that the head of the state be a Muslim, India imposes no comparable requirement, and the country has had non-Hindus (including Muslims and Sikhs) as Presidents and as holders of other prominent and influential offices in government and in the judiciary (including the Supreme Court).*

Similarly, to take another example, it is not possible, because of the secularist constitution of India, to have asymmetric laws of blasphemy, applied to one religion only, as it is in Pakistan. There *is* a difference between the legal status that Pakistan gives to Islam (as it must in an 'Islamic republic') and the lack of a comparable legal status of Hinduism in India. Not surprisingly, the 'non-existence' critique is aired much more frequently abroad than at home, and often takes the form of an implicit presumption – colouring Western analyses of the subcontinent – rather than an explicit assertion. That hardened belief turns on overlooking extensive and important features of the Indian constitution and polity.

Two qualifications should, however, be introduced here. First, the 'non-existence' critique must not be confused with the claim – not infrequently made, often by staunch secularists – that, despite the elements of legal symmetry, Hindus still have a substantive advantage over Muslims in many spheres. This would be, typically, an argument for practising secularism 'more fully' in India, rather than for discarding the secularism that is already there. Second, the rejection of the 'non-existence' critique does not identify the exact form of secularism that exists in India (nor of course assert anything like the 'superiority' of that specific form of secularism). Indeed, as was discussed earlier, the acceptance of secularism still leaves many questions

*As this essay, originally written in 1995, is republished in this volume a decade later, it is perhaps worth noting that India has, at this time, a Muslim President, a Sikh Prime Minister and a Christian head of the ruling party.

unanswered about the attitude of the state to different religions. Even when the basic need for symmetry in the political and legal treatment of different religious communities is accepted, we still have to decide on the shape that this symmetry should take, and what the exact domain and reach of that symmetry might be.

To illustrate, symmetry regarding blasphemy laws can be achieved with different formulas – varying from applying it to all religions, to applying it to none. While the latter option fits in immediately with a secularist withdrawal of the state from religious affairs, the former pursues symmetry between religions in a way that favours no religion in particular. Just as a secular state can protect the liberty of all citizens to worship as they please (or not to worship), irrespective of their religious beliefs (and this could not be seen, as was analysed earlier, as a violation of secularism), secularism can, in principle, take the form of 'shielding' every religious community against whatever that community seriously deems as blasphemy. I am not, of course, recommending such 'universal anti-blasphemy laws' – indeed, I would argue very firmly against anti-blasphemy laws in general. But my rejection of 'universal anti-blasphemy laws' is not based on seeing them as anti-secular, but on other grounds that go beyond secularism: in particular, the need to prevent religious intolerance and persecution, and the practical unfeasibility of making anti-blasphemy laws really 'universal', covering all religions in India (including those of the various tribal communities that constitute an underprivileged minority in India). The need to choose between different secular forms remains, but this is a very different contention from saying that the requirement of Indian secularism makes no difference – that it is 'immaterial'.

On the 'Favouritism' Critique

The 'favouritism' critique turns on interpreting and highlighting some legal differences between the various communities. These have been much discussed recently in the activist Hindu political literature. The difference in 'personal laws' has been particularly in focus.

It is pointed out, for example, that while a Hindu can be prosecuted for polygamy, a Muslim man can have up to four wives, in line with what is taken to be the Islamic legal position (although, in practice, this provision is extremely rarely invoked by Indian Muslims). Attention is also drawn to other differences, for example between the provision for wives in the event of a divorce, where Muslim women (in line with a certain reading of Islamic law) have less generous guarantees than those which other Indian women have – a subject that came to some prominence in the context of the Supreme Court's judgement on the famous 'Shah Bano case' (involving the right of support of a divorced Muslim woman from her estranged and more opulent husband). The existence of these differences has been cited again and again by Hindu political activists to claim that Hindus, as the majority community, are discriminated against in India, whereas Muslims are allowed to have their own 'personal laws' and 'special privileges'.

This line of reasoning has many problems. First, if these examples indicate any 'favouritism', in giving special 'privileges', in the treatment of the different communities, this can hardly be a favouritism for Muslims in general. Any unfairness that is there is surely one against *Muslim women*, rather than against *Hindu men*. A narrowly 'male' – indeed, sexist – point of view is rather conspicuous in the particular form that this political complaint often takes.

Second, it is not the case that the personal laws of the Hindus have been somehow overridden in post-independence India by some uniform civil code. The separate status of Hindu personal laws has in general survived. The issue of uniform civil codes has to be distinguished from the fact that the Hindu laws were reformed after independence, particularly during 1955 and 1956, with little opposition (indeed, they resulted from political movements within the Hindu communities). The possibility of polygamy was explicitly ruled out by reform of the Hindu laws. It did not follow from some 'uniform' civil codes being imposed on the Hindus but not the Muslims. Nor did it make the Hindu personal laws inoperative – quite the contrary. Several other provisions were introduced within the Hindu laws themselves, but the domain of Hindu personal laws continues to be quite substantial.

The makers of the Indian constitution did express some preference for 'uniformity of fundamental laws, civil and criminal', which was seen by Dr B. R. Ambedkar (the leader of the team that framed the constitution of India) as important for maintaining the unity of the country.[4] In the event, however, such uniformity was not incorporated in the constitution that emerged, and the preference for uniformity was only included as a 'Directive Principle of State Policy' – without enforceability. The principle that was adopted demanded that 'the State shall endeavour to secure for the citizens a uniform civil code throughout the territory of India'. Like all the 'Directive Principles' enunciated in the Indian constitution, this was seen as 'fundamental in the governance of the country', and it was specified that 'it shall be the duty of the State to apply' this principle, but at the same time this principle (like the other 'directive' ones) 'shall not be enforceable by any court'.[5]

It is, of course, up to the courts to see how far to go in line with this Directive Principle. In the much-debated case of the 'Shah Bano judgement', involving a Muslim woman's right to a better financial deal at the time of divorce, the Indian Supreme Court did indeed make a move in the direction of uniformity.[6] The Court also revealed some disappointment at the government's failure to move in the direction of a uniform civil code in line with the 'constitutional ideal' (and noted that this constitutional provision had 'remained a dead letter'). In fact, as one observer has noted, 'the intensity of Muslim reaction to the Supreme Court's judgment in that case was partly explained by the inclusion of this utterance and the suggestion that what the government had failed to do, the Court itself might undertake'.[7] The 'Muslim reaction' was not, however, by any means uniform, and there was support as well as criticism for the Supreme Court's judgement, from different sections of that community.[8] It was Rajiv Gandhi's Congress government that ultimately 'caved in', and made fresh legislation that further supported the 'separatist' view, rather than following the Supreme Court's push in the direction of more uniformity.

The general issue of asymmetric treatment is indeed an important one, and there would, of course, be nothing non-secular in pursuing the possibility of making the provisions of a set of uniform civil laws apply even-handedly to individuals of *all* the communities. On the other hand, as was argued earlier in this essay, the principles of secularism will also permit an arrangement by which separate personal laws continue well into the future (so long as the different religious communities are treated with symmetry). In arguing against the latter option, considerations of justice may well be raised which demand some symmetry not only in the way the different religious communities are treated, but also in the way fairness is applied across other classificatory distinctions (for example, between the different classes, between women and men, between the poor and the rich, between the 'elite' and the 'subalterns', and so on).

The choice between these two options – and intermediate ones – remains open, and certainly cannot be closed in one direction or the other by the requirements of secularism alone. To note this is not to concede the failure of secularism, but is rather an acknowledgement of its circumscribed domain, and the affirmation of the need to go beyond secularism – with other principles of fairness and justice – to identify specific legal and social forms. While there is not much substance in the charge of 'favouritism' benefiting Muslims, and certainly no general case against secularism can be constructed on that line of reasoning, it is useful to integrate the discussion on secularism with the principles – such as those of justice – that lie beyond it.

We have to distinguish, in particular, between (1) the need for symmetry among different religious communities (a secularist consideration), and (2) the question of what form that symmetry should take, a concern that has to be consolidated with other principles of justice which take us well beyond secularism into, on the one hand, the importance that may be attached to group autonomy of religious communities, and on the other, the inescapable issue of equity for different groups of Indians, classified in non-religious categories, such as class and gender.

On the 'Prior Identity' Critique

The question of political and religious identities raises issues of a rather different kind. There can be little doubt that many Indians – indeed, most Indians – have religious beliefs of one kind or another, and regard these beliefs to be important in their personal lives. The issue that is raised by the claimed priority of this identity in the political context is not the general importance of religious beliefs in personal or even social behaviour, but the specific relevance of that identity in political matters (with and without the involvement of the state).

It is useful in this context to recollect the contrast between the religiosity of political leaders in pre-independence India and their respective beliefs in a secular identity. Jinnah, the great advocate of the 'two-nation' theory and the founding father of the Islamic Republic of Pakistan, was scarcely a devout Muslim, whereas Maulana Abul Kalam Azad, the President of the Indian National Congress and a major leader of the Indian union, was a deeply religious Muslim.[9]

Similarly, Shyama Prasad Mukhopadhyay, the leader of Hindu Mahasabha, had very few Hindu practices, compared with, say, Mahatma Gandhi, who was both actively religious in personal life and in social practice (for example, he held regular prayer meetings which were open to the public) and also staunchly secularist in politics (insisting on symmetric political treatment of different religions and an effective separation of the state and religions). When Mahatma Gandhi was murdered by an extremist Hindu politician, the murderer's complaint against him was not that he did not follow Hinduism in his personal life or in his social activities, but that he was, allegedly, very 'soft' on the Muslims in political matters, and did not give adequate priority to Hindu interests.

The importance of religious identity has to be separated from its relevance in the political context. It is thus odd to require that Indians must 'go through' their religious identity first, before asserting their Indianness, and even less plausible to insist that the Indian identity must be 'built up' on the constitutive basis of the different religious identities. That assertion of priority comes not only from religious sectarians (particularly, in recent years, the so-called 'Hindu nationalists'), but also from those who have been especially worried about the usurping role of the state (as opposed to community), and about the violences committed by the state.

In this context, the issue of a national identity is often identified, misleadingly, I believe, with the philosophy of a 'nation state', thus giving an inescapably 'statist' orientation to the very conception of any political unity across religious communities and other social divisions. It is certainly true that in the emergence or consolidation of that unity, the nation state may well have an important instrumental role, but the state need not be central to the conceptual foundation of this unity, nor provide its constructive genesis. It is, for example, not a 'category mistake' to think of the Indian nation prior to 1947 as encompassing the residents of the so-called 'native states' (such as Travancore), and also of the non-British colonial territories (such as Goa), even though they did not 'belong to' the same state at all. It is a serious mistake to think that the idea of a nation requires the prior presence of a nation state.

A second problem concerns the use of this route to arrive at the proposed Hindu view of India. Even if the religious identities were somehow 'prior' to the political identity of being an Indian, one could scarcely derive the view of a Hindu India based on that argument alone. The non-Hindu communities – Muslims in particular, but also Christians, Sikhs, Jains, Parsees and others – are scarcely 'marginal' even in numerical terms in the country.

India has well over 140 million Muslims, not many fewer than Pakistan, and rather more than Bangladesh. To see India just as a Hindu country is a fairly bizarre idea in the face of that fact alone, not to mention the intermingling of Hindus and Muslims in the social and cultural life of India (in literature, music, painting and so on). Also, Indian religious plurality extends far beyond the Hindu–Muslim division. There is a large and prominent Sikh population, and a substantial number of Christians, whose settlements go back at least to the fourth century CE. There have also been Jewish settlements in India for nearly two thousand years. Parsees started moving to India twelve hundred years ago, to escape a less tolerant Iran. To this we have to add the millions of Jains, and practitioners of Buddhism, which had been for a long period the official religion of many of the Indian emperors (including the great Ashoka in the third century BCE, who had ruled over the largest empire in the history of the subcontinent).

Furthermore, large also is the number of Indians who are atheist or agnostic (as Jawaharlal Nehru himself was), and that tradition in India goes well back to the ancient times (to Cārvāka and the Lokāyata, among other atheistic or agnostic schools).* The classificatory

*The importance of scepticism in Indian traditions was discussed in Essay 1, particularly in the section headed 'Sceptics, Agnostics and Atheists'.

conventions of Indian social statistics tend to disestablish the recognition of such heterodox beliefs, since the categories used represent what in India has come to be called 'community', without recording actual religious beliefs (for example, an atheist born in a Hindu family is classified as Hindu, reflecting the so-called 'community background').

Those who framed the Indian constitution wanted to give appropriate recognition to the extensive religious pluralism of the Indian people, and did not want to derive the notion of Indianness from any specific religious identity in particular. As Dr Ambedkar, the leader of the Indian Constituent Assembly, put it: 'if the Muslims in India are a separate nation, then, of course, India is not a nation.'[10] Given the heterogeneity of India and of the Indians, there is no real political alternative to ensuring some basic symmetry and an effective separation of the state from each particular religion.[11]

The programme of deriving an Indian identity via a Hindu identity thus encounters problems from two different directions. First, it suffers from insufficient discrimination between (1) *personal* and *social* religious involvement, and (2) giving *political* priority to that involvement (against symmetric treatment of different religions). Second, it fails to recognize the implications of India's immense religious diversity.

In fact, the issue of religious plurality does not relate only to the relationship between Hindus and followers of other faiths (or none). It also concerns the divergences within Hinduism itself. The divisions do, of course, include those based on caste, and the nature of contemporary Indian politics reflects this at different levels with inescapable force. But the diversities that characterize Hinduism relate not just to caste. They also encompass divergent beliefs, distinct customs and different schools of religious thought.

Even the ancient classification of 'six systems of philosophy' in India had acknowledged deeply diverse beliefs and reasoning. More recently, in the fourteenth century, when the authoritative Hindu scholar Mādhava Ācārya (head of the religious order in Śriṅgeri in Mysore) wrote his famous Sanskrit treatise *Sarvadarśanasaṃgraha* ('Collection of All Philosophies'), his discussions brought out sharply the extent of diversity of different systems of Hindu belief.*

*This document was discussed in Essay 1.

In fact, seeing Hinduism as a unified religion is a comparatively recent development. The term 'Hindu' was traditionally used mainly as a signifier of location and country, rather than of any homogeneous religious belief. The word derives from the river Indus or 'Sindhu' (the cradle of the Indus valley civilization which flourished from around 3000 BCE) and the name of that river is also the source of the word 'India' itself. The Persians and the Greeks saw India as the land around and beyond the Indus, and Hindus were the native people of that land. Muslims from India were at one stage called 'Hindavi' Muslims, in Persian as well as Arabic, and there are plenty of references in early British documents to 'Hindoo Muslims' and 'Hindoo Christians', to distinguish them respectively from Muslims and Christians from outside India.

A pervasive plurality of religious beliefs and traditions characterizes Hinduism as a religion. The point can be illustrated with the attitude to Rama, in whose name so much of the current Hindu political activism is being invoked (including demolishing the Babri mosque in Ayodhya, claimed to be 'the birthplace of Rama'). The identification of Rama with divinity is common in the north and west of India, but elsewhere (for example, in my native Bengal), Rama is largely the heroic king of the epic *Rāmāyaṇa*, rather than God incarnate. The *Rāmāyaṇa* itself is, of course, widely popular, as an epic, everywhere in India, and has been so outside India as well – in Thailand and Indonesia, for example (even Ayutthaya, the historical capital of Thailand, is a cognate of Ayodhya). But the power and influence of the epic *Rāmāyaṇa* – a wonderful literary achievement – has to be distinguished from the particular issue of Rama's divinity.

A similar observation can be made about the claims to pre-eminent divinity of the other putatively divine characters in one part of India or another. If we must use the analogy of the 'melting pot' and the 'salad bowl', to which reference was made earlier, the Hindu traditions do not constitute a melting pot in any sense whatever. This need not, of course, prevent Hindus from living together in great harmony and mutual tolerance, but the same goes for a community of Hindus, Muslims, Christians, Sikhs, Jains, Buddhists, Parsees, Jews and people without any religion.

On the 'Muslim Sectarianism' Critique

I turn now to the issue of the alleged Muslim disloyalty to India. Spirited anecdotes abound on this subject, varying from the alleged frequency of Indian Muslims spying for Pakistan, to their tendency, we are told, to cheer the Pakistani cricket team in test matches.[12]

There is, in fact, no serious evidence for the hypothesis of the political disloyalty of Indian Muslims. A great many Muslims stayed on in post-partition India (instead of going to Pakistan) as a deliberate decision to remain where they felt they belonged. In the Indian armed forces, diplomatic services and administration, Muslims' record on loyalty to India is no different from that of Hindus and other Indians. There is no significant empirical evidence to substantiate the critique, and the unfairness of this specious line of reasoning is quite hard to beat.*

Allegations of Muslim sectarianism are sometimes linked with a certain reading of Indian history (though 'reading' may well be the wrong word to use here). Muslim kings were, it is claimed, consistently alienated from their Hindu subjects and treated them badly. Since I have discussed the biased nature of this allegation elsewhere in this book (particularly in Essay 3), I shall not pursue this specific question again here. I will, however, comment on a point of methodology, rather than of empirical history. In the context of defending the importance of secularism in contemporary India, it is not in any way essential to make any claim whatsoever about how Muslim emperors of the past had behaved – whether they were sectarian or assimilative, oppressive or tolerant. There is no intrinsic reason why a defence of India's secularism must take a position on what, say, the Moghals did

*The case of Kashmir is, of course, different in several respects, including its separate history and the peculiar politics of its accession to India and its aftermath. The evident disaffection of a substantial part of the Kashmiri Muslim population relates to the very special political circumstances obtaining there and the treatment they have received respectively from both India and Pakistan. The Kashmir issue certainly demands political attention on its own (I am not taking up that thorny question here), but the special circumstances influencing the viewpoint of 4 million Kashmiri Muslims can scarcely be used to question the strong record of national loyalty and solidarity of more than 140 million Muslims in general in India.

or did not do. The 'guilt' of Muslim kings, if any, need not be 'transferred' to the 140 million Muslims who live in India today. Also, we can scarcely form a view of the political commitments of Muslims in contemporary India, or of their political loyalties, by checking what Muslim kings might or might not have done many centuries ago.

On the 'Anti-modernist' Critique

Turning now to the 'anti-modernist' critique of secularism, is it really the case that 'as India gets modernized, religious violence is increasing' (as Ashis Nandy says)? There are certainly periods in history in which this is exactly what has happened. For example, the communal riots immediately preceding the partition of British India in 1947 almost certainly took many more lives than any violence between the different communities earlier on in the century. But as the country has moved on from there (presumably not decreasing in 'modernity'), the general level of violence has fallen from its peak in the 1940s – indeed, the number of incidents have been quite tiny in comparison with what happened half a century ago.

We must not, however, interpret Ashis Nandy's statement too literally. The thesis presented deals with a presumed shift in the long run, away from a pre-modern situation in which 'traditional ways of life' had, 'over the centuries, developed internal principles of tolerance'. There is undoubtedly some plausibility in such a diagnosis – there is some evidence that the level of communal violence did indeed increase with colonial rule. On the other hand, even in the pre-colonial past of India there were periods in which violence, especially by sectarian armed forces, had escalated sharply, and then ebbed. Nandy is right to assert that, in general, 'principles of tolerance' have tended to develop eventually, as people of different backgrounds have settled down to live next to each other. It is not, I believe, central for Nandy's thesis to check whether the time trend of communal violence has been consistently upwards, nor particularly interesting to compare the numbers killed in recent years vis-à-vis those in the past (the massive increase in the absolute size of the population would bias those comparisons anyway). The point rather is the thesis that principles of tolerance do develop in multi-community societies, unless they are disrupted by contrary moves, and Nandy sees the development of 'modernism' as just such a move.

But what exactly *is* 'modernism' that could so disrupt the process of tolerance? The concept of modernity is not an easy one to identify, even though many post-modernists seem to share the modernists' comfortable belief in the easily characterized nature of modernism. We may wish to resist being sent off on an errand to find the 'true meaning of modernism', and prefer to concentrate instead on the specific depiction of 'secularism as modernism', which is central to Nandy's thesis. The point of departure would then be the argument forcefully presented by Nandy (as was quoted earlier): 'To accept the ideology of secularism is to accept the ideologies of progress and modernity as the new justification of domination, and the use of violence to achieve and sustain ideologies as the new opiates of the masses.' This is quite an articulate – indeed, terrifying – vision, but it would seem to be a rather odd characterization of secularism. The principle of secularism, in the broader interpretation endorsed in India, demands (as was discussed earlier) symmetric treatment of different religious communities in politics and in the affairs of the state. It is not obvious why such symmetric treatment must somehow induce inescapable violence to achieve and sustain ideologies as the new opiates of the masses.

I am aware that the nation state is under grand attack these days, and I also know that in this attack it is seen as a constant perpetrator of violence. And I am also ready to accept that the state in the modern world has been responsible for many violent things (not necessarily more than in the past, but significant nevertheless). I am also aware that, in a much favoured contemporary theory, a nation state tries to 'homogenize to hegemonize'. But it seems, at best, intensely abstract to see such violence occurring whenever the state stops favouring one religious community over another.

It is thus hard to escape the suspicion that something has gone oddly wrong in the cited diagnostics. Nor is it obvious why secular symmetry should be a characteristic only of 'modernity'. Indeed, even ancient states run by, say, an Ashoka or an Akbar went a long way towards achieving just such a symmetric treatment, but there is no evidence that these historical attempts at secular symmetry increased, rather than lessened, communal violence.

It is not really helpful to see secularism and modernism in these oddly formulaic terms. Indeed, 'the principles of tolerance', on which Nandy relies, are not really so remote from taking a symmetric view of other communities, and it is less than fair to political secularism to be depicted as it is in these indictments. The development of secular attitudes and politics can surely be a part of that mechanism of tolerance, rather than running against it, unless we choose to define secularism in some specially odd way.

Also, the idea of 'modernity' is deeply problematic in general. Was Ashoka or Akbar more or less 'modern' than Aurangzeb? Perhaps the question being raised here can be illustrated with another historical example, involving differences between contemporaries. Consider the contrast between the sectarian destruction caused by Sultan Mahmud of Ghazni in the eleventh century, and the reactions of Alberuni, the Arab-Iranian traveller (and distinguished Muslim mathematician), who accompanied Mahmud to India and felt revolted by the violence he saw: 'Mahmud utterly ruined the prosperity of the country, and performed there wonderful exploits, by which Hindus became like atoms of dust scattered in all directions.'[13] He went on to suggest – perhaps overgeneralizing a little – that the Hindus, as a result, 'cherish, of course, the most inveterate aversion towards all Muslims'. That 'aversion' was, happily, not enough to prevent Alberuni from having a large number of Hindu friends and collaborators, with whose help he mastered Sanskrit and studied the contemporary Indian treatises on mathematics, astronomy, sculpture, philosophy and religion.*

However, Alberuni did not stop there, but proceeded to provide an analysis of why people of one background tend to be suspicious of those from other backgrounds, and identified the need for a balanced understanding of these problems (as was discussed in Essay 13): a 'depreciation of foreigners not only prevails among us and the Hindus, but is common to all nations towards each other'.[14] Those

*In fact, Alberuni's work and his translations of Indian mathematical and astronomical treatises had great influence in continuing the Arabic studies (well established by the eighth century) of Indian science and mathematics, which reached Europe through the Arabs.

who like 'modernism' would probably prefer to see Alberuni as a 'modern intellectual' of some kind (albeit from the eleventh century). But we need not bring in modernism – either in praise or in denunciation – at all, to recognize wisdom when we encounter it.

On the 'Cultural' Critique

I turn finally to the 'cultural' critique, and to the suggestion that India should really be seen as a 'Hindu country', in cultural terms. This, it is argued, militates against secularism in India, since secularism denies that allegedly basic recognition.

There are two questions to be raised here. First, even if it were right to see Indian culture as quintessentially Hindu culture, it would be very odd to alienate, on that ground, the right to equal political and legal treatment of minorities (including the political standing and rights of the 140 million or more Indian Muslims). Why should the cultural dominance of one tradition, even if it exists, reduce the political entitlements and rights of those from other traditions? What should remove their rights as equal citizens?

The second problem with the thesis is that its reading of Indian history and culture is extremely shallow. The cultural inheritance of contemporary India combines Islamic influences with Hindu and other traditions, and the results of the interaction between members of different religious communities can be seen plentifully in literature, music, painting, architecture and many other fields. The point is not only that so many of the major contributions in these various fields of Indian culture have come from Islamic writers, musicians, painters and so on, but also that their works are thoroughly integrated with those of others.

Indeed, even the nature of Hindu religious beliefs and practices has been substantially influenced by contact with Islamic ideas and values.* The impact of Islamic Sufi thought is readily recognizable in

*On this, see Kshiti Mohan Sen, *Hinduism* (Harmondsworth: Penguin Books, 1961, 2005). He discusses the interrelations in greater detail in his Bengali book *Bharate Hindu Mushalmaner Jukto Sadhana* (Calcutta: Visva-Bharati, 1949; extended edn., 1990).

parts of contemporary Hindu literature. Furthermore, religious poets like Kabir or Dadu were born Muslim but transcended sectional boundaries (one of Kabir's verses declares: 'Kabir is the child of Allah and of Ram: He is my Guru, He is my Pir'[15]). They were strongly affected by Hindu devotional poetry and, in turn, profoundly influenced it. There is, in fact, no communal line to be drawn through Indian literature and arts, setting Hindus and Muslims on separate sides.*

Another serious problem with the narrow reading of 'Indian culture as Hindu culture' is the entailed neglect of many major achievements of Indian civilization that have nothing much to do with religious thinking at all. The focus on the distinctly Hindu religious tradition effectively leaves out of the accounting rationalist and non-religious pursuits in India. This is a serious neglect, particularly for a country in which some of the decisive steps in algebra, geometry and astronomy were taken, where the decimal system emerged, where classical philosophy dealt extensively with epistemology and logic along with secular ethics, where people invented games like chess, pioneered sex education and initiated systematic political economy and formal linguistics.

To be sure, in his famous *History of British India*, published in 1817, James Mill did elaborate just such a view of India, an India that was intellectually bankrupt but full of religious ideas (not to mention Mill's pointer to barbarous social customs).† Mill's 'history', written without visiting India or learning any Indian language, may, in some ways, have served well the purpose of training young British officers getting ready to cross the seas and rule a subject nation, but it would scarcely suffice as a basis for understanding the nature of Indian culture.

There are good reasons to resist the anti-secular enticements that have been so plentifully offered recently. The winter of our discontent might not be giving way at present to a 'glorious summer', but the political abandonment of secularism would make India far more wintry than it currently is.

*This issue was discussed in a broader context in Essay 3.

†On the nature and influence of James Mill's reading of Indian culture, see Essays 4 and 7.

15

India through Its Calendars*

'The calendar', argued Meghnad Saha, the distinguished scientist and the leader of calendar reform in India, 'is an indispensable requisite of modern civilized life.' He could have gone further than that. The need for a calendar has been strongly felt – and well understood – well before the modern age. The calendar, in one form or another, has been an indispensable requisite of civilized life for a very long time indeed. This explains why so many calendars are so very old, and also why most civilizations, historically, have given birth to one or more specific calendars of their own. The multiplicity of calendars within a country and within a culture (broadly defined) has tended to relate to the disparate preoccupations of different groups that coexist in a country.

Calendars as Clues to Society and Culture

The study of calendars and their history, usage and social associations can provide a fruitful understanding of important aspects of a country and its cultures. For example, since calendars often have religious roles, there is sometimes a clear connection between regional religions and domestic calendars. Indeed, even the global calendars of the world are often classified as 'Christian', 'Muslim', 'Buddhist' and so on. The connection between calendars and cultures, however, goes well beyond this elementary linkage. Since the construction of calendars requires the use of mathematics as well as astronomy, and since

*This essay was first published in the *Little Magazine*, 1 (May 2000).

the functioning and utilization of calendars involves cultural sophistication and urbanity, the history of calendrical progress can tell us a lot about the society in which these developments occur.

Furthermore, given the fact that local times vary with the exact location of each place within a country, the use of a shared time and a common calendar requires the fixing of a reference location (such as Greenwich for Britain) and a principal meridian (in the case of Britain, the one that runs through Greenwich, giving us the Greenwich Mean Time, GMT). The determination of a reference location and a principal meridian is also, if only implicitly, a political decision, requiring an integrated view of the country. When GMT was imposed as the national standard in late-nineteenth-century Britain (the clinching statute came in 1880), it was not an uncontroversial decision: those in opposition included the Astronomer Royal, and also self-confident institutions that valued their independence and the 'accuracy' of their respective local times. The great clock of Christ Church in Oxford continued, for a while, to show, through an extra hand, both GMT and its local time – five minutes behind GMT – and the college tradition allowed the belief that 'one is not late till five minutes past the appointed time, that is till one is late by Oxford mean solar time as well as Greenwich'.[1] When, in 1884, at the International Meridian Conference in Washington, DC, the meridian through Greenwich was given the status of being 'the prime meridian for all nations' (by which GMT also acquired its official international position), Britain's dominant standing in world affairs certainly played an important political part.

Because of these associations, the nature, form and usage of calendars in a particular society can teach us a great deal about its politics, culture and religion as well as its science and mathematics. This applies even to as diverse a country as India, and it is in this sense that there will be an attempt in this essay to try to understand India through its calendars.

Millennial Occasions and Akbar's Concerns

This essay is being written as the second millennium of the Gregorian calendar comes to an end. That moment of passage has been interpreted in two distinct ways. In one system of counting, the Gregorian second millennium will end on 31 December 2000, but the glittering celebrations that have already occurred on 31 December 1999 indicate that the other view – according to which we are already in the third millennium – has its devoted supporters, at least among the fun-loving world population.

Even though the divisions of time that any particular calendar gives are quite arbitrary and dependent on pure convention, nevertheless a socially devised celebratory break point in time can be an appropriate occasion for reflection on the nature of the world in which we live. Different ways of seeing India – from purely Hinduism-centred views to intensely secular interpretations – are competing with each other for attention. The calendars relate to distinct religions and customs.

It is worth recollecting in this context that a little over four hundred years ago when the first millennium in the Muslim Hijri calendar was completed (the year 1000 of the Hijri era ran from 9 October 1591 to 27 September 1592), Emperor Akbar was engaged in a similar – but very much grander – exercise in the Muslim-dominated but deeply multi-religious India. Akbar's championing of religious tolerance is, of course, very well known, and is rightly seen as providing one of the major building blocks of Indian secularism. But in addition, Akbar's actions and policies also related closely to his enquiries and interpretations of India, and in that investigation, the calendrical systems had an important place.

Indeed, Akbar tried to understand the different calendars known and used in India, along with trying to study the different religions practised in the country. He went on, in the last decade of the millennium (in fact, in 992 Hijri, corresponding to 1584 CE), to propose a synthetic calendar for the country as a whole, the 'Tarikh-ilahi', just as he also proposed an amalgamated religion, the 'Din-ilahi', drawing on the different religions that existed in India. Neither of these two innovations survived, but the motivations behind the two moves – interrelated as they are – have received attention over the centuries and remain very relevant today. The present millennial occasion may well be an appropriate moment to return to some of Akbar's questions and concerns, presented at the end of a different millennium.

To this, I shall return at the end of the essay. But first I must examine the principal calendars that have governed the lives of Indians, and

Arjuna hits the target: Daswant, described by Abul Fazl as the greatest Indian painter in Akbar's court, depicts in Moghul style and letters a scene from the Mahābhārata

try to use that information for whatever understanding of India it offers. This perspective can provide clues to many different aspects of the science and society of India as well as its cultures and practices.

The Indian Calendars

India provides an astonishing variety of calendrical systems, with respective histories that stretch over several thousand years. The official Calendar Reform Committee, appointed in 1952 (shortly after Indian independence), which was chaired by Meghnad Saha himself, identified more than thirty well-developed calendars in systematic use in the country.[2] These distinct calendars relate to the diverse but interrelated histories of the communities, localities, traditions and religions that have coexisted in India. If one wanted confirmation of the pervasive pluralism of India, the calendars of India would provide fine evidence in that direction.

The authoritative *Whitaker's Almanack* reduces this long list to seven principal 'Indian eras'. It also gives the translation of the Gregorian year 2000 into these selected major calendars. Since, however, the beginning of the year in different calendars occurs at different times and in different seasons (for example, the Śaka era, the most widely used indigenous calendar in India, begins in spring, in the middle of April), these translations have to be seen in terms of substantial overlap rather than full congruence. The Gregorian year 2000 CE corresponds, *Whitaker's Almanack* reports, respectively with:

Year 6001 in the Kaliyuga calendar;
Year 2544 in the Buddha Nirvāṇa calendar;
Year 2057 in the Vikram Saṃvat calendar;
Year 1922 in the Śaka calendar;
Year 1921 (shown in terms of five-year cycles) of the Vedāṇga Jyotiśa calendar;
Year 1407 in the Bengali San calendar; and
Year 1176 in the Kollam calendar.

To this list, we can of course add other major calendars in extensive use in India, including the old Mahāvīra Nirvāṇa calendar associated with Jainism (in use for about the same length of time as the Buddha Nirvāṇa calendar), and later additions, such as the Islamic Hijri, the Parsee calendar and various versions of Christian date systems (and also the Judaic calendar, in local use in Kerala since the arrival of Jews in India, shortly after the fall of Jerusalem).

Ancient India and Its Calendars

It is clear from the table of Indian calendars in *Whitaker's Almanack* that the Kaliyuga calendar is apparently much older than – and quite out of line with – the other surviving old calendars. It also has a somewhat special standing because of its link with the religious account of the history of the world, described with mathematical – if mind-boggling – precision. (It is the last and the shortest of the four *yugas*, meant to last for 432,000 years, and has been preceded respectively by three other *yugas*, which were in length – going backwards – two, three and four times as long as the Kaliyuga, making up a total of 4,320,000 years altogether.) It is, of course, true that the Vikram Saṃvat and the Śaka calendars are also sometimes called 'Hindu calendars', and they are almost invariably listed under that heading, for example in *The Oxford Companion to the Year*. But they are mainly secular calendrical systems that were devised and used – for all purposes including, *inter alia*, religious ones – by people who happened to be Hindus. In contrast, Kaliyuga is given an orthodox and primordial religious status. Furthermore, as the ancientness of Hinduism is not in doubt, and since ancient India is often seen as primarily Hindu India, the temporal seniority of the Kaliyuga has also acquired a political significance of its own, which has a bearing in the interpretation of India as a country and as a civilization.

Interestingly enough, according to *Whitaker's Almanack* Kaliyuga too, like the Gregorian, is at the end of a millennium – its sixth. This 'double millennium' seems to offer cause for some jollity (such coincidences do not occur that often), not to mention the opportunity of inexpensive chauvinism for Indians to celebrate the completion of a sixth millennium at about the same time that the upstart Europeans enjoy the end of their modest second millennium.

How authentic is this dating of Kaliyuga in *Whitaker's Almanack*? The *Almanack* is quite right to report what is clearly the official date of the Kaliyuga calendar. Indeed, that dating is quite widely used, and even the Calendar Reform Committee reported the same convention (noting that year 1954 CE was year 5055 in Kaliyuga, which does correspond exactly to 2000 CE being 6001 Kaliyuga). However, this numbering convention raises two distinct questions, which deserve scrutiny. First, does the official Kaliyuga date correspond to the 'zero point' of the analytical system of the Kaliyuga calendar? Second, does the zero point of the Kaliyuga calendar reflect its actual historical age?

I fear I have to be the kill-joy who brings a doubly drab message. First, the zero point of Kaliyuga is not 6,001 but 5,101 years ago (corresponding to 3101–3102 BCE). Second, this zero point (5,101 years ago) is most unlikely to have been the actual date of origin of this calendar.

The first point is not in any kind of dispute, and the defenders of the pre-eminence of the Kaliyuga calendar rarely deny that the zero point is 3102 BCE. The zero point can be easily worked out from a statement of Āryabhaṭa, the great Indian mathematician and astronomer born in the fifth century, who had done foundational work in astronomy and mathematics, particularly trigonometry, and had also proposed the diurnal motion of the earth (with a corresponding theory of gravity – later expounded by Brahmagupta in the sixth century – to explain why objects are not thrown out as the earth turns). He noted that 3,600 years of the Kaliyuga calendar were just completed when he turned 23 (the year in which this precocious genius wrote his definitive mathematical treatise).[3] That was the year 421 in the Śaka calendar, which overlapped with 499 CE. From this it can be readily worked out that 2000 CE corresponds to year 5101 in the Kaliyuga calendar. This tallies also with what the Indian Calendar Reform Committee accepted, on the basis of all the evidence it had. This robs us of the opportunity of celebrating a double millennial occasion – the Gregorian second and the Kaliyuga sixth – but it still leaves the seniority of the Kaliyuga over the Gregorian quite unaffected, since 5,101 years is quite long enough (at least for chauvinistic purposes).

It is, however, important to take note of the often-overlooked distinction between a calendar's historical origin, and its zero point as a scaling device. To illustrate the distinction, it may be pointed out that the zero point in the Christian calendar was, obviously, fixed later, not when Jesus Christ was born. The zero point of the Kaliyuga calendar is clear enough, but in itself it does not tell us when that calendrical system, including its zero point, was adopted.

It has been claimed that the origin (or year zero) in Kaliyuga was fixed by actual astronomical observation in India in 3102 BCE. This has not only been stated by Indian traditionalists, it also received endorsement and support in the eighteenth century from no less an authority than the distinguished French astronomer Jean-Sylvain Bailly, who computed the orbit for Halley's comet. But as the great scientist and mathematician Laplace showed, this hypothesis is not likely to be correct. There is a clear discrepancy between the alleged astronomical observations (as reported for the zero year) and what would have been seen in the sky in 3102 BCE. Laplace had the benefit of contemporary astronomy to do this calculation quite precisely. This old calendar, ancient as it undoubtedly is, must not be taken, Laplace argued, as commemorating some actual astronomical observation.

> The Indian Tables indicate a much more refined astronomy, but everything shows that it is not of an extremely remote antiquity . . . The Indian Tables have two principal epochs, which go back, one to the year 3102, the other to the year 1491, before the Christian era . . . Notwithstanding all the arguments brought forward with the interest he [Jean-Sylvain Bailly] so well knew how to bestow on subjects the most difficult, I am still of the opinion that this period [from 3102 BCE to 1491 BCE] was invented for the purpose of giving a common origin to all the motions of the heavenly bodies in the zodiac.[4]

Let me pause a little here to note two points of some general interest. First, Laplace is disputing here the astronomical claims – often made – as to what was actually observed in 3102 BCE, and the critique is thus both of history (of the Kaliyuga calendar) and of applied astronomy (regarding what was observed and when). Second, Laplace does not treat the dating of 3102 BCE as purely arbitrary. Rather, he gives it an analytical or mathematical status, as distinct from its astronomical standing. Backward extrapolation may be a bad way of doing history, but it is an exercise of some analytical interest of its own.

Indeed, Laplace can be interpreted as adding force to the view, which can receive support from other evidence as well, that it is mathematics rather than observational science to which ancient Indian intellectuals were inclined to give their best attention. From the arithmetic conundrums of the *Atharvaveda* and the numerical fascination of the epics to the grammatical tables of Pāṇini and the numbering of sexual positions by Vātsāyana, there is a remarkable obsession in ancient India with enumeration and calculation. The plethora of Indian calendars and the analytical construction of their imagined history fit well into this reading of Indian intellectual tradition.

Returning to the Kaliyuga calendar, it is also perhaps of some significance that there is no corroboration of the use of the Kaliyuga calendar in the Vedas, which are generally taken to date from the second millennium BCE. There is, in fact, plenty of calendrical discussions in the Vedas, and a clear exposition of a system in which each year consists of twelve months of thirty days, with a thirteenth (leap) month added every five years. While the oldest of the Vedas, the *Rigveda*, outlines the main divisions of the solar year into months and seasons (four seasons of ninety days each), the more precise calculations, including the 'leap' (or intercalary) months, can be found in the *Atharvaveda*.[5] But the exact accounting system used in the Kaliyuga calculations is not found anywhere in the Vedas – at least not in the versions that have come down to us. It appears that there is no overt or even covert reference to the Kaliyuga calendar in the *Rāmāyaṇa* or the *Mahābhārata* either. Consideration of this and other evidence even prompted Meghnad Saha and his collaborators in the Calendar Reform Committee to suggest that the Kaliyuga calendar might have taken its present form precisely at the time of Āryabhaṭa, in 499 CE. Indeed, they speculated that its analytical system is 'a pure astronomical fiction created for facilitating Hindu astronomical calculations and was designed to be correct only for 499 AD'.

This may or may not be exactly right, but it is difficult to escape the conclusion that the Kaliyuga has not been in use much longer – if at all longer – than other old Indian calendars. The Vikram Saṃvat calendar, which is quite widely used in north India and in Gujarat, is traced to the reign of King Vikramāditya, and has a zero point at 57 BCE. But many of the accounts of the magnificent Vikramāditya are so shrouded in mystery, and there is so little firm evidence of its early use, that it is difficult to be sure of the exact history of the Vikram Saṃvat. In contrast, however, we do know that the Śaka calendar, which has a zero point (not necessarily its historical origin) in 78 CE, was in good use by 499 CE. Indeed, we know from Āryabhaṭa's own dating of the Kaliyuga in terms of the Śaka era (421 Śaka year) that at least by then the Śaka era is well known and in good use. While there is very little written evidence that survives on the use of the Śaka calendar (or indeed any other old calendar), it is worth noting that one well-known record (the Badami inscription) dating from 465 Śaka era or 543 CE does confirm the use of the Śaka era (not very long after the Āryabhaṭa statement, dated at the 421st Śaka year, or 499 CE).

It is hard to resist the conclusion that, unlike what appears from the table in *Whitaker's Almanack*, the Kaliyuga is not a lone forerunner of all the other extant calendars. In fact, it is even possible that among the surviving calendars today, the Buddha Nirvāṇa calendar (with a zero point in 544 BCE) may actually be significantly older than the Kaliyuga calendar. And so, quite possibly, is the Mahāvīra Nirvāṇa calendar of the Jains (with a zero point in 527 BCE). While the first uses of these calendars are hard to identify, there is solid evidence of the use of the Buddha Nirvāṇa calendar in Sri Lanka from the first century BCE – earlier than any that point firmly to the use of the Kaliyuga calendar.

Since I have been quite critical of the claims of priority of the Kaliyuga calendar as an old Indian calendar, I should make a couple of clarificatory observations, to prevent misunderstandings. First, it is not my purpose to deny that the Kaliyuga calendar may have a very old lineage. There is much evidence that it draws on older Indian calendars, including those discussed in the Vedas. But this ancient Indian inheritance is shared also by the Buddha Nirvāṇa calendar and the Mahāvīra Nirvāṇa calendar. We have to remember that ancient India is not just Hindu India, and there is an ancestry that is shared by several different religions that had their origin or flowering in India. The often-repeated belief that India was a 'Hindu country' before Islam arrived is, of course, a pure illusion, and the calendrical story fits well into what we know from other fields of Indian history.

Second, even though the sensual pleasure of celebrating the

completion of the sixth Indian millennium, compared with the ending of the second Gregorian millennium, may be denied to the Indian chauvinist, it is clear that by the time of the origin of Christianity, there were several calendars competing for attention in the subcontinent. What are now known as Christian calendars did not, of course, take that form until much later, but even the Roman calendars on which the Christian calendars (including the Gregorian) draw were going through formative stages over the first millennium BCE, precisely when the inheritance of the old Indian calendars was also getting sorted out. There is indeed much give and take between the older civilizations over this period, and it is difficult to separate out what emerged through an indigenous process in the subcontinent – or anywhere else – from what was learned by one culture from another.

There is evidence that Indians got quite a few of their ideas from the Greeks (there are several fairly explicit acknowledgements of that in the Siddhāntas), as did the Romans, but then the Greeks too had insisted that they had received a number of ideas from Indian works. As Severus Sebokt, the Syrian bishop, said in 662 CE (in a different country, in a different context): 'There are also others who know something.' If the Kaliyuga calendar loses its pre-eminence in critical scrutiny, the temptation of national chauvinism does much worse (while Hindu chauvinism does worse still).

Variations and Solidarity

The immense variety of systematic calendars in India brings out an important aspect of the country, in particular its cultural and regional variation. Yet this can scarcely be the whole story, since, despite this high variance, there is a concept of the country as a unit that has survived through history. To be sure, the presence of this concept is exactly what is denied in the often-repeated claim that India was no more than a large territory of small to medium fragments, united together, later on, by the cementing powers of British rule.

The British often see themselves as having 'authored' India, and this claim to imaginative creation fits well into Winston Churchill's belief (cited earlier) that India had no greater unity than the Equator had. It is, however, of some significance that even those who see no pre-British unity in India have no great difficulty in generalizing about the quality of Indians as a people (even Churchill could not resist articulating his view that Indians were 'the beastliest people in the world, next to the Germans'). Generalizations about Indians have gone on from the ancient days of Alexander the Great and Apollonius of Tyana (an early 'India expert') to the 'medieval' days of Arab and Iranian visitors (who wrote so much about the land and the people), to the early modern days of Herder, Schlegel, Schelling and Schopenhauer. It is also worth noting that an ambitious emperor – whether Candragupta Maurya or Ashoka or Alauddin or Akbar – has tended to assume that the empire was not complete until the bulk of the country was under his rule. Obviously, we would not expect to see, historically, a pre-existing 'Indian nation', in the modern sense, waiting anxiously to leap into becoming a nation state, but it is difficult to miss the social and cultural links and identities that could serve as the basis of one.

To this much debated issue, we can ask, what does the calendrical perspective bring? The variety of calendars, divided not only by religious connections but also by regional diversity, seems to be deeply hostile to any view of Indian unity. However, it must be noted in this context that many of these calendars have strong similarities, in terms of months, and also the beginning of the year. For example, the Kaliyuga, the Vikram Saṃvat, the Śaka, the Bengali San and several other Indian calendars begin very close to each other in the middle of April. There is evidence that their respective beginnings were typically fixed at the same point, the vernal equinox, from which they have moved over the long stretch of time in the last two millennia, during which the 'correction' for the integer value of the length of the year in terms of days has been slightly inadequate – again in much the same way.

The fact that the integer value of 365 days to the year is only approximate was, of course, known to the Indian mathematicians who constructed the calendars. To compensate for this, the periodic adjustments standardly used in many of the Indian calendars take the form of adding a leap or intercalary month (called a *mala māsa*) to bring practice in line with the dictates of computation. But the adequacy of the correction depends on getting the length of the year exactly right, and this was difficult to do with the instruments and understanding at the time the respective calendars were initiated or reformed. Indeed, the sixth-century mathematician Varāhamihira gave 365.25875 days as the true measure of the year, which, while close enough, was still slightly wrong, since the length of the sidereal year is 365.25636 days and the tropical year is 365.24220 days. The errors have moved the different north-Indian calendars away from the intended fixed points, such as the vernal equinox, but they have tended to move together, with considerable solidarity with each other.

There are, of course, exceptions to this show of unity in slight error, since the south-Indian calendars (such as the Kollam) and the lunar or luni-solar calendars (such as the Buddha Nirvāṇa) follow different rules. Indeed, it would be hard to expect a dominant uniformity in the calendrical – or indeed cultural – variations within India, and what one has to look for is the interest that different users of distinct calendars have tended to have in the practices of each other. I shall argue later that this mutual interest extends also to the calendars used by Indian Muslims after Islam came to India.

One of the tests of the presence of a united perspective in calendrical terms, already discussed, is the identification of a principal meridian and a reference location (like Greenwich in Britain). It is remarkable how durable has been the position of the ancient city of Ujjayinī (now known as Ujjain), the capital of several Hindu dynasties of India (and the home of many literary and cultural activities through the first millennium CE), as the reference location for many of the main Indian calendars. The Vikram Saṃvat calendar (with a zero point in 57 BCE) apparently originated in this ancient capital city. But it is also the locational base of the Śaka system (zero point in 78 CE) and a great many other Indian calendars. Indeed, even today, Ujjain's location is used to fix the anchor point of the Indian clock (serving, in this respect, as the Indian Greenwich). The Indian Standard Time that governs our lives still remains a close approximation of Ujjayinī time – five hours and thirty minutes ahead of GMT.

A contemporary visitor to this very modest and sleepy town may find it interesting to note that nearly two millennia ago the well-known astronomical work *Paulisa Siddhānta*, which preceded the definitive *Āryabhāṭiya*, focused its attention on longitudes at three places in the world: Ujjain, Benares and Alexandria. Ujjain serves as a good reminder of the relation between calendar and culture. We have wonderful descriptions of Ujjayinī in Indian literature, particularly from Kālidāsa in the fifth century, perhaps the greatest poet and dramatist in classical Sanskrit literature.

The elegance and beauty of Kālidāsa's Ujjayinī even made E. M. Forster take a trip there in 1914. Forster wanted to reconstruct in his mind what Ujjain looked like in the days that Kālidāsa had so lovingly described. He recollected passages from Kālidāsa, including the stirring account of evenings when 'women steal to their lovers' through 'darkness that a needle might divide'. But he could not get the old ruins there to reveal much, nor manage to get the local people to take the slightest interest in his historical and literary search. Ankle deep in the river Śipra, so romantically described by Kālidāsa, Forster abandoned his search, and accepted the prevailing wisdom: 'Old buildings are buildings, ruins are ruins.'[6] I shall not speculate whether in that abandonment of historical exactness, there is something of a unity (perhaps illustrated even by the already discussed factual uncertainty of the Kaliyuga despite its mathematical exactness). But certainly there is something very striking about the constancy of Ujjain's dominance in Indian time accounting, even though the focus of political power, and of literary and cultural pre-eminence, shifted from Ujjain itself, a long time ago.

Interaction and Integration

One of the contrasts between the different Indian calendars relates to their respective religious associations. This was a matter of particular interest to that original multiculturalist Akbar, as I have already discussed. He was especially concerned with the fact that as a Muslim he was ruling over a country of many different faiths. To that particular concern, I shall presently return, but I would like to clarify that, even before the arrival of Islam in India, India was a quintessentially multicultural and multi-religious country. Indeed, nearly all the major religions of the world (Hinduism, Christianity, Buddhism, Jainism, Judaism) were present in India well before the Muslim conquests occurred. The Indian civilization had not only produced Buddhism and Jainism (and later on, the Sikh religion as well), but India had the benefit of having Jews much longer than Europe, had been host to sizeable Christian communities before Britain had any, and provided a home to the Parsees right from the time when religious persecution began in Iran. In fact, Jews arrived shortly after the fall of Jerusalem, Christians appeared at least as early as the fourth century, and Parsees started arriving by the eighth. The different calendars associated with these religions – Buddhist, Jain, Judaic, Christian, Parsee – were already flourishing in India, along with the Hindu calendars, when the Muslim conquest of the north led to the influence of the Hijri calendar. Islam's arrival further enriched the religious – and calendrical – diversity of India.

The pioneering multiculturalism of Akbar included his taking an interest in the religion and culture of each of these groups. In his 'House of Worship' (*Ibadat Khana*), the people from diverse religions who were encouraged to attend included – as Abul Fazl noted – not only the mainstream Hindu and Muslim philosophers (of different denominations), but also Christians, Jews, Parsees, Jains and even members of the atheistic Cārvāka school.

Akbar's attempt at introducing a combined calendar paralleled his interest in floating a combined religion, the Din-ilahi. On the calendrical front, Akbar may have begun by just taking note of various calendars (Hindu, Parsee, Jain, Christian and others), but he proceeded then to take the radical step of trying to devise a new synthetic one. In 992 Hijri (1584 CE, Gregorian), just short of the Hijri millennium, he promulgated the brand new calendar, viz. the Tarikh-ilahi, God's calendar – no less. The zero year of Tarikh-ilahi corresponds to 1556 CE (the year in which Akbar ascended to the throne), but that is not its year of origin, which was 1584. It was devised as a solar calendar (like the Hindu and Iranian/Parsee calendars of the region), but had some features of the Hijri as well, and also bore the mark of a person who knew the calendrical diversity represented by Christian, Jain and other calendars in local use in Akbar's India. The Tarikh-ilahi became the official calendar, and the decrees of the ruling Moghal emperor of India (the *farmans*) henceforth carried both the synthetic Tarikh and the Muslim Hijri date, and occasionally only the Tarikh.[7]

Even though Tarikh-ilahi was introduced with a grand vision, its acceptance outside the Moghal court was rather limited, and the subcontinent went on using the Hijri as well as the older Indian calendars. While Akbar's constructive calendar died not long after he himself did, his various synthesizing efforts left a lasting mark on Indian history. But has the calendrical expression, in particular, of Akbar's synthesizing commitment been lost without trace?

Not so. There is a surviving calendar, the Bengali San, which was clearly influenced by Tarikh-ilahi, and which still carries evidence of the integrating tendency that is so plentifully present in many other fields of Indian culture and tradition (such as music, painting, architecture, and so on). It is year 1407 now (as I write in 2000 CE) in the Bengali calendar, the San. What does 1407 stand for? Encouraged by Akbar's Tarikh-ilahi, the Bengali calendar was also 'adjusted' as far as the numbering of year goes in the late sixteenth century. In fact, using the zero year of the Tarikh, 1556 CE (corresponding to year 963 in the Hijri calendar), the Bengali solar calendar, which has a procedure of reckoning that is very similar to the solar Śaka system, was 'adjusted' to the lunar Hijri number, but not to the lunar counting system. That is, the 'clock' of this solar calendar was put back, as it were, from Śaka 1478 to Hijri 963 in the newly devised Bengali San. However, since the Bengali San (like the Śaka era) remained solar, the Hijri has marched ahead of the San, being a lunar calendar (with a mean length of 354 days, 8 hours and 48 minutes per year), and the Bengali San – just turned 1407 – has fallen behind Hijri as well.

Like the abortive Tarikh-ilahi, the more successful Bengali San too is the result of a daring integrational effort, and its origin is clearly related to the synthetic experiment of the Tarikh-ilahi (and thus, indirectly, to Akbar's multicultural philosophy). When a Bengali Hindu does religious ceremonies according to the local calendar, he or she may not be quite aware that the dates that are invoked in the calendrical accompaniment of the Hindu practices are attuned to commemorating Muhammad's journey from Mecca to Medina, albeit in a mixed lunar-solar representation.

The tradition of multiculturalism in India is particularly worth recollecting at this moment in Indian history, when India's secularism is being sporadically challenged by new forces of intolerance and by politically cultivated fanaticism of one kind or another. What is under attack is not only some 'modern' notion of secularism born and bred in post-Enlightenment Europe, or some quintessentially 'Western' idea brought to India by the British, but a long tradition of accommodating and integrating different cultures which had found many articulate expressions in India's past – partly illustrated by India's calendrical history as well.

Caught as we are in India today in conflicting attempts to interpret Indian civilization and society, the calendrical perspective offers, I believe, some insights that are relevant and forceful. The calendars reveal, in fact, a great deal more than just the months and the years.

16

The Indian Identity*

Colonialism and Identity

I feel greatly honoured by the invitation to give the Dorab Tata Memorial Lectures. I appreciate this opportunity for several different reasons. First and foremost, it is wonderful to have the chance to celebrate the memory of Dorab (or Dorabji) Tata, an outstanding industrial leader, a remarkable philanthropist and a visionary human being. A second reason is that the nature of this event, and more specifically the history of the Tatas' achievements (given their deep involvement in India's future, combined with a very wide interest in the world at large), provides an occasion to examine the relationship between India and the world. Closely linked to our reading of that relationship is the difficult subject of the nature of the Indian identity, especially challenging in a rapidly changing world. That is going to be the main focus of my discussion.

My third reason for welcoming this occasion is rather personal. The development of the Tata industries, particularly iron and steel and cotton textile, is an integral part of the history of modern India, and it is a history that has enticed and fascinated me for quite a long time now.† One of the interesting questions that had to be addressed

*This essay is based on my Dorab Tata Memorial Lectures given in India (the first one in Mumbai, the second in New Delhi) in February 2001. I should acknowledge that some of the material that formed part of these lectures has been used in the introductory essays (Essays 1–4) in this volume. Those discussions are omitted here, except what has to be recapitulated for the coherence of the present essay, drawn on the two lectures.

†Indeed, the history of the entrepreneurship of the Tatas was one of my principal concerns in a paper I wrote more than forty years ago: 'The Commodity Pattern of

was the willingness and ability of Indian entrepreneurs, most notably the Tatas, to go into fields, such as iron and steel and cotton textile, that British enterprise largely shunned. I wanted to understand better the influence of values and identities on economic behaviour, over and above the general discipline that is provided by economic feasibility and commercial profitability. I was particularly keen to investigate the part that a vision of the country's needs and a specifically Indian identity and affiliation played in firing industrial imagination and innovative action. On the other hand, I was also interested in the climate of social anxiety in Britain about economic changes that could be seen as threatening established British interests in India.

As an economist I do not, I believe, need to be told that profits and commercial viability are important (though I have been lectured on that subject from time to time by friends and well-wishers who have wondered whether I manage to take sufficient note of the hard realities of the world). But within the limits of feasibility and reasonable returns, there are substantial choices to be made, and in these choices one's visions and identities could matter. There is an interesting issue as to why British investment, which came so plentifully to tea, coffee, railways, mining, mercantile establishments and even to the newly born jute industry, was so hesitant in the fields that were the pillars of British industrial establishment, to wit, cotton textile and iron and steel. There is, in particular, the difficult question about the possible perception that these fields were competitive with – and adverse to the interests of – old-established industries in Britain (in Manchester and elsewhere). There is a good deal of empirical evidence that such thoughts had crossed the minds of many responsible people in Britain, but we still have to ask whether such perceptions constituted a significant economic and social phenomenon, and to what extent they affected the pattern of British investment in India.

British Enterprise in Early Indian Industrialization 1854–1914', in the *Proceedings of the Second International Conference of Economic History* (Paris, 1965). A shortened version was published as 'The Pattern of British Enterprise in India 1854–1914: A Causal Analysis', in B. Singh and V. B. Singh (eds.), *Social and Economic Change* (Bombay: Allied Publishers, 1967). The shorter version was made somewhat more intriguing through a small misprint – with the title of the paper making the heady claim that I was presenting a 'casual' analysis.

The issue is not so much whether British investors, or for that matter British governors, might have been directly swayed by the protests that came from vested interests in Britain (for example, by the strong memorandum that the Manchester Chamber of Commerce sent to the Secretary of State for India in 1871, demanding tariff adjustment for Indian cotton textile), or by alarmist reports produced by field studies specially commissioned by established British interests (for example, by the report, in the 1870s, of John Robertson, an experienced spinner, on the growth of Indian cotton textile and its likely damaging implications for the British economy).

Rather, the question is whether a general sense of social identity and priorities, which are known to play a considerable part in economic decisions in general, exerted significant influence on the pattern of British investment in India, both through public policy and through private choice. Sir John Strachey, the well-admired and efficient English administrator with much experience of the Raj, put the central point very clearly, in his Budget speech of 28 March 1877:

> I have not ceased to be an Englishman because I have passed the greater part of my life in India, and have become a member of the Indian Government. The interests of Manchester at which foolish people sneer, are the interests not only of the great and intelligent population engaged directly in the trade in cotton but of millions of Englishmen.[1]

Identity, Nationalism and Investment

In contrast with possible British concerns, the social aspects of these investment opportunities looked enticingly different from the opposite end of the divide. As J. R. D. Tata put it in his Foreword to Frank Harris's biography of Jamsetji Tata, not only did Jamsetji understand 'the full significance of the industrial revolution in the West and its potentialities for his own country', but also 'dreamt of an industrialized and prosperous India'.[2] We can even see a progressive hold of nationalist thinking in the sequence in which Jamsetji's first cotton mills, called 'Empress Mills' and established in 1877 (just as Queen Victoria was proclaimed the Empress of India), were soon followed by the new 'Svadeshi Mills', established in 1886.* Indeed, in the year before, in 1885, Jamsetji was present at the founding of the Indian National Congress in Bombay, a cause to which he generously contributed.[3] The nationalist connections were present in different ways and to varying extents in the different economic decisions in which the early Tata enterprises were involved. They were perhaps most colourfully visible, in an anecdotal form, in his determination to establish a top world-class hotel in Bombay. There is, apparently, truth in the story that Jamsetji's decision to establish, in 1903, the ambitiously planned Tajmahal Hotel (the first building in Bombay to be lit by electricity and a place that would soon attract celebrities, from Somerset Maugham to Gregory Peck), followed his being told at Pyrke's Apollo Hotel, to which he had taken a foreign friend for a meal, that while the friend was welcome in that ('for Europeans only') hotel, he – Jamsetji – was not.[4] The anecdote adds colour to our understanding of Jamsetji's sense of identity and priorities, but the basic picture is clear enough from many other decisions as well.

Jamsetji's determination to have a flourishing iron and steel industry in India fits clearly into this pattern. There had been earlier, abortive attempts, including one by a remarkable Englishman called Josiah Marshall Heath in the 1830s (the chronicle of his misfortunes was recorded by Charles Dickens in *Household Words* in 1853).[5] Also, a small iron works was established in Barakar in 1875, which in 1889 became part of the newly formed Bengal Iron and Steel Company, and had a rather troubled history. But we can see no great groundswell of interest among British investors to go into iron and steel in India. Jamsetji's attempts in the 1880s at large-scale production of iron and steel were initially frustrated, particularly by the unwillingness of the Raj to cooperate, specifically in the arrangements for transport – a vital infrastructural requirement for the proposed iron and steel mill.

*The literal meaning of the Sanskrit term *svadeshi* is 'of one's own country', so that the name 'Svadeshi Mills' need not, in itself, convey anything more than these mills being designated as 'domestic'. But the term had already become significantly assertive in Indian nationalist politics. Indeed, the industrial entrepreneurship of the Tatas would soon be championed as an object of considerable pride by the rapidly growing 'Svadeshi' movement, which would also urge Indians to buy 'svadeshi' goods.

By the turn of the century, however, Jamsetji had received the support of the new Viceroy of India, Lord Curzon, and the coordination of the transport arrangements with industrial production was henceforth much easier to organize. Curzon even offered to help build a 45-mile rail connection from the identified hill of iron to the proposed factory. The personality of Curzon was undoubtedly important in this shift in governmental policy, but it is also worth noting that Indo-British trade relations were undergoing very major changes in this period. In particular, Britain was being displaced from its semi-monopoly position of exporting steel to India and losing ground in iron exports as well. In the middle of the 1880s, the United Kingdom was the dominant source of steel imports into India (supplying more than 90 per cent of the total imports), but by the time Curzon arrived in India in 1899, Belgium had overtaken Britain as the largest exporter of steel to India, and Germany too had become a significant source.[6]

What had not changed was the determination of the Tatas to establish a major iron and steel industry in India. There were still barriers of bureaucracy and of financing to be overcome, and when Jamsetji died in 1904, the project was yet to materialize. By 1906 matters had progressed enough for Dorabji to seek financing from London. However, the London money market was unenthusiastic, and despite protracted efforts, nothing much came of them.

And then, interestingly enough, the link with Indian identity and nationalism, which was part of the Tata motivation, itself came to the rescue. When the prospectus for the projected iron and steel works was published in August 1907, the appeal to the 'Svadeshi' movement was loud and clear. The response was immediate. As a close observer (Mr Axel Sahlin) later reported in a speech given in England:

> From early morning till late at night, the Tata Offices in Bombay were besieged by an eager crowd of native investors. Old and young, rich and poor, men and women they came, offering their mites; and at the end of three weeks, the entire capital required for construction requirements . . . was secured, every penny contributed by some 8,000 native Indians.[7]

The construction of the project began in 1908 and the much-prized output started to roll out from December 1911.

Nationalism and Global Connections

This brief history is worth recollecting, not only to pay tribute to one of the leaders of the events described, but also because it illustrates how our sense of identity and social motivation can indeed play a major part in the determination of our behaviour, including economic behaviour. Evidence of such connections emerges from different sides, including the visionary determination of Jamsetji, Dorabji and others to pursue an industrial future for India, the spontaneous support provided by an inspired Indian public, the selective reticence of British investors and the varying attitudes of British Indian government. This is not the occasion to pursue these connections further, but they are strongly suggestive of a significant role of identities and values in economic behaviour, which deserves greater attention than it tends to receive in mainstream economic analysis.[8]

There are also general issues which are raised by this historical experience, and which have significant relevance to India's relation with the world. It is, in particular, important to distinguish between the inclusionary role of identity and the exclusionary force of separatism. To want to do something in the interests of a country is not the same thing as wanting the country to be distanced from the rest of the world, or to be isolated from it. The sense of identity leaves the issue of appropriate actions and policies entirely open to scrutiny and choice. This applies to science and technology on the one hand and to economic, social and cultural relations on the other. India's relations with the world may demand significant use of the Indian identity, but they also call for critical scrutiny of specific ends and particular ways and means through which those relations may be appropriately advanced. Since identity politics and communitarian reasoning often have the effect of nurturing and promoting separatism, the distinction is important to seize.

The industrial story with which I began also illustrates this clearly enough. Despite the long history of the iron industry in India (Lovat Fraser, the historian of that industry, describes the more than 2,000-year-old massive iron column, entirely free of rust and deterioration, situated on the open ground outside the Kutub Minar in Delhi as 'a mystery greater than the building of the pyramids'[9]), the Tatas would have got nowhere in their attempt to build a modern iron and steel industry without the help of foreign expertise. They needed technical know-how from abroad, which they proceeded to obtain, well illustrated by the critical role of Charles Page Perin and the expertise he brought from Pittsburgh.[10] In general, the pursuit of what is sometimes called 'Western science and technology' was central to India's industrial and economic development. The priority the Tatas gave to modern scientific education is also well illustrated by their commitment to their educational and research agenda, such as the pioneering foundation of the Indian Institute of Science, which came into existence in 1911, and which in its turn encouraged the development of a number of other scientific institutes in the country.

A similar point can be made about the need to take note of possibly beneficial uses of interdependence in the field of trade and exchange. Considerations of identity may suggest that note be taken in economic decisions of a country's broad interests (going beyond immediate business profits), but we still have to ask how these interests will be best served. Indeed, they may, often enough, be well served by greater economic engagement with the world, rather than by shunning global association. This is a matter for actual economic assessment – not to be determined through the adoption of one or other of the simple slogans (either worshipful of markets or dismissive of their role) that bedevil critical scrutiny of such issues as trade and globalization.

This decision may call for some clarificatory remarks. The development of new enterprises tends to involve displacing existing imports, since goods for domestic consumption obviously have to come from abroad when they are not yet produced at home. There is no mystery here. As a result, import substitution is typically the initial form of industrial expansion in an economically interconnected world; this is an important but thoroughly unsurprising fact. But it does not entail anything whatsoever about the relative desirability of import substitution or export promotion.[11] The economic case for one or the other has to be worked out on the basis of economic returns both to the enterprises involved (including its employees as well as employers) and to the public at large. The experiences of many countries in the world, beginning with Japan but later on also other sizeable economies, such as South Korea and Taiwan, suggest that there is typically a strong case for moving rapidly from the import substitution phase to one of active export promotion, and that this strategy of development is perfectly consistent with the championing and promotion of a powerful national identity. Whether this would indeed be the right policy in a particular case is, of course, a matter for critical scrutiny and cannot be determined by simple formulas of one kind or another that are often championed – either favouring unrestrained trade in general or shunning it altogether.

Sharing of Global Opportunities

This gives me the occasion to move to the more general question of the pros and cons of globalization. Debates on the merits and penalties of globalization have been very active in recent years, not only within each nation (not least in India), but also in global protest movements, such as those in Seattle, Prague or Washington, DC, which drew protesters from every part of the world. In this sense, protests about globalization themselves constitute a globalized phenomenon, and should be seen as such. Globalized political resistance has tended to confront the established pattern of globalized economic relations.

I have tried to argue elsewhere that these protest movements have often been, in many ways, quite constructive, in forcefully drawing attention to problems of inequality in the world.* Indeed, the real debate on globalization is, ultimately, not about the efficiency of markets, nor about the importance of modern technology. The debate, rather, is about severe asymmetries of power, for which there is much less tolerance now than in the world that emerged at the end of the Second World War. There may or may not be significantly more economic inequality today, as is sometimes strongly asserted and equally staunchly denied (the evidence on this is conflicting, depend-

*The main argument was presented in my Commencement Address ('Global Doubts') at Harvard University in June 2000, and then more elaborately in 'How to Judge Globalism', *American Prospect*, 13 (Jan. 2002).

ing on the indicators we use), but what is absolutely clear is that people are far less willing to accept massive inequalities than they were in 1944 when the Bretton Woods agreement led to the establishment of the IMF, the World Bank and other institutions and paved the way for the present international architecture of finance and business. The global doubts partly reflect this new mood, and it is, to a great extent, the global equivalent of the within-nation protests about inequality with which we have been familiar for quite some time.

It is not at all hard to present arguments to reject many of the criticisms that have tended to figure on the posters and placards of the global protest movements. But there is a basic need to recognize that, despite the big contribution that a global economy can undoubtedly make to the prosperity of the world, we also have to confront the far-reaching manifestations of global inequality and injustice. There is, in fact, no real conflict between being determined to resist global inequality and injustice and at the same time understanding and facilitating the positive contributions of globalized economic, social and cultural relations across the world.

Indeed, resistance to global disparities calls for both global initiatives and for national and local ones. At the global level, there is need for a variety of policies. These issues were not seen clearly enough at the time of the Bretton Woods Agreement in the 1940s – when half the world was under colonial rule, when the claims of democracy and human rights were not yet widely recognized, when the massive prospects of global economic growth were not fully understood and when the tolerance of global disparities and divides was very much greater. Global initiatives are needed for a more responsive international architecture (including the strengthening of the financial viability and economic power of the United Nations), better formulation of patent laws (taking note of their actual effects on the use of technology as well as vitally important products, including medicine for severe ailments), more pressure on the richer countries to reduce trade restrictions (rather than demanding this only from the poorer and less well-placed countries), more effective institutional arrangements for defending human security and basic human rights across the world (not being content only with promoting international trade), and so on. There is need for quite a global agenda.

Domestic Policies for Global Strength

However, healthy global economic relations also call for appropriate domestic policies. For example, the feasibility of effective global participation is closely linked with the development of human resources and capabilities (for example, through educational expansion) and the development of infrastructure. Interestingly enough, the history of the Tatas has significant light to throw on the importance of both these. Indeed, Jamsetji's attempt to develop large-scale iron and steel production was initially held up, as I mentioned earlier, precisely because of the barrier of underdeveloped transport facilities, which was a crucial infrastructural handicap. There is a clear analogy here with the restrictions imposed today by infrastructural underdevelopment in India, for example in public communication and electric power, well illustrated by the debilitating – and perhaps even maddening – role of power cuts and non-working telephones. Infrastructural problems are, in many fields, still as central to the contemporary Indian economy as they were to Jamsetji's India a century ago.

The importance of education was one of the factors strongly identified by Jamsetji. This was, in fact, his reason for starting the Institute of Science. He saw the field of industrial competition being matched by one of educational competition. In praising the scholars associated with the Institute, Jamsetji could not help remarking, with some pride, that Indian students 'can not only hold their own against the best rivals in Europe on the latter's ground, but can beat them hollow'.[12] This was a matter not only of national pride, but also of India's ability to interact fruitfully and strongly in the international arena. The connection is still very important.

The central role of education also highlights the far-reaching effects of the remarkable contrast between India's neglect of school education and the massive expansion of higher education that has already occurred and continues today. The Tatas were among the pioneers in developing higher and technical education in India – a priority that Nehru, too, adopted, especially in the programme of expanding such institutions as the Indian Institutes of Technology, which were launched at his initiative and which have been critically important for the recent flowering of information technology and related developments in India. This, along with the good work of Institutes of Management, has brought many dividends and has certainly been instrumental in opening up possibilities in a powerful way to many well-placed Indians. They have done remarkably well in India and many of them abroad as well. When I went to give some lectures at Stanford University in California in January 2001, I was asked to address a group of about 800 so-called 'Silicon Indians' (in an impressive meeting arranged by The Indus Entrepreneurs: TIE), and it was quite evident that one part of the Indian community has been able to seize the opportunities offered in a very different culture and society from the one in which they were reared. Even within India, the size and speed of expansion of technology products (including computer software) have been quite extraordinary.

Yet the underdevelopment of Indian school systems, especially in socially backward regions of the country and particularly among disadvantaged groups, has been equally extraordinary. This is both deeply inefficient and amazingly unjust. The smart boy or clever girl who is deprived of the opportunity of schooling, or who goes to a school with dismal facilities (not to mention the high incidence of absentee teachers), not only loses the opportunities he or she could have had, but also adds to the massive waste of talent that is a characteristic of the life of our country. If we have not yet been able to seize the economic opportunities for the manufacture of simple products in a way that has happened in Japan, Korea, China and other countries in east Asia, not to mention the West, India's remarkable neglect of basic education has a decisive role in this handicap.*

Global economic relations have many different aspects and call for different types of policy initiatives, but many of the problems and difficulties associated with a more competitive global economy turn, to a substantial extent, on the limitations of our own domestic public policy, such as basic education, health care, micro-credit, or infrastructural planning. India's placing in the world is determined just as much within India as abroad.

*Japan's demonstration, already apparent by the early twentieth century, that school education can greatly contribute to economic development was largely ignored in India.

Global Relations and History

I want to turn now to some foundational issues about the role of global interconnections and human progress. Globalization is a complex phenomenon. Some of the fears expressed about globalization make it sound like an animal – analogous to the big shark in *Jaws* – that gobbles up unsuspecting innocents in a dark and mysterious way. We must have a good look at this alleged beast, rather than just learn to shun it.

What exactly *is* globalization? A diverse basket of global interactions are put under this broad heading, varying from the expansion of cultural influences across borders to the enlargement of economic and business relations throughout the world. It is often argued that globalization is a new folly. Is that a plausible diagnosis? I would argue that globalization, in its basic form, is neither particularly new, nor, in general, a folly. It is through global movements of ideas, people, goods and technology that different regions of the world have tended, in general, to benefit from progress and development occurring in other regions. The direction of interregional movements of ideas has varied over history, and these directional variations are important to recognize, since the global movement of ideas is sometimes seen just as ideological imperialism of the West – as a one-sided movement that simply reflects an asymmetry of power which needs to be resisted.

It may, in fact, be instructive to contemplate the nature of the world not at the end of the millennium that we have just ushered out, but at the end of the previous millennium. Around 1000 CE, globalization of science, technology and mathematics was changing the nature of the old world, even though, as it happens, the principal currents of dissemination then were typically in the opposite direction to what we see today.

For example, the high technology in the world of 1000 included paper and printing, the crossbow and gunpowder, the wheelbarrow and the rotary fan, the clock and the iron chain suspension bridge, the kite and the magnetic compass. Every one of these 'high-tech' fields of knowledge in the world a millennium ago was well established in China, and at the same time was practically unknown elsewhere. It was globalization that spread them across the world, including Europe.

We can similarly consider the impact of Eastern influence on Western mathematics. The decimal system emerged and became well developed in India between the second and the sixth centuries, and was also used extensively soon thereafter by Arab mathematicians. These procedures reached Europe mainly in the last quarter of the tenth century, and their momentous effects were felt in the early years of the last millennium. Globalization in mathematics as well as in science and engineering played a major part in the revolution of thought and social organization that helped to transform Europe into its modern shape. Europe would have been much poorer had it resisted the globalization of mathematics, science and technology at that time, and to a great extent the same – working in the converse direction – is true today. To identify the phenomenon of the global spread of ideas with an ideological imperialism would be a serious error, somewhat similar to the way any European resistance to Eastern influence would have been at the beginning of the last millennium.

India has been, like many other countries, both an exporter and importer of ideas in our world of continuing global interactions. An inadequate recognition of this two-way process sometimes leads to rather redundant controversies and conflicts. Much, for example, has been written recently about where the concept of zero, which is quite central for mathematics, developed. The claim, often made earlier, that this was an Indian contribution to the world has been strongly challenged in a number of recent publications, giving Babylon priority.* There is, in fact, considerable evidence that the concept of zero, as an idea, emerged in different cultures which may or may not have been linked. But there is evidence also for the belief that the particular symbol for zero that was adopted across the world, including in India, very likely came from Babylon via the Greeks to India, even though the Indian idea of zero in the form of *śūnya* (or emptiness) predates that arrival. It is, however, also clear that the combination of zero with a decimal place system was a particularly fruitful consolidation, and it is in

*See in particular Robert Kaplan, *The Nothing That Is: A Natural History of Zero* (Oxford: Oxford University Press, 1999), and Charles Seife, *Zero: The Biography of a Dangerous Idea* (New York: Penguin Books, 2000).

exploring the nature and implications of this integration – critically important for the use of a decimal system – that Indian mathematicians seemed to have had quite a decisive role in the early and middle parts of the first millennium. We can consider many other such examples of combining give and take, enriching the process of global intellectual interaction.*

Globalization is neither new, nor in general a folly. Through persistent movements of goods, people, techniques and ideas, it has shaped the history of the world. India has been an integral part of the world in the most interactive sense. The forces of ideological separatism may be strong in India at present, as they are elsewhere, but they militate not just against the global history of the world, but also against India's own heritage.

That acknowledgement does not, of course, undermine the overwhelming need to pay particular attention to the predicament of the vulnerable and the disadvantaged, and this is indeed an important consideration in the determination of good economic policies for the contemporary world. Global economic interactions bring general benefits, but they can also create problems for many, because of inadequacies of global arrangements as well as limitations of appropriate domestic policies. It is important that these issues receive attention. But at the same time we have to be careful that we do not shut ourselves out of the global interactions that have enriched the world over millennia.

Pluralism and Receptivity

The nature of Indian identity raises issues both of external and internal relations. I have so far concentrated on the need to resist external

*In the original lecture, I went on from here to discuss other examples of multi-directional migration of ideas, such as the impact of Indian Buddhism on the development of printing in China, Korea and Japan, and the eventual use of that achievement in India itself. There was also a discussion of international interchange leading to innovations in mathematics and science between India and the Arabs and Europeans, on the West, and China and east Asia, on the East. These cases have been discussed elsewhere, particularly in Essays 1 and 6–8, and are therefore omitted here.

isolation. It is, however, the pull towards internal separation of communities that has presented the strongest challenge in recent years to the integrity of the Indian identity. Political developments in India over the last decade or two have had the effect of forcefully challenging, in several different ways, the broad and absorbing idea of Indian identity that emerged in the days of the independence movement and that helped to define the concept of the Indian nation. If we believe that there is something of value in this inheritance, we need to understand precisely why it is valuable, and also to examine how that recognition can be adequately articulated.

It would be hard to claim that there is some exact, homogeneous concept of Indian identity that emerged during the independence movement as a kind of national consensus, or that there were no differences between the way Indianness was seen by, say, Mahatma Gandhi or Rabindranath Tagore (to consider two leading and somewhat dissimilar voices that helped to teach us what we are). The general idea of a spacious and assimilative Indian identity, which Gandhi and Tagore shared, was interpreted with somewhat different emphases by the two, and there were other differences in the characterization of Indian identity by other theorists and intellectual leaders of the independence movement.

These distinctions were – and remain – important in many contexts, for example in interpreting the respective roles of science, ethics and analytical reasoning in India's past and in its future.* But these varying interpretations all share an inclusionary reading of Indian identity that tolerates, protects and indeed celebrates diversity within a pluralist India. They also reflect an understanding of India's past as a joint construction in which members of different communities were involved. Tagore and Gandhi differed substantially, both in their respective cultural predispositions and in their religious beliefs and personal practice. But in interpreting India and the Indian identity, they shared a general refusal to privilege any one narrowly circumscribed perspective (such as an exclusively religious approach, or, more specifically, a Hindu view).

It is the combination of internal pluralism and external receptivity

*Essay 5 goes into some of the differences between Gandhi and Tagore.

that has been most challenged in recent decades by separatist viewpoints, varying from communitarian exclusion and aggressive parochialism on the one side to cultural alienation and isolationist nationalism on the other. These challenges and their practical manifestations give some urgency to subjecting the idea of Indian identity to critical scrutiny and assessment.

Identities and Decisions

It is useful to recollect Rabindranath Tagore's remarkable claim, made in a letter to C. F. Andrews in 1921, that the 'idea of India' itself militates 'against the intense consciousness of the separateness of one's own people from others' (a visionary statement that was also quoted earlier in this collection of essays).[13] Note that there are two distinct implications of this claim. First, internally, it argues against an idea of India as a mixture of separated and alienated cultures and communities, sharply distinguished according to religion, or caste, or class, or gender, or language, or location. Second, externally (that is, in relation to the world), Tagore's claim argues against an intense sense of the dissociation of Indians from other people elsewhere. It also rejects, as we know from Tagore's other writings too, the temptation to see Indian culture as frail and fragile, something that will break if touched by other cultures and which has to be protected through isolation from outside influences.

Tagore's claim involves, therefore, an integrative message – internally as well as externally – and it proposes an inclusionary form for the idea of Indian identity. It is this integrative notion that has recently been challenged, and both its internal and external claims have been chastised. Challenges have come, on the one side, from separatism within India (particularly with the privileging of one community over others and one cultural tradition over others), and on the other side, from separatism vis-à-vis the world (with the rejection of our constructive connections with others on the globe). In assessing these attacks we have to look carefully at the notion of identity in general.

Indeed, it is very important to be clear about the demands of what can be called the discipline of identity.* In particular, we have to resist two unfounded but often implicitly invoked assumptions: (1) the presumption that we must have a single – or at least a principal and dominant – identity; and (2) the supposition that we 'discover' our identity, with no room for any choice.

To take up the former question first, even though exclusivity of identity is often presumed (typically implicitly), this claim is in fact preposterous. Each of us invokes identities of various kinds in disparate contexts. The same person can be of Indian origin, a Parsee, a French citizen, a US resident, a woman, a poet, a vegetarian, an anthropologist, a university professor, a Christian, a bird watcher, and an avid believer in extraterrestrial life and of the propensity of alien creatures to ride around the cosmos in multicoloured UFOs. Each of these collectivities, to all of which this person belongs, gives him or her a particular identity. They can all have relevance, depending on the context. There is no conflict here, even though the priorities over these identities must be relative to the issue at hand (for example, the vegetarian identity may be more important when going to a dinner rather than to a Consulate, whereas the French citizenship may be more telling when going to a Consulate rather than attending a dinner).

The second false move – or what I claim is a false move – is to assume that one's identity is a matter of discovery rather than choice. This is asserted often enough, particularly in communitarian philosophy. As Professor Michael Sandel has explained this claim (among other communitarian claims): 'community describes not just what they *have* as fellow citizens but also what they *are*, not a relationship they choose (as in a voluntary association) but an attachment they discover, not merely an attribute but a constituent of their identity.'[14] In this view, identity comes *before* reasoning and choice.

But that claim is difficult to sustain, since we do have the opportunity to determine the relative weights we would like to attach to our

*The discussion that follows draws on the conceptual analyses presented in my 1998 Romanes Lecture at Oxford University, published as *Reason before Identity* (Oxford: Oxford University Press, 1999), and the 2000 Annual Lecture of the British Academy, 'Other People', published both by the British Academy and in a slightly shortened form in *New Republic*, 18 Dec. 2000.

different identities. For example, an Australian citizen of Indian origin would have to decide whether to root for Australia or for India in a test match between the two countries; he cannot, in any obvious sense, simply 'discover' the result of his own choice.

Perhaps the confusion in promoting the 'discovery' view arises from the fact that the choices we can make are constrained by feasibility, and sometimes the constraints are very exacting. The feasibilities will certainly depend on circumstances. For example, the constraints may be particularly strict when considering the extent to which we can persuade others to take us to be different from what they take us to be. A person of Jewish origin in Nazi Germany may not have been able to alter that identity as he or she wished. Nor could an African-American when faced with a lynch mob, or a low-caste agricultural labourer threatened by a gunman hired by upper-caste activists in, say, North Bihar. Our freedom in choosing our identity, in terms of the way others see us, can sometimes be extraordinarily limited.

Even in general, whether we are considering our identities as we ourselves see them, or as others see us, we choose within particular constraints. But this is not a surprising fact – it is in fact entirely unremarkable. Choices of all kinds are always made within particular constraints, and this is perhaps the most elementary aspect of any choice. For example, as any student of even elementary economics would know, the theory of consumer's choice does not deny the existence of a budget, which of course is a constraint. The presence of budget constraint does not imply that there is no choice to be made, only that the choice has to be made within the budget. The point at issue is not whether any identity whatever can be chosen (that would be an absurd claim), but whether we have choices over alternative identities or combinations of identities, and perhaps more importantly, whether we have some freedom in deciding what priority to give to the various identities that we may simultaneously have. People's choices may be constrained by the recognition that they are, say, Jewish or Muslim, but there is still a decision to be made by them regarding what importance they give to that particular identity over others that they may also have (related, for example, to their political beliefs, sense of nationality, humanitarian commitments or professional attachments).

Identity is thus a quintessentially plural concept, with varying relevance of different identities in distinct contexts. And, most importantly, we have choice over what significance to attach to our different identities. There is no escape from reasoning just because the notion of identity has been invoked. Choices over identities do involve constraints and connections, but the choices that exist and have to be made are real, not illusory. In particular, the choice of priorities between different identities, including what relative weights to attach to their respective demands, cannot be only a matter of discovery. They are inescapably decisional, and demand reason – not just recognition.

Religions, Heterodoxy and Reason

The issues of plurality and of choice are immensely relevant to the understanding and analysis of the idea of Indian identity. In arguing for an inclusionary form of the Indian identity, Tagore and Gandhi did not deny the presence and contingent importance of other identities. Rather, in terms of political coherence, social living and cultural interactions, both emphasized the fact that the Indian identity could not favour any particular group over others within India.

Tagore was different from Gandhi in having a less conventional view of his Hindu identity, and indeed in *The Religion of Man* pointed to the fact that his family was a product of 'a confluence of three cultures, Hindu, Mohammedan and British'.[15] Gandhiji's Hindu identity was more assertive, and he held regular prayer meetings, in a largely Hindu form (even though other religions were also invoked). But Gandhi was just as opposed as Tagore to letting his Hindu identity overwhelm his overarching commitment to an Indian identity in political and social matters. Indeed, Gandhiji gave his life in the cause of secularism and fairness, at the hands of someone with a simpler view of the congruence of Indian and Hindu identities.

Those who argue that the Indian identity has to be in some way derived from a Hindu identity point out not only that the Hindus constitute a large majority of people in India, but also that, historically, Hinduism has been the mainstay of the Indian civilization. These descriptions can, to a considerable extent, be taken to be true. But they do not in any way indicate that the Indian identity has to be basically derivative from the Hindu identity, or that the Indian identity must privilege the Hindu identity over others.*

Perhaps I should comment briefly on the role of three distinct issues that are involved in the approach I am trying to defend. First, identity is not a matter of discovery – of history any more than of the present – and has to be chosen with reasoning. Even if it were the case (as it certainly is not) that Indian history were largely Hindu history, we would still have to determine how a pluralist and multi-religious population can share an Indian identity without sharing the same religion. This, of course, is the basis of secularism in India, and our reasoning about priorities in dealing with competing conceptions of Indian identity need not be parasitic on history. The makers of the Indian constitution recognized that fully, as did the United States in adopting a largely secular constitution for a mostly Christian population. The need to reason and choose cannot be given over to the mere observation of history, and this point relates to the more general claim, which I have defended elsewhere, that while we cannot live *without* history, we need not live *within* it either.†

The second point is more historical. As was discussed in Essays 1–4, India has been a multi-religious country for a very long time, with Jews, Christians, Parsees and Muslim traders arriving and settling in India over the first millennium. Sikhism was born in India, in the same way that Buddhism and Jainism originated in the country. Even pre-Muslim India was not, as is sometimes claimed, mainly a Hindu country, since Buddhism was the dominant religion in India for many hundreds of years and Jainism has had an equally long history and in fact a large continuing presence today. Since there is so much politically generated antagonism these days against Hindus converting to any other religion, it is perhaps worth remembering that Ashoka (arguably the greatest emperor of India) did convert to

*This issue was discussed in Essay 3.

†See my *On Interpreting India's Past* (Calcutta: The Asiatic Society, 1996); also published in Sugata Bose and Ayesha Jalal (eds.), *Nationalism, Democracy and Development: Reappraising South Asian States and Politics in India* (Delhi: Oxford University Press, 1999).

Buddhism from what would have been the then form of Hinduism and sent emissaries propagating Buddhism to many other countries.*

Indeed, even in terms of Vedic and Upaniṣadic contributions, Buddhism and Jainism are as much the inheritors of that tradition as are later forms of Hinduism. The one university for which India was outstandingly famous, namely Nālandā, which attracted scholars from China and elsewhere, and which came to an end after many hundred years of existence just around the time when the universities of Oxford and Cambridge were being founded (in the thirteenth century), happened to be a Buddhist university.

I come now to the third reason against making the Indian identity dependent on the Hindu identity. Hindus are defined in two quite distinct ways. When the number of Hindus is counted, and it is established that the vast majority of Indians are in fact Hindu, this is not a counting of religious beliefs, but essentially of ethnic background. But when generalizations are made about, say, the divinity of Rama, or the sacred status of the *Rāmāyaṇa*, beliefs are invoked. By using the two approaches together, a numerical picture is constructed in which it is supposed that a vast majority of Indians believe in the divinity of Rama and the sacred status of the *Rāmāyaṇa*. For a large proportion of the Hindus, however, that attribution would be a mistake, since hundreds of millions of people who are defined as Hindu in the first sense do not actually share the beliefs which would be central to the second approach.

Indeed, by making this attribution, the champions of Hindu politics undermine the rich tradition of heterodoxy that has been so central to the history of the Hindu culture. As was discussed earlier, Sanskrit (including its variants, Pāli and Prākrit) has a larger literature in the atheistic and agnostic tradition than exists in any other classical language (Greek, Roman, Hebrew or Arabic). In the fourteenth century, Mādhava Ācārya's remarkable book called *Sarvadarśanasaṃgraha* ('The Collection of All Philosophies'), which has one chapter each on

*The spread of Buddhism from India to nearly half the world is one of the great events of global history. For an excellent account of that remarkable process, see H. Bechert and Richard Gombrich, *The World of Buddhism* (New York: Thames and Hudson, 1987). See also Richard Gombrich, *Theravada Buddhism* (London and New York: Routledge and Kegan Paul, 1988).

the major schools of Hindu belief, devoted the entire first chapter to arguments in favour of the atheistic position. The history of that tradition goes back at least two millennia and a half, to the sixth century BCE, when the Lokāyata and Cārvāka schools had their origin, in a climate of heterodoxy in which Buddhism and Jainism were also born.*

Something similar can be said about alleged cultural attitudes of the Hindus. I do not doubt that some Hindus do indeed find, as reported recently in the newspapers, that even Valentine's Day cards are offensive as being allegedly sexually explicit – a point made with much force by some politically activist Hindus. But Hindus vary in their attitude to issues of this kind, as the sculptors of the temples in Khajuraho could readily explain. I take the liberty of speculating that the greatest Sanskrit poet, Kālidāsa, with his eloquence on the beauty of female forms bathing in the river Śipra in his native Ujjayinī, would have found Valentine's Day cards to be deeply disappointing. The term Hindu can be sensibly used in either of two alternative forms, reflecting respectively membership of a community, or the holding of particular religious views and cultural attitudes, but the numerical force of the Hindus that is marshalled in favour of censorial uses is obtained through a conceptual confounding of two distinct notions.

A Concluding Remark

I want to make one last point on a different issue related to the role of religion and community in general (not Hinduism in particular) as a route to the Indian identity. Should the Indian identity be seen as something of a 'federal' concept that draws on the different religious communities, perhaps even including non-religious beliefs within the list of the constituents of a 'federation of cultures'? A question of a very similar type was raised in Britain in an important document produced by the Runnymede Trust, called the *Report of the Commission on the Future of Multi-ethnic Britain*. The report gives partial and qualified backing to a federal view of contemporary Britain, as 'a

*See the discussion in Essay 1 of the presence of heterodox beliefs in India throughout its history going back even to the *Rigveda*.

looser federation of cultures held together by common bonds of interest and affection and a collective sense of being'.[16]

This is a well-articulated position, and the Commission provides plausible arguments for it (without ruling out other interpretations). I would, nevertheless, argue that such a 'federal' view would be a great mistake for Britain as well as for India. The issue relates directly to the plurality of identities I have already discussed, and to the scope for choice in the determination of identity. People's relation to Britain, or to India, need not be mediated through the 'culture' of the family in which they may have been born, nor through its religion. People may choose to seek identity with more than one of these predefined cultures, or, just as plausibly, with none. People are also free to decide that their cultural or religious identity is less important to them than, say, their political convictions, or their literary persuasions, or their professional commitments. It is a choice for them to make, no matter how they are placed in the 'federation of cultures'.

To conclude, the inclusionary view of Indian identity, which we have inherited and which I have tried to defend, is not only not parasitic on, or partial to, a Hindu identity, it can hardly be a federation of the different religious communities in India: Hindu, Muslim, Sikh, Christian, Jain, Parsee and others. Indian identity need not be mediated through other group identities in a federal way. Indeed, India is not, in this view, sensibly seen even as a federal combination of different communities.

I quoted earlier a statement of Jamsetji Tata of an affirmatively nationalist kind, when – commenting on the excellence that young Indians can achieve through education – he said that Indian students 'can not only hold their own against the best rivals in Europe on the latter's ground, but can beat them hollow'. That expression of pride – even perhaps of arrogance – is not the pride of a Parsee who happened to be an Indian, but of an Indian who happened to be a Parsee. There is a distinction here, and it is, I would argue, both important and in need of some understanding right now.

Notes

ESSAY 1. THE ARGUMENTATIVE INDIAN

1. Arjuna is supposed to have ended with abject surrender: 'I stand firm with my doubts dispelled. I shall act according to Thy word' (Sarvepalli Radhakrishnan, *The Bhagavadgita*, New Delhi: HarperCollins, 1993, p. 381).
2. In collaboration with Swami Prabhavananda (Madras: Sri Ramakrishna Math, 1989).
3. Jawaharlal Nehru, who quotes Humboldt, does however point out that 'every school of thought and philosophy . . . interprets [the *Gītā*] in its own way' (*The Discovery of India*, Calcutta: The Signet Press, 1946; repr. Delhi: Oxford University Press, 1981, pp. 108–9).
4. T. S. Eliot, 'The Dry Salvages', in *Four Quartets* (London: Faber & Faber, 1944), pp. 29–31.
5. For a good discussion of some other interesting arguments in the *Mahābhārata*, see Bimal Matilal, *Moral Dilemmas in the Mahabharata* (Shimla: Indian Institute of Advanced Study, and Delhi: Motilal Banarasidass, 1989). See also his collection of papers, edited by Jonardan Ganeri, *The Collected Essays of Bimal Krishna Matilal*, vol. ii: *Ethics and Epics* (Delhi and Oxford: Oxford University Press, 2002). Shashi Tharoor conveys well the excitements offered by the stories and substories in the *Mahābhārata*, in his adapted tale, *The Great Indian Story* (Harmondsworth: Penguin, 1990).
6. See Len Giovannitti and Fred Freed, *The Decision to Drop the Bomb* (London: Methuen, 1957).
7. See *In the Matter of J. Robert Oppenheimer: USAEC Transcript of the Hearing before Personnel Security Board* (Washington, DC: Government Publishing Office, 1954). See also the play, based on these hearings, by Heinar Kipphardt, *In the Matter of J. Robert Oppenheimer*, trans. Ruth Speirs (London: Methuen, 1967).

8. This extract and the others that follow, on the Gārgī–Yājñavalkya debate, are taken from *Brihadāraṇyaka Upaniṣad*, sections 3. 8. 1 to 3. 8. 12. They correspond to the English translations of this Upaniṣad published by Sri Ramkrishna Math (Madras, 1951), pp. 242–53, and by Advaita Ashrama (Calcutta, 1965), pp. 512–29, but the English versions given here include my slight emendations of these earlier translations, based on the original Sanskrit text.

9. See Antonia Fraser, *Boadicea's Chariot: The Warrior Queens* (London: Weidenfeld and Nicolson, 1988). For other biographies of the Rani, who – widowed at an early age – rose to be a major leader in the growing resistance to British rule and died valiantly on the battlefield, see Joyce Lebra-Chapman, *The Rani of Jhansi: A Study of Female Heroism in India* (Honolulu: University of Hawaii Press, 1986), and Mahasweta Devi, *The Queen of Jhansi*, translated from Bengali by Mandira and Sagaree Sengupta (Calcutta: Seagull Books, 2000).

10. *Brihadāraṇyaka Upaniṣad*, sections 2. 4. 2 and 2. 4. 3; in the Advaita Ashrama translation, pp. 352–4.

11. Draupadī was in fact married to all five Pāṇḍava brothers, of whom Yudhiṣṭhira was the eldest: this is one of the rare cases of polyandry in the epics.

12. Trans. Indira Viswanathan Peterson, *Design and Rhetoric in a Sanskrit Court Epic* (New York: State University of New York Press, 2003), pp. 191–4.

13. On these references and the discussion that follows, see Kshiti Mohan Sen, *Hinduism* (Harmondsworth: Penguin Books, 1961, 2005), pp. 27–31.

14. The proposal to dilute democracy came from no less a statesman than Indira Gandhi, the Prime Minister of India. The firmness with which one of the poorest electorates in the world rejected the proposed move to authoritarianism had a salutary effect in discouraging other temptations in that direction. After being voted out of office, Indira Gandhi changed tack, strongly reasserted her earlier commitment to democracy, and regained the Prime Ministership in the general elections of 1980.

15. For a discussion of this general connection as well as illustrations from the histories of various parts of Asia and Africa, in addition to Europe, see my 'Democracy and Its Global Roots', *New Republic*, Nov. 2003.

16. See John Rawls, *A Theory of Justice* (Cambridge, Mass.: Harvard University Press, 1971). Indeed, Rawls saw 'the exercise of public reason' as the central feature of democracy: see his *Justice as Fairness: A Restatement*, ed. Erin Kelly (Cambridge, Mass.: Harvard University Press, 2001), p. 50. See also Juergen Habermas, *Toward a Rational Society* (Boston: Beacon

Press, 1971), and *The Theory of Communicative Action* (Boston: Beacon Press, 1987).

17. James M. Buchanan, 'Social Choice, Democracy, and Free Markets', *Journal of Political Economy*, 62 (1954), p. 120.

18. See my 'Democracy and Its Global Roots'.

19. As explained in the Preface, I have taken the liberty of spelling Aśoka as Ashoka, since that name is more familiar to people outside India in that spelling.

20. *Robert's Rules of Order: Simplified and Applied*, Webster's New World (New York: Simon and Schuster Macmillan, 1999).

21. See Irfan Habib (ed.), *Akbar and His India* (Delhi and New York: Oxford University Press, 1997), for a set of fine essays investigating the beliefs and policies of Akbar as well as the intellectual influences that led him to his heterodox position. Two of the essays in this volume ('Secularism and Its Discontents' and 'India through Its Calendars') include discussions of the intellectual significance of the interreligious interchanges in Akbar's time. Shirin Moosvi's book *Episodes in the Life of Akbar: Contemporary Records and Reminiscences* (New Delhi: National Book Trust, 1994), gives a vividly informative account of how Akbar arrived at social decisions through the use of reasoning.

22. Akbar was, obviously, not obliged, as the emperor, to follow what emerged in the discussions he arranged (they had only an advisory role), and he could have stopped the deliberations that occurred at his invitation whenever he chose. Since the freedom to present their respective viewpoints that the participants enjoyed in practice would have been conditional on Akbar's acceptance, it would not count as 'genuine freedom' when assessed in the 'republican' perspective (as advanced by Philip Pettit, *Republicanism: A Theory of Freedom and Government*, Oxford: Clarendon Press, 1997), or in terms of the 'neo-Roman' theory of freedom (as developed by Quentin Skinner, *Liberty before Liberalism*, Cambridge: Cambridge University Press, 1998).

23. On different concepts of secularism, see the collection of essays in Rajeev Bhargava (ed.), *Secularism and Its Critics* (Delhi: Oxford University Press, 1998).

24. On the histories involved, see Shalva Weil (ed.), *India's Jewish Heritage* (Mumbai: Marg Publications, 2002), and the literature cited there.

25. There were also pre-Christian Greek settlements in north-west India from the second century BCE. On the early relations between India, Greece and Rome, see the lucidly illuminating essay by John Mitchener, 'India, Greece and Rome: East–West Contacts in Classical Times' (mimeographed, 2003), and also the large literature cited there.

26. These statements of Ashoka occur in Edict XII (on 'toleration') at Erragudi; I am using here the translation presented by Vincent A. Smith in *Asoka: The Buddhist Emperor of India* (Oxford: Clarendon Press, 1909), pp. 170–71, except for some very minor emendations based on the original Sanskrit text.

27. Translation in Vincent A. Smith, *Akbar: The Great Mogul* (Oxford: Clarendon Press, 1917), p. 257.

28. See Iqtidar Alam Khan, 'Akbar's Personality Traits and World Outlook: A Critical Reappraisal', in Habib (ed.), *Akbar and His India*, p. 78.

29. Akbar's principal adviser, Abul Fazl, was a great scholar in Sanskrit as well as Arabic and Persian. One of the generals in Akbar's forces, Rahim (or Abdurrahim Khankhana), himself a Muslim, wrote rather beautiful poems that draw, *inter alia*, on Sanskrit literature and Hindu philosophy.

30. See Kshiti Mohan Sen, *Medieval Mysticism of India*, with a Foreword by Rabindranath Tagore (1930), and *Hinduism* (1961, 2005).

31. Edict XII, in Smith, *Asoka*, p. 171; italics added.

32. A. C. Bouquet, *Comparative Religion* (Harmondsworth: Penguin, 5th edn., 1956), p. 112. Sarvepalli Radhakrishnan, the great commentator on Indian philosophy, went even further, and argued that 'the chief mark of Indian philosophy in general is its concentration upon the spiritual' (S. Radhakrishnan and S. A. Moore, in the introduction to their collection, *A Sourcebook in Indian Philosophy*, Princeton: Princeton University Press, 1957, p. xxiii). That point of view is disputed, with textual evidence, by Bimal Matilal (who was, as it happens, a successor of Radhakrishnan as Spalding Professor of Eastern Religions and Ethics at Oxford): *Perception: An Essay on Classical Indian Theories of Knowledge* (Oxford: Clarendon Press, 1986).

33. See Debiprasad Chattopadhyaya, *Lokayata: A Study of Ancient Indian Materialism* (New Delhi: People's Publishing House, 1959), and *Indian Atheism* (Calcutta: Manisha, 1959).

34. In a series of recent studies on ancient India in Bengali (including one on 'doubt and atheism in the Vedic literature', 2000), Sukumari Bhattacharji has substantially enriched our understanding of the nature and reach of this heterodoxy. Even Yājñavalkya, who was referred to earlier as being identified by the woman interlocutor, Gārgī, as the best-informed scholar on God, gives some evidence of entertaining serious doubts about the existence and role of God. Among Sukumari Bhattacharji's earlier contributions, those in English include: *The Indian Theogony* (Cambridge: Cambridge University Press, 1970; London: Penguin, 2000); *Literature in the Vedic Age*, 2 vols. (Calcutta: K. P. Bagchi, 1984, 1986); and *Classical Sanskrit Literature* (Calcutta: Orient Longman, 1990).

35. D. N. Jha, *Ancient India* (New Delhi: Manohar, 1977, rev. edn. 1998), pp. 69–70.
36. *The Sarva-Darsana-Samgraha or Review of Different Systems of Hindu Philosophy by Madhava Acharya*, trans. E. B. Cowell and A. E. Gough (London: Trübner, 1882; repr. New Delhi: Cosmo Publications, 1976).
37. Ibid., p. 2.
38. Ibid., pp. 2–3.
39. Ibid., p. 10.
40. *Arthaśāstra* can be literally translated as: 'the discipline of material prosperity'. For an English translation, see R. P. Kangle, *Kautilya's Arthasastra* (Bombay: University of Bombay, 1970). Kauṭilya's approach to politics as well as economics is governed by an overarchingly consequential priority. This is discussed, *inter alia*, in my *Money and Value: On the Ethics and Economics of Finance*, The First Baffi Lecture (Rome: Bank of Italy, 1991), repr. in *Economics and Philosophy*, 9 (1993).
41. On this, see my Inaugural Address to the Indian History Congress in January 2001: 'History and the Enterprise of Knowledge', distributed by the Congress; repr. in *New Humanist*, 116 (2 June 2001).
42. On this, see particularly Matilal, *Perception*.
43. Trans. Makhanlal Sen, *Ramayana: From the Original Valmiki* (Calcutta: Rupa, 1989), pp. 174–5.
44. *Sarva-Darsana-Samgraha*, trans. Cowell and Gough, p. 6.
45. Ibid.
46. Ibid. On the epistemological issues pursued here and in related texts, see also Matilal, *Perception*.
47. See Debiprasad Chattopadhyaya, *Lokayata*, pp. 2–3; and Ramendranath Ghosh, in his Bengali essay on 'Cārvāka Materialism' in Dipak Bhattacharya, Moinul Hassan and Kumkum Ray (eds.), *India and Indology: Professor Sukumari Bhattacharji Felicitation Volume* (Kolkata [Calcutta]: National Book Agency, 2004), p. 242.
48. Repr. in B. H. G. Wormald, *Francis Bacon: History, Politics and Science, 1561–1626* (Cambridge: Cambridge University Press, 1993), pp. 356–7.
49. *Alberuni's India*, trans. E. C. Sachau, ed. A. T. Embree (New York: Norton, 1971), p. 111. Further discussion of this controversy can be found in my essay 'History and the Enterprise of Knowledge'.
50. Nelson Mandela, *Long Walk to Freedom* (Boston: Little, Brown & Co., 1994), p. 21.
51. In the presence of multiple and interdependent causation, which factor we decide to emphasize must depend on what features are being highlighted already. Facing a different act of balancing in the context of British history,

Eric Hobsbawm discussed, half a century ago, why it was important for Marxist historians (he was writing as one) to bring out the role of 'ideals, passions and movements' (increasingly neglected by orthodox historians), rather than concentrating mainly on material conditions – the traditional focus of Marxist analysis: 'In the pre-Namier days Marxists regarded it as one of their chief historical duties to draw attention to the material bases of politics. . . . But since bourgeois historians have adopted what is a particular form of vulgar materialism, Marxists have had to remind them that history is the struggle of men for ideas, as well as a reflection of their material environment' ('Where Are British Historians Going?', *Marxist Quarterly*, 2 Jan. 1955, p. 22).

52. Rabindranath Tagore, *The Religion of Man* (London: Unwin, 1931, 2nd edn., 1961), p. 105.

53. From *Gitanjali*. See also Essay 5.

ESSAY 2. INEQUALITY, INSTABILITY AND VOICE

1. See Louis Dumont, *Homo Hierarchicus: The Caste System and Its Implications* (Chicago: University of Chicago Press, 1980). For critical assessment of Dumont's reading of Indian stratification and related theses, see André Béteille, *The Idea of Natural Inequality and Other Essays* (Delhi: Oxford University Press, 1983); Arjun Appadurai, 'Is Homo Hierarchicus?', *American Anthropologist*, 13 (1986); Dipankar Gupta (ed.), *Social Stratification* (Delhi: Oxford University Press, 1991); Nicholas Dirks, 'Castes of Mind', *Representations*, 37 (1992), and *Castes of Mind: Colonialism and the Making of Modern India* (Princeton: Princeton University Press, 2001).

2. See e.g. Charles Taylor, *Philosophy and the Human Sciences: Philosophical Papers* (Cambridge: Cambridge University Press, 1986); and Nancy Fraser and Axel Honneth, *Redistribution or Recognition? A Political-Philosophical Exchange* (London: Verso Books, 2003). The underlying issues in the idea of recognition are also discussed by Emma Rothschild, 'Dignity or Meanness', *Adam Smith Review*, 1 (2004).

3. Ambedkar himself played an important part in the policy of affirmative actions in favour of disadvantaged social groups (the 'scheduled castes' and 'scheduled tribes') included in the constitution of the Indian Republic. But his own sense of growing social pessimism led him, eventually, to embrace the egalitarianism of Buddhism, in a powerfully evocative public ceremony of religious conversion. See *The Essential Writings*

of B. R. Ambedkar, ed. Valerian Rodrigues (Delhi: Oxford University Press, 2002).

4. The connections are discussed in Jean Drèze and Amartya Sen, *Hunger and Public Action* (Oxford: Clarendon Press, 1989), and *India: Development and Participation* (Delhi and Oxford: Oxford University Press, 2002). Activist movements for women's rights and equity, in different forms varying from self-help organizations to participation in public discussion through meetings and publications (*Manushi*, ed. Madhu Kishwar, a pioneering feminist journal), have had considerable success in changing the agenda of political and social change in India. An engaging account of some of the developments can be found in Radha Kumar's elegant book, *The History of Doing: An Illustrated Account of Movements for Women's Rights and Feminism in India* (New Delhi: Kali for Women, 2nd edn., 1997). The variety of issues in which the women's movement have to be engaged include the relatively neglected field of ownership in general and land ownership in particular, on which see the classic study of Bina Agarwal, *A Field of One's Own* (Cambridge: Cambridge University Press, 1994). The social correlates of the new departures of the 'invisible women' are beautifully described by Anees Jung, *Beyond the Courtyard: A Sequel of Unveiling India* (New Delhi: Penguin Books, 2003).

5. There are also important issues of governance, in particular what Mark Tully and Gillian Wright call the 'peculiarly Indian form of bad governance' (*India in Slow Motion*, London: Penguin Books, 2003, p. xv). However, the prospects of improving governance in India are linked, ultimately, with the vigour of its democratic practice, as Tully and Wright themselves note. On that connection, see also Drèze and Sen, *India: Development and Participation*, ch. 10.

6. For references to these and related points of view, see Essay 1, and also Kshiti Mohan Sen, *Hinduism* (1961, 2005).

7. Yi Jing, *A Record of the Buddhist Religions as Practised in India and Malay Archipelago*, trans. J. Takakusu (Oxford: Oxford University Press, 1896), p. 136.

8. Indeed, even the pre-imperial travellers from Britain also tended to see India as a country. This clearly applies, for example, to that determined English tourist, Ralph Fitch, who roamed around India in the sixteenth century. See William Foster (ed.), *Early Travels in India* (Oxford: Oxford University Press, 1921).

9. E. M. Forster, 'Nine Gems of Ujjain', in *Abinger Harvest* (Harmondsworth: Penguin Books, 1936, 1974), pp. 324–7.

10. Trans. from Barbara Stoler Miller, *The Plays of Kalidasa* (Delhi: Motilal Banarasidass, 1999), pp. 5–6.

11. The history of the partition has been the subject of considerable critical analysis. See particularly Ayesha Jalal, *The Sole Spokesman: Jinnah, the Muslim League and the Demand for Pakistan* (Cambridge: Cambridge University Press, 1985). See also Gyanendra Pandey's analysis of the causation, intensity and lasting effects of the violence in the process of partition, *Remembering Partition: Violence, Nationalism and History in India* (Cambridge: Cambridge University Press, 2001).
12. The role of civil society for the development of a South Asian community is illuminatingly discussed by Rehman Sobhan, *Rediscovering a South Asian Community: Civil Society in Search of Its Future* (Colombo: International Centre for Ethnic Studies, 1997).

ESSAY 3. INDIA: LARGE AND SMALL

1. Kshiti Mohan Sen, *Hinduism* (Harmondsworth: Penguin, 1961), pp. 39–40.
2. The translation is from Makhanlal Sen, *Ramayana: From the Original Valmiki* (Calcutta: Rupa, 1989), p. 174, with minor emendations based on the original Sanskrit text.
3. On the nature and use of these claims, see Sunil Khilnani, *The Idea of India* (London: Penguin Books, extended edn., 2003), pp. 150–52.
4. The contrast between that broad tradition and the narrowness of contemporary political Hinduism is brought out in several of the essays in Tapan Raychaudhuri's wide-ranging anthology of essays on colonial and post-colonial India, *Perceptions, Emotions, Sensibilities: Essays on India's Colonial and Post-Colonial Experiences* (New Delhi and Oxford: Oxford University Press, 1999).
5. In addition to the consolidating role that Indian nationalism played during the struggle for independence, it did also have other – including some less agreeable – social features. See, among other contributions, Bipan Chandra, Amales Tripathi and Barun De, *Freedom Struggle* (New Delhi: National Book Trust, 1972); Ayesha Jalal, *The Sole Spokesman: Jinnah, the Muslim League and the Demand for Pakistan* (Cambridge: Cambridge University Press, 1985); and Barun De, *Nationalism as a Binding Force: The Dialectics of the Historical Course of Nationalism* (Calcutta: Centre for Studies in Social Sciences, 1987).
6. The discussion here draws on an earlier essay, 'What Is the Indian Nation?', *Taj Magazine* (2003).
7. The book was originally published under the nom de plume 'A Maratha'

(*Hindutva*, Nagpur: V. V. Kelkar, 1923). It was later republished under Savarkar's own name in various editions, including *Hindutva* (Bombay: Veer Savarkar Prakashan, 6th edn., 1989).

8. Indeed, Savarkar himself had gone on trial – and been released on somewhat technical grounds – for alleged complicity in Gandhi's murder. This history is discussed in some detail by A. G. Noorani, *Savarkar and Hindutva* (Delhi: Leftword Books, 2002). It is a sign of how the times have changed that a portrait of Veer Savarkar was installed in 2004 in the central hall of the Indian parliament, on the initiative of the coalition government (led by the BJP) then in office in New Delhi, even though many parliamentarians boycotted the event.

9. On different aspects of sectarian conflicts and challenges to secularism in India, see Veena Das (ed.), *Mirrors of Violence* (Delhi: Oxford University Press, 1990), including, among other essays, Ashis Nandy, 'The Politics of Secularism and the Recovery of Religious Tolerance'; K. M. Panikkar (ed.), *Communalism in India: History, Politics and Culture* (New Delhi: Manohar, 1991); Upendra Baxi and Bhikhu Parekh (eds.), *Crisis and Change in Contemporary India* (New Delhi: Sage, 1995); Rafiq Zakaria, *Widening Divide: An Insight into Hindu–Muslim Relations* (London: Viking, 1995); Kaushik Basu and Sanjay Subrahmanyam (eds.), *Unravelling the Nation: Sectarian Conflict and India's Secular Identity* (Delhi: Penguin, 1996); Sugata Bose and Ayesha Jalal (eds.), *Nationalism, Democracy and Development: State and Politics in India* (Delhi: Oxford University Press, 1997); Achin Vanaik, *The Furies of Indian Communalism* (London: Verso, 1997); Rajeev Bhargava, *Secularism and Its Critics* (1998); Neera Chandoke, *Beyond Secularism: The Rights of Religious Minorities* (Delhi and Oxford: Oxford University Press, 1999); A. G. Noorani, *The RSS and the BJP* (Delhi: Manohar Publishers, 2001); Ashutosh Varshney, *Ethnic Conflict and Civic Life: Hindus and Muslims in India* (New Haven: Yale University Press, 2002), among other contributions.

10. The failure of the ruling Congress government to prevent, and even to probe adequately, the riots following Indira Gandhi's assassination in 1984, in which a great many Sikhs lost their lives, has also seriously tarnished Congress's political record.

11. Samuel Huntington, *The Clash of Civilizations and the Remaking of World Order* (New York: Simon and Schuster, 1996).

12. *Alberuni's India*, trans. E. C. Sachau, ed. A. T. Embree (New York: Norton, 1971), p. 22.

13. Rabindranath Tagore, 'The Message of Indian History', *Visva-Bharati Quarterly*, 22 (1902), p. 105. Sunil Khilnani discusses the nature of this

diagnosis in his insightful book *The Idea of India* (London: Penguin Books, extended edn. 2003), pp. 166–70.

14. Dinesh Chandra Sen, *History of Bengali Language and Literature* (Delhi: Gian Publishing House, 1986), pp. 10–12.

15. The sense of astonishment and disapproval about BJP's use of its official position to radically rewrite Indian history on its own lines, often in direct conflict with well-known features of India's past, also had a political impact against the BJP, in alienating many Indian intellectuals, who were previously sitting on the fence. There is a lesson here also for the other political parties not to deploy temporal political strength in messing with the history that children have to read. See also Ramachandra Guha's argument that the left had also earlier used their own official position to give a particular direction to the study of Indian history ('The Absent Liberal: An Essay on Politics and Intellectual Life', *Economic and Political Weekly*, 15 Dec. 2001). Even though that diagnosis of events has been contested, Guha's demand for efforts to pursue objectivity and to avoid partisan bias in producing textbooks and other official accounts of history is surely important.

16. One of the first acts of the reconstituted Indian Council of Historical Research was to put into cold storage a history of India's struggle for independence (called 'Towards Freedom') that had been commissioned earlier on – before its reorganization – by the ICHR itself. The decision was apparently connected with the expectation – probably correct enough – that the authors of the study, two distinguished historians (K. M. Panikkar and Sumit Sarkar), were likely to go into the divisive role of Hindu political activists during India's struggle for national independence.

17. *Hindusthan Times*, 5 Oct. 2002.

18. 'Inventing History', *Hindu*, 14 Oct. 2002.

19. Chitra Srinivas, a history teacher in a school in New Delhi, who was asked to comment on the textbooks but whose advice (like those of many other history teachers) was comprehensively neglected, commented later that the aim of the textbooks seemed to be the generating of the feeling 'that our freedom struggle was basically a religious struggle against Christian missionaries and Muslim communalists'. Srinivas, who comes from a Hindu background herself, lamented: 'The problem is I love India and admire its multicultural society too much. . . . I am unable to accept distortions in the writing of India's history that will go against the very spirit of her existence' ('Whither Teaching of History?', in *Saffronised and Substandard*, New Delhi: SAHMAT, 2002, pp. 69–71).

20. See Mortimer Wheeler, *Indus Civilization* (Cambridge: Cambridge University Press, 1953); John Mitchener, *Studies in the Indus Valley*

Inscriptions (New Delhi: Oxford University Press, 1978); B. B. Lal and S. P. Gupta (eds.), *Frontiers of the Indus Civilization* (New Delhi: Books & Books and Indian Archaeological Society, 1984); Bridget and Raymond Allchin, *Origins of a Civilization: The Prehistory and Early Archaeology of South Asia* (New Delhi: Viking, 1997); D. N. Jha, *Ancient India: In Historical Outline* (New Delhi: Manohar, 1998).

21. Aside from these specific misattributions of scientific history, there is a general methodological problem, which Meera Nanda has discussed in her highly engaging book, *Prophets Facing Backward: Postmodern Critiques and Hindu Nationalism in India* (New Brunswick, NJ: Rutgers University Press, 2003). Nanda argues that at the heart of the Hindutva ideology lies 'a postmodernist assumption: that each society has its own norms of reasonableness, logic, rules of evidence, and conception of truth'. She presents a forceful critique both of that assumption and of the use she argues the Hindutva movement makes of that assumption.

22. For example, the Social Science textbook made by NCERT for Class VI attributed Āryabhaṭa's fifth-century clarifications about the diurnal motion of the earth – as opposed to the sun going round the earth – to the Vedic period, thousands of years earlier. See the extract in *Saffronised and Substandard*, p. 31.

23. Natwar Jha and N. S. Rajaram, *The Deciphered Indus Script* (New Delhi: Aditya Prakashan, 2000).

24. 'Horseplay in Harappa', *Frontline*, 17 (13 Oct. 2000).

25. See R. E. Latham (ed.), *The Travels of Marco Polo* (Harmondsworth: Penguin Books, 1958), pp. 250–51.

26. As Aijaz Ahmad has argued, commenting on the violence of the historical process that led to the partition of India, 'neither the high-caste Hindu nor the genteel and propertied Muslim, neither the fatefully communal forms of our modernity nor the exclusivist practices of our anti-colonial reform movements' were entirely free of cultivating the 'savageries of the politics of identity' (*Lineages of the Present: Ideology and Politics in Contemporary South Asia*, London: Verso, 2000, pp. xi–xii).

27. From a letter to C. F. Andrews, dated 13 March 1921, published in *Letters to a Friend* (London: Allen & Unwin, 1928). See also Essay 5.

ESSAY 4. THE DIASPORA AND THE WORLD

1. Samuel P. Huntington, *The Clash of Civilizations and the Remaking of World Order* (New York: Simon and Schuster, 1996), p. 71.

2. Trans. Vincent A. Smith, *Akbar: The Great Mogul* (Oxford: Clarendon Press, 1917), p. 257.
3. See M. Athar Ali, 'The Perception of India in Akbar and Abu'l Fazl', in Irfan Habib (ed.), *Akbar and His India* (Delhi and New York: Oxford University Press, 1997), p. 220, and also my essay, 'The Reach of Reason: East and West', *New York Review of Books*, 47 (20 July 2000), included in this volume as Essay 13.
4. Other features of the many-sided colonial impact on ideas and emotions in India have been studied by a number of distinguished historians in India. See e.g. Tapan Raychaudhuri, *Perceptions, Emotions, Sensibilities: Essays on India's Colonial and Post-Colonial Experiences* (New Delhi and Oxford: Oxford University Press, 1999), and Sumit Sarkar, *A Critique of Colonial India* (Calcutta: Papyrus Publishing House, 2000). The important subject of the origins of nationality in the subcontinent during British rule is investigated in C. A. Bayly, *Origins of Nationality in South Asia: Patriotism and Ethical Government in the Making of Modern India* (Delhi and Oxford: Oxford University Press, 1998).
5. T. B. Macaulay, 'Indian Education: Minute of the 2nd February, 1835', repr. in G. M. Young (ed.), *Macaulay: Prose and Poetry* (Cambridge, Mass.: Harvard University Press, 1952), p. 722.
6. The gripping story that William Dalrymple tells in his masterly novel *White Mughals* (London: Flamingo, 2002) about love in eighteenth-century India, when a third of the British in India were living with Indian women, is a distinctly early empire phenomenon. As the Raj solidified over the following century, with its theories of distance between the British and Indian peoples (a line of thinking of which James Mill was a principal theorist), the mainstream of social relations radically changed, even though there were many individual cases of close personal ties stretching over the nineteenth and twentieth centuries.
7. Ranajit Guha, *Dominance without Hegemony* (Cambridge, Mass.: Harvard University Press, 1997).
8. Max Müller, *Sacred Books of the East*, 50 vols. (Oxford: Clarendon Press, 1879–1910).
9. James Mill, *The History of British India* (London, 1817; repr. Chicago: University of Chicago Press, 1975), pp. 223–4.
10. Quoted ibid., Introduction by John Clive, p. viii.
11. As Romila Thapar has noted, James Mill's reading of India, which gained ground rapidly and by the middle of the nineteenth century became almost 'axiomatic' in England to 'the understanding of Indian society and politics', 'suited the imperial requirements' rather well (see her *Interpret-*

ing Early India, Delhi: Oxford University Press, 1982, pp. 5–6, 33–4).
12. *Alberuni's India*, trans. E. C. Sachau, ed. A. T. Embree (New York: Norton, 1971), pp. 276–7.
13. Mill, *The History of British India*, pp. 225–6.
14. Ibid., p. 247.
15. On the importance of 'third-person perspectives' in the development of 'identities' in the presence of asymmetries of power, see Akeel Bilgrami, 'What Is a Muslim?', in Anthony Appiah and Henry L. Louis Gates (eds.), *Identities* (Chicago: Chicago University Press, 1995). See also Ayesha Jalal, *Self and Sovereignty: Individual and Community in South Asian Islam since 1850* (London: Routledge, 2000).
16. Partha Chatterjee, *The Nation and Its Fragments* (Princeton: Princeton University Press, 1993), p. 6.
17. Jawaharlal Nehru, *The Discovery of India* (Calcutta: Signet Press, 1946; centenary edn., Delhi: Oxford University Press, 1989).
18. See *The Essential Writings of B. R. Ambedkar*, ed. Valerian Rodrigues (Delhi: Oxford University Press, 2002), particularly essay 32 ('Basic Features of the Indian Constitution').
19. An interesting comparison can be made between the ideas of two of the stalwarts of political thinking in ancient India, viz. Kauṭilya and Ashoka. The continuing relevance of their respective viewpoints and the contrasts between them have been engagingly examined by Bruce Rich, *To Uphold the World: The Message of Ashoka and Kautilya for the 21st Century* (forthcoming).
20. *Nihongi: Chronicles of Japan from the Earliest Times to A.D. 697*, trans. W. G. Aston (Tokyo: Tuttle, 1972), pp. 128–33.
21. Nakamura Hajime, 'Basic Features of the Legal, Political, and Economic Thought of Japan', in Charles A. Moore (ed.), *The Japanese Mind: Essentials of Japanese Philosophy and Culture* (Tokyo: Tuttle, 1973), p. 144.
22. In fact, the Diamond Sutra was translated into Chinese many times – perhaps even a dozen times. But it is Kumārajīva's translation of this Sanskrit document in 402 CE that was printed in what became the first dated printed book in the world. On this, see Essay 8 below.
23. The scroll was found in 1907 by the archaeologist Sir Marc Auriel Stein in one of the 'Caves of the Thousand Buddhas' in north-west China. The given date of printing translates, in the Gregorian calendar, as 11 May 868.
24. See Thomas McEvilley, *The Shape of Ancient Thought: Comparative Studies in Greek and Indian Philosophies* (New York: Allworth Press, 2002), pp. 368–70. In general, McEvilley provides an admirably illuminating account of Greek–Indian interactions in the ancient world.
25. *Alberuni's India*, p. 20. The Arabic word then used for Hindu or Indian

was the same, and I have replaced Sachau's choice of the English word 'Hindu' in this passage by 'Indian', since the reference is to the inhabitants of the country.

ESSAY 5. TAGORE AND HIS INDIA

1. Rabindranath Tagore, *The Religion of Man* (London: Unwin, 1931, 2nd edn., 1961), p. 105. The extensive interactions between Hindu and Muslim parts of Indian culture (in religious beliefs, civic codes, painting, sculpture, literature, music and astronomy) have been discussed by Kshiti Mohan Sen in *Bharate Hindu Mushalmaner Jukto Sadhana* (in Bengali) (Calcutta: Visva-Bharati, 1949: extended edn., 1990) and *Hinduism* (Harmondsworth: Penguin, 1961, 2005).

2. Rabindranath's father Debendranath had in fact joined a reformist religious group, the Brahmo Samaj, which rejected many contemporary Hindu practices as aberrations from the ancient Hindu texts.

3. *Selected Letters of Rabindranath Tagore*, ed. Krishna Dutta and Andrew Robinson (Cambridge: Cambridge University Press, 1997). This essay draws on my Foreword to this collection. For important background material on Rabindranath Tagore and his reception in the West, see also the editors' *Rabindranath Tagore: The Myriad-Minded Man* (New York: St Martin's Press, 1995), and *Rabindranath Tagore: An Anthology* (New York: Picador, 1997).

4. See *Romain Rolland and Gandhi Correspondence*, with a Foreword by Jawaharlal Nehru (New Delhi: Government of India, 1976), pp. 12–13.

5. On Dartington Hall, the school, and the Elmhirsts, see Michael Young, *The Elmhirsts of Dartington: The Creation of an Utopian Community* (London: Routledge, 1982).

6. Yasunari Kawabata, *The Existence and Discovery of Beauty*, trans. V. H. Viglielmo (Tokyo: Mainichi Newspapers, 1969), pp. 56–7.

7. W. B. Yeats, Introduction, in Rabindranath Tagore, *Gitanjali* (London: Macmillan, 1913).

8. The importance of ambiguity and incomplete description in Tagore's poetry provides some insight into the striking thesis of William Radice (one of the major English translators of Tagore) that 'his blend of poetry and prose is all the more truthful for being incomplete' (Introduction to his *Rabindranath Tagore: Selected Short Stories*, Harmondsworth: Penguin, 1991, p. 28).

9. Reported in Amita Sen, *Anando Sharbokaje* (in Bengali) (Calcutta: Tagore Research Institute, 2nd edn., 1996), p. 132.

10. B. R. Nanda, *Mahatma Gandhi* (Delhi: Oxford University Press, 1958; paperback, 1989), p. 149.
11. The economic issues are discussed in my *Choice of Techniques* (Oxford: Blackwell, 1960), appendix D.
12. Mohandas Gandhi, quoted by Krishna Kripalani, *Tagore: A Life* (New Delhi: Orient Longman, 1961, 2nd edn., 1971), pp. 171–2.
13. For fuller accounts of the events, see Dutta and Robinson, *Rabindranath Tagore: The Myriad-Minded Man*, ch. 25, and Ketaki Kushari Dyson, *In Your Blossoming Flower-Garden: Rabindranath Tagore and Victoria Ocampo* (New Delhi: Sahitya Akademi, 1988).
14. Published in English translation in *Rabindranath Tagore: A Centenary Volume, 1861–1961* (New Delhi: Sahitya Akademi, 1961), with an Introduction by Jawaharlal Nehru.
15. English trans. from Kripalani, *Tagore: A Life*, p. 185.
16. 'Einstein and Tagore Plumb the Truth', *New York Times Magazine*, 10 Aug. 1930; repr. in Dutta and Robinson, *Selected Letters of Rabindranath Tagore*.
17. Hilary Putnam, *The Many Faces of Realism* (La Salle, Ill.: Open Court, 1987). On related issues, see also Thomas Nagel, *The View from Nowhere* (New York: Oxford University Press, 1986).
18. Isaiah Berlin, 'Rabindranath Tagore and the Consciousness of Nationality', in his *The Sense of Reality: Studies in Ideas and Their History* (Boston: Farrar, Straus and Giroux, 1997), p. 265.
19. E. P. Thompson, Introduction to Tagore's *Nationalism* (London, Macmillan, 1991), p. 10.
20. For a lucid and informative analysis of the role of Subhas Chandra Bose and his brother Sarat in Indian politics, see Leonard A. Gordon, *Brothers against the Raj: A Biography of Indian Nationalists Sarat and Subhas Chandra Bose* (New York: Columbia University Press, 1990).
21. Kawabata made considerable use of Tagore's ideas, and even built on Tagore's thesis that it 'is easier for a stranger to know what it is in [Japan] which is truly valuable for all mankind' (*The Existence and Discovery of Beauty*, pp. 55–8).
22. Tagore, *Letters from Russia*, trans. from Bengali by Sasadhar Sinha (Calcutta: Visva-Bharati, 1960), p. 108.
23. See Satyajit Ray, *Our Films Their Films* (Calcutta: Disha Book/Orient Longman, 3rd edn., 1993). I have tried to discuss these issues in my Satyajit Ray Memorial Lecture, included in this book as Essay 6. See also Andrew Robinson, *Satyajit Ray: The Inner Eye* (London: André Deutsch, 1989).

24. *Guardian*, 1 Aug. 1991.
25. Shashi Tharoor, *India: From Midnight to the Millennium* (New York: Arcade Publishing), p. 1.
26. On this and related issues, see Jean Drèze and Amartya Sen, *India: Economic Development and Social Opportunity* (Delhi and Oxford: Oxford University Press, 1996), particularly ch. 6, and also Drèze and Sen (eds.), *Indian Development: Selected Regional Perspectives* (Delhi and Oxford: Oxford University Press, 1996).
27. Edward Thompson, *Rabindranath Tagore: Poet and Dramatist* (Oxford: Oxford University Press, 1926).
28. Quoted in Tharoor, *India*, p. 9.

ESSAY 6. OUR CULTURE, THEIR CULTURE

1. Satyajit Ray, *Our Films Their Films* (Calcutta: Disha Book/Orient Longman, 3rd edn., 1993), p. 154.
2. An insightful analysis of the different processes involved in cultural interactions and their consequences can be found in Homi Bhabha, *The Location of Culture* (London: Routledge, 1994).
3. See particularly Partha Chatterjee, *The Nation and Its Fragments* (Princeton: Princeton University Press, 1993).
4. See W. S. Wong, 'The Real World of Human Rights', mimeographed, Vienna, 1993.
5. Repr. in *Our Films Their Films*, pp. 42–3.
6. Ibid., p. 12.
7. Ibid., p. 160.
8. Ibid., p. 5.
9. Ray, *My Years with Apu: A Memoir* (New Delhi: Viking, 1994), p. 4.
10. In addition to Satyajit Ray's own autobiographical accounts in *Our Films Their Films* and *My Years with Apu*, his involvement in ideas and arts from many different places is discussed in some detail in Andrew Robinson's *Satyajit Ray: The Inner Eye* (London: André Deutsch, 1989).
11. Ray, *Our Films Their Films*, p. 9.
12. Chatterjee, *The Nation and Its Fragments*, p. 5.
13. The 'last summer' referred to here was the summer of 1995, preceding the Ray Lecture given in December 1995. In the original version of this Satyajit Ray Lecture, I also discussed the transmigration of mathematical ideas and terms from and to India, often going full circle. That discussion has been dropped in this reprint, since similar points have been made in other essays in this volume (see e.g. pp. 178–9).

14. Isaiah Berlin, *Four Essays on Liberty* (Oxford: Oxford University Press, 1969), p. xl.
15. Orlando Patterson, *Freedom*, vol. i: *Freedom in the Making of Western Culture* (New York: Basic Books, 1991).
16. I have discussed this issue in 'Is Coercion a Part of Asian Values?', presented at a conference in Hakone, Japan, in June 1995. A later version of this paper was given as a Morgenthau Memorial Lecture at the Carnegie Council on Ethics and International Affairs, on 1 May 1997, published by the Council as a pamphlet, and also as an essay, 'Human Rights and Asian Values', *New Republic*, 14 and 21 July 1997.

ESSAY 7. INDIAN TRADITIONS AND THE WESTERN IMAGINATION

1. Edward W. Said, *Orientalism* (New York: Random House, 1978; Vintage Books, 1979), p. 5; italics added.
2. Ibid., p. 5.
3. In the earlier article, 'India and the West', on which this essay draws, the third category was called 'investigative' rather than 'curatorial'; the latter is more specific and I believe somewhat more appropriate.
4. See *Alberuni's India*, trans. E. C. Sachau, ed. A. T. Embree (New York: Norton, 1971).
5. See Wilhelm Halbfass, *India and Europe: An Essay in Understanding* (New York: State University of New York Press, 1988), ch. 2.
6. *Alberuni's India*, p. 246. The same Arabic word was commonly used for 'Hindu' and 'Indian' in Alberuni's time. While the English translator had chosen to use 'Hindus' here, I have replaced it with 'Indians' in view of the context (to wit, Alberuni's observations on the inhabitants of India). This is an issue of some interest in the context of the main theme of this essay, since the language used here in the English translation to refer to the inhabitants of India implicitly imposes a circumscribed ascription.
7. Ibid., p. 20.
8. William Jones, 'Objects of Enquiry During My Residence in Asia', in *The Collected Works of Sir William Jones*, 13 vols. (London: J. Stockdale, 1807; repr. New York: New York University Press, 1993).
9. I have discussed the 'positional' nature of objectivity, depending on the placing of the observer and analyst vis-à-vis the objects being studied, in 'Positional Objectivity', *Philosophy and Public Affairs*, 22 (1993), and 'On Interpreting India's Past', in Sugata Bose and Ayesha Jalal (eds.), *Nationalism, Democracy and Development: State and Politics in India* (Delhi: Oxford University Press, 1997).

10. Quoted in Eric Stokes, *The English Utilitarians and India* (Oxford: Clarendon Press, 1959), p. 250.
11. James Mill, *The History of British India* (London, 1817; repr. Chicago: University of Chicago Press, 1975), pp. 225–6.
12. Ibid., p. 248.
13. Ibid., p. 247.
14. *Alberuni's India*, pp. 174–5.
15. For a modern account of the complex history of this mathematical development, see Georges Ifrah, *From One to Zero* (New York: Viking, 1985).
16. Mill, *The History of British India*, pp. 219–20.
17. Mill found in Jones's beliefs about early Indian mathematics and astronomy 'evidence of the fond credulity with which the state of society among the Hindus was for a time regarded', and he felt particularly amused that Jones had made these attributions 'with an air of belief' (Mill, *The History of British India*, pp. 223–4). On the substantive side, Mill amalgamates the distinct claims regarding (1) the principle of attraction, (2) the daily rotation of the earth, and (3) the movement of the earth around the sun. Āryabhaṭa's and Brahmagupta's concern was mainly with the first two, on which specific assertions were made, unlike the third.
18. Mill, *The History of British India*, pp. 223–4.
19. *Alberuni's India*, pp. 276–7.
20. Ibid., p. 277.
21. See Harold Isaacs, *Scratches on Our Minds* (Cambridge, Mass.: MIT Press, 1958); repr. as *Images of Asia: American Views of India and China* (New York: Capricorn Books, 1958). See also the discussion of this issue in the Introduction in Sulochana Glazer and Nathan Glazer (eds.), *Conflicting Images: India and the United States* (Glen Dale, Md.: Riverdale, 1990).
22. Lloyd I. Rudolph, 'Gandhi in the Mind of America', in Glazer and Glazer (eds.), *Conflicting Images*, p. 166.
23. Ashis Nandy, *Traditions, Tyranny, and Utopias: Essays in the Politics of Awareness* (Delhi: Oxford University Press, 1987), p. 8.
24. On this, see Glazer and Glazer (eds.), *Conflicting Images*. The influence of magisterial readings on American imaging of India has been somewhat countered in recent years by the political interest in Gandhi's life and ideas, a variety of sensitive writings on India (from Erik Erikson to John Kenneth Galbraith), and the Western success of several Indian novelists in English. Since the early 1990s, when this essay was written, the success of Indian science and technology, especially in informational fields, has added another dimension to the re-evaluation of India in American discussions.

25. Quoted in John Drew, *India and the Romantic Imagination* (Delhi and New York: Oxford University Press, 1987), p. 95.
26. J. G. Herder, *Auch eine Philosophie der Geschichte*, in *Samtliche Werke*; trans. Halbfass, *India and Europe*, p. 70.
27. Trans. Halbfass, *India and Europe*, pp. 74–5. Halbfass provides an extensive study of these European interpretations of Indian thought and the reactions and counter-reactions to them.
28. A. Schopenhauer, *Parerga und Paralipomena*; trans. Halbfass, *India and Europe*, p. 112.
29. See John H. Muirhead, *Coleridge as a Philosopher* (London: G. Allen & Unwin, 1930), pp. 283–4, and Drew, *India and the Romantic Imagination*, ch. 6.
30. The nature of exoticist reading has typically had a strongly 'Hindu' character. This was, in some ways, present even in William Jones's curatorial investigations (though he was himself a scholar in Arabic and Persian as well), but he was to some extent redressing the relative neglect of Sanskrit classics in the previous periods (even though the version of the Upaniṣads that Jones first read was the Persian translation prepared by the Moghal prince Dara Shikoh, Emperor Akbar's great-grandson). The European Romantics, on the other hand, tended to identify India with variants of Hindu religious thought.
31. William Davis, *The Rich* (London: Sidgwick and Jackson, 1982), p. 99.
32. On this issue, see Bimal Matilal, *Perceptions: An Essay on Classical Indian Theories of Knowledge* (Oxford: Clarendon Press, 1986). See also Ronald Inden, *Imagining India* (Oxford: Blackwell, 1990).
33. On this issue in general, and on the hold of 'a predominantly third-person perspective' in self-perception, see Akeel Bilgrami, 'What Is a Muslim? Fundamental Commitment and Cultural Identity', *Critical Inquiry*, 18 (4) (1992).
34. Jawaharlal Nehru, *The Discovery of India* (Calcutta: Signet Press, 1946; centenary edn., Delhi: Oxford University Press, 1989), p. 158.
35. While the constitution of independent India has been self-consciously secular, the tendency to see India as a land of the Hindus remains quite strong. The confrontation between 'secularists' and 'communitarians' has been an important feature of contemporary India, and the identification of Indian culture in mainly Hindu terms plays a part in this. While it is certainly possible to be both secular and communitarian (as Rajeev Bhargava has noted in 'Giving Secularism Its Due', *Economic and Political Weekly*, 9 July 1994), the contemporary divisions in India tend to make the religious and communal identities largely work against India's secular commitments (as

Bhargava also notes). I have tried to scrutinize these issues in my paper 'Secularism and Its Discontents', in Kaushik Basu and Sanjay Subrahmanyam (eds.), *Unravelling the Nation: Sectarian Conflict and India's Secular Identity* (Delhi: Penguin, 1996); Essay 14 in this volume. See also the other papers in that collection, and the essays included in Bose and Jalal (eds.), *Nationalism, Democracy and Development*.

36. Partha Chatterjee, *The Nation and Its Fragments* (Princeton: Princeton University Press, 1993), p. 6.

37. The most effective move in that direction came under the leadership of Ranajit Guha; see his introductory essay in *Subaltern Studies I: Writings on South Asian History and Society*, ed. Ranajit Guha (Delhi: Oxford University Press, 1982). See also the collection of 'subaltern' essays ed. Ranajit Guha and Gayatri Chakravorty Spivak, *Selected Subaltern Studies* (New York: Oxford University Press, 1988).

38. *Alberuni's India*, p. 32.

39. I have tried to discuss this general issue in 'Description as Choice', *Oxford Economic Papers*, 32 (1980), repr. in *Choice, Welfare and Measurement* (Oxford: Blackwell; Cambridge, Mass.: MIT Press, 1982; repr. Cambridge, Mass.: Harvard University Press, 1997), and in 'Positional Objectivity', *Philosophy and Public Affairs*, 22 (1993).

40. This contrast is discussed in my joint paper with Martha Nussbaum, 'Internal Criticism and Indian Rationalist Traditions', in Michael Krausz (ed.), *Relativism: Interpretation and Confrontation* (Notre Dame, Ind.: University of Notre Dame Press, 1989).

41. For example, the fourteenth-century book *Sarvadarśanasaṃgraha* ('Collection of All Philosophies') by Mādhava Ācārya (himself a good Vaishnavite Hindu) devotes the first chapter of the book to a serious presentation of the arguments of the atheistic schools.

42. Trans. H. P. Shastri, *The Ramayana of Valmiki* (London: Shanti Sadan, 1959), p. 389.

43. Ifrah, *From One to Zero*, p. 434.

44. Voltaire, *Les Œuvres complètes*, vol. 124; translated by Halbfass, *India and Europe*, p. 59.

ESSAY 8. CHINA AND INDIA

1. The exact question that Yi Jing asked was: 'Is there anyone, in the five parts of India, who does not admire China?' See J. Takakusu's translation of Yi Jing's book *A Record of the Buddhist Religions as Practised in India and Malay Archipelago* (Oxford, 1896), p. 136. Yi Jing's name (as in Pinyin

– now standard) is also spelt as I-tsing and I-Ching, among other earlier renderings.

2. Faxian's name has also been spelt in English as Fa-Hsien and Fa-hien, and Xuanzang's name as Hiuan-tsang and Yuang Chwang (among other variants). Many of the documents cited in this essay use these earlier spellings, rather than the Pinyin versions used here.

3. See Prabodh C. Bagchi, *India and China: A Thousand Years of Cultural Relations* (Calcutta: Saraswat Library, revised edn., 1981), p. 7. Zhang Qian is spelt as Chang Ch'ien in this and some other earlier works.

4. Tansen Sen, *Buddhism, Diplomacy, and Trade: The Realignment of Sino-Indian Relations, 600–1400* (Honolulu: University of Hawaii Press, 2003), p. 184.

5. In his well-researched study *Buddhism, Diplomacy, and Trade*, Tansen Sen shows that the size and continuity of Sino-Indian trade relations are often underestimated. For example, in contrast with the common presumption that the trade between the two countries died out in the second millennium, Sen argues that Sino-Indian exchanges were very extensive between the eleventh and the fourteenth centuries. Also, Sen provides evidence to conclude that Buddhism, too, continued to flourish simultaneously in Song dynasty China and in eastern India in the early part of the second millennium.

6. See Bagchi, *India and China*, especially pp. 197–8; Lokesh Chandra, 'India and China: Beyond and the Within', ignca.nic.in/ks_41023.htm.

7. The weakening of the hold of Buddhism in China is sometimes assigned to the ninth century, under the persecution of Buddhists by the Tang emperor Wuzong. These persecutions were important, but, as is argued by Tansen Sen (in *Buddhism, Diplomacy, and Trade*), Buddhism had plenty of life left in China in the centuries to follow. However, by then the form of Buddhism in China was turning more indigenous and less dependent on Indian Buddhism.

8. This book (see n. 1 above) was followed by another monograph containing detailed accounts of Yi Jing's reflections, *Records of the High Monks Who Went Out to Seek for the Books of the Law in the Tang Time*.

9. There is a translation by James Legge, *The Travels of Fa-Hien or Record of Buddhist Kingdoms* (New York: Dover, 1965; Patna: Eastern Book House, 1993). There is a useful extract from this book in Mark A. Kishlansky (ed.), *Sources of World History*, vol. i (New York: HarperCollins, 1995), pp. 154–8.

10. See Samuel Beal, *Life of Hieun Tsang* (London: Kegan Paul, 1914), and Sally Hovey Wriggins, *Xuanzang: A Buddhist Pilgrim on the Silk Road* (Boulder, Colo.: Westview Press, 1996). There are also two perceptive recent books that draw on Xuanzang's travels and their continuing significance today: Richard Bernstein, *Ultimate Journey: Retracing the Path of an Ancient*

Buddhist Monk Who Crossed Asia in Search of Enlightenment (New York: Knopf, 2001), and Sun Shuyun, *Ten Thousand Miles without a Cloud* (London: HarperCollins, 2003).

11. Among other things, Xuanzang noted King Harṣa's strong praise of the Chinese Tang ruler, Tang Taizong. In his book *Buddhism, Diplomacy, and Trade*, Tansen Sen has questioned the authenticity of Xuanzang's report, on the grounds, among others, that Harṣa's description of Taizong as a 'saintly lord' seems clearly inaccurate (he had gained the throne by murdering his brothers); Sen argues that Xuanzang, who knew and had the support of the Tang ruler, may have deliberately doctored the account. We have to judge, of course, whether it is more plausible that the Chinese scholar Xuanzang, with a great reputation for accuracy and authenticity, just heard wrong (rather than fabricating a story), or that the Indian emperor was simply misinformed about the Chinese monarch, at some considerable distance from him.

12. See Bagchi, *India and China*, p. 250.

13. Through Arthur Waley's English translation of it (*Monkey*, London: Allen & Unwin, 1942), the story achieved considerable popularity in Europe and America as well. Waley's translation, however, is incomplete. A complete translation can be found in Anthony Yu, *The Journey to the West*, 4 vols. (Chicago: Chicago University Press, 1977–83).

14. Charles O. Hucker, *China's Imperial Past: An Introduction to Chinese History and Culture* (Stanford: Stanford University Press, 1975), p. 216.

15. Leon Hurvitz and Tsai Heng-Ting, 'The Introduction of Buddhism', in Wm. Theodore de Bary and Irene Bloom (eds.), *Sources of Chinese Tradition*, vol. i (New York: Columbia University Press, 2nd edn., 1999), pp. 425–6.

16. Ibid., p. 425; the translators could not identify which 'commentary' is quoted here at the beginning of the passage.

17. Chinese Buddhist scholars did, however, eventually succeed (by about the eighth century) in making China something of a second 'homeland' of Buddhism, complete with stories of prior sightings of Buddha in Chinese territory as well as prominent displays of Buddhist relics brought from India. On this see Tansen Sen, *Buddhism, Diplomacy, and Trade*.

18. This striking feature was noted in *The Descriptive Catalogue of the Imperial Library* (1795) in the entry on Faxian's book, *Record of Buddhist Kingdoms*. The commentator, well versed in the Chinese perspective, saw in this nothing more than an attempt to glorify Buddhism: 'In this book we find India regarded as the Middle Kingdom, and China as a frontier country. This is because the ecclesiastics wish to do honour to their religion and is braggart-fiction which is not worth discussing.'

19. *Alberuni's India*, trans. E. C. Sachau, ed. A. T. Embree (New York: Norton, 1971), p. 19.

20. In Legge's translation (1965), p. 58.

21. Quoted in Joseph Needham, *Science and Civilization in China* (Cambridge: Cambridge University Press, 1956), vol. i, pp. 209–10.

22. Jean-Claude Martzloff, *A History of Chinese Mathematics*, with a Foreword by Jacques Gernet and Jean Dhrombres (Berlin and London: Springer, 1997), p. 90.

23. Needham, *Science and Civilization in China*, vol. iii (1959), pp. 146–8.

24. Martzloff, *A History of Chinese Mathematics*, p. 91.

25. John Kieschnick, *The Impact of Buddhism on Chinese Material Culture* (Princeton: Princeton University Press, 2003), p. 166.

26. Needham, *Science and Civilization in China*, vol. ii (1956), p. 427.

27. Needham also points to the possibility that some Chinese ideas that appear to have been influenced by Indian Buddhism might have been 'really Taoist' (vol. iii, p. 427).

28. See Bagchi, *India and China*, pp. 249–51.

29. See Howard Eves, *An Introduction to the History of Mathematics* (New York: College Publishing House, 1990), p. 237: and Martzloff, *A History of Chinese Mathematics*, p. 100.

30. *Kaiyvan Zhanjing*, in Pinyin, is often referred to as *Khai-Yuan Chan Ching* in earlier spelling.

31. See Needham, *Science and Civilization in China*, vol. iii (1959), p. 202; also pp. 12 and 37. Note that Needham's spelling of the Chinese version of Gautama's name, 'Chhütan', corresponds to 'Qutan' in Pinyin, and he was referred to in that spelling earlier as 'Qutan Xida'. Yang Jingfeng is spelt as Ching-Feng in Needham's description. A general account of Indian calendrical systems is presented in my 'India through Its Calendars', *Little Magazine*, 1 (2000); Essay 15 below.

32. Kieschnick, *The Impact of Buddhism on Chinese Material Culture*, pp. 199–214.

33. Yi Jing, *A Record of the Buddhist Religions as Practised in India and Malay Archipelago*, trans. Takakusu, p. 169.

34. Kieschnick, *The Impact of Buddhism on Chinese Material Culture*, p. 164.

35. Wm. Theodore de Bary, 'Neo-Confucian Education', in de Bary and Bloom (eds.), *Sources of Chinese Tradition*, vol. i, p. 820.

36. From the translation of Legge, *The Travels of Fa-Hien or Record of Buddhist Kingdoms* (1993), p. 79.

37. Trans. Bagchi, *India and China*, p. 134.

ESSAY 9. TRYST WITH DESTINY

1. I have discussed this issue in 'Democracy and Secularism in India', in Kaushik Basu, *India's Emerging Economy: Problems and Prospects in the 1990s and Beyond* (Cambridge, Mass.: MIT Press, 2004), which contains a number of fine essays providing helpful assessments from different perspectives.
2. A collection of wide-ranging investigations of continuing social inequalities in India and the policy issues they raise can be found in Ramachandra Guha and Jonathan P. Parry (eds.), *Institutions and Inequalities: Essays in Honour of André Béteille* (New Delhi and Oxford: Oxford University Press, 1999).
3. On these and related assessments, see Jean Drèze and Amartya Sen, *India: Development and Participation* (Delhi and Oxford: Oxford University Press, 2002).
4. For the economic case for the reforms introduced by Manmohan Singh, see the essays included in Isher Judge Ahluwalia and I. M. D. Little (eds.), *India's Economic Reforms and Development: Essays for Manmohan Singh* (New Delhi and Oxford: Oxford University Press, 1998).
5. A perceptive – and upbeat – diagnosis of India's achievements and prospects in the global economic route can be found in Gurcharan Das's forceful book, *India Unbound* (London: Viking/Penguin Books, 2000). See also his later study, *The Elephant Paradigm: India Wrestles with Change* (London: Penguin Books, 2002). A less buoyant assessment of the process of economic reform in India, China and Russia can be found in Prem Shankar Jha, *The Perilous Road to the Market* (London: Pluto Press, 2002).
6. On this, see Drèze and Sen, *India: Development and Participation*. See also Angus Deaton and Jean Drèze, 'Poverty and Inequality in India: A Re-examination', *Economic and Political Weekly*, 7 Sept. 2002. See also the large literature on Indian poverty that is cited in these writings.

ESSAY 10. CLASS IN INDIA

1. In the Nehru Lecture on which this essay is based, I not only paid tribute to Nehru as a maker of modern India, but also celebrated the intellectual contributions of a visionary thinker. For example, Nehru's attempts at radically re-examining the history of India and of the world in his two remarkable collections (*The Discovery of India* and *Glimpses of World History*) were innovative as well as inspirational, and the underlying visions deserve more systematic attention than they have tended to get.

2. On the interdependences between different sources of adversity, see also Stuart Corbridge and John Harriss, *Reinventing India* (Cambridge: Polity Press, 2000), and Jean Drèze and Amartya Sen, *India: Development and Participation* (Delhi and Oxford: Oxford University Press, 2002).

3. See my *Inequality Reexamined* (Oxford: Clarendon Press, and Cambridge, Mass.: Harvard University Press, 1992); and jointly with Jean Drèze, *India: Economic Development and Social Opportunity* (Delhi and Oxford: Oxford University Press, 1996), and *India: Development and Participation*.

4. Jean Drèze and Amartya Sen, *Hunger and Public Action* (Oxford: Clarendon Press, 1989).

5. See Peter Svedberg, *Poverty and Undernutrition: Theory, Measurement and Policy* (Oxford: Clarendon Press, 2000; Delhi: Oxford University Press, 2002). See also S. R. Osmani, 'Hunger in South Asia: A Study in Contradiction', and Peter Svedberg, 'Hunger in India: Facts and Challenges', *Little Magazine*, Dec. 2001.

6. See Nevin Scrimshaw, 'The Lasting Damage of Early Malnutrition', World Food Programme, mimeographed, 31 May 1997.

7. See Siddiq Osmani and Amartya Sen, 'The Hidden Penalties of Gender Inequality: Fetal Origins of Ill-Health', *Economics and Human Biology*, 1 (2003).

8. I have discussed this issue, jointly with Jean Drèze, in *India: Economic Development and Social Opportunity*, and also in its follow-up study, *India: Development and Participation*.

9. See particularly the PROBE report: *Public Report on Basic Education in India* (Delhi: Oxford University Press, 1999).

ESSAY 11. WOMEN AND MEN

1. I have addressed this issue in 'Many Faces of Gender Inequality', *New Republic*, 17 Sept. 2001, and *Frontline*, Nov. 2001.

2. The nature and significance of this distinction have been discussed in my 'Well-being, Agency and Freedom: The Dewey Lecture 1984', *Journal of Philosophy*, 83 (Apr. 1985), and *Inequality Reexamined* (Oxford: Clarendon Press, and Cambridge, Mass.: Harvard University Press, 1992). Related empirical issues are discussed in my *Development as Freedom* (New York: Knopf, and Oxford: Oxford University Press, 1999).

3. The discussion that follows draws on my earlier essay, 'Many Faces of Gender Inequality'.

4. 'India and Africa: What Do We Have to Learn from Each Other?', in

Kenneth Arrow (ed.), *The Balance between Industry and Agriculture in Economic Development* (London: Macmillan, 1988).

5. The numbers as well as the causal influences that tend to produce 'missing women' were presented in my 'More Than a Hundred Million Women Are Missing', *New York Review of Books*, Christmas Number 1990, and in 'Missing Women', *British Medical Journal*, 304 (Mar. 1992). In the debate that followed, some commentators missed the fact that I had used the sub-Saharan African ratio as the standard, rather than the much higher European or North American ratio (which would have given far larger estimates of 'missing women'). The misunderstanding led to the mistaken argument that I was comparing developing countries like China and India with advanced Western ones (in Europe and North America), which have high longevity and a different demographic history; see e.g. Ansley Coale, 'Excess Female Mortality and the Balances of the Sexes in the Population: An Estimate of the Number of "Missing Females"'. *Population and Development Review*, 17 (1991). In fact, however, my estimates of 'missing women' were based on contrasts *within* the so-called Third World, in particular using the sub-Saharan African ratio as the basis for estimating the numbers missing in Asia and North Africa.

6. See Stephan Klasen, '"Missing Women" Reconsidered', *World Development*, 22 (1994), and his joint paper with Claudia Wink, 'Missing Women: Revisiting the Debate', *Journal of Feminist Economics*, 9 (July/Nov. 2003).

7. Note, however, that the Chinese and Korean figures cover children between 0 and 4, whereas the Indian figures relate to children between 0 and 6. However, even after adjustment for age coverage, the relative positions remain much the same.

8. A tiny exception, within the north and west of India, is the small territory of Dadra and Nagar Haveli, with less than a quarter of a million people altogether.

9. On this see Jean Drèze and Amartya Sen, *India: Development and Participation* (Delhi and Oxford: Oxford University Press, 2002), ch. 7, esp. pp. 232–5 and 257–66.

10. There is, as identified in n. 8, the tiny exception of the minute territory of Dadra and Nagar Haveli.

11. There is also a possible political connection, in that the incidence of sex-specific abortion is, in general, significantly higher in those regions of the country in which religion-based politics has a strong hold (for example, Rajasthan, Gujarat or Jammu and Kashmir, in contrast with, say, Assam or West Bengal or Kerala). On the numerical association, see Drèze and Sen, *India: Development and Participation*, sect. 7.5, pp. 257–62, and my essay '"Missing Women" Revisited', *British Medical Journal*, 327 (6 Dec. 2003).

This association requires much further scrutiny before it can be concluded that the two phenomena are indeed causally linked directly, or perhaps indirectly through the influence of some third variable.

12. See e.g. Irawati Karve, *Kinship Organization in India* (Bombay: Asia Publishing House, 1965); Pranab Bardhan, 'On Life and Death Questions', *Economic and Political Weekly*, Special Number, 9 (1974); David Sopher (ed.), *An Exploration of India: Geographical Perspectives on Society and Culture* (Ithaca, NY: Cornell University Press, 1980); Barbara Miller, *The Endangered Sex* (Ithaca, NY: Cornell University Press, 1981); Tim Dyson and Mick Moore, 'On Kinship Structure, Female Autonomy, and Demographic Behaviour in India', *Population and Development Review*, 9 (1983); Monica Das Gupta, 'Selective Discrimination against Female Children in Rural Punjab', *Population and Development Review*, 13 (1987); Alaka M. Basu, *Culture, the Status of Women and Demographic Behaviour* (Oxford: Clarendon Press, 1992); and Satish Balram Agnihotri, *Sex Ratio Patterns in the Indian Population* (New Delhi: Sage, 2000).

13. See William St Clair, *The Godwins and the Shelleys* (New York: Norton, 1989), pp. 504–8.

14. See Bina Agarwal, *A Field of One's Own* (Cambridge: Cambridge University Press, 1994).

15. World Health Organization, *Handbook of Human Nutrition Requirement* (Geneva: WHO, 1974).

16. See the empirical literature cited in my *Development as Freedom*. Among later contributions, see particularly Gita Sen, Asha George and Pireska Östlin (eds.), *Engendering International Health: The Challenge of Equity* (Cambridge, Mass.: MIT Press, 2002).

17. I have tried to discuss the importance of freedom of thought for rationality as well as freedom in general in the Introduction to my *Rationality and Freedom* (Cambridge, Mass.: Harvard University Press, 2002).

18. Gender divisions within the family are sometimes studied formally as 'bargaining problems', taking off from Nash's classic framework, but introducing critically important variations in its exact formulation. The literature includes, among other contributions, Marilyn Manser and Murray Brown, 'Marriage and Household Decision Making: A Bargaining Analysis', *International Economic Review*, 21 (1980); M. B. McElroy and M. J. Horney, 'Nash Bargained Household Decisions: Toward a Generalization of Theory of Demand', *International Economic Review*, 22 (1981); Shelly Lundberg and Robert Pollak, 'Noncooperative Bargaining Models of Marriage', *American Economic Review*, 84 (1994).

19. Attempts to discuss the causal influences and the implicit ethics underlying

the treatment of cooperative conflicts within the family can be found in my *Resources, Values and Development* (Cambridge, Mass.: Harvard University Press, 1984), chs. 5 and 16, and 'Gender and Cooperative Conflict', in Irene Tinker (ed.), *Persistent Inequalities* (New York: Oxford University Press, 1990). See also Nancy Folbre, 'Hearts and Spades: Paradigms of Household Economics', *World Development*, 14 (1986); J. Brannen and G. Wilson (eds.), *Give and Take in Families* (London: Allen & Unwin, 1987); and Marianne A. Ferber and Julie A. Nelson (eds.), *Beyond Economic Man* (Chicago: Chicago University Press, 1993), among other contributions.

20. See the discussion and the large literature cited in my joint books with Jean Drèze, *India: Economic Development and Social Opportunity* (Delhi and Oxford: Oxford University Press, 1996), and *India: Development and Participation*.

21. Mamta Murthi, Anne-Catherine Guio and Jean Drèze, 'Mortality, Fertility and Gender Bias in India: A District Level Analysis', *Population and Development Review*, 21 (1995), and also in Jean Drèze and Amartya Sen, *Indian Development: Selected Regional Perspectives* (Delhi and Oxford: Oxford University Press, 1996). See also Jean Drèze and Mamta Murthi, 'Fertility, Education and Development: Evidence from India', *Population and Development Review*, 27 (2001).

22. See, among other important contributions, J. C. Caldwell, 'Routes to Low Mortality in Poor Countries', *Population and Development Review*, 12 (1986); and J. R. Behrman and B. L. Wolfe, 'How Does Mother's Schooling Affect Family Health, Nutrition, Medical Care Usage, and Household Sanitation?', *Journal of Econometrics*, 36 (1987).

23. See the papers of Mamta Murthi and Jean Drèze cited earlier, and also Drèze and Sen, *India: Development and Participation*.

24. On this see Drèze and Sen, *India: Economic Development and Social Opportunity*, and *India: Development and Participation*.

25. This pioneering research has been led by Professor David Barker of Southampton University. See D. J. P. Barker, 'Intrauterine Growth Retardation and Adult Disease,' *Current Obstetrics and Gynaecology*, 3 (1993); 'Fetal Origins of Coronary Heart Disease', *British Medical Journal*, 311 (1995); *Mothers, Babies and Diseases in Later Life* (London: Churchill Livingstone, 1998). See also P. D. Gluckman, K. M. Godfrey, J. E. Harding, J. A. Owens, and J. S. Robinson, 'Fetal Nutrition and Cardiovascular Disease in Adult Life', *Lancet*, 341 (1995).

26. On this, see Siddiq Osmani and Amartya Sen, 'The Hidden Penalties of Gender Inequality: Fetal Origins of Ill-Health', *Economics and Human Biology*, 1 (2003).

ESSAY 12. INDIA AND THE BOMB

1. *Times of India*, 28 June 1998.

2. On this, see George Perkovich, *India's Nuclear Bomb: The Impact on Global Proliferation* (Berkeley: University of California Press, 1999). See also T. Jayaraman, 'Science, Politics and the Indian Bomb: Some Preliminary Considerations', mimeographed, Institute of Mathematical Sciences, CIT Campus, Chennai, 2000.

3. Praful Bidwai and Achin Vanaik, *New Nukes: India, Pakistan and Global Nuclear Disarmament* (Oxford: Signal Books, 2000), p. 1.

4. For a graphic account of this episode and the chain of events related to it, see Robert Jungk, *Brighter Than a Thousand Suns: A Personal History of Atomic Scientists* (New York: Penguin Books, 1960).

5. Kenzaburo Oe, *Hiroshima Notes*, trans. David L. Swain and Toshi Yonezawa (New York: Grove Press, 1996), p. 182.

6. Pankaj Mishra, 'A New, Nuclear India?' in Robert B. Silvers and Barbara Epstein (eds.), *India: A Mosaic* (New York: New York Review of Books, 2000), p. 230. The essay is dated 28 May 1998.

7. Amitav Ghosh, 'Countdown: Why Can't Every Country Have the Bomb?', *New Yorker*, 26 Oct. and 2 Nov. 1998. See also his later book, *Countdown* (Delhi: Ravi Dayal, 1999), which further develops some of his arguments.

8. N. Ram, *Riding the Nuclear Tiger* (New Delhi: LeftWord Books, 1999), p. 106. See also his Preface to Silvers and Epstein (eds.), *India: A Mosaic*.

9. See Ghosh, *Countdown*.

10. Arundhati Roy, 'The End of Imagination', *Frontline*, 27 July 1998; repr. in *The Cost of Living* (New York: Modern Library, 1999). See also her Introduction to Silvers and Epstein (eds.), *India: A Mosaic*.

11. Arundhati Roy, 'Introduction: The End of Imagination', in Bidwai and Vanaik, *New Nukes*, p. xx.

12. Ghosh, 'Countdown', pp. 190 and 197.

13. C. Rammanohar Reddy, 'Estimating the Cost of Nuclear Weaponization in India', mimeographed, *Hindu*, Chennai, 1999.

14. Bidwai and Vanaik, *New Nukes*, pp. xiii, xv.

15. Eric Arnett, 'Nuclear Tests by India and Pakistan', in *SIPRI Yearbook 1999* (Oxford: Oxford University Press, 1999), p. 377.

16. Even though it is not clear whether Fernandes knew about the dates of the impending tests, he would certainly have seen – and in part been in charge of – the connection between Indian defence postures and its international pronouncements.

17. 'Nuclear Anxiety: India's Letter to Clinton on the Nuclear Testing', *New York Times*, 13 May 1998, p. 4.

18. Mark W. Frazier, 'China–India Relations since Pokhran II: Assessing Sources of Conflict and Cooperation', *Access Asia Review*, National Bureau of Asian Research, 3 (July 2000), p. 10.
19. UNDP, *Human Development Report 1994* (New York: United Nations, 1994), pp. 54–5, and table 3.6.

ESSAY 13. THE REACH OF REASON

1. Jonathan Glover, *Humanity: A Moral History of the Twentieth Century* (London: Jonathan Cape, 1999; New Haven: Yale University Press, 2000), p. 7. Glover, a leading light in Oxford philosophy for many decades, is also the author of *Responsibility* (London: Routledge, and New York: Humanities Press, 1970) and *Causing Death and Saving Lives* (Harmondsworth: Penguin, 1977), among other works of note. He is now the Director of Medical Law and Ethics at King's College, London.
2. Trans. Vincent A. Smith, *Akbar: The Great Mogul* (Oxford: Clarendon Press, 1917), p. 257.
3. See Irfan Habib (ed.), *Akbar and His India* (Delhi and New York: Oxford University Press, 1997), for a set of fine essays investigating the beliefs and policies of Akbar as well as the intellectual influences that led him to his heterodox position.
4. The last century, however, was subjected to a searching scrutiny by Eric Hobsbawm, a few years before the century and the millennium came to an end, in *The Age of Extremes: A History of the World, 1916–1991* (London: M. Joseph, and New York: Vintage, 1994). See also Garry Wills, 'A Reader's Guide to the Century', *New York Review of Books*, 15 July 1999.
5. An eminent example can be found in John Gray, *Enlightenment's Wake: Politics and Culture at the Close of the Modern Age* (London: Routledge, 1995). See also the perceptive review of this work by Charles Griswold, *Political Theory*, 27 (1999), pp. 274–81.
6. Kenzaburo Oe, *Japan, the Ambiguous, and Myself* (Tokyo and New York: Kodansha, 1995), pp. 118–19.
7. An important collection of perspectives on this is presented in Rajaram Krishnan, Jonathan M. Harris and Neva R. Goodwin (eds.), *A Survey of Ecological Economics* (Washington, DC: Island Press, 1995). A far-reaching critique of the relationship between institutions and reasoned behaviour can be found in Andreas Papandreou, *Externality and Institutions* (Oxford: Oxford University Press, 1994).
8. I have discussed this question in my *On Ethics and Economics* (Oxford: Blackwell, 1987), ch. 1.

9. On this, see Emma Rothschild, *Economic Sentiments* (Cambridge, Mass.: Harvard University Press, 2001).
10. David Hume, *Enquiries concerning Human Understanding and concerning the Principles of Morals*, ed. L. E. Selby-Bigge (Oxford: Oxford University Press, 1962), p. 172.
11. Thomas Nagel, *The Last Word* (Oxford: Oxford University Press, 1997), p. 102.
12. On the role of reasoning in the development of attitudes and feelings, see particularly T. M. Scanlon, *What We Owe to Each Other* (Cambridge, Mass.: Harvard University Press, 1999).
13. Adam Smith, *The Theory of Moral Sentiments* (London: T. Cadell, 1790; repr. Oxford: Oxford University Press, 1976), pp. 319–20.
14. Samuel P. Huntington, *The Clash of Civilizations and the Remaking of World Order* (New York: Simon and Schuster, 1996), p. 318.
15. Clifford Geertz, 'Culture War', *New York Review of Books*, 30 Nov. 1995. This is a review of Marshall Sahlins, *How 'Natives' Think About Captain Cook, for Example* (Chicago: University of Chicago Press, 1995), and Gananath Obeyesekere, *The Apotheosis of Captain Cook: European Mythmaking in the Pacific* (Princeton: Princeton University Press, 1992).
16. Gertrude Himmelfarb, 'The Illusions of Cosmopolitanism', in Martha Nussbaum with Respondents, *For Love of Country* (Boston: Beacon Press, 1996), pp. 74–5.
17. See Huntington, *The Clash of Civilizations*, p. 69.
18. On this and related issues, see my *Development as Freedom* (New York: Knopf, and Oxford: Oxford University Press, 1999), ch. 10, and the references cited there.
19. See my *Human Rights and Asian Values* (New York: Carnegie Council on Ethics and International Affairs, 1997); a shortened version came out in *New Republic*, 14 and 21 July 1997.
20. See Basil Davidson, F. K. Buah and J. F. Ade Ajayi, *A History of West Africa 1000–1800* (Harlow: Longman, new rev. edn., 1977), pp. 286–7.
21. See M. Athar Ali, 'The Perception of India in Akbar and Abu'l Fazl', in Habib, *Akbar and His India*, p. 220.
22. See Pushpa Prasad, 'Akbar and the Jains', in Habib, *Akbar and His India*, pp. 97–8. The one missing group seems to be the Buddhists (though one of the early translations included them in the account by misrendering the name of a Jain sect as that of Buddhist monks). Perhaps by then Buddhists were hard to find around Delhi or Agra.
23. See Iqtidar Alam Khan, 'Akbar's Personality Traits and World Outlook: A Critical Reappraisal', in Habib, *Akbar and His India*, p. 96.
24. See also Martha Nussbaum, *Cultivating Humanity: A Classical Defense*

of Reform in Liberal Education (Cambridge, Mass.: Harvard University Press, 1997).

25. Michael Sandel, *Liberalism and the Limits of Justice* (Cambridge University Press, 2nd edn., 1998), p. 150.

26. I discuss this issue in *Reason before Identity: The Romanes Lecture for 1998* (Oxford: Oxford University Press, 1999).

27. New Delhi: National Book Trust, 1994.

28. *Alberuni's India*, trans. E. C. Sachau, ed. A. T. Embree (New York: Norton, 1971), p. 20. See also Essay 7.

ESSAY 14. SECULARISM AND ITS DISCONTENTS

1. See e.g. T. N. Madan, 'Coping with Ethnic Diversity: A South Asian Perspective', in Stuart Plattner (ed.), *Prospects for Plural Societies* (Washington, DC: American Ethnological Society, 1984), and 'Secularism in Its Place', *Journal of Asian Studies*, 46 (1987); and Ashis Nandy, 'An Anti-Secular Manifesto', *Seminar*, 314 (1985), and 'The Politics of Secularism and the Recovery of Religious Tolerance', *Alternatives*, 13 (1988).

2. See Ashutosh Varshney's helpful characterizations of different claims associated with 'Hindu nationalism', in his 'Contested Meanings: Indian National Unity, Hindu Nationalism, and the Politics of Anxiety', *Daedalus*, 122 (1993), pp. 230–31; see also Ashis Nandy, 'The Ramjanmabhumi Movement and the Fear of Self', mimeographed paper, presented at the Harvard Center for International Affairs, April 1992.

3. Nandy, 'The Politics of Secularism and the Recovery of Religious Tolerance', pp. 188, 192. See also Madan, 'Secularism in Its Place'.

4. On the history of this aspect of Indian laws, see John H. Mansfield, 'The Personal Laws or a Uniform Civil Code?', in Robert Baird (ed.), *Religion and Law in Independent India* (Delhi: Manohar, 1993), which also provides a balanced review of the pros and cons of the case for submerging different personal laws in India in a 'uniform civil code'. See also Tahir Mahmood, *Muslim Personal Law, Role of the State in the Indian Subcontinent* (New Delhi: Vikas Pub. House, 1977; 2nd edn., Nagpur, 1983).

5. *Constitution of India*, Article 37.

6. This was done by the Supreme Court by giving priority – over the provisions of Islamic law for divorce settlements – to 'section 125 of the Code of Criminal Procedure', which requires a person of adequate means to protect from destitution and vagrancy their relations (including spouse, minor children, handicapped adult children and aged parents). For critical analyses of the rather complex considerations involved in the Shah Bano case, see

Asghar Ali Engineer, *The Shah Bano Controversy* (Delhi: Ajanta Publishers, 1987), and Veena Das, *Critical Events* (Delhi: Oxford University Press, 1992), ch. IV. Also see Mansfield in Baird (ed.), *Religion and Law in Independent India*.

7. Mansfield in Baird (ed.), p. 140.

8. The Supreme Court had also taken this opportunity of commenting on the disadvantaged position of women in India (not just among the Muslims, but also among the Hindus), and had called for more justice in this field. The Shah Bano case did, in fact, get much attention from women's political groups as well.

9. In fact, Azad was among the 'traditionalist' Muslims, as opposed to the 'reformers' (for example from the Aligarh school). On the intricacies of Azad's religious and political attitudes, see Ayesha Jalal, 'Exploding Communalism: The Politics of Muslim Identity in South Asia', in Sugata Bose and Ayesha Jalal (eds.), *Nationalism, Democracy and Development: Reappraising South Asian States and Politics in India* (Delhi: Oxford University Press, 1997). Jalal also discusses the much broader question of a general misfit between (1) the reformism–traditionalism division among Muslims in pre-partition India, and (2) the division between Muslims who favoured an undivided India and those who wanted a separate Pakistan. In particular, quite often the Muslim traditionalists opted for staying on in India (as Azad himself did), especially after the Khilafat movement.

10. In his perceptive paper, 'Hindu/Muslim/Indian' (*Public Culture*, 5 (1), Fall 1992), Faisal Devji begins with this (and another) quotation from Ambedkar, and goes on to scrutinize critically the relation between different identities (raising issues that are much broader than those addressed in this essay).

11. See also Nur Yalman, 'On Secularism and Its Critics: Notes on Turkey, India and Iran', *Contributions to Indian Sociology*, 25 (1991). See also Gary Jeffrey Jacobsohn, 'Three Models of the Secular Constitution', mimeographed, Williams College, 1995, and the literature cited there.

12. Whether or not Indian Muslims do this in any significant numbers, I ought to confess that this non-Muslim author has often done just that, either when the Pakistani team plays as well as it frequently does, or when a Pakistani win would make the test series (or the one-day series) more interesting.

13. *Alberuni's India*, trans. E. C. Sachau, ed. A. T. Embree (New York: Norton, 1971), p. 22.

14. Ibid., p. 20.

15. See *One Hundred Poems of Kabir*, trans. Rabindranath Tagore (London: Macmillan, 1915), verse LXIX. See also Kshiti Mohan Sen, *Hinduism*

(Harmondsworth: Penguin Books, 1961, 2005), chs. 18 and 19, and his collection of Kabir's poems and his Bengali commentary in *Kabir* (Calcutta: Visva-Bharati, 1910, 1911), reissued with an Introduction by Sabyasachi Bhattacharya (Calcutta: Ananda Publishers, 1995).

ESSAY 15. INDIA THROUGH ITS CALENDARS

1. See *The Oxford Companion to the Year*, ed. Bonnie Blackburn and Leofranc Holford-Strevens (Oxford: Oxford University Press, 1999), p. 664.
2. See M. N. Saha and N. C. Lahiri, *History of the Calendar* (New Delhi: Council of Scientific and Industrial Research, 1992).
3. Ibid., pp. 252–3; also S. N. Sen and K. S. Shukla, *History of Astronomy in India* (New Delhi: Indian National Science Academy, 1985), p. 298.
4. Marquis Pierre-Simon de Laplace, as quoted in W. Brennand, *Hindu Astronomy* (London, 1896), p. 31.
5. On this, see O. P. Jaggi, *Indian Astronomy and Mathematics* (Delhi: Atma Ram, 1986), ch. 1.
6. E. M. Forster, 'Nine Gems of Ujjain', in *Abinger Harvest* (Harmondsworth: Penguin Books, 1936, 1974), pp. 324–7.
7. See Irfan Habib (ed.), *Akbar and His India* (Delhi and New York: Oxford University Press, 1997).

ESSAY 16. THE INDIAN IDENTITY

1. Quoted in Lady Betty Balfour, *The History of Lord Lytton's Indian Administration 1876 to 1880* (London, 1899), p. 477.
2. F. R. Harris, *Jamsetji Nusserwanji Tata: A Chronicle of His Life* (London: Blackie, 2nd edn., 1958), p. vii.
3. R. M. Lala, *The Creation of Wealth* (Bombay: IBH, 1981), p. 6.
4. Ibid., p. 47.
5. Lovat Fraser, *Iron and Steel in India: A Chapter from the Life of Jamsetji N. Tata* (Bombay: The Times Press, 1919), p. 3.
6. See S. B. Saul, *Studies in British Overseas Trade 1870–1914* (Liverpool: Liverpool University Press, 1960), p. 199. The shifting trade pattern and its implications were investigated by the so-called Chamberlain Inquiry of 1895, *Trade of the British Empire and Foreign Competition*, C. 8449 of 1897.
7. Fraser, *Iron and Steel in India*, pp. 52–3.
8. Comparisons with alternative causal explanations are discussed in my paper, 'The Commodity Pattern of British Enterprise in Early Indian

Industrialization 1854–1914', in the *Proceedings of the Second International Conference of Economic History* (Paris, 1965). I have examined the general relevance of values and commitments in behavioural choices in *On Ethics and Economics* (Oxford: Blackwell, 1987), and, more technically, in 'Maximization and the Act of Choice', *Econometrica*, 65 (1997), included in my *Rationality and Freedom* (Cambridge, Mass.: Harvard University Press, 2002).

9. Fraser, *Iron and Steel in India*, p. 1.

10. Perin wrote that when Jamsetji came to interview him, this 'stranger in a strange garb' asked: 'Will you come to India with me?' '"Well," I said, "yes, I'd go." And I did' (quoted in Lala, *The Creation of Wealth*, p. 20).

11. There is, furthermore, a significant distinction between import substitution and endogenous domestic expansion. In a joint paper with K. N. Raj, 'Alternative Patterns of Growth under Conditions of Stagnant Export Earnings' (*Oxford Economic Papers*, 13, 1961), I was concerned with the latter, whereas it has sometimes been interpreted, quite mistakenly, as a defence of import substitution against export promotion – an issue that was not even addressed in the paper. The so-called Raj–Sen model considered neither import substitution nor export promotion, and concentrated instead on alternative patterns of endogenous development, focusing in particular on issues of growth theory and the implications of stock–flow relationships.

12. Harris, *Jamsetji Nusserwanji Tata*, p. 118.

13. From a letter to C. F. Andrews, dated 13 March 1921, published in Rabindranath Tagore, *Letters to a Friend*, with essays by C. F. Andrews (London: Allen & Unwin, 1928).

14. See Michael Sandel, *Liberalism and the Limits of Justice* (Cambridge: Cambridge University Press, 2nd edn., 1998), pp. 150–52.

15. Rabindranath Tagore, *The Religion of Man* (London: Unwin, 1931; 2nd edn., 1961), p. 105.

16. This is how the issue was presented by its distinguished chairman, Lord Parekh, in 'A Britain We All Belong To', *Guardian*, 11 Oct. 2000. See, however, the much richer analysis of social identity presented by Bhikhu Parekh himself in *Re-thinking Multi-culturalism: Cultural Diversity and Political Theory* (Basingstoke: Palgrave, 2000).

Index of Names

General Index